The Biology of Organisms

THE BIOLOGY OF CELLS
Herbert Stern and David L. Nanney

THE BIOLOGY OF ORGANISMS
William H. Telfer and Donald Kennedy

THE BIOLOGY OF POPULATIONS
Robert H. MacArthur and Joseph H. Connell

THE BIOLOGY
OF ORGANISMS

WILLIAM H. TELFER University of Pennsylvania

DONALD KENNEDY Stanford University *, 1931-*

John Wiley & Sons, Inc., New York · London · Sydney

Library of Congress Catalog Card Number: 65–19472
Printed in the United States of America

FOREWORD

The idea for this series of three books was conceived in June 1960 at a meeting sponsored by John Wiley & Sons and involving Professors David Nanney (University of Illinois), Robert MacArthur (University of Pennsylvania), Joseph Gall (Yale University), Peter Ray (University of Michigan), William Van der Kloot (New York University Medical School), and Clifford Grobstein (Stanford University). A year later the three books were outlined, discussed, and interrelated during a second meeting held at the Morris Arboretum of the University of Pennsylvania. Most of the authors participated in this second meeting, which profited from the courtesy and counsel of Professor David Goddard (University of Pennsylvania). A sense of common objective emerged from the two meetings, and it is hoped that the books reflect it.

What was this common objective? In broadest terms it was to demonstrate the conviction that the teaching of biology could be reoriented to convey more effectively and forcefully the intellectual revolution which biology was undergoing. We were delighted to find that we shared not only the conviction but also a vision of how to realize it. It is now clear—but was not then—that this vision was common to many biologists. Revision of biological curricula at the university level is rapid and widespread because teachers (many of whom also are investigators) have almost simultaneously seen how far pedagogy lags behind the swift advance of research.

The vision was embodied in several basic decisions on organization of the three volumes. The first decision was adoption of the "levels" approach. This recognizes that the living world is composed of a hierarchy of organizational patterns that can best be encompassed by explicit discussions of cells, organisms, and populations. In parallel with the various levels of organization treated in the physical sciences, each level has its own set of characteristics. These compel the biologist to be concerned with the relation of properties and behavior at one level to each of the other levels. We believe (unlike the vitalists of an earlier era) that much of the behavior of living things is referable to the properties of their components—although we also recognize that many of the properties of the components cannot be ascertained in isolated systems alone. We recognize, also, that biological entities at lower levels of organization are markedly dependent upon the properties of those at higher levels of which they are part. The properties of biological systems have developed from both molecular mechanisms and evolutionary forces; these opposing poles account for much of the pattern and unity of life.

A second decision was to emphasize the uniformities of nature as opposed to its variety. The great generalizations of biology are those that apply to life in all (or many) of its manifestations. The endless diversity of life is a fact, but its endless documentation is inappropriate as an introduction where the major focus should be on life *in toto*.

A third decision concerned assumptions about the previous background of the student. How much information and experience relevant to biology are students entering college likely to have? Improvements in secondary school preparation have been dramatic, not only in biology but also in mathematics and the physical sciences. The prospect is that we shall see increasing numbers of well-prepared students for whom most past college introductions to science are inappropriate and obsolete. Accepting the near-impossibility of accommodating all levels of prior training, we need deliberate attempts to build upon the enriched experience of these students who have already been effectively exposed to some of the basic concepts of physics, chemistry, mathematics, and biology.

Finally, we decided that—although science is frequently regarded as a "body of knowledge," and presented in an up-to-date summary of that body—any such treatment is doomed to early obsolescence. Science is more than a body of knowledge; it also is a process. In the long run, comprehension of the process is more significant than knowledge of any of its particular products. Therefore, it is important to present the intellectual roots of as many topics as possible and the elements essential to their growth.

These were the decisions and the intentions. Their validity, and the effectiveness of our execution, must now be judged in practice. Each of these books may be used alone as a presentation of its particular level. Each, however, has been written under the explicit assumption that no one level of biological organization is fully comprehended without consideration of the other two. Accordingly, the three books will be most meaningful if used together and in their intended sequence—Cell, Organism, Population. Only in this way is the student likely to benefit from the great continuity and cohesiveness that are the products of the last two decades of biological investigation.

The Authors and Clifford Grobstein, *Series Consultant*

PREFACE

While most biologists would agree on what an organism is, there is, paradoxically, no common understanding on what constitutes the *biology* of organisms. After cell and population biologists have claimed what seems rightly to be theirs, the residue appears, at first sight, to consist of scattered blocks of unrelated information. A serious challenge to the utility of subdividing biology according to the three levels of organization is thus the question of whether an acceptable framework can be found to accommodate the subject matter of organism biology.

It seemed to us that what remained consisted most prominently of the traditional studies of anatomy, reproduction and embryology, comparative and environmental physiology, and behavior. Though alarmed at the outset by the prospects for being able to do more than simply pack these topics together in a single book cover, it occurred to us that a beginning student who is not already steeped in the curricular traditions of biology might find the usual separations between them somewhat artificial. Thus fortified, we identified not one but three pervasive biological concepts to serve as unifying agents. One was the cell theory, the second was the concept of adaptation, and the third was the organism's universal requirement for mechanisms of integration. Our aim became therefore to analyze how a cell or an aggregate of cells develops and functions in unitary fashion as an organism that is superbly equipped to exploit a restricted environmental niche.

We strongly suspect that many of our colleagues will feel that we have arranged a shotgun wedding between their respective fields, and we may ourselves worry about this in retrospect. We hope, however, for a more charitable treatment from their students—some of whom will one day be able to improve on our effort.

We gratefully acknowledge the help of numerous colleagues who read portions of the manuscript, including William G. van der Kloot, Winslow R. Briggs, Richard Holm, Paul Ehrlich, Sidney Rodenberg, Paul B. Green, Ralph O. Erickson, and W. John Smith; we also thank the authors of the other volumes in the series for similar assistance. Clifford Grobstein was involved in the planning of the book from the outset, and read it in several different stages; we thank him both for the practical worth of his suggestions and for his insistence that we adhere to the original intention of the series in the face of temptations to depart from it. Finally, we salute the patience and tact of our respective wives, who not only survived the experience but found time to act as innkeeper and critic (Mary A. Telfer) and indexer (Jeanne Kennedy).

William H. Telfer

Donald Kennedy

Philadelphia, Pennsylvania
Stanford, California
April 1965

CONTENTS

The Biology of Organisms

1

The Problem of Diversity

The organism is a concept that is familiar to everyone from routine observation. Even the most inexperienced reader has a working knowledge of organisms, a grasp of the fantastic range in their size and appearance, and an appreciation of their activities and requirements. In viewing the whole range of structures that can be regarded as organisms, questions of criterion and definition arise in only a few special instances. In some colonial forms, for instance, the individual is so intimately associated with its siblings that its physical and functional discreteness are lost; and it is not clear whether the colony or the individual member should be regarded as an organism. Such cases raise special semantic problems rather than practical difficulties of a general character, and thus do not dim the clarity of our concept of the organism as a discrete and living individual.

Our primary concern in this text is with the individual organism—how it comes into being, what kind of structure it has, how it functions. Any attempt to achieve this objective, however, is brought face to face with a practical problem of major dimensions. Between one and two million species of organisms have been described in the journals of biology. The magnitude of this figure testifies to the enormous energy of the taxonomists who have collected, described, and classified each of these species—and whose work, incidentally, is still far from completed. The figure is of immediate concern because it expresses concisely and eloquently the diversity of organisms. What general statements can be made about two million kinds of organisms with two million different structures and two million different ways of making a living? Is there

1

really an *organism biology*—a set of principles and problems that are relevant from *Escherichia coli* to *Sequoia sempervirens,* from the amoeba to the elephant, and from the viper to the lily? Or must we be content with the totally impractical objective of trying to understand each of the two million kinds in its turn or, at best, of trying to understand the structures and operations of a few dozen examples?

One of the theses of this volume is that a general biology of organisms is not as impractical an objective as the diversity of species makes it seem. The organism is the middle ground between two levels of biological organization, the cell and the population, in which principles generally relevant to all forms of life are readily identified. As the casting in the mold, the organism has had general properties impressed on it by the die on either side. Every organism is a unit in a population of many organisms of similar structure and behavior; the resulting competitions, which are among the primary concerns of the population biologist, have had profound consequences for the nature of the individual organism. And every organism is itself either a cohesive population of cells or a single cell. This fact also has general consequences for the structure of organisms and how they operate. We can profitably begin by exploring each of these relationships in turn.

THE POPULATION AND THE ORGANISM

Population biology has dealt, apparently with some success, with the evolution of diversity. We need not look in detail at either the mechanisms proposed or their justification, since these are treated in an accompanying volume.* They have been conceived from analyses of the nature of organisms and of the manner in which they interact. The salient points for our immediate purpose are as follows:

At some stage in their life histories organisms generally leave progeny whose subsequent life history, structure, and behavior resemble those of their progenitors. Hence it is necessary to conceive of the existence of mechanisms of heredity. Heredity mechanisms can be accidentally altered however and hereditary variants, or mutants, can arise as a consequence; the accumulation of such events over long periods leaves the species with a substantial store of mutations. Thus a population of organisms—even if it satisfies the criteria for being a single species—consists of individuals with dissimilar hereditary complements. In sub-

---

* Robert MacArthur and Joseph Connell, *The Biology of Populations,* Wiley, to be published.

sequent generations the composition of the population may change. By the process of natural selection the offspring of some individuals become relatively more numerous than others, and these are thereby defined as more fit. By the continued action of mutation, gene recombination, and natural selection, the structure, physiology, and behavior of the organisms comprising the population may change progressively through successive generations. The nature of the change generally is not simply random or indifferent; for fitness is related in a poorly defined but critically important way to the effectiveness of the organism in obtaining energy and matter from the environment and in converting these into progeny.

Adaptation and the Efficiency of Organisms

It is of profound importance for the nature of the organism that, due to natural selection, the evolutionary changes in organisms have either moved relentlessly in the direction of efficiency or have kept them attuned to a changing environment. The expected consequence would be the evolution of organisms that are lean and efficient—organisms that have little energy to spare for activities that might detract from the essential operations of obtaining matter and energy, of developing to a state of reproductive competence, and of propelling their progeny into the next lap of the race. Evolutionary adaptation thus suggests an extremely fine attunement between organism and environment. The organism doesn't merely get along; its whole life mode has been tempered and refined by the successful competition of generations of its ancestors with a multitude of differing genotypes. Thus even in the finest details of their organization, organisms are constructed and operate in a manner which makes sense in terms of the way they make their living.

Consider, for example, the relations between the structure and the function of a leaf. As the site of photosynthesis in the plant, the leaf must be the point of convergence of the energy and all the materials necessary for assembling molecules of carbohydrate. Its anatomy is consistent with this function. Chloroplasts equipped with the necessary pigments for absorbing light are abundantly present. As a consequence of the flattened shape of the leaf, the chloroplasts are arranged so that they do not significantly shade each other; and neighboring leaves are arranged on the stem in a manner that reduces the extent of shading (Fig. 1-1). The tree thus develops in such a way that a minimal amount of energy and matter is expended in the formation of leaves and chloroplasts which are shaded by other parts of the same plant. The thickened

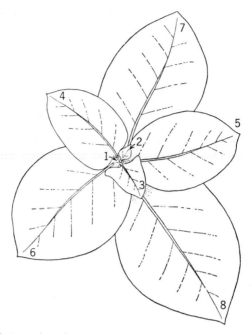

Fig. 1-1. Apical view of a tobacco stem showing the arrangement of eight successive leaves. (From K. Esau, *Plant Anatomy,* Wiley, 1953, p. 341.)

veins and petioles serve to support the leaf so that its flattened surface intercepts the path of the sunlight rather than lying parallel to it. The veins ramify in the blade of the leaf so that all chloroplast-containing cells are less than a millimeter from the conductile elements which bring it water and remove its photosynthetic products (Fig. 1-2). The surface

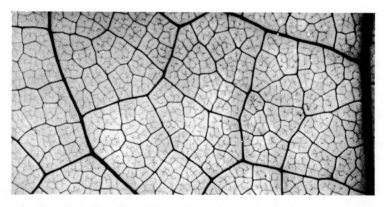

Fig. 1-2. Venation of a tulip tree leaf. The mid-rib is the thicker vein on the right. (From Esau, *Plant Anatomy,* p. 687.)

of the leaf is covered with a wax, suberin, and the under surface is dotted with stomata—microscopic air vents, which may be opened or closed by the action of the two guard cells which surround them (Fig. 1-3). This arrangement allows the control of evaporation of water and exchange of gases. It is an eminently suitable compromise between the necessity of gas exchange and the hazard of desiccation, and indirectly provides a critical function in the transport of mineral nutrients from the roots (p. 235).

Even at the level of molecular architecture the appropriateness of the design is apparent. Each chloroplast contains pigment molecules whose absorption spectra are appropriate for trapping some of the wavelengths in sunlight. Moreover, within the chloroplast the chlorophyll molecules are arrayed with other molecules in highly ordered, semicrystalline arrays (the *grana*); the spacing of layers within a granum appears appropriate for electronic energy transfer between molecules. And more and more evidence suggests that these energy-trapping arrays are structurally related to the metabolic machinery of energy utilization.

Although the appropriateness of organization thus extends from gross to molecular dimensions, the usefulness of some hereditary features in the leaf is not so obvious. Oak leaves have lobed edges, for instance; in the white oak these are rounded, while in the black oak they are pointed and tipped with a spine (Fig. 1-4). The under surface of the black oak leaf bears epidermal hairs to a much greater extent than that of the white oak. What accounts for hereditary differences such as these? Are

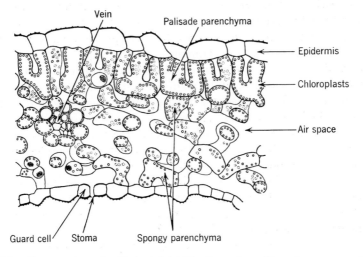

Fig. 1-3. Cross-section of a lily leaf ($\times$ 260). (From Esau, *Plant Anatomy*, p. 417.)

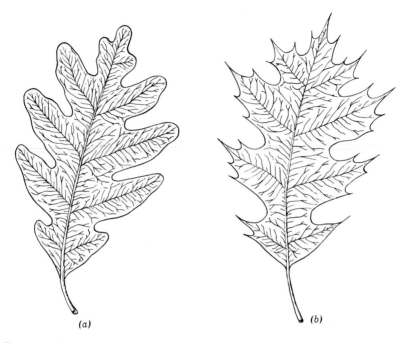

Fig. 1-4. Comparison of the leaves of white oak (a) and black oak (b). (From *Common Trees of Pennsylvania*, Penna. Dept. of Forests and Waters, p. 10 and 12.)

hairs and spines in the black oak to be considered superfluous structures, suggestive of valuable energy and matter spent frivolously on useless frills? Such situations are often rationalized by assuming that if we only understood the organism a bit better we *could* specify a significant function, or that the structure *once* had an appropriateness which has now vanished. Thus the human appendix and the second and fourth digits of the horse, which walks so effectively on its third digits, are frequently relegated to the status of vestigial holdovers—structures that were useful to an ancestor but are now on their way to disappearance. A final possibility is that some aspects of an organism have no relevance to the effectiveness of its activities. A leaf must have an edge, but the precise shape of the edge—whether lobed, rounded, or saw-toothed—makes no difference to the operation of the organism. Its precise shape may thus have been determined largely by historical accident. Since none of these alternatives can be subjected to critical proof, perhaps the best course is to be satisfied with the fact that *most* features of an organism are recognizably *adaptive* and that none of them significantly detracts from its ability to succeed in its special way of life.

The Restrictive Character of Adaptation

Let us, finally, define more precisely the role of adaptation in accounting for the diversity encountered in the world of organisms. The result of natural selection has been the achievement of congruence between the demands and opportunities of the environment and the structure and capabilities of the organism. But the war of selection is fought on small battlefields; the environment is not homogeneous, but divided into sectors. The population biologist proposes that the very process of natural selection that fits the organism so well for any given subenvironment also makes it *less* fit for all others. As a corollary he predicts that "specialists" will outperform "generalists" if the competition is held on the specialist's own ground. Such a notion would, in turn, predict a continual pressure in the direction of diversification. In the next few paragraphs we shall examine the evidence for this restrictive effect of adaptation.

The earth's surface is roughly subdivided into three major physical environments: the salt water seas and oceans, the freshwater lakes and streams, and dry land. Already we see the restrictions of adaptation at work, for most organisms are limited to just one of these three physical media and generally are unable to do well in the other two. There are, of course, organisms such as the varied spectrum of intertidal algae and invertebrates whose unique attribute is a capacity to close up shop and survive periodic stranding on dry land when the tide has ebbed. It can hardly be said that they cope equally well with both environments; they thrive in one and merely tolerate the other.

A more serious exception might be those organisms that spend part of their lives in one environment and part in another; but on closer examination these appear instead to strengthen the argument that adaptation is restrictive. The Pacific salmon develops from an egg deposited in the headwaters of a freshwater stream, feeds for a period in its stream, migrates to the ocean to spend several years feeding and growing, and finally returns to the same stream to breed. The Great Lakes eel, by contrast, performs precisely the reverse migration. It breeds in the Sargasso Sea of the tropical Atlantic and migrates to freshwater continental streams, there continuing its development to maturity. The transition from water to land is illustrated by those insects and amphibians that breed in freshwater streams and lakes, spend a long larval feeding period there, and then leave the water for a period of time to be spent on land. In all of these instances a change in diet and in the physiological mechanisms of water and salt balance (Chapter 6) must be achieved, and particularly for the water to land transformation new modes of locomotion are required. Such transformations can be marked, therefore, by an extensive remodeling of the organism. In insects such as mayflies and dragonflies the metamorphosis is so extensive that the aquatic nymph, which would have desiccated or starved on land, becomes an adult which would drown if immersed in water (Fig. 1-5).

The restrictive nature of adaptation also operates on a far more subtle scale. Within each of the three major physical media other variables —light intensity, temperature, the concentration of dissolved gases and salts in aquatic environments, and the humidity of the air overlying the terrestrial environment—combine to introduce a multitude of microhabitats to which organisms have become adapted. And again, adaptation to a particular set of conditions has diminished the organism's capacity to get along in other sets of conditions.

A few days travel on the western coast of the United States provides a spectacular example of restriction. A storm moving from the Pacific Ocean inland may deposit several inches of warm rain at the lower elevations in the coastal valleys, two feet of snow on the colder mountain tops of the Sierra Nevada and Cascade Mountains, and very little precipitation on the high plateau between the coastal mountains and the

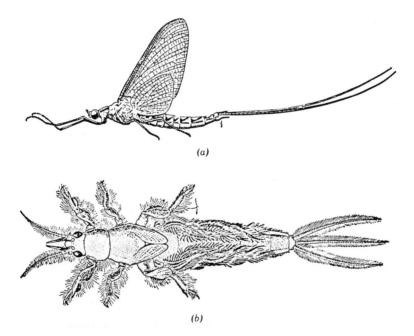

(a)

(b)

Fig. 1-5. Adult (a) and nymphal (b) forms of a mayfly. (From V. A. Little, *General and Applied Entomology,* Harper & Row, 1963, p. 120.)

Rocky Mountains. The correlation between the vegetation and the form and amount of precipitation is striking. Coastal valleys, which in some areas receive over one hundred inches of rain per year, are populated by lush forests of western hemlock, Sitka spruce, and Douglas fir in the north and by firs and coast redwoods in the south—many of these trees attaining heights of well over two hundred feet. The high mountains with their lower temperatures, heavy snow, and poorer soil are populated by very different species of trees, such as the slower and more compactly growing mountain hemlock and alpine fir. And on the interior plateau, which may receive as little as ten inches of precipitation per year, sage brush and juniper trees grow in the north and cactus and Joshua trees in the south. There are, of course many intermediate conditions between these extremes which give areas their characteristic vegetation—chapparal hillsides in coastal California and yellow pine forests of the inland mountains. Although such extreme contrasts may not always be apparent, comparable correlations between vegetation and climate can be made in almost any other region of the world.

Interspecies Competition

Restrictive adaptations to varied physical conditions clearly account for much of organic diversity, but competition with other organisms greatly complicates the picture. It is frequently found that an organism can tolerate a far wider range of physical conditions than characterize its actual distribution. That interspecies competitions account for the difference is often confirmed by the experiences of the amateur gardener. His carefully tended flowers and vegetables may do quite well as long as he fights their battles for them. But the local flora, with its long history of successful competition for water, minerals, and light in precisely the climate and soil which prevail in the gardener's garden, will quickly take over if it is not assiduously weeded out.

The winter wren, which inhabits most of the forests of temperate North America, provides an additional example. Eight species of wrens inhabit the United States and Canada. Collectively they occupy a wide range of habitats: cactus deserts, marshes, deep forests for the winter wren, and even the dooryard for the house wren. In Europe the winter wren appears in the absence of other wren species; and there it successfully populates a variety of habitats, including the dooryard which the house wren dominates in America. Examples of this sort are sufficiently diverse to suggest that many organisms could get along quite well in a much wider range of habitats than they normally occupy were it not for the fact that competing species can grow more vigorously in the extremes of their range of tolerance.

Hence the organism must be genetically endowed with developmental, behavioral, and physiological strategies for coping with a set of physical circumstances and also with the avaricious behavior of a variety of competing and predatory species. The result has been the evolution of organisms that are superbly equipped for a restricted way of life in a very restricted environment. We can note, for instance, that even in North America the winter wren still inhabits the forests to the exclusion of every other species of wren. Confinement to ecological niches has in some cases become so extreme that we find species of ants that live by herding aphids, and others that culture fungi; a species of moth that lives only in the fruits produced by Yucca flowers; and a constellation of organisms on intertidal rocks, which is vertically zoned according to the percentage of time that each level of the rock is submerged by water.

Above all else, therefore, it has been the evolution of restrictive adaptations to narrow ecological niches which has led to the magnitude of diversity confronting the organism biologist.

COPING WITH DIVERSITY:
THE CLASSIFICATION OF ORGANISMS

The most direct effort to cope with organic diversity has been made by the taxonomists who catalog organisms in a system of classification. Although there are a number of objectives entailed in constructing a classification system one of its greatest benefits is that it gives the biologist a clearer understanding of where he is working in the world of organisms. A system of classification is an extremely practical device for creating order out of what otherwise would be a chaos of scientific conflict and misunderstanding. A full understanding of the theory and methods by which the established system operates requires a background in population biology. The product is so useful to organism biology, however, that several comments concerning its mode of operation are essential here.

It must first be recognized that the criteria used in arranging organisms in a system of classification could be basically arbitrary. Organisms could be classified by their size, color, or habitat. Indeed, there are specific instances in which it is useful to group organisms by one of these criteria, but for most purposes such groupings would have very little meaning. The most generally useful system, in terms of understanding the similarities and differences between organisms, has instead been based on a broad spectrum of criteria, most of them relating to the general body plan of the organism.

Philosophically, it has been conventional to classify organisms in a manner that is presumed in most instances to reflect their evolutionary history. Thus organisms that are believed to have a common ancestry are grouped together, and subgroups established within the major group encompass organisms whose common ancestry is more recent. As a practical matter, however, there is very little direct information available on the ancestry of most organisms, and relationships must therefore be inferred, often in a highly speculative manner, from similarities in the anatomy and reproduction of contemporary organisms.

From the point of view of organism biology, the utility of the present system as an orienting device is derived from the fact that it is based on a number of relatively stable features in the structure of organisms, rather than on single characteristics which are more responsive to the whimsies of mutation and natural selection. An equally useful system could be developed by any philosophy of classification that was based on a broad spectrum of similarities and differences. The antecedent of the present system was first published in 1735 by Linnaeus, and it is interesting to note that Linnaeus believed in the doctrine of special creation. Despite the philosophical intent of his system, the fact that Linnaeus endeavored to classify organisms according to their basic anatomical features led to his establishing groups that are for the most part still incorporated in the present post-Darwinian system.

A system of classification provides a relatively simple method of identifying organisms. In biology, as in any other science, repeatability of observations by others is the disciplining feature that encourages careful experiments and thoughtful reporting, and the identification of the species in which the observations were made is a frequent prerequisite to repeatability. For this purpose, it is essential to be able to place an organism in the appropriate slot in the system of classification conveniently and accurately. Alphabetical and numerical systems of ordering items are useful wherever there is an obvious sequence in which they should be arranged—as in the ordering of words in a dictionary. There is no obvious sequence in the classification of organisms, however, and thus it has been necessary to establish a system of hierarchies of groupings as a guide through the intricacies of classification. The system of hierarchies proposed by Linnaeus which remains the convention at the present time is as follows:

Kingdom
Phylum
Class
Order
Family
Genus
Species

(There are additional steps such as the superorder and suborder in common usage at the present time, but these refinements have in no way altered the mode of operation of the system.)

The utility of the hierarchy of groupings for nonsequentially arranged items can be demonstrated in the following comparison. Let us say that there are two kingdoms, ten classes in each phylum, ten orders in each class, and so on up to ten species in each genus for a total of two million species. (In fact the number of subgroupings at each step in the hierarchy varies with the diversity of the group.) A biologist would then have to make only seven choices out of sixty-two possibilities in order to identify a species. Thus he must decide that the species he is trying to identify is in one of the two kingdoms, in one of the ten phyla in that kingdom, and so forth. Without a hierarchical system he would have to make one positive decision and around two million negative decisions in order to identify a species with assurance.

To the extent that taxonomists have achieved a consensus about the relationships of organisms, the system of classification has a stable structure. It is a fact, however, that consensus has not been achieved about many points. To the confusion of both the students and practitioners of organism biology, some taxonomists divide organisms into two kingdoms, and some into three or four. The number of phyla described varies from about twenty to about forty. And what one person considers as three phyla may be grouped by another as three classes in a single phylum. Such disputes reflect the difficulties entailed in fitting organisms, as they exist, into an arbitrary system of classification so that their similarities and differences are meaningfully highlighted. Fortunately they do not significantly detract from the overriding utility of the system.

An abbreviated classification of organisms is presented. The classification is designed for the orientation of a student using the present text. Specific organisms or groups of organisms taken as examples throughout this text are mentioned in such a manner that reference to Tables 1-1 and 1-2 will indicate their positions in the animal and plant kingdoms.

THE CELL AND THE ORGANISM

The realization that organisms are composed of cells has perhaps done more than any other biological concept to transform the study of organisms into a cohesive subject. It has led to an awareness that the basic mechanisms of heredity, growth and metabolism are the same in all organisms and that diversity is an expression of the ways

Table 1-1   Plant Kingdom

Phylum	Class	Type of organism
Schizomycophyta		bacteria
Cyanophyta		blue-green algae
Chlorophyta		green algae
Euglenophyta		euglenoids
Phaeophyta		brown algae
Rhodophyta		red algae
Chrysophyta		diatoms and others
Myxomycophyta		slime molds
Eumycophyta	Phycomycetes Ascomycetes Basidiomycetes	fungi
Bryophyta	Hepaticae Musci	liverworts mosses
Tracheophyta	(Several primitive classes) Filicinae Gymnospermae Angiospermae	ferns conifers flowering plants (monocots and dicots)

Table 1-2   Animal Kingdom

Phylum (Subphylum)	Class	Type of organism
Protozoa	Flagellata Sarcodina Ciliata Sporozoa	flagellates amoebae ciliates sporozoans (mainly parasitic)
Porifera		sponges
Coelenterata	Hydrozoa Scyphozoa Anthozoa	Hydra, Obelia, etc. jellyfish sea anemones, corals
Ctenophora		comb jellies

Table 1-2   (continued)

Platyhelminthes	Turbellaria	free-living flatworms
	Trematoda	parasitic flukes
	Cestoda	tapeworms
Aschelminthes	Rotifera	rotifers
	Nematoda	roundworms
	(others)	
Nemertea		proboscis worms
Mollusca	Gastropoda	snails, etc.
	Pelecypoda	clams, etc.
	Cephalopoda	squids, octopuses
	(others)	
Annelida	Polychaeta	marine segmented worms
	Oligochaeta	earthworms
	Hirudinea	leeches
Arthropoda		
(Arachnomorpha)	Xiphosura	horseshoe crabs
	Arachnida	spiders, scorpions, ticks
	(others)	
(Crustacea)		lobsters, shrimps, crabs, etc.
(Labiata)	Chilopoda	centipedes
	Diplopoda	millipedes
	Insecta	insects
Echinodermata	Crinoidea	sea lilies
	Holothuroidea	sea cucumbers
	Asteroidea	starfish
	Echinoidea	sea urchins
	Ophiuroidea	brittle stars
Chordata		
(Urochordata)		Tunicates
(Cephalochordata)		*Amphioxus*
(Vertebrata)	Agnatha	lampreys
	Chondrichthyes	sharks and rays
	Osteichthyes	bony fish
	Amphibia	frogs, toads, salamanders
	Reptilia	snakes, lizards
	Aves	birds
	Mammalia	mammals

that cells, singly or in association with each other, are able to exploit their environment. Before we can live comfortably with this unifying concept, however, we need to define the boundary between cell biology and organism biology; there would be little justification for a separate biology of organisms if it sufficed to think of organisms simply as a series of special manifestations of cells.

While it is true that in microorganisms the cell and the organism are different terms for the same object, in larger forms the cell has the status of a subunit in the construction of the organism. One way to seek a distinction between the two fields therefore is to ask why it is that ten million yeast cells in a culture tube are considered ten million organisms, while ten million cells in the form of a moss plant or a bee are only one organism? The simplest answer to this question is that the cells comprising the moss and the bee cohere in a single mass, whereas the yeast cells are suspended in the culture medium as individual cells, or at most as aggregates of a few siblings. An additional answer is that, except for being in different phases of their growth and division cycles, the yeast cells all look about the same and can all do about the same things; the moss and the bee, by contrast, include many different kinds of cells, and the differences are generally permanent rather than cyclical.

But there is more to the problem than this. Indeed, it can be proposed that cohesion and differentiation are merely expressions of a more fundamental attribute. What really convinces us that the bee cells are subunits of one organism is the extent to which the activities of the individual cell are subservient to the whole population. In general the individual yeast cell competes with its partners for the nutrients present in the culture tube. Every individual has sufficient capacity for growth and reproduction to utilize, with its progeny, all the materials available; each can be counted on to produce a clone of cells that will take what it can until all nutrients are exhausted, or until crowding factors limit its growth. While other more subtle relationships may exist between cells, competition is the predominant form of interaction in the growing culture.

By contrast, the multicellular organism is not an association of freely competing cells. Prominent among the differences between cells are differences in their capacity to utilize nutrients for growth. The cells of a mature leaf or of the skeletal muscle of a vertebrate normally do not proliferate at all, even under the most optimal conditions of nutrition. Other cells, such as those at the apex of the shoot in a plant or the basal cells in the epidermis in a mammal, may grow; but generally they do so only in what may be considered the best interests of the organism as a whole. Thus the next season's leaves are produced by the growth of cells at the apex of the stem while rubbed-off, superficial layers of skin are replaced by the proliferation of epidermal cells. The problem of producing progeny may be left to a special set of cells, which have thereby come to be known as germ cells. These may even be nourished by the synthetic products of cells which are not themselves destined to participate in reproduction. Thus the cells of the moss, or the bee, or any other multicellular organism act in an integrated way that is quite different from the predominantly competitive interaction of yeast cells. Whether the number of cells is a few hundred, as in rotifers and some of the algae, or billions, as in many trees and vertebrates, they act collectively in obtaining matter and energy from the environment, in converting these into the growth of the organism, and in leaving progeny.

Returning to the cell that is also an independent organism, it is clear that cohesion, differentiation, and integration of sub-units are just as fundamental to it as to the multicellular organism. There is, therefore, a set of problems that are relevant to all organisms, and a discussion of the biology of organisms must be to a major extent concerned with these. But what does this do to reduce the problem of diversity to manageable proportions? Although the requirement of integration may be universal, may not the mechanisms of integration be just as varied as the organisms?

At this juncture we will acknowledge a capitulation to diversity in one respect. In microorganisms the mechanisms of cohesion, differentiation, and integration are essentially those of a single cell. The subunits are molecules and molecular aggregates, and their interactions, so far as they are understood, can be described by thermodynamic and chemical equations. These topics have been introduced in the first volume of this series* and will not be repeated here. The bulk of the present volume therefore concerns the multicellular organism.

What are the mechanisms of integration that make unity of action in the multicellular organism possible? What are the cues which the individual cell takes from its environment and which govern its activities? What does the individual cell do to influence its brethren? How are the cells organized so that the sum total of their activities and interactions will be manifested in effective feeding, development, and reproduction? What features distinguish integration between cells from integration within a cell? These are the central questions that distinguish biology at the organism level from biology at the cell level. The answers that can be provided are largely incomplete, for the integration of the orga-

---

* Herbert Stern and David Nanney, *The Biology of Cells*, Wiley, 1965, referred to throughout simply as Stern and Nanney.

nism is a field of vigorous contemporary investigation. But the questions—and questions are just as important as answers—form some of the major themes of organism biology.

ORGANISM BIOLOGY

Cell biology, on the one hand, deals with the general mechanisms and behavior of the basic unit from which organisms are constructed whereas population biology explains the origins of the present diversity of organisms and in so doing emphasizes the importance of adaptation and specialization. Both fields have attained their present stature with the benefit of dramatic theoretical developments. The theory of natural selection aroused the entire literate world in the last century. After seventy years or so of acceptance as a satisfactory general explanation, it has in recent decades begun to be used as the starting point for inductive considerations that reveal the basic properties of ecological systems. The revelation that cells could be studied as physicochemical systems has culminated in recent advances in molecular genetics that promise to do for cell biology what natural selection has done for population biology. It is interesting to note that both fields had their historical roots in the analysis of organisms—that organism biology has therefore served as a progenitor for the other two major areas of general biology. And now we must ask what is left of the parent.

The concept of the organism as a cell, or a cohesive aggregate of cells that lives as a highly competent specialist in a qualitatively restricted environment seems to us to give rise to a series of general questions concerning the strategies and mechanisms of operation of organisms. Every organism must nourish itself and reproduce; and its behavior, development, and other operations must be carefully integrated to accomplish these ends in a hazardous and competitive environment. Since the cell is a basic unit of structure and function in all organisms, it is apparent that the mechanistic solutions to these problems must also have a great deal in common. In short, each kind of organism is a variation on a theme, rather than a totally novel entity; and we can propose that a full understanding of the common theme should be the first objective of a text on the biology of organisms. It also seems to us that a second objective, a survey of the basic strategies employed by organisms, can be conveniently achieved in the course of exploring the problems and mechanisms that they share in common.

The order of events by which we attempt to achieve these objectives is as follows. First, the more prominent solutions to the problems of nutrition and reproduction are described (Chapters 2, 3, and 4). The organisms used as examples in these chapters span the full range of size and complexity from the viruses to multicellular plants and animals. In the last three chapters the internal mechanisms of operation in multicellular organisms are considered, with particular emphasis on development (Chapter 5), the special problems in metabolism and housekeeping (Chapter 6), and intercellular integrating mechanisms—the endocrine and nervous systems (Chapter 7).

Throughout the book the reader should be aware that we are trying to focus on principles, citing specific systems in order to provide examples or experimental proofs for them. We have made an honest effort to make each illustration count—to require that each problem considered in detail contributes to some significant theme of the nature of the organism, and not qualify for inclusion just because it has always been taught to biologists. Although diversity is at times the organism biologist's most exciting weapon, it may also be his enemy, robbing him of the chance to formulate sweeping questions about organisms as systems and substituting instead a fascination for the special event, the unique form, the clever stratagem. But he may be equally betrayed if he supposes that the comforting unity of the cell can be mobilized to provide a complete set of statements that apply without exception to all organisms. In steering this difficult course—recognizing diversity and using it to illustrate, yet seeking unifying principles wherever they can be found—the danger is that one becomes too superficial. We must leave to the reader's own energies the correction of this potential fault.

2

The Biology of Microorganisms

Organisms exist at several levels of complexity. Some of the algae and protozoa are single cells whose average diameter generally falls within the range of 10-50 μ. The bacteria, on the other hand, are much smaller cells having a more compact construction and a diameter generally 1-5 μ. They contain functional equivalents of the nuclei and mitochondria of more conventional cells, but these are not at all the discrete, membranous organelles that reside in the cytoplasm of the algae and protozoa. The viruses are relatively simple macromolecular aggregates which have a diameter no greater than a few tenths of a micron and in some cases as small as 25 mμ. At the other end of the scale are the multicellular organisms. Within any single life history the multicellular organisms develop through a series of levels of complexity, from that of a single cell to that of a structure which in extreme cases consists of more than 10^{10} cells organized into an arrangement akin to a tree or a mammal.

In this chapter the structures and the ways of life of the viruses, the bacteria, and the unicellular plants and animals are described. These are creatures whose strategies for making a living and leaving progeny are relatively unobscured by structural and mechanistic complexity. On the other hand they are sufficiently diverse so that a comparative analysis can distinguish between the general attributes of organisms and the specific strategies which they individually employ. Against this background the more complex problems of multicellular organization will then be analyzed.

VIRUSES

Intracellular Parasitism

A virus exhibits a partial sample of the properties of organisms. Those viruses which have been isolated in sufficient purity to be analyzed chemically contain at least two classes of the basic macromolecular constituents of cells—proteins and either RNA or DNA. They also possess that most fundamental property of organisms, the capacity to reproduce. As an essential correlate of reproduction the virus exhibits genetic properties: the progeny of a tobacco mosaic virus are invariably tobacco mosaic viruses, rather than bushy stunt, or yellow fever, or poliomyelitis viruses. And within these limits of hereditary constancy mutations occur just as in other organisms (Stern and Nanney, Chap. 14). Thus the viruses show what is in a sense the most basic attribute of living systems: hereditary continuity through a mechanism of replication which is subject to mutation.

The attribute which sets a virus apart from more conventional organisms is its subcellular construction. It is an obligate parasite which possesses little if any of the synthetic machinery required for reproduction. Although it carries the genetic material which specifies the quality of synthesis, the virus depends on the cell which it infects to energize, catalyze, and nourish its reproduction. It is thus a subcellular particle which can behave like an organism only with the metabolic assistance of its victim.

By using the present technology for observing the structure of cells, a virus in the early phases of infection cannot be distinguished from the structural elements of the host cell. Even in its extracellular phase when it is no longer to be confused with the substance of the cell, a virus is too small to be detected by means of the light microscope. Consequently the biology of viruses, like the study of chemicals, has been largely inferential. Even the existence of a virus may pass unobserved, unless it exhibits a combination of two properties. First, it must alter in some manner either the appearance or the behavior of its host. In the more conspicuous cases the virus does this by killing its host, or by stunting its growth, or by making it temporarily ill. Second, and equally important, the virus must be infectious: it must move from victim to victim in contagious fashion.

Contagion in the absence of visible phenotypic effects would be likely to go unnoticed, and it is quite possible that numerous viruses exist which for this reason have never been detected. On the other hand, phenotypic effects without contagion would fall within the operational definition of hereditary characters. Such a virus would have to pass from generation to generation through the reproductive cells of its host, and its effects on the phenotype would be difficult to distinguish from those of the host's more conventional nuclear genes. There are a variety of hereditary phenotypes caused by agents which are recognized as viruses, or virus-like, only because they are contagious under special circumstances. The case of lysogeny is a useful example.

It is possible to isolate from nature individual bacteria of the species *Escherichia coli,* which will grow luxuriantly in an appropriate culture medium but whose progeny release small amounts of a virus (or *bacteriophage*) to the medium. (The manner in which the released viruses are detected will become apparent in the following paragraphs.) Observation of the behavior of individual bacteria taken from such a culture indicate that all cells in the culture do not release virus particles continuously. Rather, virus particles are suddenly liberated from occasional cells which are lysed and killed in the process. Strains of bacteria which behave in this fashion are described as lysogenic. Other strains of *E. coli* do not liberate virus particles spontaneously; but if they are mixed with some of the medium in which the lysogenic strain grew, they may lyse in large numbers within an hour.

The explanation of this phenomenon now seems well established. The lysogenic bacterium contains bacteriophage nucleic acid which reproduces in synchrony with the bacterium itself. This agent, which has become known as *prophage,* may be carried by the clone of bacteria through many successive divisions (right hand cycle in Fig. 2-1). However, an occasional cell becomes activated by unknown mechanisms to produce the virus nucleic acid at an accelerated rate, and to initiate the synthesis of the virus proteins. The growth of the cell itself essentially ceases. Infectious virus particles are assembled from these constituents and are finally released from the cell when it lyses. Cells which already carry prophage are for some reason immune to infection by the virus particles released from their hapless brethren. But cells which do not carry prophage can be infected, and such cells are presented to the virus when it is mixed with the culture of cells which are not lysogenic. On entering a new cell, the virus may again give rise to prophage, but it will more probably become a rapidly reproducing infectious virus. Thus most of the sensitive cells cease growing and lyse subsequent to exposure to the virus (left-hand cycle of Fig. 2-1).

In the absence of lysis it is clear that the prophage would go undetected, and any phenotypic effect of the prophage on the bacterium

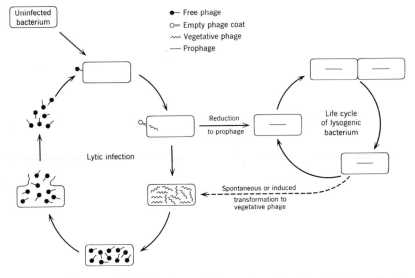

Fig. 2-1. A diagram of the infectious and lysogenic cycles of bacteriophage, beginning at the upper left with the exposure of uninfected bacteria to free phage particles. (From R. Y. Stanier, M. Doudoroff, and E. A. Adelberg, *The Microbial World,* Prentice-Hall, 1963, p. 202.)

would be interpreted simply as one of its numerous inherited characteristics. This is not simply an academic argument; such phenotypic effects actually occur, the immunity of lysogenic cells to infection by additional virus particles being an example.

The viruses which most conspicuously fulfill the requirements for ready detectability are those which cause epidemic diseases. Most of what we know of the behavior of viruses has been revealed by analyses of a few of these unambiguous parasites.

The Isolation and Structure of Viruses

Toward the end of the nineteenth century rapidly developing techniques for isolating and culturing microorganisms permitted a large number of diseases to be attributed to infectious bacteria. Yet some diseases remained refractory to such analyses. Neither a bacterium nor any other organism could be isolated from afflicted individuals and grown in culture. Such diseases were clearly contagious, for they frequently occurred as epidemics and extracts or secretions of infected tissues produced the disease when injected into a new host. Passing such an extract through a filter capable of retaining particles the size of bacteria did not clear it of the infectious agent, however, and microscopic examination of the filtrate revealed nothing comparable to a bacterium.

Finally, in 1935, the virus causing the mosaic disease in tobacco plants was induced by Stanley to form crystals. Each crystal represented an aggregate of many particles, but it was at least a visible manifestation of the infectious agent; crystalization was a major step in its purification for chemical analysis. Within the next two decades, when techniques such as ultracentrifugation and more refined chemical fractionation were applied to the problem, a number of additional viruses were purified. The electron microscope led to direct observation of the virus particle (Fig. 2-2). The capacity of such purified preparations to infect other organisms confirmed that the particles visualized with the electron microscope were indeed the infectious agent. The blame for a number of famous diseases, including yellow fever, poliomyelitis, and many varieties of influenza and colds, has thus been placed on the viruses.

Chemical analyses, electron microscopy, and other techniques have yielded information about the structure of many virus particles. Some idea of their structure and diversity is given here with brief descriptions of five examples. The virus causing the mosaic disease in tobacco plants

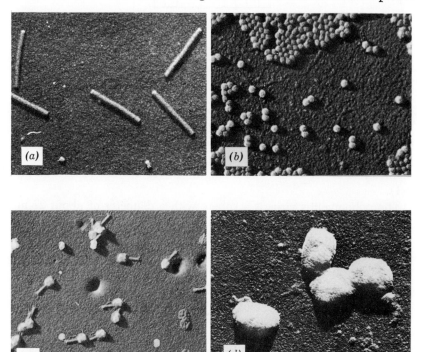

Fig. 2-2. Electron micrographs of virus particles shadowed with heavy metal; all magnified $\times$ 50,000. *(a)* Tobacco mosaic virus. *(b)* Poliomyelitis. *(c)* T$_4$ bacteriophage *(d)* Vaccinia. (Photographs courtesy of Robley C. Williams.)

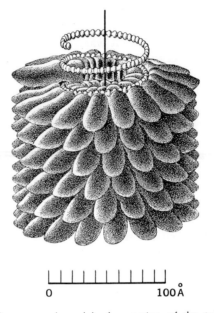

0   100 Å

Fig. 2-3. A recently proposed model of a section of the tobacco mosaic virus particle showing the central helix of RNA enclosed by a cylinder of protein molecules. (From A. Klug and D. L. D. Caspar in *Advances in Virus Research,* Vol. 7, ed. by K. M. Smith and M. A. Lauffer, Academic, 1960, p. 274.)

consists of a helix of RNA, which is probably in the form of a single molecular strand and which constitutes 6% of the mass of the virus. The nucleic acid component is embedded in an aggregate of 2000–3000 protein molecules which form a hollow cylinder with an outside diameter of about 17 mμ and a length of over 300 mμ (Fig. 2-2*a* and 2-3).

The poliomyelitis virus is a sphere with a diameter of about 27 mμ (Fig. 2-2*b*) and consists of 25% RNA and 75% protein. Since the virus is not inactivated by exposure to the enzyme RNA-ase, the RNA is presumed to lie, like that of the tobacco mosaic virus, within a protective jacket of protein.

T$_2$ bacteriophage has a much more complex configuration, including at least five different proteins arranged around a core of DNA. It contains nearly equal amounts of DNA and protein. Part of the protein forms a narrow, cylindrical tail, about 100mμ long, with several fine fibers attached to one end, while a polyhedral head enclosing the DNA and measuring about 60 × 80 mμ comprises the other end (Fig. 2-4 and, for the related T$_4$, Fig. 2-2*c*).

The vaccinia virus has been described as brick-shaped with dimensions of 280 × 220 × 220 mμ. Like T$_2$, it is relatively complex,

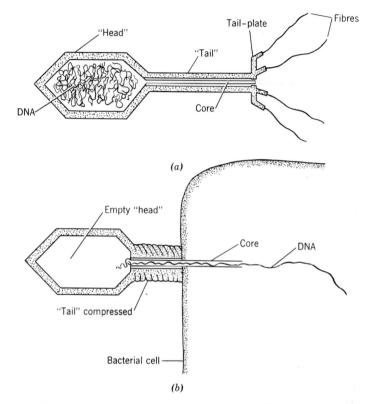

Fig. 2-4. Diagram of a model of T_2 bacteriophage. *(a)* Free phage. *(b)* After contacting a bacterial cell. $\times$ 92,500 (From K. M. Smith, *Viruses*, University Press, Cambridge, 1962, p. 48.)

probably consisting of a lipoid membrane and at least two protein envelopes surrounding a DNA-protein core (See Fig. 2-2d).

Finally, in the polyhedral diseases of insects, 100 or more individual virus particles may be trapped in more or less haphazard distribution in a crystal of protein (Fig. 2-5). Depending on the virus, the particles may be either spherical or cylindrical. The shape of the crystal varies characteristically with the type of virus; in extreme cases it may have a diameter as great as 10 μ.

The Life History of Viruses

The life history of the pathogenic virus takes it through a series of phases. The particles crystallized by Stanley as well as those observable by means of the electron microscope represent the infectious stage

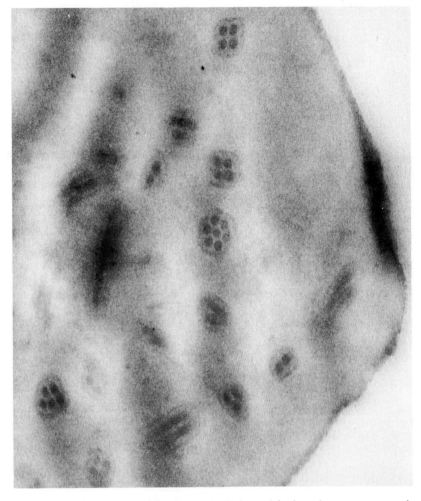

Fig. 2-5. Electron micrograph of a section of a polyhedron from a gypsy moth. Bundles of two to seven rod-shaped virus particles are embedded in a crystalline matrix of protein. (From C. Morgan, G. H. Bergold, D. H. Moore, and H. M. Rose, *J. Biophys. & Biochem. Cytol.,* **1**, 190 (1955).)

which can be transmitted from cell to cell. The nucleic acid moiety of a virus must enter the host cell in order to achieve infection, while at least in some cases the proteins remain mainly outside. The best current guess is that the protein and other components of the extra-cellular virus play a critical role in stabilizing the nucleic acid, in attaching the particle to the surface of the susceptible cell, or in injecting the nucleic acid into the cell. Although the exact functions of the protein coats may vary from virus to virus, they may be considered in general as synthetic products which abet the transmission of the nucleic acid from cell to cell.

Penetration of the virus into a new host is in some cases a passive phenomenon. In many plant diseases the virus enters the cell through lesions made by an insect which is feeding on the plant. Virologists accomplish the same result by abrading the surface of a leaf while spreading a suspension of virus particles on it. In other cases the protein plays an active role in penetration. T_2 bacteriophage attaches to the surface of the cell by the end of its tail (Fig. 2-1), the forces of attachment presumably being analogous to those by which an enzyme combines with its substrate, or an antibody with its antigen. In an incompletely understood series of events, which include the contraction of the tail (Fig. 2-4), the cell wall in the vicinity of the point of attachment is modified and the DNA is injected into the cell. A number of animal viruses such as those causing influenza possess an enzyme capable of hydrolyzing neuraminic acid, a component of the cell surface. It is reasonable to presume that such an enzyme plays a role in the process of penetration, but again the exact mechanism of penetration is poorly understood.

Having entered the cell, the virus effectively recruits the synthetic machinery of the cell for its own purposes. It has been proposed that the lipoid coat on the vaccinia virus may be nothing more than a piece of the cell membrane taken from its former host. The various virus proteins, however, and the nucleic acid, are unique synthetic products which are not detectable in uninfected cells. The problem of assembling these synthetic products into infectious particles is one of the major gaps in the understanding of viruses. Within twenty minutes after infecting a bacterium with T_2, and within eight hours after infecting animal tissue culture cells with the vaccinia virus, synthetic processes have proceeded far enough so that new infectious particles can be detected in the cell by the electron microscope.

Although there may be a good deal of variability between individual cells, the number of progeny produced after a single particle has entered a cell is of the order of magnitude of 100 in both the T_2 and poliomyelitis viruses. A single cell in the leaf may produce as many as 10,000 particles of tobacco mosaic virus.

A variety of mechanisms accounts for the release of the infectious particles from the cell. Bacteriophage is released by the lysis of its victim. By contrast, the tobacco mosaic virus is believed to move from cell to cell through cytoplasmic connectives, the plasmodesmata (Chapter 5, p. 178). This method of transmission is largely inferred from the observation that the virus cannot move across the thick cellulose wall which surrounds the plant cell. Finally, some animal cells can release virus without actually lysing—the process being accompanied by the production of cytoplasmic processes at the cell surface containing virus particles (Fig. 2-6).

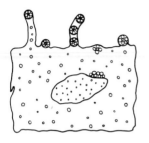

Fig. 2-6. Fowl-plague virus being extruded from a cell. (From K. M. Smith, *Viruses,* University Press, Cambridge, 1962, p. 50.)

The success of a bacterial virus after leaving the cell depends on its chance contact with another susceptible host. Not just any bacterium will do, for there is a high degree of specificity involved in the attachment to the cell surface and in the capacity of the nucleic acid to recruit the synthetic mechanisms of the cell. T_2, for instance, will detectably infect only *Escherichia coli* cells and, as we have noted, only those which do not already carry prophage.

In the viruses infecting multicellular organisms, at least until the host has succumbed or initiated successful immune reactions, the virus may simply spread from cell to cell. Different modes of transmission from host to host must be relied on. Aerial transmission, whereby the new host inhales or ingests the virus, suffices for many animal viruses; the common cold viruses notoriously rely on this mode of transmission. The polyhedral viruses of insects are apparently spread by rain and wind from the carcasses or feces of infected individuals, and new individuals are readily infected by feeding on contaminated vegetation. Other viruses, including the yellow fever virus of mammals and many plant viruses, are transmitted from host to host by insects. The classical experiment demonstrating insect transmission was Walter Reed's proof in 1900–1901 that individuals are infected with yellow fever when bitten by a mosquito that has previously bitten a person suffering from the disease—though at the time of Col. Reed's experiments and for several decades thereafter, it was not known that yellow fever is caused by a virus.

Among the most thoroughly studied of the insect-borne viruses are a series of plant viruses carried by the insects known as leaf hoppers. These insects feed on plant juices by sinking their proboscis into a leaf, much as a mosquito feeds on the blood of mammals. If the plant is infected, virus particles are unavoidably drawn in along with the plant juices. Depending on the virus, there is a great deal of variability in subsequent events. In some cases the insect, after a lag period of over a week (during which the virus becomes established in its tissues), is able to infect other plants for the rest of its life. In the leaf hopper which carries the virus causing rice stripe disease, the progeny of a female which has fed on an infected plant also transmit the disease. In one remarkable experiment performed in Japan, twenty-three successive generations of insects were able to infect rice plants without having any opportunity to be reinfected by feeding on diseased plants. Such results leave little doubt that the virus can reproduce in both the plant and the insect, and that it can be transmitted from generation to generation of insect through the eggs. So far as is known in these cases, insect does not infect insect, except in hereditary fashion, and plant does not infect plant. Thus there is an obligatory cycle of infections between the two types of organisms. A similar obligatory cycle occurs between mammals and mosquitoes in yellow fever.

The Origin of Viruses

The capacity of the virus to disappear into the fabric of the cell, and its utter reliance on the metabolic machinery of the host, detract from its status as an organism and bias one toward considering it instead as a formerly normal constituent of the cell which has become infectious. The question is thus frequently raised as to whether it is legitimate to consider the virus an organism.

The question really has two parts, the first concerning the evolutionary origin of the virus. Was the ancestor of a contemporary virus an independent organism which transformed by mutation and natural selection into an intracellular parasite, or was it a normal part of the genome of the cell which somehow achieved a small measure of independence? At the present time this question cannot be answered in a verifiable manner; and the answer, if available, would contribute little to an understanding of the virus as an organism. To the pragmatic organism biologist the question is therefore a poor one. (Fortunately, not all biologists are always pragmatic, and thus questions such as this have not been altogether forgotten.)

The second part of the question concerns the definition of an organism. Whether we call a virus an organism depends on how broad we make the definition; but this is more a matter of taste or convention than of biological insight. We will avoid the issue entirely here by asserting that whatever we call it, a virus is a subcellular parasite with many of the properties of more conventional organisms.

A final property of viruses which relates to, but does not solve, the question of how they evolved concerns their status in natural selection. Hypothetically, a virus which behaved exclusively as part of the cell even to the point of reproducing in synchrony with the cell, as bacterial prophage does, would be subjected to natural selection in tandem with its host. To the extent that the presence of virus impaired the reproduction of the host, and thereby rendered it less fit than its competitors, the future of the virus would also be jeopardized. But when the virus possesses the additional attribute of being able to break out of its host and to infect other individuals, natural selection should treat it as an independent genetic entity. It need no longer behave benignly toward its host; as long as the virus possesses effective mechanisms of transmission to a new organism, it can even afford to kill its host, as a predator does its prey.

BACTERIA

The smallest of the free-living organisms are the bacteria. Unlike the viruses, they are large enough to be seen through the light microscope. They were, in fact, described by Antoni von Leeuwenhoek in a series of letters to the Royal Society of London (1676 to 1683) describing the organisms which he observed with his remarkable home-made microscopes (Fig. 2-7). The microscopists coming after Leeuwenhoek were able to observe bacteria along with other microorganisms in a wide variety of forms and situations. Wherever putrefaction occurred (generally wherever solutions of organic materials were allowed to sit around for a day or so), bacteria could be found in many forms and in abundance. Decaying plants and animals essentially became a suspension of bacteria and other microorganisms. A clear idea of the meaning of their apparent materialization out of nowhere, and of their varieties of form, required technical advances and scientific insight which are classics in the history of biology. Before it could be demonstrated that bacteria conform to the general properties of organisms, two critical ideas had to emerge. One of these was that the bacteria of putrefaction arise by reproduction, rather than by spontaneous generation, and the second was that they possess a mechanism of inheritance governing both their structure and physiological activities.

It has long been common knowledge that food which has been cooked and then sealed in an airtight container while still hot can be stored for a year or more without going bad. But if, after the contents cool, the seal is broken for an instant and is then resealed, putrefaction

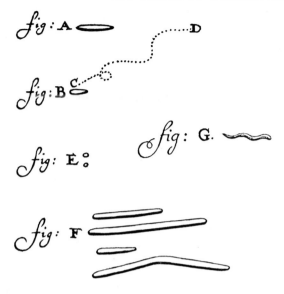

LEEUWENHOEK'S FIGURES OF BACTERIA FROM THE HUMAN MOUTH
(Letter 39, 17 Sept. 1683)
Enlarged (× 1½) from the engravings published in *Arc. Nat. Det.*, 1695.

Fig. A, a motile *Bacillus*.
Fig. B, *Selenomonas sputigena.* C . . . . D, the path of its motion.
Fig. E, Micrococci.
Fig. F, *Leptothrix buccalis*.
Fig. G, A spirochæte—probably "*Spirochaeta buccalis*," the largest form found
in this situation.

Fig. 2-7. A copy of one of Leeuwenhoek's diagrams and identifications proposed by Clifford Dobell. (From Clifford Dobell, *Antoni von Leeuwenhoek and his Little Animals,* Harcourt, Brace, 1932, p. 239.)

is likely to occur. The interpretation of this event seems straightforward at the present time, but was in fact the product of a century or more of ingenious experimentation. The effects of cooking are easy to understand: cooking kills most forms of life and severely impairs the capacity for growth of microorganisms, although there are some heat-resistant spores which can withstand brief exposure to boiling water. But why does temporarily breaking the seal encourage putrefaction?

When food is sealed while hot and then allowed to cool, a vacuum is created. Breaking the seal allows a sudden influx of air which is sufficiently vigorous to produce a hissing sound. One early nineteenth-century answer was that the air contains an ingredient which is essential for the spontaneous generation of bacteria from the dead organic materials in the cooked preparation. A second explanation was that cooking does not kill all of the organisms present. Since many forms of life require oxygen, the admission of oxygen makes the exploitation of food much more likely for some of the spore-forming organisms that have survived the cooking process. The final and most likely explanation was that the inrushing air carries a quantity of microorganisms. This indeed proved to be the case when methods were devised for allowing the admission of air which had been filtered or otherwise cleaned of particulate matter. Louis Pasteur accomplished this purpose in 1861 by cooking the organic nutrients in a flask whose neck was sufficiently long, curved, and moisture-coated so that dust particles in the air passing through it were caught on its sides. The modern bacteriologist routinely plugs his flasks of culture medium with sterile cotton—an effective dust trap through which the gases of air can readily diffuse. Such methods have sufficed to demonstrate that in the time span of most biological experiments, new bacteria arise only by the reproduction of bacteria.

A second point of confusion solved by the nineteenth-century studies of bacteria was the nature of their morphological and physiological diversity. That many forms of bacteria are visible microscopically in a putrefying broth can at the present time be explained by the fact that the broth was seeded with a corresponding array of bacteria. Demonstration of the validity of this interpretation required knowledge of the forms which would appear if a culture medium were seeded with a single strain of bacterium. The most convenient technical solution to this problem entails growing the bacteria on the surface of a culture medium which has been solidified with agar, an amino polysaccharide which is extracted from certain marine algae and which most bacteria are unable to degrade. The initial insight which ultimately led to this technique was achieved by Robert Koch in 1881 when he observed patches of bacteria growing on the cut surface of a potato. The progeny of a single bacterium which has landed on the surface of a solid medium cannot mix freely with the progeny of other bacteria which have been introduced simultaneously at other points on the surface.

A clone of bacteria growing as a compact mass on the surface of a culture medium has been designated as a colony; both microscopic and metabolic analyses have demonstrated that the members of a colony exhibit a good deal less structural heterogeneity than is apparent in a liquid culture which has been inoculated by exposure to air or water or by any other technique allowing multiple seeding. Through such methods it has become apparent that bacteria exhibit a high degree of genetic specificity. Bergey's *Manual of Determinative Bacteriology* lists approximately 1500 types of bacteria which are distinguishable from each other by a combination of metabolic and morphological characteristics, and which breed true for these characteristics over prolonged periods in pure-strain cultures. Mutations and environmentally induced changes are, of course, known, but these do nothing to weaken the concept of hereditary specificity among bacteria and in fact have done much to allow characterization of its physical basis (Stern and Nanney, Chap. 14).

Despite earlier views to the contrary, bacteria have thus been found to conform to the rules of reproduction and inheritance which hold for all other organisms. That there should ever have been confusion about this fact is due entirely to their exceedingly small size—to their ability to get around without the investigator seeing them. Genetic analyses of the bacteria have in the last decade extended the similarities. Such analyses are applicable only to organisms in which some form of genetic interchange occurs, and such an exchange was fortunately found in several bacteria. In *Escherichia coli* it occurs by two mechanisms: by sexual fusion with the transfer of the chromosome from one individual to the other, and by virus transport (Stern and Nanney, Chap. 14). There is as yet little knowledge of the extent to which these phenomena occur in natural populations.

Structure

Viewed through the light microscope, the bacteria are too small to permit direct visualization of their detailed substructure. The longest dimension of *Pasteurella tularensis*, an extreme case, is less than 1 μ; since under optimal conditions the limit of resolution of the light microscope is 0.1 μ, very little of the substructure of such an organism can be observed. Yet the bacterium is an independent organism which contains all the synthetic mechanisms necessary for growth and reproduction. We are unavoidably intrigued by the possibility that the bacterium is the minimum organism—the smallest entity that can contain all of the physiological components and organization required for feeding, growth, and reproduction.

When observed by techniques with greater resolution than the light microscope, the bacterium exhibits all of the complexity which is so apparent in other organisms. To an organic chemist, the bacterium is just as heterogeneous as any other organism, for virtually all the major categories of biological compounds are present. The biochemist working with enzyme systems finds that any single bacterium contains most of the metabolic pathways present in other cells, although there may be important differences between the various kinds of bacteria. The cell biologist attempting to visualize how the organic molecules and macromolecules extractable from bacterial cells are arranged and interact in a functional organism finds that the bacterium is the same old bewildering box of puzzles.

Electron microscopy has demonstrated some real and consistent differences between the bacterium and most other cells (Fig. 2-8). A compact nucleus is not present; there are instead several regions of interconnected material which are identified as nuclear because staining reactions indicate that they contain DNA. The nucleus is not demarked from the rest of the cell by a membrane such as envelops the nuclei of most other organisms. The system of membranes in the

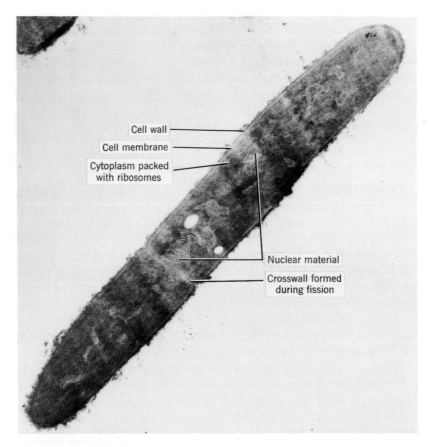

Fig. 2-8. Electron micrograph of a section of a bacterium near the completion of cell division. (Courtesy of George B. Chapman.)

cytoplasm, the endoplasmic reticulum, is not present, or at least is not as extensive as in most plant and animal cells. Membranous organelles such as the mitochondria are absent. (The electron transport enzymes which characterize the mitochondrion in other cells are closely associated instead with the cell membrane.) Flagella, when present, appear in the electron microscope as simple fibers, rather than as the complex of fibers and enveloping membrane which characterize the cilia and flagella of plants and animals. The cytoplasm of bacteria is tightly packed with particles about the size of the ribonucleoprotein granules which are known to be an important site of protein synthesis in other cells. Photosynthetic pigments, in those forms which possess them, are located in minute ovoid chromatophores quite unlike the much larger lamellar chloroplasts of green plants.

All bacteria are surrounded by a cell wall which is about 10–20 mμ thick. Isolation and chemical analysis of the cell wall indicates that it is a complex polymer of amino acids and amino sugars together with varying amounts of lipids, carbohydrates, and other substances. It is thus usually quite different chemically from the cellulose and pectin wall of the plant cell, although it serves just as effectively some of the same functions. It has sufficient tensile strength, for instance, to prevent the osmotic swelling which would occur when the cell is immersed in water, and which actually does occur when the bacterium is deprived of an effective cell wall by enzymatic digestion. Finally, the cell wall may be surrounded by additional capsules of polysaccharides or polypeptides. (One of the best known of these is the polysaccharide sheath which can surround the *Pneumococcus* cell if it contains the appropriate DNA (Stern and Nanney, Chap. 12).)

The bacterium is thus constructed at a level of structural organization—of heterogeneity and complexity—higher than that of the virus particle; and the differences undoubtedly reflect the fact that the bacterium can make its own way as an organism without relying on the metabolic machinery of other cells for its growth and reproduction.

From the point of view of its properties as an organism, the most important outcome of the small size and relative simplicity of the bacterium is their consequence for development and reproduction. The life cycle of a single bacterium consists of growth, which doubles the size or number of each protoplasmic subunit, followed by cell division. Although this process is biosynthetically the equivalent of growth and reproduction in larger organisms, it is morphologically direct and simple, and can be achieved at a far faster rate. The bacterium is thus capable of rapid exploitation of any transitory situation which favors its growth.

Nutrition and Metabolism

Compared with the monotony of viral parasitism, the bacteria exhibit a rich diversity in ways of making a living. Some are photoautotrophs; that is, they convert carbon dioxide into organic compounds with the assistance of energy obtained by absorbing light. Others, the chemoautotrophs, accomplish the same result with energy obtained by the oxidation of inorganic substances such as iron, magnesium, sulfur, or ammonia. The majority of known bacteria, however, are heterotrophic organisms which rely on energy and matter in the form of various organic compounds; a myriad of marine, aquatic, and soil bacteria, and of parasitic and symbiotic types falls into this category. In no other group of organisms do members display so much variety in their modes of nutrition.

The nutritional specializations of bacteria can be illustrated by the transformations in the state of nitrogen which result from their metabolic activities (Fig. 2-9). Protein, for instance, is an excellent source of energy and materials for the growth of many heterotrophic organisms. Proteins are not readily absorbed by bacteria, but some kinds, such as *Pseudomonas* and *Clostridium,* secrete proteolytic enzymes which hydrolyze the protein into amino acids and polypeptides which can be absorbed.

Many kinds of heterotrophic bacteria are able to grow in laboratory cultures with amino acids as their only source of energy, carbon, and nitrogen. Some of the amino acid molecules are utilized directly in the synthesis of bacterial protein, or, with modifications, in the synthesis of other organic compounds comprising the bacterial cell. Protein synthesis as well as other activities of the growing bacterium require energy, however, and this is obtained by degrading the rest of the amino acid. When degradation occurs, the products generally include nitrogen in the form of ammonium salts. Here ammonium salts are products of metabolism, but under other circumstances they may serve as an essential nutrient. Thus a culture of bacteria which *produces* ammonia when fed amino acids or protein may instead *utilize* ammonia for the synthesis of amino acids when it is fed primarily carbohydrates. This is a necessary attribute of those bacteria (such as *Escherichia coli*) which can be cultured on sugar, ammonium salts, and inorganic ions. Autotrophic bacteria which utilize carbon dioxide as their source of carbon must also be able to utilize ammonium salts in the synthesis of amino acids.

A number of chemosynthetic bacteria which grow in the soil can use ammonia as a source of energy as well as of nitrogen for amino acid

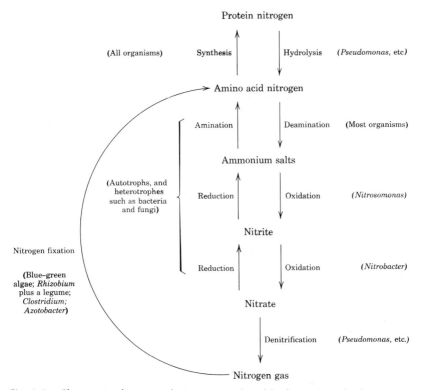

Fig. 2-9.   Changes in the state of nitrogen catalyzed by bacteria and other microorganisms.

synthesis. Winogradsky demonstrated in 1890 that the soil bacterium *Nitrosomonas* can grow in a solution of ammonium and other inorganic salts, with carbon dioxide as the only carbon source. The explanation of these remarkably simple nutritional requirements lies in the fact that *Nitrosomonas* has the capacity to oxidize ammonia, transforming it to nitrite. The energy yielded by this reaction is then used for the fixation of carbon dioxide and the synthesis of the various organic compounds which comprise the protoplasm of the growing bacterium. Energetically, the process is comparable to the utilization of sunlight for carbon dioxide fixation by photosynthetic organisms (Stern and Nanney, Chap. 2).

Winogradsky discovered an additional bacterium, *Nitrobacter*, which has equivalent abilities except that the energy for carbon dioxide fixation is provided by the oxidation of nitrite to nitrate. Neither *Nitrosomonas* nor *Nitrobacter* is able to grow on organic nitrogen sources.

Many bacteria which can use ammonia as a source of nitrogen when growing on sugar can also use nitrate for the same purpose. They must first reduce the nitrate to ammonia, however, and they must expend metabolic energy to do so. Thus their effect is precisely opposite to that of *Nitrosomonas* and *Nitrobacter*. Like ammonia, nitrate may thus be either a metabolic product or a nutrient, depending on the organism and the situation.

We will finally note that certain bacteria can convert soil nitrogen into atmospheric nitrogen (N_2), and that still others can perform the opposite feat, incorporating atmospheric nitrogen into amino acids and finally into proteins. Many species of bacteria can release energy from organic compounds by using substances other than oxygen as reducing agents. Several soil bacteria, *Pseudomonas* among them, can use nitrate for this purpose, reducing it to gaseous nitrogen. The utilization of atmospheric nitrogen to form organic nitrogen is a process which is an exclusive attribute of certain bacteria and their near relatives, the blue-green algae. Although some bacteria such as *Azotobacter* can fix nitrogen as free-living organisms, a better known example is the bacterium which can do so only when living in the roots of leguminous plants. This is a striking example of a symbiosis in which there is a physical association of two independent organisms to the mutual advantage of both.

Unlike most other higher plants, legumes such as peas and clover are often able to grow satisfactorily in nitrogen-poor soil. Since the growing plants contain more nitrogen than the seeds from which they germinate, it is necessary to conclude that they can somehow take nitrogen from the atmosphere. The capacity of the legume to fix nitrogen is curtailed, however, if the seeds are allowed to germinate in soil which has been sterilized; this result suggests that in order to fix nitrogen the plant must first be infected with a microorganism. Indeed, the roots of legumes grown under conditions favoring nitrogen fixation form nodules which can be shown by microscopic examination to contain a bacterium known as *Rhizobium*.

In 1888 Beijerinck isolated and cultured the nodule bacterium and demonstrated that, like the legume, it is unable to fix nitrogen by itself. Both of these organisms can thus grow independently of the other as long as they are given a suitable source of nitrogen, such as nitrate. *Rhizobium* probably grows normally in a free state in the soil, and when the seeds of the legume germinate, the two come in contact. The bacteria enter the plant through the root hairs and move to the center of the root where many of the cells come to appear filled with bacteria. Only when "infection" has occurred are the two, acting in concert, able to fix nitrogen.

In focusing the discussion of bacterial nutrition and metabolism around the utilization and production of the various forms of nitrogen, we have taken some measure of the breadth and diversity of their nutritional requirements. Just from this sampling it should be apparent that there must be numerous kinds of nutritional situations occurring in nature which a particular group of bacteria is uniquely equipped to exploit. The range of diversity of these environments would appear even greater had we also discussed bacterial photosynthesis and other forms of chemosynthesis and heterotrophy. The present description only scratches the surface of an enormous and complex subject.

The Bacterial Way of Life

The conversions in the state of nitrogen described in the preceding section have been determined by isolating and culturing the bacteria concerned, determining what nutrients are necessary for their growth, and measuring the products of their metabolism. Such information inevitably leads a biologist to speculate about the problems and opportunities of the bacterium in its natural environment. The knowledge that *Nitrosomonas* and *Nitrobacter* collectively require ammonia as an energy source would suggest that wherever ammonia is available in nature, there is an opportunity available for these two bacteria. Wherever ammonia disappears and is replaced by nitrate, as is apt to be the case in a pile of decomposing manure, or when ammonium fertilizers are added to the soil, we can suspect that these bacteria have actually been taking advantage of the opportunity. The suspicion is confirmed if the appropriate bacteria can be isolated from the scene of conversion. Yet we cannot actually observe the bacteria in action and be sure that they alone are responsible for nitrate production. Nor is it easy to understand where they were and what they were doing before the ammonium was presented to them, or what their fate will be when it is exhausted.

Under favorable laboratory conditions many bacteria can grow exceedingly rapidly. *Escherichia coli* in a solution containing nitrate, phosphate, and other inorganic salts, and with glucose as a source of carbon and energy, can grow and divide once every twenty minutes. At this rate a single bacterium can yield a clone of cells whose number and mass have doubled 36 times in twelve hours, yielding 7×10^{10} bacteria. But to what extent is the bacterium apt to find such ideal circumstances in nature? Are there naturally occurring circumstances which will allow it to grow, only at a slower rate? Under what conditions will it simply become quiescent, yet capable of growth if conditions change for the better? In short, what are the problems and conditions for which natural selection has adapted the bacterium?

There are few natural situations in which relatively ideal conditions as defined by laboratory studies occur. The bacteria inhabiting the digestive tract of vertebrates, *E. coli* among them, live in a nutritionally rich and physically constant environment. Conditions are so favorable for their growth that about a third of the dry weight of fecal matter may consist of bacterial cells. In soil also it is conceivable that the nutritional value of the environment may be reasonably constant, though the growth rate of *E. coli* in this situation must be a good deal slower than under laboratory conditions. A closer look at the soil, however, indicates that this is in many regards a fickle environment in which the joy of living must have its ups and downs.

Soil is a complex mixture of mineral particles, decaying organic matter, and living organisms. It may be alternately waterlogged, damp, and dry. When damp or dry, soil is often aerated, making an abundance of oxygen available to the organisms residing in it. When it is waterlogged, the air is entirely replaced by water, transforming the soil into an anaerobic environment, encouraging the growth of anaerobic bacteria, and discouraging those which require oxygen. In temperate and subarctic climates it is apt to be frozen for weeks or months of the year.

Organic nutrients, primarily in the form of dead leaves or grass and other vegetable matter, are added to the surface of the soil annually, and are continually invaded from beneath by the bacteria and other organisms which initiate their decomposition. A gram of fertile soil has been estimated to contain more than 10^9 living bacterial cells, but many other organisms are present which affect the abundance and activity of the bacteria as profoundly as do variations in the physical and nutritional properties of the soil. In terms of the *mass* of organisms present, the fungi—heterotrophic competitors of the bacteria —are equally abundant in many soils. Fungi affect bacteria in several ways, besides acting as competitors for nutrients. In culture, a number of soil fungi produce substances which kill or inhibit the growth of bacteria. These well known "antibiotics," which have so remarkably enhanced the ability of the modern physician to cope with bacterial infections, are probably also produced and effective in localized regions of the soil. On the other hand some metabolic products of the fungi, such as ammonia, will serve as food for certain bacteria, and dead fungal hyphae will provide nutrition for others.

Other heterotrophic organisms occurring in the soil include protozoa and small multicellular animals, especially a variety of nematodes and arthropods. These comprise a ruthless society whose members make their way by devouring bacteria, fungi, and each other. Finally, there are photosynthetic plants, including some algae and mosses at the surface of the soil and, at greater depths, the roots of vascular land plants. These are the autotrophic organisms whose synthetic activities provide the complex society of soil organisms with organic matter on which to feed. In localized regions of the soil they must also compete with bacteria for ammonia and other inorganic nutrients. It is apparent that there is plenty of opportunity for the lucky soil bacterium which finds itself in the right place at the right time, but that the bacterium must be frequently confronted with distressing circumstances. Freezing, water-logging (or drought), antibiotics, and predation are all likely occurrences; and if it escapes these, there is always the probability of running out of food.

When starvation occurs in laboratory cultures, most of the cells die. This must also be the fate of most of the cells which are passed out of the digestive tract of a vertebrate, and must frequently happen in localized regions of the soil. Yet we know from the simple experiment of exposing a sterile Petri plate containing a nutrient medium to air, or tap water, or a piece of clothing, that the environment is abundantly populated with dormant bacteria which are still capable of growth. Some of these have entered a special dormant condition by forming spores which can transform again into vegetative cells when they are exposed to an environment suitable for growth (p. 43). Others, however, have the appearance of vegetative cells and can be considered dormant only because they reside in an environment which is incompatible with growth.

It is possible in the laboratory to prolong the life of the bacterium at a slow rate of growth. If a culture growing on the surface of a nutrient agar is covered with mineral oil and placed in a refrigerator, it can be maintained in a viable state for weeks or months longer than would be possible under more optimal conditions for growth. We can speculate that under special circumstances the bacterium may achieve the same results in its natural environment.

The picture which thus emerges is that the bacterium operates in an exceedingly hazardous and tenuous environment. The strategy for coping with the situation is quite clear: reproduce as fast as you can when you have the chance; if you produce enough progeny, some of them may be fortunate enough to happen on transitory good times. This may not seem like a very happy prospect for the individual bacterium; the chance that any given organism will be well enough fed to give rise to a clone may be exceedingly slight under many circumstances. But the bacterial way of life as a device for assuring the continuance of the line is obviously quite successful. The ubiquity of dormant bacteria and their capacity to exploit rapidly any transitory conditions favoring their growth are impressive indeed to the human being who leads such a very different life.

Adaptation

Several features of the bacterial system, in addition to high rate of reproduction and the capacity to survive in a dormant condition, significantly enhance the capacity of these organisms to succeed. One of these features concerns the rate at which genetic mutations become established in a population. Mutation rates are ordinarily expressed for a given gene as the number of mutations occurring per new individual in the population. In most organisms these have been found to be in the range of 10^{-5} to 10^{-8}; in other words, we would have to look at between 100 thousand and 100 million progeny of parents containing a particular gene before we would be apt to find a mutation of that gene. Bacteria are not exceptional in this regard, and thus by this criterion their mutation rate is standard. However, under optimal growing conditions the rate of formation of new progeny is so high compared with most other organisms (particularly multicellular ones), that the frequency of new mutations per unit of time is unusually high. Natural selection can therefore occur at a high rate, so that a population of bacteria can with relative speed adapt genetically to many environmental changes. A population of *E. coli* sensitive to penicillin, for instance, can give rise to a substantial population of a penicillin-resistant strain within a few days' time. Such a potential clearly has a very high adaptive value.

Besides such population responses, the individual bacterium can take actions which increase the probability of its being able to grow or to survive impoverished circumstances. Three examples will be cited here.

Many bacteria are motile, their movements arising from the action of their flagella. In several cases it can be shown that they are able to respond to environmental factors in such a fashion as to assure that they will find themselves in favorable circumstances for growth. Motile photosynthetic bacteria, for instance, will aggregate in the light if they have an opportunity to move freely between an illuminated and a nonilluminated region. Other forms can respond similarly to oxygen, avoiding it if they are anaerobic and aggregating in oxygenated regions if they are aerobic.

Adaptive enzyme formation provides a second example. *Escherichia coli,* for instance, will synthesize the enzyme which hydrolyzes galactose-containing disaccharides (such as lactose) only in the presence of such a sugar. When grown on sucrose, the bacterium does not expend the energy and molecular subunits required to synthesize this enzyme. From the point of view of natural selection, this behavior is most easily interpreted as an adaptation allowing a more economical expenditure of energy.

Finally, spore formation can be considered as an adaptive response of the individual to the environment. Several forms of rod-shaped bacteria are stimulated to form spores by such factors as the depletion of nutrients in their environment. The nuclear material and other constituents of the protoplast form a spherical or ovoid mass within the cell, and a thick wall of hexosamine-containing peptides is deposited around the mass. The spore thus formed has no measurable metabolism, and it can withstand prolonged desiccation or even boiling for short periods of time. If later exposed to conditions adequate for growth, the cell rehydrates, breaks out of its capsule, and resumes its growth and reproduction.

The bacterial level of organization is thus equipped with a respectable gamut of adaptive reactions. Although much is left to chance in the bacterial way of life, responses such as these serve to increase the probability that the genome will perpetuate itself.

UNICELLULAR PLANTS AND ANIMALS

Multicellular plants and animals are compounded of cells which are unlike the bacterial cell in many regards. When viewed through the light microscope, they appear much larger and more heterogeneous than most bacteria; by means of the electron microscope they are observed to have a more pronounced emphasis on membranous organelles. Such cytological characteristics are not, however, exclusive correlates of being multicellular, for there are many unicellular organisms which possess a similar structure. These include representatives of both the animal and plant kingdoms: the protozoa among the animals; and among plants several groups of unicellular algae and fungi.

Like the bacteria, these organisms display considerable diversity in their ways of making a living. Autotrophy is represented by the algae, which make their way as photosynthetic organisms; heterotrophy is practiced by protozoa and yeasts. A number of intermediate organisms get along on either mode of nutrition, and still others must simultaneously indulge in both photosynthesis and heterotrophy.

The adaptive problems of the photosynthetic and heterotrophic representatives have such profound consequences for their structure and behavior that they can be most profitably introduced separately.

The Organization of a Unicellular Alga

The flagellated green alga *Chlamydomonas* is one of several unicellular algae whose structure has by now been analyzed with the electron microscope. It has also been the subject of many light microscope studies, and its structure is thus well enough known to serve as an example for introducing the structure of the unicellular plants (Fig. 2-10).

Chlamydomonas is an oval cell measuring about 6×8 μ, and is thus a good deal larger than most bacteria. It is surrounded by a thin cellulose wall (about 40 mμ thick), which is in turn surrounded by an equally thin capsule of gelatinous polysaccharide. Two flagella emerge

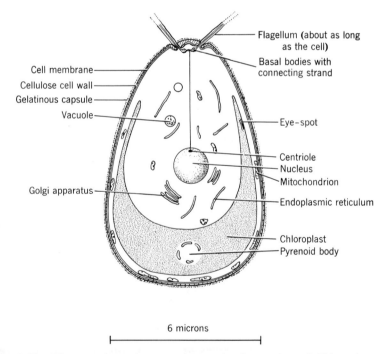

Flagellum (about as long as the cell)

Basal bodies with connecting strand

Cell membrane

Cellulose cell wall

Gelatinous capsule

Vacuole

Eye-spot

Centriole

Nucleus

Mitochondrion

Golgi apparatus

Endoplasmic reticulum

Chloroplast

Pyrenoid body

6 microns

Fig. 2-10. Diagram of an electron micrograph of a section of *Chlamydomonas*. (Adapted from R. Sager, *Science*, **132**, 1459 (1960) and other sources.)

through pores in the cell wall at the anterior end of the cell, and the whipping action of these pulls the cell in an anterior direction. Each flagellum is attached to a basal body just inside the cell wall; a short thread in turn connects the basal bodies to each other. (Although it has not yet been observed in the electron microscope, an additional thread has been seen connecting the paired basal bodies with a centriole lying just inside the nuclear membrane; when the cell divides, the old motor apparatus disintegrates and the division products of the centriole are said to give rise to the new motor apparati in the daughter cells.)

The cytoplasm is dominated by a large, cup-shaped chloroplast enclosed within a limiting membrane and composed of many groups of lamellae arranged somewhat like the grana in the chloroplasts of higher plants. Special differentiations of the chloroplast include a single pyrenoid body which serves as a site of starch grain formation, and a red "eye-spot" consisting of two plates containing carotenoid pigments and believed to function in orienting the movements of the cell toward light. In addition to the chloroplast, the cytoplasm includes mitochondria, endoplasmic reticulum, ribonucleoprotein granules, and Golgi apparati, all of which can be presumed to function as the corresponding organelles in other cells. A pair of contractile vacuoles at the anterior end play a role in water secretion (p. 55). Finally, one or a variety of kinds of vacuoles containing particulate inclusions may be present.

The nucleus is located at the center of the cell. As in most other plants and animals a limiting membrane separates its contents from the cytoplasm, and it contains chromosomes which may be clearly resolved by the light microscope during mitotic and meiotic divisions. The nuclear membrane, unlike that in most plant and animal cells, appears to remain intact during mitosis, and the centrioles and spindle remain within its confines.

It must not be supposed that *Chlamydomonas* is a representative algal cell in all ways. Some unicellular algae have no detectable cell wall, and when present the cell wall may have a very different form and composition, as will be exemplified with the diatoms and dinoflagellates in the next section. Contractile vacuoles occur prominently only in freshwater algae with fairly weak cell walls in which the osmotic uptake of water must be battled by secretory processes. Flagella and the associated basal bodies and centrioles are altogether absent from many algae. In many cases the single large chloroplast is replaced by numerous small ones. Finally, *Chlamydomonas* does not exhibit one of the most pronounced characteristics of most multicellular plant cells—a large central vacuole with the cytoplasm arranged for the most part around the periphery adjacent to the cell wall. Despite such differences, the general level of organization of *Chlamydomonas* and the fine structure of many of its cytoplasmic organelles are representative of those in other plant and animal cells and contrast strikingly with the fine structure of the smaller bacterium.

Adaptation in the Pelagic Algae

Our next concern must be with the way in which the unicellular alga makes its living, and for this purpose it is instructive to consider the organisms of the open ocean—an environment in which the unicellular algae predominate. The most abundant algae in this environment are the diatoms and dinoflagellates. Both groups include species which occur in fresh water; some diatoms inhabit terrestrial surfaces, but they occur most conspicuously in the pelagic environment.

Both are unicellular forms, having diameters of approximately 20 μ, and are thus a good deal larger than *Chlamydomonas*. The dinoflagellates are usually enclosed in plates of cellulose which give them an armored appearance (Fig. 2-11*a*), and possess two flagella, one characteristically extended away from the organism and a second wrapped around it in a groove between cellulose plates. The diatoms are enclosed in a pair of siliceous shells (Figs. 2-11*b* and 2-15). Some of them are motile, a feat which is achieved in a unique fashion: cytoplasm and aqueous environment come in contact in a long groove on each shell, and it has been proposed that the flowing of the cytoplasm in the groove is responsible for propelling the cell. Both groups differ from *Chlamydomonas* in having a large number of small chloroplasts.

As in the studies of bacteria, it is not possible to determine with assurance the critical nutrient and physical conditions required for the growth of these organisms in their natural environment; but we can conjecture about these conditions from what is known of their behavior in the laboratory, where a limited number of photosynthetic dinoflagellates and diatoms have been successfully cultured. For reasons which are not at present apparent, many of these require, in addition to light, carbon dioxide and inorganic salts, a supplementary source of vitamins. If these requirements are representative of what they also need in their natural environment, it must be assumed that cohabitation with other organisms is an essential feature of their existence. Indeed, some of the dinoflagellates have been observed ingesting other organisms, which might thus be thought of as the dinoflagellates' equivalent of a vitamin pill. (It should be pointed out that

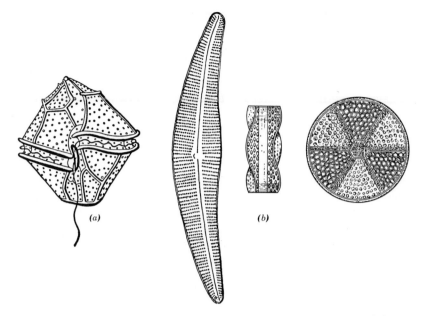

Fig. 2-11. Pelagic algae. *(a)* The dinoflagellate, *Gonyaulax.* (From R. Buchsbaum, *Animals without Backbones,* Univ. Chicago Press, 1948, p. 42.) *(b)* The diatoms *Cymbella* (on the left) and *Isthmia. Isthmia* is shown in two views. The longest diameter of these forms is 20–40 microns. (From G. M. Smith, *Cryptogamic Botany,* Vol. I, McGraw-Hill, 2nd ed., 1955, pp. 197–198.)

this is not a generalized requirement; many other unicellular algae, such as the green alga *Chlorella,* will grow luxuriantly under laboratory conditions in illuminated and aerated solutions of inorganic salts alone.)

We might anticipate that the marine diatoms and dinoflagellates, living in the relative physical constancy of the ocean, would have a reasonably constant abundance. But this is not the case; in many seas they undergo dramatic fluctuations in populations, rendering clear waters opaque within a few days or weeks and then just as rapidly disappearing again. A closer examination of their environment and the conditions required for their growth provides a plausible explanation of this behavior. Light, water, carbon dioxide, and inorganic salts such as nitrate and phosphate must be simultaneously available in one place for effective growth of the unicellular algae. Water and carbon dioxide are no problem, since they are ubiquitous, but light and the essential salts have a more uneven distribution. Even the clearest ocean waters absorb and scatter light sufficiently so that no more than 1% of the incident sunlight reaches a depth of 300 feet; and plants generally require at least this amount of light in order to grow. When conditions for growth are good, the amount of light absorption and scattering due to the algae themselves greatly reduces the depth of light penetration so that growth may be possible only in the top 5 to 10 feet. Where the light intensity is sufficient to support growth, the algae may promptly deplete the water of inorganic nitrogen, phosphate, and other mineral nutrients. Thus, after a brief period of flourishing, they may themselves render their environment unfit for further growth.

The alga which has depleted its environment has two obvious possible fates: it may be devoured by one of the many animal predators which graze the surfaces of the oceans, or it may participate in the "rain" of organisms which falls into the black and unproductive ocean depths. Here also it may be eaten or die. Bacteria exist at all levels of the ocean, feeding on the synthetic products of the algae, and these recycle the minerals released as organic compounds from the dying organisms. The rapid incorporation of inorganic nitrogen and phosphates into organisms in the illuminated surfaces and their production from organic matter in the depths thus tend to keep these essential nutrients at an adequate level for growth only where there is insufficient light. The chances are, therefore, that an algal cell will always find itself under conditions which are ideal for growth *except that just one essential ingredient is absent*—an ingredient which is apt to be in great abundance just a few feet away.

A prerequisite for algal blooms in the open oceans is a set of conditions which remedy this situation by bringing inorganic nutrients from the depths to the illuminated surface. This may be achieved to some degree merely by the process of diffusion, or as a result of turbulence due to storms. But it occurs in far more spectacular fashion when conditions lead to convection currents that turn the waters over. Off the west coasts of South America and Africa, turning over occurs where the predominantly offshore winds tend to push the surface water away from land so that it must be replaced by water from greater depths. In regions of the ocean where there are pronounced seasonal changes it is induced by fluctuations in the temperature of the surface water. As the surface water cools in the winter, it becomes more dense than the warmer water underneath it; the resulting turnover may bring up mineral-rich waters from depths of a thousand feet or more, and such waters will remain nutritionally rich until the algae have grown sufficiently to deplete them once again.

A photosynthetic organism which operates in an environment such as this must have certain features in order to flourish. Capacity to survive long periods of quiescence is one. Bathed in the relative constancy of the ocean, the alga need not be equipped to survive the dehydration or extremes of temperature which are apt to confront a terrestrial organism; its problem is more apt to be nutritional deficiency. When it finds conditions just right, as in the hypothetical case of a diatom which is accidentally caught in a rising current, it must be prepared for rapid exploitation. Once such a diatom has been presented with light, it must be able to produce a clone of offspring which will capture a fair share of the available nitrate and phosphate before these nutrients have been incorporated by competing organisms.

An entirely comparable sequence of events may occur in freshwater lakes in which an annual turnover in the water occurs every spring. In tropical oceans, in the absence of seasonal cooling, convection mixing does not occur as dramatically as farther north and south, and such waters tend to have a low, constant rate of photosynthetic activity.

Comparison of the Algae with the Photosynthetic Bacteria

From what has been said in Chapter 1 concerning the restrictive nature of adaptation, it is reasonable to inquire whether there are any obvious differences between the algae and the bacteria with regard to the environmental conditions in which they can achieve photosynthesis. Such questions are not always answerable, but in this case there appear to be some striking correlations. With few exceptions the algae yield oxygen as a product of photosynthesis, while the bacteria never do. In fact, some photosynthetic bacteria are even killed by oxygen, a feature which they share in common with strictly anaerobic heterotrophs. The photosynthetic bacteria are thus generally restricted to anaerobic environments such as stagnant water and sulfur springs, while the unicellular algae predominate in the surface waters of the oceans and in freshwater lakes and streams.

An interesting group of photosynthetic organisms, which combine some of the characteristics of the bacteria and the green algae, are the blue-green algae (Fig. 3-4). They are cytologically similar to the bacteria in possessing neither mitochondria nor membrane-limited nuclei. Their cell wall and extracellular secretions of mucoid and gelatinous substances are also akin to those of the bacteria. Their chlorophyll is not located in laminar chloroplasts like those of the algae, nor in minute, ellipsoidal chromatophores like those in photosynthetic bacteria. At the present time the evidence points to pigment localization in the cell surface, and in a folded membrane which penetrates the cytoplasm from the cell surface. Oxygen is a product of their photosynthesis as it is in algae; but like some bacteria, many of them are able to fix nitrogen.

Almost any environment which is moist and light enough to support photosynthesis is apt to include a few species of blue-green algae. The explanation for their ubiquity, and for their success in competition with other photosynthetic organisms, is not as yet apparent.

Heterotrophy: The Protozoa

The protozoa possess many of the basic structural features of the algae. It is in fact difficult to assign some unicellular organisms unequivocally to one group or the other. Although basically these two groups represent two different ways of making a living, intermediate cases exist which make it impossible to establish a clear line of demarcation. The euglenoids and the dinoflagellates, for instance, each include some species which are photosynthetic, some species which are heterotrophic, and some which are both. Behaviorally and structurally they exhibit a combination of classical plant and animal properties. A dinoflagellate which is surrounded by plates of cellulose, but which can engulf other organisms between the plates while at the same time carrying on photosynthesis, is a splendid example of this ambiguity.

There are nevertheless a number of protozoa which no botanist would wish to claim and which might be considered as prototypes of the various amoeboid, flagellated, or ciliated cells occurring in multicellular animals. Taxonomists commonly subdivide the protozoa into groups on the basis of their adaptations to the problems of movement and feeding. In this scheme the flagellates, as the name implies, include those forms which possess one to several flagella (Fig. 2-11a). They include all of the protozoa which are photosynthetic or otherwise reminiscent of the unicellular algae, and a variety of closely related heterotrophic organisms. The ciliates possess hundreds or thousands of cilia, arranged in rows on the cell surface and functioning in their motility and feeding (Fig. 2-12). They also frequently have two types of nuclei—one or several micronuclei and a highly polyploid macronucleus. The amoebae, or sarcodines, constitute a third group. The fourth includes the sporozoa, amoeba-like organisms which are classified separately because of their unique mode of reproduction (p. 57).

Nutrition of the Protozoa

Heterotrophy takes a form among the protozoa which is very different from the pattern found among bacteria. The experimental difficulties encountered in growing protozoa in chemically defined media

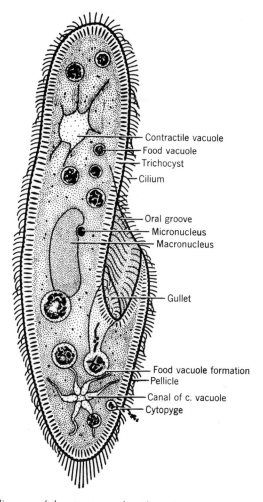

Fig. 2-12. A diagram of the structure of a ciliate, *Paramecium*. (From A. M. Elliott, *Zoology,* Appleton-Century-Crofts, 1963, p. 171.)

contrast sharply with the ease of culturing bacteria. These difficulties have resulted in large part from the complexity of protozoan nutritional requirements.

As has been noted, *Escherichia coli* can grow satisfactorily in a culture medium containing glucose and inorganic nutrients, including nitrate. This implies that the bacterium is able to reduce nitrate and combine it with the products of glucose metabolism in the synthesis of each of the twenty or so amino acids which comprise its proteins. In addition, the carbon chain of glucose can be transformed and combined with nitrogen, phosphorus, or sulfur to yield all of the other organic monomers—sugars, amino sugars, nucleotides, and lipids—found in the structure of the bacterial cell.

The protozoa have only a fraction of this number of synthetic capacities. *Tetrahymena,* one of the few ciliates to be grown on a chemically defined culture medium, must be provided with at least ten different amino acids. It has limited powers of converting some amino acids into others, but it cannot synthesize any from the more elementary raw materials. The chemical composition of a culture medium which will support the growth of *Tetrahymena paravorax* (Table 2-1) is an eloquent statement of its nutritional differences from the bacterium. And it should be noted that *Tetrahymena* is fairly representative of animal cells both in the complexity and in many of the details of its organic nutritional requirements.

Table 2-1 Composition of a culture medium for Tetrahymena paravorax. *The amount of each constituent is expressed as the weight added to 100 ml of the final medium.*

L-Arginine·HCL	20 mg	Nicotinic acid	100 μg
L-Glutamine	5 mg	D-Pantothenate, Ca	100 μg
Glycine	20 mg	Thiamine·HCL	100 μg
L-Histidine·HCL·H$_2$O	25 mg	Riboflavin-5′-mono-	
L-Isoleucine	10 mg	phosphate (Na)	25 μg
L-Leucine	15 mg	Pyridoxamine·2HCl	50 μg
L-Lysine·HCL	30 mg	Pyridoxal·HCl	50 μg
DL-Methionine	10 mg	Biotin	1 μg
DL-Phenylalanine	10 mg	DL-6-Thioctic acid	1 μg
L-Proline	10 mg	Folic acid	1 μg
DL-Serine	15 mg		
DL-Threonine	10 mg	K$_2$HPO$_4$	50 mg
L-Tyrosine	10 mg	MgSO$_4$·7H$_2$O	35 mg
L-Tryptophan	10 mg	CaCO$_3$	2.5 mg
DL-Valine	10 mg	Citric acid·H$_2$O	20 mg
Na$_3$guanylate·4H$_2$O	5.4 mg		
(2′ & 3′)		Fe	34 μg
Uracil	4 mg	Zn	50 μg
		Mn	20 μg
		Cu	4 μg
		Co	5 μg
		Mo	0.6 μg
		Glucose	0.5 g

From G. G. Holz, J. A. Erwin, and B. Wagner, *Journal of Protozoology,* **8,** 298, (1961).

Questions then arise as to where the protozoa can find such a rich and varied diet. The answer is quite simple: they find it ready-made in "prewrapped" packages, for most protozoa feed by engulfing other organisms. Soil, the oceans, and freshwater lakes and streams are all populated with amoebae, flagellates, and ciliates which are predatory primarily on the smaller organisms—the bacteria and unicellular algae —which are found there.

Once the principle of the predator-prey relationship is established the results are endless, for animal predator can in turn serve as prey for other animals. The giant amoeba, *Pelomyxa*, and the ciliate, *Didynium*, can both thrive by feeding on *Paramecium*, a ciliate which feeds largely on bacteria. The pattern established here recurs again and again throughout the animal kingdom. Among plants adaptation primarily concerns the range of physical conditions under which the organism can simultaneously find light, water, and mineral nutrients; but for animals the kind of organisms on which the individual preys and the predators it must evade join the physical environment as the major determining features of adaptation.

Adaptation for Predation

The mechanical problems of eating other organisms have been solved in several ways by protozoans. Most commonly, a pocket is formed in the cell surface at the point where contact is made with the prey, and the pocket is then pinched off to become a vacuole lying within the cytoplasm (see Fig. 2-12). Since the structure of the victim can be seen to degrade within the vacuole, it can be inferred that digestion is accomplished by the secretion of hydrolytic enzymes and that the products of hydrolysis are then absorbed through the erstwhile cell membrane which lines the vacuole.

In the amoeba engulfment can occur at any point on the cell surface which contacts the food; but in many ciliates and flagellates which possess a semirigid covering, or pellicle, a particular point on the cell surface is especially differentiated for the formation of vacuoles. This point is generally set in a depression, the gullet, into which water currents created by the action of the cilia or flagella carry the food particles (see Fig. 2-12). The vacuole may remain in the cytoplasm for a time and finally disappear; or it may move to the surface again and open out, emitting any residual undigested contents. In some ciliates this too occurs at a discrete point on the cell surface, where a pore in the pellicle serves the function of an anus.

Alternatively, it is possible to eat another organism from the inside rather than from the outside, and this is the approach taken by the many parasitic protozoa which dwell in the blood and tissues of various multicellular animals. (Plants are not significantly parasitized by protozoa. We may conjecture that the protozoa are unable to cope with the cell wall and the lack of extracellular fluids in plants. The most successful plant parasites are the viruses, which are small enough to pass through plasmadesmata and which often rely on intracellular inoculation by insects, and the fungi, which penetrate the cell wall by secreting hydrolytic enzymes.)

Like other organisms, the free-living protozoa are faced with the problem of finding food. Among their adaptive features for this, their ability to move about is preeminent. Movement, like particle feeding, is achieved by the amoeba by means of an undifferentiated cell surface. Any point on the surface of an amoeba can be the focus of production of a pseudopod into which the animal flows in achieving movement. The ciliate, with its highly structured cell surface, represents the opposite extreme. More than 2000 cilia are arranged in discrete rows on the surface of a *Paramecium*. The action of such a large population of subunits must be coordinated; if 2000 cilia were to beat randomly in direction and in time, their thrust would be likely to average zero. Microscopic observations reveal that neighboring cilia beat almost synchronously with a short but orderly time lag between neighbors, so that at any moment all phases of a beat are exhibited by a row of cilia (Fig 2-13). The resulting *metachronous* waves produce a thrust which is sufficient to propel the organism at about 1 mm per second. The direction and strength of the thrust can be controlled so as to stop the animal in less than one second, back it up, and change its direction. The organism can and does use maneuvers of this sort to get around solid obstacles in its path, to avoid conditions such as anoxia and irritating solutes, and to hunt suitable concentrations of prey. Integration of the cilia is presumed to be mediated by a system of fibers through which the basal bodies of adjoining cilia are associated, but beyond this there is little understanding of the mechanisms involved.

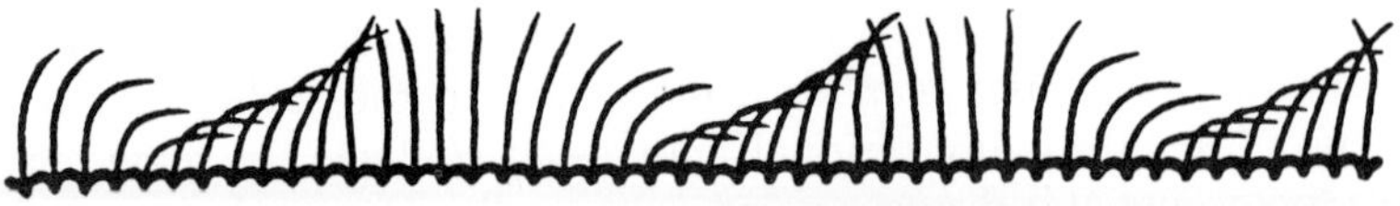

Fig. 2-13. Metachronous beating of the cilia of *Paramecium*. (From R. Buchsbaum, *Animals without Backbones*, Univ. Chicago Press, 1948, p. 23.)

There are additional problems in survival which motility will not solve. Natural populations of free-living protozoa often fluctuate in the extreme manner of the unicellular marine algae. This is to be expected for a predator whose prey occurs in unstable populations. In addition, small ponds which freeze over in the winter or dry up during droughts are often populated with protozoa in abundance. Protozoa must thus be endowed with the capacity to survive periods of impoverishment and distress. As with other cases of dormancy described earlier in this chapter, observation and experimental analysis have not yet satisfyingly demonstrated what reason predicts; for starving or dehydrating or freezing a laboratory culture of protozoa generally kills the animals rather than plunging them into dormancy. The clearest examples are provided by some of the parasitic forms. The amoebae that infect the lining of the intestines in man, producing a form of dysentery, can encase themselves in a thick proteinaceous wall. In this form they can forego feeding and reproduction and avoid desiccation for prolonged periods of time. When a cyst has been defecated by the host it can infect a new host when ingested incidentally with food or drinking water.

Perhaps a more common mode of transmission is that of the sporozoans, which cause malaria, and of the trypanosomes which cause African sleeping sickness and Chagas' disease. These are carried from host to host by blood-sucking insects, much in the manner of the insect-borne viruses. The general features of parasitism discussed in connection with the viruses hold also for the protozoa, and the two groups show interesting parallels in their adaptations for transmission from host to host.

A final problem concerning functional adaptations of the protozoa is particularly pertinent to those free-living forms that live in fresh water. The cytoplasm of freshwater organisms is necessarily hypertonic to the environment, a relationship that results in a continuous osmotic influx of water. The bacteria and many aquatic plant cells rely on the tensile strength of the cell wall to oppose the osmotic forces of swelling. The protozoa rely instead on secretory devices. A conspicuous feature in many protozoa and some of the motile, freshwater algae such as *Chlamydomonas* (p. 45) is one or more contractile vacuoles that alternately fill with water and then contract, forcing the water through a pore to the outside of the cell (see Fig. 2-12). That the contractile vacuole serves to bail water out of the cell is confirmed by the fact that it is always more conspicuous and active in freshwater species than in marine forms. Such secretory processes may well be expensive in terms of energy expenditure.

But they enable the organism to maintain a free existence, unimprisoned by cell walls, and they thereby preserve the agility which is a hallmark of the animal cell and a basic requirement of its predatory way of life.

Heterotrophy in Yeasts

For the sake of completeness in treating the unicellular heterotrophs mention should be made of the yeasts, which are specialists in the exploitation of fruits, nectar, and other sugary products of flowering plants. From such sources they are able to absorb sugars and the inorganic nutrients which are the minimal requirements for their growth. The ability of many species to produce ethyl alcohol under anaerobic conditions has been utilized in the production of a wide variety of beverages.

Yeasts have a simplicity of nutritional requirements which is reminiscent of the bacteria and quite unlike the protozoa. On the basis of their cellular structure and their mode of sexual fusion and spore formation, which are similar to those of the *Ascomycetes* such as *Neurospora* described in Stern and Nanney, Chap. 2, yeasts have been classified as unicellular fungi. Under certain environmental conditions some species form filamentous multicellular hyphae like the more conventional fungi. They can thus be added to the list of organisms (to be described in the next chapter) that form a bridge between unicellular and multicellular organizations.

REPRODUCTION AND DEVELOPMENT

It is apparent that, as in the bacteria, a key feature in the success of unicellular algae and protozoa is their ability to reproduce at a rapid rate whenever the opportunity presents itself (and to remain in a viable, dormant condition when it does not).

Reproduction in these forms still basically consists of alternating cycles of growth and cell division. Some of the algae depart from this pattern and display the beginning of the rich variety of reproductive mechanisms which plagues the student of multicellular plants. Some forms such as *Chlamydomonas* and *Chlorococcus,* undergo at certain times a phenomenon termed zoospore formation (Fig. 2-14). The protoplast divides to form 2, 4, 8, or 16 cells, all within the original cell wall and without a period of growth intervening between successive divisions. The products, which are in most instances flagellated cells, eventually break out of the parent cell wall and lead an independent existence. In many cases these will grow and reproduce for a time in the conventional pattern of vegetative cell division and then repeat the process of zoospore formation; in others zoospore formation is the only mode of reproduction.

Among the protozoa a similar process is exhibited by the sporozoans. *Plasmodium vivax*, after a period of growth in a human erythrocyte, may divide successively several times to produce as many as forty cells, which then break out of the erythrocyte and invade other cells. This mode of reproduction is a unique feature that sets the sporozoans apart from other protozoa.

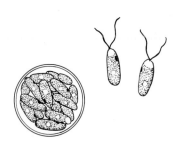

Fig. 2-14. Zoospore formation in *Chlorococcum*. The left-hand figure shows the spores produced by repeated division of a single vegetative cell. Liberated zoospores are shown to the right. (From G. M. Smith, *Cryptogamic Botany*, Vol. 1, McGraw-Hill, 2nd ed., 1955, p. 90.)

In either mode of reproduction one of the paramount problems faced by unicellular plants and animals is differentiation at the time of cell division. The larger size of these organisms and their more extensive differentiation of special cellular organelles such as siliceous shells, gullets, and cilia make the process of reproduction more cumbersome than in the bacteria. With increased complexity arise a number of problems in the control and genesis of structure that, although not unique to this level of organization, are much more apparent than in the smaller microorganisms, and effectively foreshadow some of the primary concerns in the study of multicellular forms. It would be appropriate to defer consideration of these problems to Chapter 5 were it not for the advantage to be gained in discussing them while the structure and adaptive problems of unicellular organisms are still fresh in our minds. The problem is partly a matter of the mechanics of the division process—to take an extreme example, how does a cell encased in glass, as a diatom, go about dividing in two? It is also a problem in the maintenance of specificity, as discussed by Stern and Nanney. For every structure present in the cell before division, there must ultimately be one for each of the two daughter cells.

The most thoroughly analyzed organelles in terms of replication and the mechanics of distribution to the daughter cells are unquestionably the chromosomes (see Stern and Nanney, Chapter 2). There are also a number of cytoplasmic organelles about which the available information is less definitive. For present purposes we may divide these into two categories. One includes structures such as the mitochondria, chloroplasts, and basal bodies of the cilia, all of which are potentially self-reproducing structures. A second group includes the siliceous shells of diatoms, the oral apparatus of many ciliates, and other structures that do not appear to be self-reproducing but arise during cell division at a particular point in the cytoplasm some distance from their preexisting counterpart in the parent cell.

In algae that possess a single chloroplast reproduction is accompanied by cleavage of the chloroplast and donation of each half to a daughter cell. The chloroplast then enlarges during the growth phase of the reproductive cycle, gradually reassuming its characteristic shape. In organisms that possess many chloroplasts cell division occurs in such a way that some chloroplasts are given to each daughter cell; by the time of the next cell division the number of chloroplasts has approximately doubled, due to growth and division of the preexisting chloroplasts. Mitochondria are similarly distributed at mitosis, but the mode of origin of new mitochondria during the growth phase following reproduction, whether by growth and divisions of preexisting mitochondria or by their formation from other structures in the cell, has not been conclusively demonstrated. In all these cases there is the tantalizing suggestion that the cytoplasmic organelles are each involved in some way in their own reproduction—but whether their role is as directors of the quality of synthesis, in the fashion of chromosomes, or merely as the site at which synthetic products are condensed and organized into microscopic structures is not apparent. The first alternative is increasingly favored by evidence that DNA is present in these replicating structures.

In contrast, there are those cases in which new organelles are apparently formed quite independently of their preexisting homologues. In the diatoms, whose cell wall consists of two discrete plates (or valves) of silicon dioxide, each valve is given to one of the daughter cells at the time of cell division, while the second one must be formed *de novo*, on the opposite side of the daughter cell (Fig. 2-15). Making the new valve is not simply a question of laying down a sheet of silicon dioxide, for each valve is elaborately decorated with a pattern of pits or grooves which are so precisely arranged that

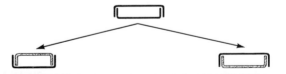

Fig. 2-15.   Valve formation after cell division in a diatom. The parental valve retained by each daughter cell is shaded black. (From G. M. Smith, *Cryptogamic Botany*, Vol. 1, McGraw-Hill, 2nd ed., 1955, p. 204.)

they serve as diagnostic characteristics for identifying the 5000 or so species of diatoms. It is difficult to see how the preexisting valve could influence the pattern of the new one. Indeed, during the process of sexual fusion (p. 65) both valves are shed before the two cells come together, and both new valves must then be formed in the absence of old ones. The protoplast itself is thus able to form and pattern the valves, but—as in so many other instances of the genesis of structure—there is no information on how this remarkable feat is achieved.

An especially imposing problem in reproduction is presented by the highly differentiated cell surface of a ciliate. The problem can be exemplified by the formation of the mouth and associated structures in *Stentor* (Fig. 2-16). This is a large, cone-shaped ciliate which

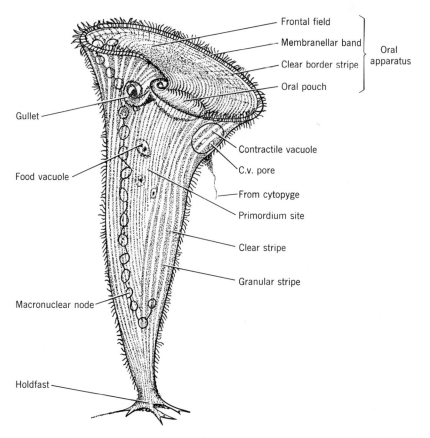

Fig. 2-16. A diagram of the structure of *Stentor*. (From V. Tartar, *Biology of Stentor*, Pergamon, 1961, p. 8.)

feeds while anchored to the substratum by a hold-fast at the point of the cone. The flat surface of the cone is covered by rows of cilia, shaped in a whorl, which terminate in a depression containing the mouth. The rim of the oral surface carries a series of cilia in plate-like clusters. This whole complex of structures, which functions in sweeping particulate food material from the surrounding water into the mouth, is termed the oral apparatus.

During cell division the second oral apparatus is formed at a characteristic point some distance from the old one. The factors controlling its site of formation have been explored in a series of observations and experiments which have revealed a mechanism having much in common with the developmental control mechanisms to be met in later chapters.

The conical sides of *Stentor* are adorned with longitudinal pigment stripes alternating with rows of cilia and contractile threads (Figs. 2-16 and 2-17). The width of these pigment stripes varies in a characteristic fashion. Beginning with the broadest stripe and moving around the animal in counterclockwise direction, the stripes become progressively narrower; the finest stripes thus lie adjacent to (and are intercepted by) the broadest one at the starting point. Observations of dividing animals have indicated that the locus of formation of the new oral apparatus early in cell division is the zone containing the finest stripes (Fig. 2-18). The progress in its formation and growth is closely correlated with the process of division itself. In the final stages of division the new oral apparatus enlarges, moves basally, and gradually intercepts all of the stripes, the basal sections of which

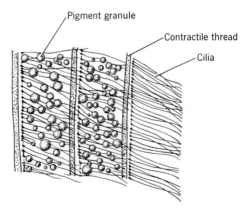

Fig. 2-17. Enlarged view of the pigment granules, which form the granular stripes in Fig. 2-16, and the rows of cilia. (From L. H. Hyman, *The Invertebrates, Protozoa through Ctenophora*, McGraw-Hill, 1940, p. 166.)

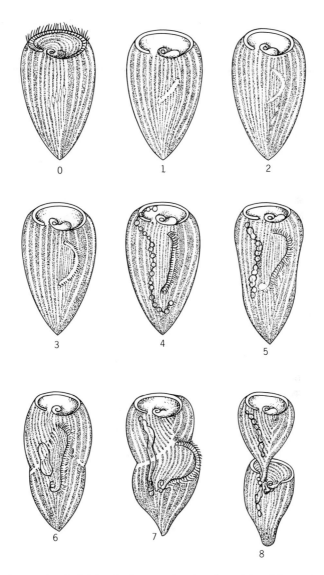

Fig. 2-18. Stages of cell division in *Stentor,* showing the origin of the oral apparatus. Structural details of the oral apparatus have been omitted from drawings of
stages 1–8. The macronucleus has been omitted from stages 0–3. (From V. Tartar,
Biology of Stentor, p. 68.)

become associated with the new oral apparatus, while the apical portions retain their earlier association with the old apparatus.

Stentor is particularly adept at the process of regeneration. Thus if the oral apparatus is cut off, the animal can successfully form a new apparatus; and, as in cell division, the new apparatus is initiated in the fine-stripe zone adjacent to the point of discontinuity in stripe width.

We are prone to suspect that there is something unique and unseen in the fine-stripe zone which gives rise to the new oral apparatus. That something essential to oral apparatus formation is unseen is quite true; but regeneration and grafting experiments indicate that it is not unique, in the sense of being restricted to only one region of the cell surface. In these experiments not only the oral apparatus but also the fine-stripe zone was removed. The superficial cytoplasm containing the residual stripes then spread out to close the resulting wounds, and thereby a new point of discontinuity in stripe width was formed. A new oral apparatus was formed by these animals in the region containing the finest remaining stripes.

It has also been possible to graft pieces of the surface of *Stentor* into cuts made in the surface layer of other individuals. For instance, a piece containing broad stripes can be grafted into the fine-stripe zone. When the oral apparatus is removed from such an animal, not one but three new oral apparati are regenerated—one on each side of the graft, in addition to the one normally formed by the host (Fig. 2-19). The most obvious conclusion is that many regions of the cell surface which do not normally form an oral apparatus can be made to do so. The conditions responsible for oral apparatus formation can also be described at this point. It is always formed at a point of discontinuity in stripe width—more exactly, in a fine-stripe zone

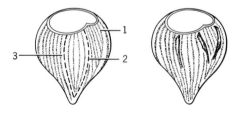

Fig. 2-19. Formation of oral apparati following insertion of a sector containing wide stripes into the zone of fine stripes of an animal whose oral apparatus had been cut off. Regeneration occurred at three sites, the normal host primordium site (1) and the two fine stripe zones adjacent to the graft (2 and 3). (From V. Tartar, *14th Growth Symposium,* D. Rudnick, ed., Princeton Univ. Press, 1956, p. 78.)

directly adjacent to a broad-stripe zone. Thus the graft of broad stripes inserted in a region of fine stripes induced two oral apparati because two discontinuities in stripe width resulted, one at each border of the graft.

We cannot assert that the pigment stripes themselves are involved in determining the locus of mouth formation, for a gradient of as yet undefined entities in the surface cytoplasm associated with the pigment stripes might equally well be involved. What we can state at this point is that *Stentor* has a clearly defined mechanism for determining the locus at which the materials incorporated into the oral apparatus are condensed and organized. There are two important consequences of this mechanism. Under normal circumstances it operates in such a manner that a single oral apparatus is present in each daughter cell at the time of cell division. In addition, it achieves an accurate positioning of the mouth with relation to the other surface differentiations of the animal. The problem of where the oral apparatus will form is the first of several cases of spatial coordination in the genesis of structure analyzed in this text. In most organisms accurate positioning of new structures during development is absolutely essential to the viability of the individual.

In addition to illustrating the problem of positioning, the formation of the oral apparatus can also be used as an example of temporal coordination. The oral apparatus does not arise at any time in the life cycle of *Stentor*, but always at a discrete phase in the division process, and thus in close coordination with nuclear and cytoplasmic division. The fact that many regions of the organism act more or less simultaneously in cell division indicates a diffuseness in the mechanisms of temporal coordination which contrasts vividly with spatial coordination.

An even clearer example of temporal coordination is seen in the giant amoebas of the genus *Pelomyxa*, which may contain up to 1000 nuclei scattered in their cytoplasm. Here, as in many other multi-nucleate cells, mitosis commences in all nuclei simultaneously when it occurs. (As in the distribution of chloroplasts and mitochondria, many nuclei in the giant amoeba are presented to each daughter cell during cytoplasmic division.) It is quite apparent in these instances that a change has occurred which is spatially diffuse—because all nuclei scattered throughout the cytoplasm respond to it—but which is temporally discrete—because all nuclei commence mitosis simultaneously. Temporal and spatial control mechanisms are *sine qua non* to the development of highly differentiated organisms, and thus a major portion of Chapter 5 is devoted to them.

Sexuality

Sexual fusion occurs in most groups of unicellular organisms, although in some forms, including many of the amoebae and dinoflagellates, it has never been observed. In many life-cycles nuclear fusion is preceded by cellular fusion (Figs. 2-20 and 2-21); in others, notably among the ciliates, the individual cells retain their identity, but a temporary bridge of cytoplasm is established across which gamete nuclei are exchanged (Fig. 2-22e).

Fertilization yields a single diploid nucleus from two haploid nuclei, and it is necessary for the process of meiosis to occur at some time in the life history of the individual in order to achieve a return to the haploid condition in the gametes of subsequent generations. There are some interesting contrasts in the time at which meiosis occurs. In the ciliates and in most of the diatoms which indulge in sexuality, meiosis occurs directly before sexual fusion (Fig. 2-21 and Fig. 2-22a–c). The zygote yielded by fertilization then undergoes mitotic reproduction to initiate a clone of vegetative cells, all of which contain diploid nuclei. In other forms, such as the green alga *Chlamydomonas*, meiosis intercedes after fertilization and before the resumption of reproduction by mitosis. Each of the four haploid products of meiosis can then produce a clone of vegetative, haploid cells (Fig. 2-20f).

It is thus a well-established fact that some microorganisms normally possess haploid nuclei, while some possess diploid nuclei. As will be seen in Chapter 4, vegetative cells in other organisms may be either haploid or diploid, depending on the phase of their life cycle. Since

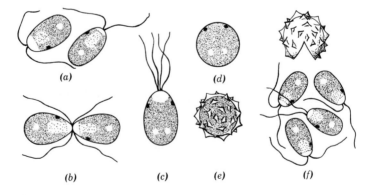

(a)   (d)

(b)   (c)   (e)   (f)

Fig. 2-20. Sexual fusion in *Chlamydomonas*. Nuclear fusion occurs at the stage shown in *(e)*, the resting zygote stage. Meiosis occurs prior to germination *(f)*. (From G. M. Smith, *Cryptogamic Botany,* Vol. 1, McGraw-Hill, 1st ed., 1939, p. 31.)

all of these organisms function effectively, it is difficult to identify the advantages to the individual of either haploidy or diploidy. The one consequence that is quite clear concerns the expression of mutations. In a haploid individual the effect of a mutation will be immediately felt, whereas in a diploid individual its effects can be masked or altered by the presence of the allelic gene on the homologous chromosome. The fact that both kinds of organisms flourish suggests that heterozygosity is of advantage to some organisms and not to others, but at the present juncture nothing more precise can be said.

The Problem of Size in Protozoa

A final point to be made in this chapter concerns the large size which is achieved by many species of protozoa. *Paramecium aurelia*, which is not an exceptionally large ciliate, measures 100 μ long and 30 μ wide. Some of the larger amoebae may be approximately 1000 μ (1 mm) long.

Many zoologists prefer to think of such animals as being composed of many cells which have failed to preserve their separating membranes.

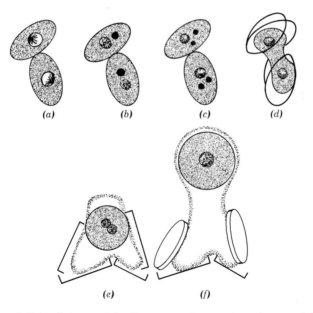

Fig. 2-21. Cellular fusion and fertilization in *Cocconeis*, a diatom. Cellular contact is followed by meiosis, with all except one haploid nucleus disintegrating in each cell *(a-d)*. The cells abandon their glass valves *(d, e)*. Nuclear fusion occurs *(f)*. (From G. M. Smith, *Cryptogamic Botany*, Vol. 1, McGraw-Hill, 2nd ed., p. 206.)

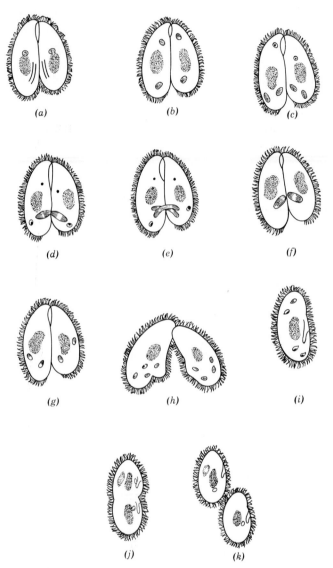

Fig. 2-22. Conjugation and fertilization in *Paramecium*. *(a)* Newly conjugated pair. *(b, c)* Meiosis of the micronucleus with degeneration of all meiotic products except one. *(d)* Beginning of mitosis of the remaining haploid nucleus to form two gamete nuclei, one of which migrates to the mate *(e)*. *(f)* Fusion of gametes to form diploid zygote nucleus. *(g, h, i)* Mitotic division of the zygote nucleus, and the termination of conjugation. *(j, k)* Two of the mitotic products form macronuclei while the old macronucleus disintegrates. After the first cell division *(k)* each daughter nucleus has one macronucleus and one micronucleus, all derived mitotically from the diploid zygote nucleus in *(f)*. (From R. Wichterman, *The Biology of Paramecium*, Blakiston, 1953, pp. 280, 281.)

There is a multiplicity in the substructure of many large protozoa which justifies this view. As we have seen, the ciliates contain two nuclear bodies: a micronucleus with a diploid set of chromosomes, and a highly polyploid macronucleus. After sexual interchange, which involves an exchange of the meiotic products of the micronucleus, the macronucleus disintegrates and a new one is formed by the growth of a mitotic product of the micronucleus (Fig. 2-22f–k). The macronucleus and the micronucleus are thus genetically equivalent, and the macronucleus might be thought of as a device for enhancing the amount of genetic material in a cell containing an unusually large amount of cytoplasm. A similar explanation can be offered for the multinucleate condition of the giant amoebae. When to these facts is added the information that a ciliate may contain thousands of cilia, it is clear that large size has been achieved not by the addition of something qualitatively new, but by compounding the basic elements possessed by smaller cells.

Ciliates may have a volume which is between a hundred thousand and a million times as great as the volume of a small bacterium. Presumably a size difference of this magnitude has a number of consequences, many of them of adaptive significance. It is an empirical fact, for instance, that small organisms generally reproduce faster than large organisms. It takes a gram of *E. coli* less than thirty minutes to become two grams of *E. coli*, under optimal conditions, while *P. aurelia* requires about seven hours to achieve the same feat. We can thus speculate that natural selection would favor small size wherever rapid exploitation is a key to fitness, as appears to be the case in the bacteria and the marine algae. On the other hand, a predatory organism, just for mechanical reasons, needs to be larger than the prey which it ingests, and this could well be the key selective factor which leads to large size in protozoa and in animals generally.

SUMMARY

From this review of the biology of microorganisms it is apparent that a broad range of structures is encompassed by both the unicellular and the subcellular organisms. The range in size from the relatively simple molecular aggregate which constitutes an infectious virus particle to the largest ciliates and amoebae is enormous. It would take about 10^{12} of the smallest bacteria, for instance, to make a volume equal to that of the largest amoebae, and about an equal number of the latter to achieve the volume of a large conifer. Equally divergent are the stratagems which these organisms employ in feeding themselves. Parasitism, symbiosis, and free-living autotrophy and heterotrophy all occur, and each in a variety of ways.

But despite this diversity, they are all single cells (with the exception of the viruses) which must operate within the rules of physiology and genetics explored in Volume I. All of them can reproduce at a fairly rapid rate relative to multicellular organisms, and in all cases reproduction is synonymous with cell division. As we have moved from the smaller to the larger microorganisms, however, problems in the genesis of structure have tended to become more obvious, and these have in turn called attention to the necessity of both spatial and temporal precision in the molecular events underlying reproduction and development. Such problems will become increasingly apparent in later chapters dealing with multicellular organisms.

Sexuality occurs in all major groups, although it has never been demonstrated in some species, and it is accompanied by a sampling of the variety of haploid-diploid life cycles which also occur in the multicellular organisms.

Most forms exhibit an elementary behavior which allows them to respond to environmental stimuli within the restrictions of a limited repertoire of movements and development.

Feeding and reproduction, the central problems facing all organisms, occur here in relatively unadorned and elementary fashion, however. One of our purposes in introducing the microorganisms separately from the multicellular organisms has been to provide a panoramic view of all aspects of some relatively simple and unembellished organisms before considering the mechanistic complexities of the multicellular state.

3

Multicellular Organisms

In Chapter 2 we were concerned with organisms that exist throughout their lives as single cells, each one independently extracting
matter and energy from the environment and utilizing them for
growth and reproduction. The rest of this volume is concerned with
the biology of multicellular organisms—aggregates of cells in which
the growth and maintenance of the individual cell is dependent on a
close functional association with its fellows.

Several different levels of complexity in the broad spectrum of
multicellular organisms will be considered in an attempt to extract
some principles that can be generally applied to this kind of biological
organization. In beginning such an effort, it is helpful to consider
forms whose structures are intermediate between unicellular and
multicellular organization. One warning is necessary: whenever an
analysis progresses through increasing levels of biological complexity,
there is a temptation to attribute an evolutionary significance to what in
fact is only an arbitrarily constructed series of contemporary organisms.
Surely such a progression must have taken place during evolution, but
not necessarily in precisely the same way. What matters for the purpose
of this chapter is that structural and functional organizations occurring
at a number of levels of complexity are available in the present world
for direct experimental analysis.

INTERMEDIATE FORMS

There are today a number of organisms that seem to function at
the edge of multicellularity. An interesting series with increasing

multicellular tendency occurs in the family of green algae known as the *Volvocales*. In this group the individual cell is a typical biflagellated, chlorophyll-containing algal cell (Fig. 3-1*b*). The unusual feature of the group is most spectacularly illustrated by *Volvox*, long a favorite organism of the general biology laboratory. Its 2000 or so cells are compacted into a spherical, hollow-centered mass (Fig. 3-1*a*) that carries out its activities in an impressively unitary fashion. The unity may be related to the existence of fine protoplasmic strands connecting the member cells. Biologists have often referred to *Volvox* as a *colony*; some would now prefer to use the term *multicell*, implying something closer to an organism. The distinction between these terms underlines the difficult question which such a cellular aggregate poses: namely, at what point and on the basis of what kind of relationships between component cells is the concept of organism properly applied to the whole rather than to the cellular unit?

Volvox moves as a whole in a nonrandom way. Instead of rolling about aimlessly, the sphere has head- and tailness—that is, a particular region always goes first in locomotion. We can thus define a pair of hemispheres, one of which *precedes* while the other *follows*. Other indications of functional differentiation are also present. Occasional cells in the posterior hemisphere resume growth and cell division to form inverted daughter aggregates, which protrude into the central cavity. These then turn inside out and detach from the wall of the mother aggregate, remaining inside the sphere until liberated by its death or destruction. Cells in the same region may also produce sexual gametes at certain seasons. Regardless of which type of reproduction is practiced, however, the reproductive cells occur *only in the "following" hemisphere.* Although the slight structural and size differences between cells of the two hemispheres might be explained by the fact that the "preceding" hemisphere is on top and hence receives more light, such evidences of segregated function persuade us that real differentiation has occurred among the cells of different regions.

Experiments suggest that the development of the multicellular state has resulted in an obligatory reliance of the individual cells on each other. If a single *Volvox* cell is detached from the mass and cultured separately, it never regenerates a new aggregate. Comparable experiments have been performed on the related forms *Eudorina, Pandorina,* and *Gonium*. These algae form masses considerably smaller in cell number than *Volvox: Eudorina* is intermediate in cell number, while aggregates of the latter two contain only a dozen or so cells (Fig. 3-2). Single cells isolated from *Eudorina* form abnormal masses, while regeneration from single *Gonium* or *Pandorina* cells is apparently per-

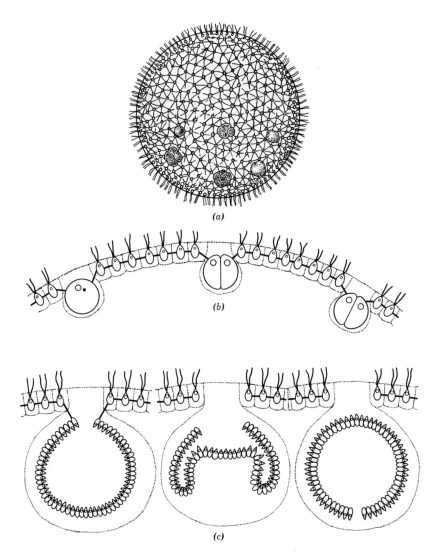

Fig. 3-1. (a) *Volvox,* with daughter colonies in the posterior hemisphere. (b) An enlarged view showing biflagellate cells with cytoplasmic connectives and several cells which have commenced daughter colony formation. (c) Inversion of the daughter colony after formation of the definitive cell number. (a and b from L. Hyman, *The Invertebrates, Protozoa through Ctenophora,* McGraw-Hill, 1940, p. 106; c from G. M. Smith, *Cryptogamic Botany,* Vol. I, 2nd ed., McGraw-Hill, 1955, p. 40.)

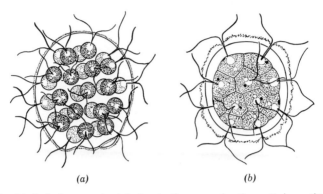

(a)   (b)

Fig. 3-2. (a) Eudorina, a colonial alga in the same family as Volvox. (b) Gonium, an even smaller and more compact alga (From G. M. Smith, Cryptogamic Botany, Vol. I, 2nd ed., McGraw-Hill, 1955, pp. 36 and 37.)

fect. It may well be that these related algae form a series of increasing size and complexity, in which the process of differentiation goes farther in the larger aggregates and, in Volvox, cuts off from the individual cell certain abilities that are necessary for adequate development of a normal aggregate. Most biologists would agree that such evidence of differentiation, especially if it is normally irreversible, is one likely criterion for calling an aggregate an organism.

The cellular slime molds point to some additional criteria; the following description applies to Dictyostelium discoideum, but may be extended to others with some modification. For a time the slime molds exist as single amoeboid cells, each derived from a single spore. Cultured on agar in the laboratory (or, in nature, wandering about on rotting logs or some similar environment), these cells live as independently as most other microorganisms, feeding on bacteria, growing, and reproducing. A remarkable phenomenon brings this separate feeding stage to an end, often at the very time when the food supply is exhausted. Amoebae begin to stream toward an aggregation center, piling up on one another and eventually forming a sausage-shaped slug (stages A–G in Fig. 3-3). The slug then migrates as a unit, always with a particular end first and often following temperature or light gradients. It then stops, rounds up, and engages in a precise series of morphogenetic movements during which a ball of cells (originally located in the posterior half of the slug) climbs up a growing stalk formed from anterior cells (stages H–N in Fig. 3-3). The final result looks like a ping-pong ball stuck on the point of an inverted golf tee. It is in fact a reproductive structure. The cells in the spherical sorus atop the stalk transform into spores which, on landing in a suitable environment, will release a

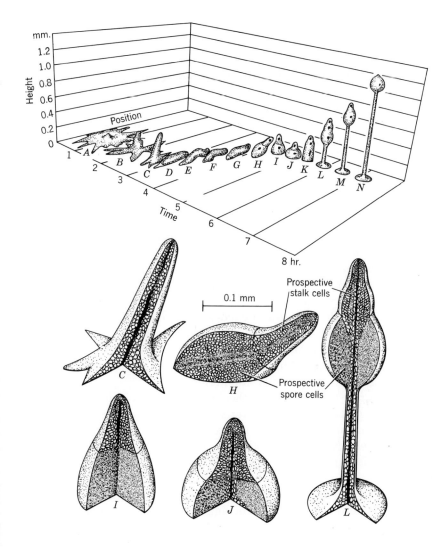

Fig. 3-3.   Development of the fruiting structure in *Dictyostelium discoideum*. The timetable is given above in a three-dimensional graph which also shows position. Sections *C-L* show the cell structure at selected stages. (From J. T. Bonner, *The Cellular Slime Molds*, Princeton, 1959, p. 26.)

new generation of amoebae; the stalk itself is a supporting structure, strongly reinforced with cellulose.

Clearly a marked differentiation in both the behavior and structure of these cells takes place during the formation of the delicate and complex fruiting structure. The anterior cells push down through the posterior mass to form the lower part of the stalk (stage J in Fig. 3-3); the stalk elongates by vacuolization of these cells and by the addition of other cells that have climbed to its apex. As the column rises, these cells synthesize cellulose and contribute it to the common stalk sheath. They eventually die, leaving their own cell wall as the structural unit of the stalk. Spore cells originating in the posterior cell mass also secrete cellulose walls after climbing the stalk to their definitive position; but they do not become vacuolated, and remain as viable cells within.

Considerable experimental effort has gone into attempts to determine how much differentiation is already present among cells of the migrating phase. It is evident that the polarity of movement of the slug indicates, as with *Volvox*, some functional differentiation. Moreover at the beginning of culmination, anterior and posterior cells already differ in their morphogenetic fates: they produce stalk and sorus respectively, as revealed by experiments in which the movements of marked regions (sometimes produced by grafting red-stained anterior halves onto colorless posterior ones) are followed. In a histological search for other evidences of differentiation, it was revealed that the anterior cells are larger and that they stain more weakly with hematoxylin. Certain enzymes are also more active in anterior cells.

Let us pursue this question further and consider the independent free-amoeba stage. Here the cells differ somewhat in size, but the distribution is continuous; there is no evidence for separate populations of large and small cells. Nor have any other consistent morphological differences been revealed among free amoebae. At the conclusion of the feeding phase aggregation centers are formed, and we might expect to find some special properties in the cells which form the centers. Experiments on the nature of the stimulus for aggregation have shown that it is basically a chemotactic process: that is, cells at the center produce a chemical that orients the movement of their neighbors toward the focus. This chemical, called *acrasin,* does more than direct locomotion. It also alters the properties of cells subjected to it so that they too begin to produce acrasin and to become sticky through the secretion of a slimy material. In the later stages of aggregation, therefore, the streams of cells moving toward the center are coherent, and actually set up subgradients of the attracting substance which in turn induct cells from farther away. When the aggregation process is completed, the slug is encased in a slimy sheath and the cells within it all engage in motion. The tip is apparently formed of cells having the highest rate of acrasin production, with the result that the posterior cells follow it in all movements; the following is helped, of course, by the coherence established by sticky extracellular materials in the sheath.

Are centers of aggregation formed by special cells? This has been a somewhat controversial question over the past several years. The evidence indicates that the process of initiation depends on some particular cell reaching the stage of acrasin production before its fellows—just as, in the heart, a number of cells are capable of initiating a beat, the specific identity of the "pacemaker" being determined by which one recovers its excitability and fires first. The pacemaker hypothesis of aggregation would thus argue against a rigorously specific differentiation of free amoebae into initiator and follower cells. The indications are rather that differentiation proceeds during the multicellular phase of the life cycle.

What happens if we deliberately interfere with the cellular balance produced by the differentiation of anterior and posterior cells within the migrating mass? When the slug is divided transversely in two along the border between anterior and posterior cells, two viable masses are produced. Both subsequently undergo culmination and form perfect, though small, fruiting structures. This is preceded by a redifferentiation of cells—a change of posterior to anterior cells in one of the masses, and the reverse change in the other—which reestablishes the ratio between cells destined to form stalk and those destined to form spores. In some fashion information about the proportion of cell types present can be exchanged among cellular members of the aggregate, which can then *regulate* the quality of differentiation of its members.

What lessons can be learned from these two evolutionary experiments along the borderlines of multicellularity? In accord with the questions raised in Chapter 1, we would hope to be able to identify a strategic advantage which was conferred on the individual cell as a consequence of being associated with its siblings. In *Dictyostelium* the amoebae can feed and reproduce with obvious effectiveness as individual cells, and the transformation to multicellularity is clearly directed toward dispersal. A clone of amoebae that has depleted its surroundings of food, or otherwise come upon distressing circumstances, can elevate a substantial proportion of its members above the moist substratum, where they will transform into spores and be disseminated by the wind. Only one of the thousands of spores produced needs to lodge in more congenial circumstances to make the operation a complete success in terms of the continuity of the genome. In *Volvox* the strategic advantage of multicellularity is not so obvious, unless it resides in the motor apparatus which is efficient enough to allow these organisms to swim with the velocity of a good-sized ciliate. Whatever the adaptive advantage may be, it is clearly different from that of multicellularity in the slime molds. This fact warns us that there may be many reasons for the origins and success of this cumbersome way of life.

A second point made in Chapter 1 and confirmed in these very primitive organisms is that any advantage which may be conferred by the multicellular condition is dependent on the simultaneous establishment of integrating mechanisms. The secretion of acrasin, the much less well understood mechanism by which a proper balance is established between the number of stalk and spore cells in slime molds, and the coordination of flagellar activity in *Volvox* are not only elegant examples of intercellular coordination but are very likely *sine qua non* for the success of these organisms in their natural world.

Finally, it is possible to see in these two groups of organisms many of the anatomical principles manifested on a grander scale in other multicellular organisms. Before describing the strategic consequences and the functional mechanisms of multicellularity, we will briefly explore these anatomical problems.

THE STRUCTURE OF MULTICELLULAR ORGANISMS

Manifested in the organisms just described are three aspects of multicellular structure that will be fundamental to many problems discussed in the following chapters. First, *cohesiveness* is evidently important and may be brought about in different ways. In the *Volvocales* it results from the failure of division products to separate; in the slime molds a special swarming mechanism brings free cells together secondarily. In both groups a substantial amount of noncellular material is present in the structure, and the formation and functions of these materials raise a second category of problems. Finally, multicellularity is accompanied in both cases by differentiation in which the cell population becomes diversified and specialized. In *Volvox* this is limited to a distinction between reproductive and somatic cells. In the cellular slime molds more profound changes result in the production of a complex fruiting structure with clear differences between spore cells and stalk cells. In discussing these problems it is reasonable to begin with cohesion—the most fundamental mechanistic requirement of multicellularity.

The Problem of Sticking Together

The failure of daughter cells to separate after mitosis is basic to the cohesiveness of most multicellular organisms. When a reproductive cell has divided to form two cells, these continue to adhere to each other, as do all subsequent mitotic products. A general exception to this rule occurs in reproduction, the essence of which is the separation of viable cells, individually or in groups, from the parent body.

On reexamining the unicellular organisms and their reproduction, it is clear that many of these also have a pronounced tendency to remain associated after cell division. In some instances this is apparently due to the trapping of daughter cells within the coat of extracellular gelatinous material that was secreted by the parent cell. Cohesion by entrapment of component cells is particularly evident among some of the blue-green algae. Here the daughter cells, following mitosis, soon become separated from each other by further secretion of gelatinous matrix; but they still remain trapped within the common sheath that was secreted when they were a single cell before division (Fig. 3-4a).

In other cases there is a suggestion that cohesion consists of more than entrapment. Cells of the filamentous blue-green algae, in particular, remain closely apposed to each other after cell division (Fig. 3-4b). Although they secrete a cylindrical sheath of gelatinous material surrounding the filament of cells, the matrix material never appears between cells to an appreciable degree. And even where they protrude from the sheath at its ends, the cells continue to adhere to each other. (In conformity with the general use of these terms, *adhesion* is defined here as the sticking of one object to another, while *cohesion* refers to the ability of a single object to resist disintegration. Cohesion is thus the integrated effect of many adhesions: an organism is cohesive either because its cells adhere to each other or because they are mechanically trapped in a matrix whose molecules adhere to each other.)

When cell division occurs in most multicellular plants, each daughter cell lays down a wall of cellulose adjacent to its sibling, the two walls being separated by a *middle lamella* of intercellular substances (Fig. 3-5, b–d). For a time the two remain within the lateral cell wall of the parent cell from which they were derived (a–c). Apparently by a process of digestion the edge of the new plate of middle lamella eventually penetrates the parent cell wall, however, and thus each daughter cell becomes continuously surrounded by middle lamella. The new cell wall and the space between neighboring cells becomes permeated with polysaccharides, the calcium pectinates, whose cementing action effec-

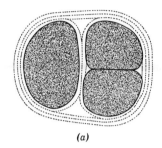

(a)

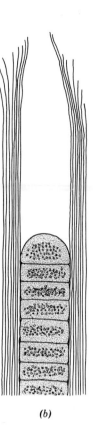

Fig. 3-4. (a) The blue-green alga, Chroococcus, showing daughter cells trapped in the gelatinuous matrix secreted earlier by their common parent. (b) A filamentous blue-green alga, Porphyrosiphon. Gelatinous material surrounds the filament, but is not produced between cells. In such forms the cells adhere even if the filament protrudes from the sheath. (From G. M. Smith, Cryptogamic Botany, Vol. I, 2nd ed., McGraw-Hill, 1955, pp. 277 and 278.)

(b)

tively glues the adjoining cells together. The pectinates can be dissolved in the laboratory, either by chemical treatment or by enzymatic hydrolysis (utilizing the pectinase extracted from the disgestive glands of snails); when this is done the cells lose much of their adhesiveness and can be more readily pulled apart. Multicellular plants thus rely on both mechanical trapping and adhesives to maintain their physical integrity.

The filamentous green alga, Oedogonium, foregoes the initial contribution of the parent cell wall to cohesion. In this case a crack develops in the wall near one end of the cell at the completion of division (Fig. 3-6a). When the two daughter cells elongate, their point of adhesion shifts freely within the parent cell wall. The latter can therefore contribute nothing to holding the two cells together; from the time of cell division adhesion rather than entrapment must be relied on.

Much of the mechanical strength of animals is due to the secretion of fibrous proteins such as collagen and to a number of other tough matrix materials such as bone, cuticle, and chondroitin sulfate. Animal

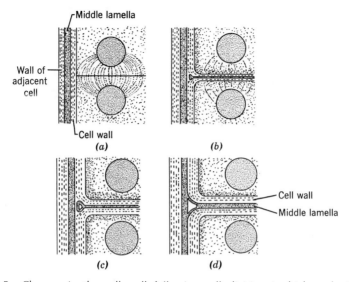

Fig. 3-5.   Changes in the cell wall following cell division in higher plants. (a) Parent cell wall still intact. (b-d) Formation of the middle lamella between daughter cells, accompanied by digestion of the parent cell wall around the edge of the new lamella. (From A. J. Eames and L. H. McDaniel, *An Introduction to Plant Anatomy*, 2nd ed., McGraw-Hill, 1947, p. 29.)

embryos, on the other hand, possess few of these entrapping materials and depend instead on cell-to-cell adhesion for their mechanical integrity. Most animal embryos are covered with protective membranes of various sorts. If the embryo is removed from these, it remains as a cohesive structure, but it is generally an extremely fragile one until it has differentiated to the point where it can synthesize extracellular components such as collagen. If such an embryo is briefly treated with a proteolytic enzyme, its cells can be made to separate from each other. The cells of many embryos will also disaggregate if they are bathed in an artificial salt solution that imitates their normal environment in every respect except that it is deficient in calcium ions or has an elevated pH. On the subsequent restoration of normal conditions, the cells will reaggregate. In some cases reasonably normal development ensues, indicating that the cells have not been irreparably damaged by the treatment (see Chapter 5, p. 167). There is as yet no clear indication whether calcium is essential to the effectiveness of an intercellular glue analogous to the pectinates of plants.

Finally, we should point out that the function of some cells, such as reproductive cells and the red blood cells of vertebrates, is dependent on their being nonadhesive (though clearly an egg must eventually

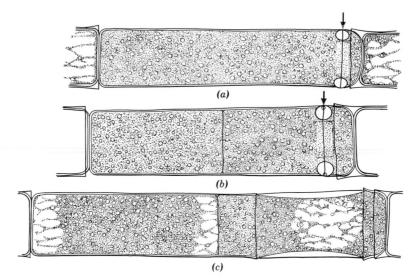

Fig. 3-6. Cell division in *Oedogonium*. The arrows in (a) and (b) indicate a ring of new cell wall material. When the daughter cells elongate after cell division (c), the parent cell wall breaks at this point. (From G. M. Smith, *Cryptogamic Botany*, Vol. I, 2nd ed., McGraw-Hill, 1955, p. 70.)

adhere to a sperm). Thus both in the mechanism and the occurrence of cohesion multicellular organisms show a good deal of versatility which has been manipulated to cope with specific needs.

The Noncellular Components

The organism has a surface, a boundary between itself and its environment, which is in all cases clearly defined. Yet everything within the boundary is not necessarily living cells. The bark which lies in thick flakes on the trunk of a tree, for instance, and the fibers and vessels of wood are both nonliving residues of cells (see Chapter 5, p. 182), whereas the layer of wax that coats the surface of the leaves is a cellular secretion.

Wood consists in large part of xylem cells which, in their final stages of differentiation, lose both cytoplasm and nuclei (Chapter 5, p. 176). Remaining as a residue is the cell wall with its cellulose fibrillae, a trace of the intercellular layer of pectinates, and significant amounts of lignins, which form a tough matrix surrounding the cellulose fibrillae and render the structure mechanically stronger. There are thus several synthetic products involved, and these have combined to form a structure that simultaneously contributes to the mechanical strength of the stem and functions in the transport of water and minerals to the leaves from the roots.

Additional examples can be given of noncellular products that comprise a significant portion of the total mass of the organism; most of them are as familiar as wood. Keratin, for instance, is a fibrous protein whose presence accounts for the horny quality of the scales of reptiles, the feathers of birds, and the hair of mammals. Like wood, these structures have a cellular origin: they are composed of the transformed carcasses of cells, the transformation consisting of the synthesis of large amounts of keratin and the subsequent dissolution of cytoplasm and nuclei. In other cases the cells remain as living, mechanically fragile structures that either line the surface of or are embedded in the cohesive matrix which they have produced (Fig. 3-7). The bone and cartilage of vertebrates, the cuticle that covers the body surfaces of insects and other arthropods, the calcareous shells of snails and clams, and the "jelly" of the jellyfish are examples of these.

Such cells are reminiscent of the microorganism that surrounds itself with a shell of polysaccharide or protein. In the multicellular organism the results can be an achievement of very different dimensions. A large group of cells located in a particular region of the organism and all synthesizing the same matrix material can yield, for instance, an elephant's thigh bone, measuring 5 feet in length and supporting one quarter of the animal's 2 ton weight or, by suitable reduction in numbers and activity of cells, the thigh bone of a shrew, measuring less than half an inch and supporting one quarter of the shrew's tenth of an ounce weight.

Prominent in any list of the noncellular components in a multicellular organism are the circulating fluids—the matrix of the blood of animals, and the sap and other fluids which are transported by the vascular tissue of plants. As is noted in Chapter 6, the composition of the circulating fluids can be greatly modified by variations in the physical environment, a sensitivity that is related to the fact that they are engaged in the transport of substances between the environment and the cells. They are also engaged in the transport of materials between different regions of the organism, however, and thus their composition is determined in large measure by the activities of cells that both add solutes to and remove them from their immediate environment. The circulating fluids, like the noncellular structural components, must therefore be considered the product of cellular activities. (Whether a secreted substance becomes a local structural component depends in large measure on its solubility and on its capacity to combine chemically with other structural or circulating substances.)

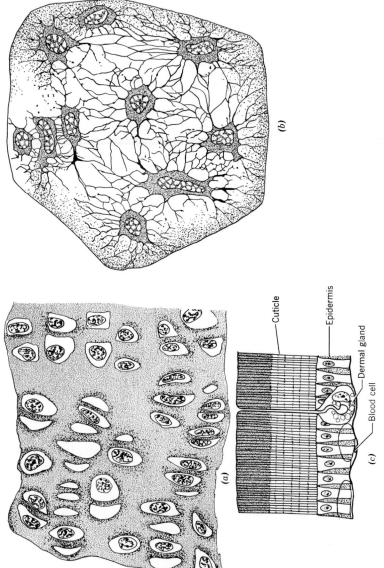

Fig. 3-7. (a) Cartilage from the xiphoid process of a rat. The cells remain embedded in the interstitial substance which they have secreted. 750 X. (b) Transparent membrane bone of a mouse. 700 X. (c) Cuticle and epidermis of an insect. 200 X. (a and b from W. Bloom and D. W. Fawcett, *A Textbook of Histology*, Saunders, 1962, pp. 145 and 154; c from V. B. Wigglesworth, in *Biological Reviews*, **23**, 409 (1948).)

The immediate environment of a cell in a multicellular organism thus includes not only the other cells that it can actually touch, but also various secretory products—some its own, some those of its immediate neighbors, and some which reach it via the circulating fluids, the products of its more distant siblings in the organism. In the following pages there will be frequent references to these substances, to the various functions they serve, and to their role as vehicles for communication between cells.

The Arrangement and Differentiation of Cells

Multicellular organization has an extraordinary plasticity, which has permitted the evolution of a seemingly limitless variety of forms. Basic to this versatility is the fact that a multicellular organism, rather than being a haphazard structure, is formed with precision. The individual reproductive cell has a rigidly limited genetic endowment, which leads it to develop to a predetermined shape and size, and any significant deviation from that form is generally disastrous to the biological success of the individual. Nevertheless, the hereditary mechanisms which govern development have been sufficiently responsive to mutation and natural selection to have yielded the degree of diversity that we have come to expect among biologically successful species.

Broadly speaking, a description of this all-important anatomy has three components. They are the shape and size of the organism, the kinds of cells and cellular secretions that constitute it, and the manner in which these constituents are distributed. As we have seen, all three components are necessary for a precise description of the anatomy of even rudimentary multicellular aggregates such as *Volvox* and of transitory ones such as the fruiting body of *Dictyostelium*. As the size and complexity of the organism increases, complete descriptions of this sort begin to be more difficult to achieve. There are, however, some basic patterns that are helpful in understanding the anatomy of more complex organisms; for example, the cells are frequently arranged in hollow cylinders or in flattened sheets. These two simple configurations account for the structure of *Ulva*, a common marine alga often called "sea lettuce," and the familiar freshwater coelenterate, *Hydra*.

Epithelial Organization. Ulva (Fig. 3-8) consists of an irregular sheet of cells, the *blade*, growing up from a holdfast that attaches the plant to the substratum. The blade is formed by two closely compressed layers of photosynthetic cells embedded in a tough gelatinous matrix that arises by the confluence of materials secreted by adjacent cells. (In both

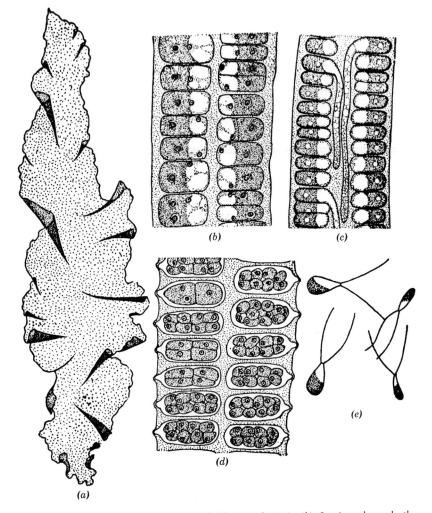

Fig. 3-8. (a) The blade of *Ulva* (one half natural size). (*b*) Section through the blade. (*c*) Rhizoidal outgrowths of blade cells near the hold-fast. (*d*) Blade cells forming gametes. (*e*) Mature gametes. (From G. M. Smith, *Cryptogamic Botany*, Vol. I, 2nd ed., McGraw-Hill, 1955, p. 62.)

plants and animals layers of cells of this sort are termed *epithelia.*) Many cells near the base of the *Ulva* produce long rhizoids that grow down through the matrix (Fig. 3-8*c*). The holdfast is composed of bundles of these rhizoids that emerge from the base of the blade.

Reproduction occurs when each cell of the blade divides several successive times to form 16 to 32 flagellated cells. Like the zoospores described in the last chapter, these cells break out of the parent cell wall and swim away (Fig. 3-8d and e). Every cell in the blade, beginning at the periphery, abandons the plant in this fashion, and a new blade is then regenerated from the perennial holdfast. Depending on environmental conditions, the zoospores possess either two or four flagella. When they have four flagella, after swimming for a short distance, they settle to the bottom and generate new plants. When they possess only two flagella they serve as gametes, each of which must first fuse with a similar cell from another plant. Development begins in both cases with a mitotic division giving rise to two cells; one of these forms the holdfast and the other produces the leaf-like blade. Growth and division of the latter cell and its progeny give rise at the outset to a filamentous structure like the definitive form of many other algae. After several cell divisions growth in other planes commences, and a two-dimensional sheet forms from the linear file. The blade produced may be a foot or more long and thus is a good deal larger than any organism that we have thus far considered. Until reproduction begins, the only cellular differentiation apparent is between the blade and the rhizoid cells, and thus the enhanced size entails very little in the way of increased complexity.

Cellular differentiation is substantially more complex in *Hydra*, even though the geometry of the individual can still be expressed in simple terms. *Hydra* is a cylindrical organism with a crown of elongated tentacles (Fig. 3-9); at the base of these is the single opening to the hollow interior, which serves as a digestive tract. The body wall consists of two layers, an inner and an outer epithelium (Fig. 3-10). The inner layer or *endodermis* is composed of nutritive cells which ingest food particles, and secretory cells which produce digestive enzymes. In the outer layer or *epidermis* are the epithelio-muscular cells, with elongated, contractile bases, and the nematoblasts—remarkable cells containing an internal capsule (the nematocyst) with a barbed shaft and thread, which is ejected upon stimulation of a mechanically and chemically sensitive trigger.

Every cell in such organisms is in more or less direct contact with the environment; in *Hydra*, which is heterotrophic and therefore has more complex needs, the digestion, absorption, and some transport of nutrients is handled by the endodermal cells. Each, of course, requires O_2 and produces CO_2, but these exchanges also are carried out between individual cells and the environment without the intervention of transport and control mechanisms like those of larger organisms.

Hydra, being an animal, albeit a comparatively sessile one, shows rather rapid coordinated responses, though their integration is not well worked out. *Hydra* normally feeds on small aquatic organisms that

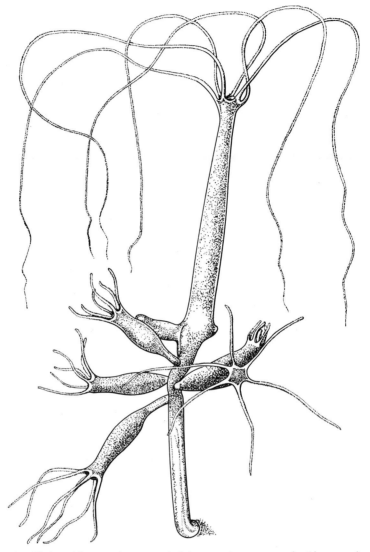

Fig. 3-9.   Hydra with tentacles expanded for trapping prey, and with a number of buds forming on the body column. (From P. Brien, in American Scientist, **48,** p. 460 (1960).)

blunder into its crown of tentacles and are then pulled into the gastro-vascular cavity by coordinated contractions. Capture of the prey by the tentacles is a totally uncoordinated process: nematocysts are fired inde-pendently by mechanical stimuli (possibly aided by local chemical stim-ulation). Some of the nematocysts merely entangle the prey in sticky

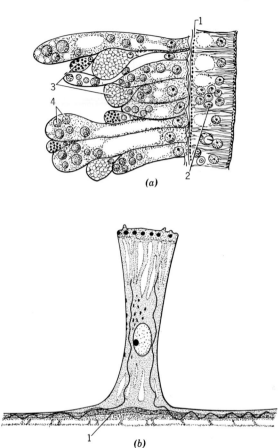

Fig. 3-10. (a) Section through the gastric region of the body wall in Hydra; 1. muscle fibers at the base of the epidermal cells; 2. interstitial cells forming nematocysts; 3. secretory cells in the endodermis; 4. engulfed food particles in a nutritive cell. (b) An epitheliomuscular cell. (From L. Hyman, *The Invertebrates, Protozoa through Ctenophora*, McGraw-Hill, 1940, p. 374.)

threads. Others actually penetrate its integument with barbed spears, and release toxins that paralyze the prey. Once the animal is trapped in the tentacles, a feeding response is elicited, which involves coordinated movements of the tentacles and mouth by the epithelio-muscular system. It is probable that the movements are controlled by the same kind of diffuse, net-like nervous system that is responsible for muscular activity in other coelenterates.

Recent experiments with animals grown in cultures suggest that gamete production in *Hydra* is evoked by crowded conditions, sometimes apparently in response to high local concentrations of CO_2 produced by the organisms, though temperature changes can also stimulate the process. The "interstitial cells" of the outer epidermis (Fig. 3-10a), which normally transform as needed into nematoblasts, are stimulated under these conditions to produce eggs or sperm. In the absence of the stimuli eliciting gamete formation and as long as the individual is well nourished, *Hydra* reproduces by forming buds, which develop into miniature adults while still attached to the parent. They ultimately drop off and form an independent attachment to the substratum.

Hydra has an odd potential kind of immortality in that its total cell population "turns over" in a very few weeks. The Belgian zoologist Brien demonstrated in 1950 that a patch of cells, identified by staining with a vital dye and grafted into the body column of another hydra just below the point of attachment of the tentacles, gradually moves toward the base of the body column where it ultimately disappears. Similarly, cells lying closer to the tentacles gradually move into the tentacles, travel their length, and disappear at the tips. It has been concluded from such experiments that new cells are continually produced in a growth zone in the body column close to the base of the tentacles and that old cells are destroyed at the base of the body column and at the tips of the tentacles. All cells except those remaining in the growth zone, therefore, are gradually displaced toward the sites of cellular destruction. We can thus think of *Hydra* as maintaining its form in the same way a whirlpool might: through a permanent structure, a ceaselessly changing set of cellular elements is formed, moves along, grows old, and departs.

Three-Dimensional Organs. It is possible to describe in fairly brief fashion the arrangement and differentiation of every cell type in organisms such as *Volvox, Dictyostelium* and *Ulva*, to account for the developmental history of each cell, and to relate its activities to the major functions performed by the organism. Such an undertaking would be much more difficult in *Hydra* where there are about ten kinds of cells produced, and would become laborious indeed in a higher plant which contains around 20 discrete cell types and in animals such as arthropods and vertebrates where the number is between 50 and 100. Hand in hand with the increased cellular differentiation is a far greater organizational complexity, which not only makes an anatomical description more cumbersome but also obscures the basic facts.

Hydra and *Ulva* exhibit what is commonly called the "tissue level" of organization; that is, the major features of body form are derived from foldings or outpocketings of simple epithelia. Furthermore, beyond a few distinctions such as blade *vs.* holdfast and tentacles *vs.* body column, differentiated cells are not highly organized into organs with morphological identity and corporate functional tasks. *Hydra* lacks a brain; *Ulva* lacks flowers. Functions analogous to those associated with brains and flowers in more complex organisms are performed by scattered cells.

In more complex organisms there are many more different types of cells, and these are arranged in a three-dimensional anatomy that cannot be interpreted in terms of one or two layers of folded epithelia. So far as the animal is concerned, the inner and outer layers of epithelia that were apparent in *Hydra* are still prominent—such tissues form the lining of the digestive tract, for instance, and the outer layer of the skin. These are now separated from each other, however, by a middle layer, the *mesoderm*, which takes over the vascular, contractile, and connective functions, and in the vertebrates and echinoderms serves as the skeletal system. Indeed, most of the mass of these organisms is comprised of mesodermal structures; and (as we will see in Chapter 5) most organs that are not exclusively mesodermal are composite in origin, consisting of either endoderm or ectoderm in association with mesoderm. Not only does this composite character increase the potential architectural complexity of the organism; it now appears that the opportunity thus provided for physiological interactions between different tissues during growth is important in regulating the final shape of the organism. Similarly in higher plants, growth is characterized by a distinct third-dimensional component quite unlike the laminar growth of *Ulva* or the filamentous growth of *Oedogonium*.

Fortunately, even in these more complex situations the arrangement of cells in discrete layers or groupings is a characteristic feature. The anatomy of a tree, for instance, can be grossly described in terms of leaves, roots, and stems. Such a description is particularly useful because these anatomically defined subunits also possess functional significance; the leaf is the site of photosynthesis, the root tip is the site of mineral and water absorption, and the stem and root provide the means of conduction between the two as well as support for the leaves. The anatomy and activities of a leaf, root, or stem can in turn be analyzed in terms of the shape, arrangement, and activities of the cells that comprise it. Even here, however, we are apt to think of the structure of a leaf or stem, not in terms of individual cells but of layers or groups of cells. Thus the upper and lower surfaces of the leaf are each covered with an epidermis while between these two layers is a thick layer of chloroplast-containing cells and vascular bundles (p. 5). In effect, cells are arranged in layers, or groups, which are frequently termed tissues. Various tissues are grouped into functional associations that have been termed organs, and the whole mass is cemented together in the form of an organism which, for a tree, is thus three orders of complexity greater than the individual cell.

In animals a good example is the intestine of a vertebrate, which receives partially digested food from the stomach, and completes the process of digestion and absorption. Like the leaf, the intestine is subdivided into a series of layers of cells, each of which performs a discrete set of functions (Fig. 3-11). The innermost layer is a folded epithelium, one cell thick, which is formed into finger-like processes, the villi, protruding into the lumen of the intestine, and glandular pockets, the intestinal glands, opening at the base of the villi. Absorption of sugars, amino acids, lipids, and other products of digestion is performed by the cells coating the villi, while the gland cells secrete a number of digestive enzymes. Surrounding the intestinal glands and forming the core of the villi are layers of connective tissue, including a number of cells that synthesize the protein collagen. Collagen occurs in extracellular fibers whose mechanical properties account for much of the tensile strength of the intestine. The epithelium and associated connective tissue form a morphologically discrete layer, the *mucosa,* which is separated by a thin layer of muscle from the *submucosa,* an additional layer of connective tissue. Surrounding the connective tissue are two layers of smooth muscle cells, one layer oriented so that its contraction shortens the intestine, and the other to constrict it. These two layers accomplish the churning and mixing of food and digestive enzymes, and finally push the partially digested mixture posteriorly. An additional layer of connective tissue surrounds the smooth muscle, forming the peritoneum (the tough outer lining of the intestine) and connecting it to the mesenteries which suspend it in the cavity of the abdomen. The whole set of tissues is permeated with blood vessels and lymphatic vessels, and the muscles in particular are connected with a plexus of nerves. All of these layers and the component cell types comprising each of them are essential to effective activity of the intestine as a digestive organ.

In analyzing the operations of the organism, it is necessary to acknowledge the position, shape, functions, and interconnections of the intestine with all of the other multicellular subunits. The human intestine was accurately diagramed in the sixteenth century by the European physician and anatomist, Vesalius, and much of its anatomy was undoubtedly known to others much earlier. The digestive juices that are secreted by the epithelial glands of an adjacent organ, the stomach, were collected by Spallanzani in 1790 by the surprising procedure of swallowing a sponge on a string and then pulling it out again. Having obtained his gastric juices, Spallanzani demonstrated their capacity to cause the dis-

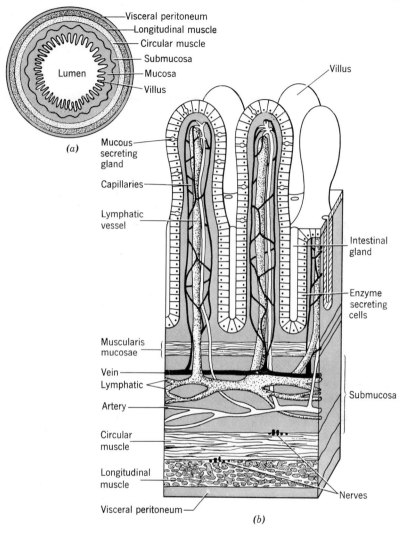

Visceral peritoneum
Longitudinal muscle
Circular muscle
Submucosa
Mucosa
Lumen
Villus
Villus

(a)

Mucous secreting gland

Capillaries

Lymphatic vessel

Intestinal gland

Enzyme secreting cells

Muscularis mucosae

Vein
Lymphatic
Artery

Submucosa

Circular muscle

Longitudinal muscle

Nerves

Visceral peritoneum

(b)

Fig. 3-11. A diagrammatic section of the small intestine of a mammal. (From C. A. Villee, W. F. Walker, and F. E. Smith, *General Zoology,* Saunders, 1963, p. 487.)

solution of food. An accurate concept of the gross structure and some of the functions of such organs had thus been established *at least two centuries before their cellular structure was revealed.*

This discussion is not intended to discourage the analysis of plants and animals in terms of cells. We wish only to indicate the practical limitations of such an analysis, and to emphasize the importance of the functional associations of large populations of cells in the form of tissues and organs. Organ-level analysis is an indispensable step in understanding the structure and function of multicellular organisms. To explain the mechanisms whereby an organ such as a leaf or intestine carries out its functions, however, it is ultimately necessary to think in terms of the differentiation, arrangement, and activities of individual cells.

Finally, we must reaffirm the status of the cell as the "least common denominator" of multicellular organisms. The diversity of organisms is patently manifested in their multicellular subunits: the organs of vertebrates are subunits only for vertebrates, while other organisms such as trees have their own special multicellular components which are not at all relevant to the analysis of vertebrates. Regardless of this fact, the hierarchy of levels of anatomical organization is seen in all multicellular organisms that consist of more than a few hundred cells. Not until organisms are examined at the level of the individual cell does it become apparent that they have a common structural basis.

MULTICELLULARITY AS AN ADAPTIVE STRATEGY

We must now pose the question of the significance of multicellular organization as a strategic device enabling its practitioners to maintain their foothold in a world which must have been dominated by microorganisms during the period of their origin and which remains so to a significant degree even today. It is not enough merely to call attention to the grand opportunities for specialization, differentiation, and intercellular communication; these advantages can accrue to the single-celled organism by exploitation of molecular architecture, and have done so—in spite of size limitations—in the more complex ciliated protozoa. We must find, instead, opportunities for the establishment of unique ways of earning a living through this kind of organization. We can only guess at what attributes might have accomplished this for the first multicellular organisms. Samples of these early multicells are not available to us; we have to look at present-day forms and by evaluating their distribution and achievements try to decide the basis for their success.

It seems fairly clear that this problem must be separately considered for plants and animals. Although there are notable exceptions (the fungi, for example), plants are in general photoautotrophs; they make demands on the environment which are entirely different from those of heterotrophic animals. It is felt by almost all biologists that the advent of multicellularity was a separate evolutionary event in the two cases—there is, in fact, no guarantee that there were not *more* than two such origins.

The distribution of autotrophic plants reveals several striking facts. The terrestrial environment is dominated by multicellular plants, while in marine environments these organisms have not enjoyed significant success. The vast bulk of marine photosynthesis (which, in turn, accounts for at least half of the carbon dioxide fixation occurring on the earth) is carried out by unicellular algae—especially the diatoms and dinoflagellates (page 46). The multicellular red, brown, and green algae occur primarily at shallow depths, around the rims of continents; their contribution to the total biomass of the oceans is insignificant, although they certainly dominate the shorelines. These facts can be explained by assuming that unicellular plants have flourished wherever all the necessities of life are available in one place, while multicellular forms have tended to predominate wherever there has been a strategic advantage to be gained from large size and a consequent ability to be in two places at once. Multicellular organization appears to have been the most successful method of obtaining a really large size. We may cite two supporting considerations: first, no unicellular organisms of large size are known, a finding that suggests that there are strong practical reasons why it *hasn't* worked; second, there are theoretical reasons for believing that it *shouldn't* work. These are related to the surface/volume ratio. As single cells become very large, this ratio decreases, and the exchanging cell surface becomes unable to supply the cytoplasmic volume; in addition, the nucleus must become impractically large in order to service the synthetic activities of this cytoplasmic volume, and this undoubtedly has drastic consequences for division mechanics and the genetic system.

Among plants it is especially apparent that enhanced size has been of great advantage in situations that required the individual organism to be, effectively, in two places at once, as opposed to the situation among microorganisms where rapidity of exploitation is a key feature. Hence the open sea is a good environment for the unicellular plant (Chapter 2, p. 47). Light penetrates well through clear oceanic water, and at least in many places CO_2 and mineral nutrients are available in adequate amounts. Finally, the density of sea water is not radically different from that of cytoplasm, and the difference is readily resolved by adaptations of the single algal cell which retard its sinking rate. Marine diatoms and dinoflagellates often possess elaborate spines, cytoplasmic oil droplets, or other flotation mechanisms, particularly in tropical waters where the density of sea water is decreased by its high temperature. In such a situation, where there is no apparent advantage to be gained by being multicellular, the more rapidly growing unicellular forms have predominated.

The relative success of multicellularity at the ocean's rim is due to a unique set of opportunities and requirements. Mineral nutrients are constantly available in many of these regions because of the interaction of oceanic currents with the continental shelf and streams, and thus there is a definite advantage here if an organism can root itself to the substratum. However, the turbidity characteristics of the water arising from the action of the breakers, as well as shading by neighboring plants, make it advantageous to grow toward the surface from the rooted point on the substratum. For this combination of necessities the bulk and length made possible by multicellularity is an advantage.

Terrestrial plants are in a very different situation from aquatic ones. Such plants must go into the ground for water and mineral nutrients; but unfortunately, this shuts off the supply of light energy. So terrestrial photoautotrophs must occupy two environments at once, maintaining a photosynthetic, quantum-trapping apparatus where the water isn't and a water-absorbing system where the light isn't. As with the attached marine algae, increased size is necessary for leading such a two-environment existence, and multicellular organization provides it. Confirmation of this argument is to be found in the striking fact that more than 99% of the photosynthetic biomass in most terrestrial regions is composed of multicellular plants.

This explanation is not helpful, of course, in accounting for heterotrophic plants such as the multicellular fungi, which absorb nutrients from the organically rich medium in which they live. It is likely that the requirement of spore dissemination that we have already explored in slime molds (p. 75) is a major contributing factor. Most fungi feed by growing into the substance of either living or dead organisms or the organic matter of soil. When faced with the problem of dissemination, they emerge from the substratum in which they have been immersed and form a complex fruiting body (Fig. 3-12). Most members of the *Phycomycetes,* one of the three classes of fungi, go only part way along the route to multicellularity during the feeding stage. Their branching tubular hyphae are not subdivided into cells, but contain a freely mixing, multinucleate cytoplasm. In the *Ascomycetes* the partition between adjacent cells is often perforated, permitting intermixing of the cytoplasm and occasionally of nuclei, while in the *Basidiomycetes* the hyphae are subdivided completely into cells. Even in the *Phycomycetes* and *Ascomycetes* the fruiting bodies are strictly multicellular. Thus while a substantial increase in size can be achieved by a syncytial structure with all the elements of multicellularity except the crosswall, the differentiations prerequisite to invading the second environment and disseminating spores are always accompanied by the final partitioning off of cells.

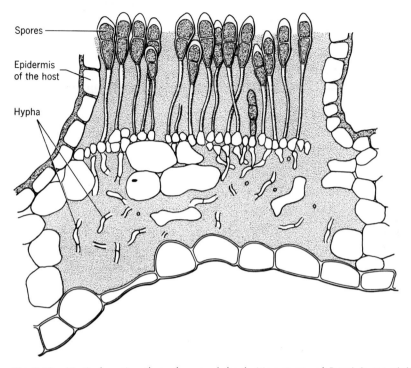

Spores

Epidermis
of the host

Hypha

Fig. 3-12. Vertical section through one of the fruiting stages of *Puccinia graminis,* the wheat rust fungus. The fungus is producing spores to be liberated through the ruptured epidermis, while the feeding component, the hypha, remains embedded in the tissues of the leaf. (From G. M. Smith, *Cryptogamic Botany,* Vol. I, 2nd ed., McGraw-Hill, 1955, p. 501.)

Animals, whose nutritional pattern is heterotrophic, stimulate a different sort of speculation. For them increased size is adaptive not because it enables them to live in two environments at once, but because it permits more effective exploitation of a single one. Most unicellular heterotrophic organisms feed by active uptake of relatively small food particles. For many the size is molecular, and the mode of uptake is essentially an active transport system. Others feed phagocytically on particles in the bacterial size range. But the level to which the environment can be exploited for "living food" is always limited, because for most simple feeding mechanisms the prey must be very much smaller than the eater. Multicellularity opened up a new size range of possible prey, and it seems very likely that it is within this context that the new mode of organization flourished.

The obvious exception to this reasoning, of course, is the parasitic animal. A substantial number of organisms have been able to avail themselves of the nutritional opportunities afforded by the tissues of multicellular plants and animals by remaining small enough to reside there without immediately disturbing the viability of their host. This is the only way in which protozoa can prey upon the larger organisms, but there are many multicellular plants and animals that are also parasitic. These are generally closely enough related to the more prevalent free-living organisms to allow the conclusion that parasitism arose in these forms well after the developmental and functional patterns of multicellularity had been established.

EVOLUTIONARY ORIGINS OF MULTICELLULARITY

For reasons already given we have thus far avoided speculating on how multicellular organisms arose, in favor of exploring their adaptive advantages. But it seems unfair to leave the issue of the origin of multicellularity without a brief consideration of such an obvious question.

Most botanists agree that multicellular plants have arisen several times from unicellular precursors, probably flagellated green algae. The present-day *Bryophyta* and *Tracheophyta* probably arose from a branched, filamentous, multicellular green alga of uncertain identity; brown and red algae may well have had entirely separate origins from unicellular forms. At the core of all hypotheses is the assumption that multicellularity in plants arose through the kind of cohesion displayed in the *Volvocales*—in other words, by cells failing to separate after division.

The origin of the metazoa (multicellular animals) has been classically viewed as a similar process. The three most primitively constructed groups of metazoa are the sponges (*Porifera*), the coelenterates, and the flatworms (*Platyhelminthes*). Because of their differences from the other two phyla and their clear relationship to certain flagellates (the choanoflagellates), the sponges are now widely regarded as having had an origin separate from the rest of the metazoa (Fig. 3-13). The coelenterates (Fig. 3-14) possess a larval stage (the *planula*), which shows an appealing resemblance to some "colonial" algal types; and certain flatworms do not depart radically from this form. Some planula-like organism, then, itself derived from a presently unknown aggregate of non-photosynthetic flagellates, has been regarded widely as the common "ancestor" of coelenterates and flatworms—and thereby of the rest of the multicellular animals.

An alternative view is that aggregation of unicellular forms had nothing to do with metazoan origins; that instead, multicellularity in

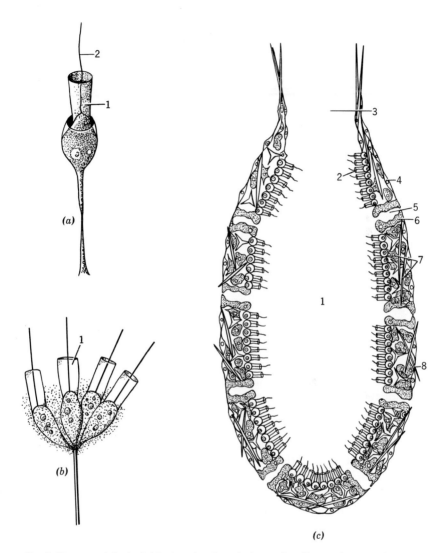

Fig. 3-13. a and *b*, Individual and colonial choanoflagellates, showing the collar (1) and flagellum (2) which characterize the feeding apparatus of this group of protozoa. (c) Diagrammatic drawing of a simple sponge with the spongocoel (1) lined by choanocytes (2). Other features include the osculum (3), epidermis (4), pores (5), porocytes (6), mesenchyme cells (7) and spicules, the skeletal elements (8). The flagella of the choanocytes create a current of water which enters through the pores and leaves through the osculum. (From L. Hyman, *The Invertebrates, Protozoa through Ctenophora*, McGraw-Hill, 1940, p. 108 and 289.)

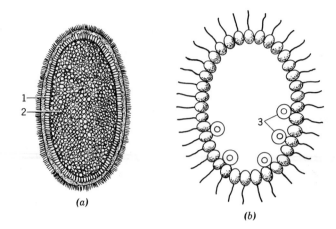

(a)

(b)

Fig. 3-14. (a) Planula larva of a living hydroid coelenterate showing ectoderm (1) and endoderm (2) which, with subsequent development, will be organized in a manner similar to that of *Hydra*. (b) Hypothetical flagellated ancestor of the planula with germ cells (3) occupying the position of the endoderm. Note the similarity to *Volvox*. (From L. Hyman, *The Invertebrates, Protozoa through Ctenophora*, McGraw-Hill, 1940, p. 251.)

animals arose through the *cellularization* of some multinucleate unicell. The ciliate protozoa, as described in Chapter 2, often show this multinucleate condition and indeed have achieved great complexity. Certain flatworms (the *Acoela*) are themselves syncytial organisms; that is, except for the gametes (which are complete cells), the entire adult organism consists of a common, undivided cytoplasm with many nuclei. It has been proposed, on the basis of similarities between certain multinucleate ciliates and the acoel flatworms, that the latter represent an intermediate between the multinucleate and multicellular condition. The cellularization argument, however, is weakened by the fact that the acoel flatworms themselves go through a normal cleavage series during development and only subsequently lose their cellular boundaries.

Differences of opinion such as these which arise in the course of speculations about the *specific* evolutionary routes are not always readily resolved. Fossil records of the transitions are lacking, and controversy thrives best when hypotheses cannot be tested.

4

Reproduction in
Multicellular Organisms

At some stage of its career every organism spends a substantial proportion of its time and energy on the problem of leaving progeny. Natural
selection suggests that this is so because the genome of an organism
that does not reproduce is permanently lost with the death of the individual. The mechanisms of the reproductive process vary enormously
among species of multicellular organisms, and may even have a series
of alternate forms within a single species. Despite this range of variation, some general characteristics of reproduction can be stated, which
are so obvious that they are frequently overlooked and yet so fundamental that the analysis would be grossly incomplete if they were not
made explicit.

One is that reproduction entails the dissociation from the individual of viable fragments. In some organisms, such as most higher plants,
certain generations of offspring may remain parasitic on the parent
plant. In others, such as the vegetatively reproducing land plants and
many of the bryozoa, coelenterates, and tunicates, a clone of individuals
may remain physically associated in the form of a colony. Such cases
testify that reproduction, like the other activities of organisms, has
been modified in all sorts of special ways to contend with special adaptive requirements. Despite the interesting exceptions most cases of
reproduction are recognized as such primarily because physically independent progeny are produced.

A second generalization is that the viable fragments which form the
progeny are cellular in nature. As will be described shortly, they are
sometimes multicellular structures but, more frequently, single cells.

Of great importance is the fact that they are never subcellular. Over a century ago Virchow's doctrine that cells all come from preexisting cells was first explicitly enunciated. One of the severest tests of Virchow's doctrine was the elucidation of the nature of spores and gametes. It was demonstrated during the nineteenth century that these structures, though highly differentiated for their specific functions, can nevertheless be interpreted as cells, and modern biochemistry and electron microscopy have confirmed this conclusion. In no case has a multicellular organism been found to generate progeny from subcellular entities.

A third general characteristic of reproduction is its interdependence and cyclical relationship with development. Since the newly formed progeny are of necessity smaller and more simply constructed than the parent organism from which they dissociated, growth, reorganization, and differentiation must follow before the progeny will themselves achieve reproductive competence. In the life history of the individual, therefore, development is a prerequisite to reproduction, while reproduction, in turn, imposes on the offspring the necessity of further growth and differentiation.

These three generalizations can be illustrated by analyzing the cellular origins and the initial form of the progeny of a series of organisms.

THE FORMS OF REPRODUCTION

In its simplest form among microorganisms the cycle of reproduction and development consists of cell division, preceded by a period of synthesis and accompanied by a duplication of all of the structural components of the cell. It is finally consummated by the separation of the daughter cells from each other. Similarly, at the multicellular level a flatworm such as *Planaria* can reproduce by constricting at its midsection to form two masses of cells, one without a head and one without a tail, which finally go their separate ways. Within a few days each half has reconstituted its missing structures and is capable of feeding, growing, and repeating the whole process.

Although fission in the planarian and cell division in the unicellular organism are very different mechanisms, they both exhibit the essential features of reproduction. In both a single individual converts itself into two independent individuals. In addition, the progeny, though endowed with half of the parental mass and structure, are morphologically incomplete and must undergo a period of synthesis and development before they are fully competent to reproduce in turn.

In most multicellular organisms the parent does not endow its off-spring so lavishly with preformed equipment (concomitantly, the parent retains its identity at the conclusion of the process). As a result, much more must be achieved in the subsequent period of development than is the case with the flatworm. Although the initial form of the progeny varies greatly among different organisms, for our purposes they may be classified into two kinds: (1) multicellular reproductive forms, or buds, which were exemplified in Chapter 3 by *Volvox* and *Hydra;* and (2) unicellular structures, the spores and gametes.

Reproduction from multicellular buds is further illustrated in a number of flowering plants. A strawberry plant, for instance, produces special stems called *stolons* that grow away from the plant along the ground by the growth and proliferation of cells at their tip. At a distance of a foot or so roots are generated from the stolon, and from a neighboring point a bud may arise that grows into a leafy shoot (Fig. 4-1). The original stem that produced the new plant may eventually dry up or be cut, thereby effecting a separation of the offspring from its parent.

Some marine Coelenterates related to *Hydra* are among the many examples of sessile animals that can reproduce from multicellular buds to form colonies. A stolon consisting of ectoderm and endoderm grows out from the organism along the rock or other substratum to which the hydroid is attached. The stolon branches periodically, and each branch gives rise to a new individual (Fig. 4-2).

Stolon formation is just one of many forms of reproduction from multicellular, vegetative structures among higher plants. In some plants adventitious shoots arise on underground roots. This is particularly conspicuous in a potato plant in which the shoots arise on tubers—expanded

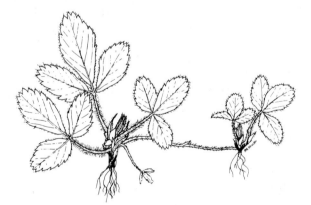

Fig. 4-1. Strawberry plant reproducing from a stolon. (From V. A. Greulach and J. E. Adams, *Plants: An Introduction to Modern Botany,* Wiley, 1962, p. 414.)

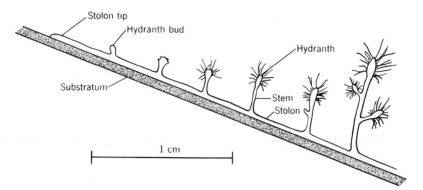

Fig. 4-2.   Reproduction from a stolon in *Cordylophora,* a coelenterate. (From C. Fulton, in *The Biology of Hydra,* H. M. Lenhoff and W. E. Loomis, eds., Univ. Miami Press, 1961, p. 288.)

regions of the root that serve as carbohydrate storage depots. In the ferns and many grasses an underground stem (or *rhizoid*) analogous to the stolon can give rise to both new leaves and adventitious roots. In raspberries and Forsythia bushes roots and shoots are produced when a leafy shoot bends over and touches the ground at its tip. Bulbs, which are fleshy, underground stems in tulips and crocuses, and clusters of fleshy leaves in an onion, may form branches that can then break away and lead an independent existence. And in a few plants a shoot and roots may arise wherever the ground is touched by a leaf (Fig. 4-3). In most of these instances the process leads to a cluster of genetically identical plants that live in close association, although they are sufficiently independent of each other so that the connecting bridge may eventually break without impairing the subsequent growth of the individuals.

In contrast to the unicellular organism or the planarian undergoing fission, the new individual in all of these cases has a long way to go before it can be recognized as a replica of its parent or is competent to reproduce. Although the parent provides the energy and matter required to get the new individual organized, the starting point of the offspring is a relatively unorganized region of the stolon, rather than half the structure of the parent plant. Even more extreme is the problem of generating new individuals from single cells. With few exceptions all multicellular organisms, including those which arise from multicellular reproductive units, can also produce single cells which are able to form progeny. Such organisms thus exist temporarily at the level of organization of a unicellular organism, and must embark on a period of growth, cell multiplication, and differentiation—during which they gradually assume the

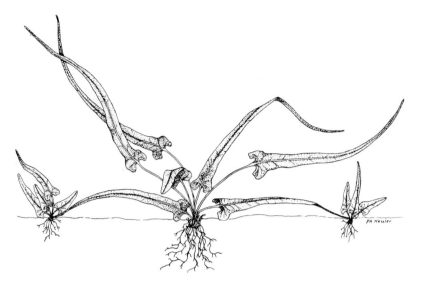

Fig. 4-3.   Reproduction from leaf tips in the walking fern. (From V. A. Greulach and J. E. Adams, *Plants: An Introduction to Modern Botany*, Wiley, 1962, p. 417.)

cellular arrangements and patterns characteristic of a reproductively competent individual. The capacity of the individual organism to climb the scale of complexity in this fashion introduces a whole new set of problems that were not encountered in the analysis of microorganisms.

For reasons that will be considered shortly, most multicellular plants and animals combine the function of reproduction from single cells with the function of sexual fusion. Here the reproductive cells have been termed *gametes*. In some of the lower plants and protozoa the gametes from different parents are morphologically similar to each other. *Ulva* (p. 85) can be cited as an example of this. Among most multicellular plants and animals, however, a clear distinction between two forms of gametes is the general rule. The female gamete or *egg* is generally nonmotile. It either has a placental relationship with its parent, as in the flowering plants and mammals; or, as in birds (to cite a familiar example), it carries sufficient nutrient reserves within its cytoplasm to provide energy and matter for the early development of the offspring. The male gamete, or *sperm*, is a much smaller cell that is endowed with the ability to transport its nucleus to the egg. Motility and the storage of food reserves are two essentially incompatible functions, and it is not surprising that natural selection has separated them into different cells.

Gametes are the only kinds of unicellular reproductive units produced by multicellular animals. Plants, on the other hand, can generally produce progeny from single cells which we will refer to as spores. As has been noted, the term *spore* is used by microbiologists to denote the thick-walled form in which unicellular organisms can endure periods of stress and privation. The use of the same term for the nonsexual reproductive cells of multicellular plants is a reflection of the fact that here also they may be a highly durable form of the organism.

The algae, the fungi, and some of the land plants such as mosses and ferns are particularly adept at spore formation. The flowering plants, as will be demonstrated shortly, have veiled this talent by permitting their spores to germinate into modest-sized individuals—the pollen grain in the male and the embryo sac in the female—which never become independent and self-sufficient organisms.

THE MECHANISMS OF REPRODUCTION

With these comments on the general problems and forms of reproduction, it should now be possible to examine a few of the special mechanisms of reproduction in greater detail without losing a sense of perspective. Particular attention will be paid to the differentiation of gametes, the mechanisms of sexual fusion, and the complex relations of reproduction with mitosis, meiosis, and fertilization.

The Differentiation of Gametes in Animals

An examination of the details of gamete formation as it occurs in animals reveals some striking examples of the differentiation of single cells for the requirements of reproduction.

The sperm, or spermatozoa, are the transformation products of germ cells located in the testes. Here they occur in association with several other kinds of cells, including connective tissue cells which give the testes a mechanical discreteness, and various other cells with special accessory functions. In the vertebrates (Fig. 4-4b) the latter include the *interstitial cells,* which secrete the hormone *testosterone* during periods of sexual competence. Testosterone stimulates the development of secondary sexual characteristics such as the antlers of deer, the nuptial plumage of birds, and other accoutrements of courtship and battle. In addition to the interstitial cells, the vertebrate testis includes the *Sertoli cells,* elements of poorly defined function to which the maturing sperm are attached. Germ cells and Sertoli cells combine to form a number of tubules which are coiled up within the testes, (Fig. 4-4a) while the interstitial cells lie between the tubules. When their

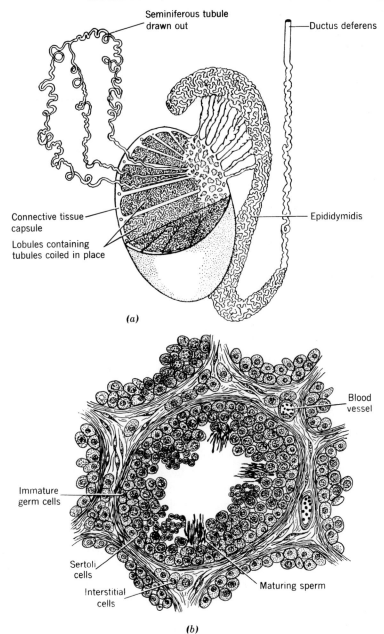

Seminiferous tubule drawn out

Ductus deferens

Connective tissue capsule

Lobules containing tubules coiled in place

Epididymidis

(a)

Blood vessel

Immature germ cells

Sertoli cells

Interstitial cells

Maturing sperm

(b)

Fig. 4-4. (a) A diagram of the mammalian testis, showing seminiferous tubules. One tubule is drawn out to indicate its extent; the others remain in normal positions, coiled within the lobules. (b) Microscope section of a seminiferous tubule. (a from C. D. Turner, *General Endocrinology,* Saunders, 1948, p. 265; b from J. F. Fulton, *Textbook of Physiology,* 16th ed., Saunders, 1949, p. 1198.)

differentiation has been completed, the sperm are released to the lumen of the tubule through which they move to a duct leading to the external environment. (The detailed anatomy of the ducts and the accessory glands, which store and nourish the spermatozoa, varies considerably among the various groups of animals.)

In the mature testis the germ cells can proliferate mitotically, maintaining in many animals a continuing reservoir of diploid cells that can be drawn on for the formation of spermatozoa. The timing of the differentiation of spermatozoa varies with the species. In some, spermatozoa are seasonally produced, while in others, including man, they are more continuously produced. Analysis of testes of the latter type which have been fixed, sectioned, and stained for microscopic examination reveals that all stages in the differentiation of germ cells into spermatozoa may be simultaneously present. The steps in the transformation of a single cell can be inferred by piecing together in what seems to be an appropriate sequence the various configurations visible in a single preparation.

A germ cell begins its differentiation into a spermatozoan when it undergoes meiosis. When meiosis is completed the cytoplasmic organelles of the four haploid products commence a remarkable series of maneuvers. The centriole, which had heretofore served as a focus of mitotic and meiotic spindle formation, remains closely associated with the nucleus, but a conventional, eleven-stranded flagellum grows away from it toward the lumen of the tubule. The mitochondria, which had been dispersed in the cytoplasm of the germ cell, come together in a compact mass which assumes a spiral configuration around the base of the flagellum (Fig. 4-5). On the opposite side of the nucleus, and in association with the Golgi apparatus, a cap-like vesicle appears. The acrosome, as this structure is known, lies close to the nuclear membrane. The nucleus itself becomes highly compact and assumes a shape characteristic for the species; frequently it is elongate. All remaining cytoplasm moves to the flagellar end of the sperm cell, leaving the cell membrane tightly apposed to the acrosome, the nucleus, the mitochondria, and finally to the flagellum. Most of the cytoplasm that does not fit into this compact structure drops off the sperm, leaving it a greatly trimmed-down cell, uniquely adapted to its task of carrying the male nucleus to the sedentary egg and its lavish dowry of yolk.

The ovary is constructed for the maturation of a much smaller number of germ cells. In vertebrates it is often an oval mass of cells, sometimes hollow and sometimes solid, with the germ cells tending to be located near its periphery. The germ cells are a good deal larger than the cells of the tissues in which they are embedded—primarily vascular

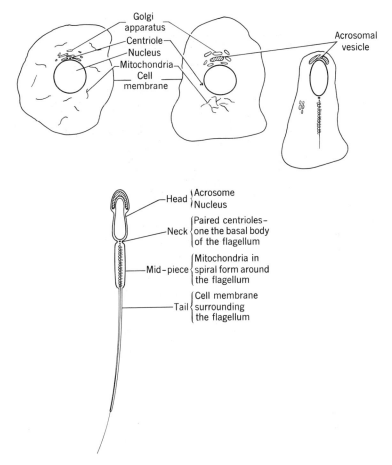

Golgi apparatus
Centriole
Nucleus
Mitochondria
Cell membrane

Acrosomal vesicle

Head { Acrosome
       { Nucleus

Neck { Paired centrioles–
     { one the basal body
     { of the flagellum

Mid-piece { Mitochondria in
          { spiral form around
          { the flagellum

Tail { Cell membrane
     { surrounding
     { the flagellum

Fig. 4-5. Diagrammatic drawing of the differentiation of animal spermatozoa.

tissue, connective tissue, and the follicle cells which will be described shortly (Fig. 4-6*a*). As in the male, the onset of germ cell differentiation is marked by the initiation of meiosis. The meiotic divisions take a very different course here, however, for the process is arrested at a mid-point in the prophase of the first meiotic division. The chromosomes, which have by this time undergone synapsis and the preliminary stages of shortening, interrupt their preparation for division. The egg cell then commences a period of cytoplasmic growth that varies tremendously from species to species. At the very least, it results in the formation of an inordinately large cell. Deposited within the cytoplasm are extensive amounts of nucleic acid, glycogen, fat droplets, proteins, and conjugated proteins, which are collectively referred to as yolk. In extreme cases,

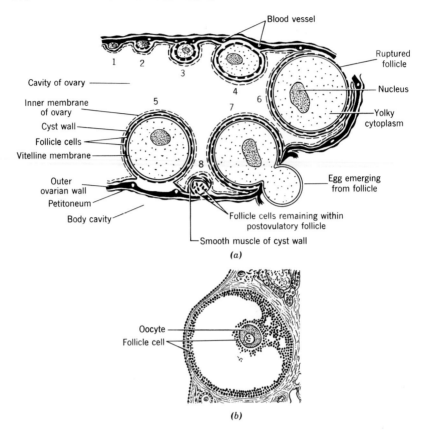

Fig. 4-6. (a) Diagrammatic section through a lobe of the frog's ovary. 1, 2, 3, 4, and 5 illustrate stages in the growth of the ovarian follicle; 6, breaking of the rupture area, an early event in ovulation; 7, emergence of the egg from the ruptured follicle; 8, a postovulatory follicle. (b) A single follicle from a mammalian ovary, showing the greatly reduced size of the oocyte relative to the follicle. (From C. D. Turner, *General Endocrinology*, Saunders, 1949, pp. 270 and 370.)

such as the eggs of larger birds, the process does not cease until the egg is thousands of times larger than undifferentiated germ cells.

During this period of growth the egg cell of vertebrates is invested with an epithelium-like layer of follicle cells, which may preside over the transfer into the growing egg cell of materials derived from the blood vessels of the ovary. The follicle cell layer itself grows rapidly enough so that it continues to invest the expanding egg until the end of the growth period. In mammals, which produce an unusually small and yolk-free egg, the layer of follicle cells nevertheless grows to a substantial size. It primarily envelops a large, fluid-filled chamber (Fig. 4-6*b*), rather than a yolk-charged egg such as that characteristic of other vertebrates.

The number of egg cells that differentiate simultaneously varies systematically with other factors in the natural history of the organism. In fish such as the salmon several thousand eggs may be laid at one time near the end of the female's life. Many amphibians lay several hundred eggs during a few days in the spring and repeat this behavior annually. Where the hazards faced by the progeny are not so great— as in reptiles, which deposit massively yolky eggs in a well-hidden nest, or in birds or mammals, which engage in some degree of parental care —the picture changes drastically. A good laying hen can produce one egg per day for several years. If she has been mated, however, and is allowed to incubate her eggs, she will stop maturing eggs after about a dozen have been laid and will devote her energies to the successful rearing of these. Human females usually mature one egg per month unless fertilization is achieved, in which case further differentiation of eggs is delayed until after the birth of the infant.

When the formation of yolk has been completed, the nucleus resumes meiosis. The yolky deposits are reserved for a single cell, however, rather than being equally distributed among the four haploid products. This result is achieved by meiotic divisions in which the chromosomes are distributed in the conventional manner, but in which the cytoplasm is divided in a one-sided fashion. In its commonest form the first meiotic spindle appears at the upper pole of the egg, and one of the daughter cells, containing half of the chromosomes and a negligible proportion of the cytoplasm, is pinched off as a small body, the *first polar body*, at the surface of the relatively enormous egg cell (Fig. 4-7).

In most vertebrates meiosis is again arrested during the second meiotic division until some time after the egg has left the ovary. When it occurs, however, it follows the pattern of the first, with only a small fragment of cytoplasm, the *second polar body*, being pinched off with one of the two haploid nuclei. The egg thus retains the bulk of the yolk, while the polar bodies are exceedingly small structures which eventually disintegrate.

Insemination

When it has reached maturity, the egg is ready to leave the ovary. In most vertebrates the release awaits a specific stimulus in the form of a hormone, the luteotropic hormone, secreted by the pituitary gland. Since the egg is buried in the tissues of the ovary, its release entails

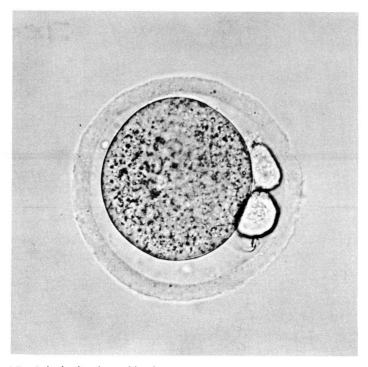

Fig. 4-7. Polar bodies formed by the mouse egg. (From T. W. Torrey, *Morphogenesis of the Vertebrates,* Wiley, 1962, p. 73.)

the dissolution of the follicle cell layer and the fibrous connective tissues that separate the follicle from the surface. The egg is then liberated into the body cavity (Fig. 4-6a) and in many forms is swept to the opening of the oviduct by ciliary action of the cells that line the coelom. In other animals the ovaries open through an oviduct directly to the environment.

The subsequent history of the egg varies with the group of animals in question. In most aquatic animals, including fishes and amphibians among the vertebrates, it is pushed down the length of the oviduct by muscular contractions along with hundreds or thousands of other eggs and liberated to the external environment where sperm are simultaneously released by an awaiting male. In terrestrial animals (the reptiles, birds, mammals and insects in particular) and in some aquatic forms the male deposits the sperm internally in the reproductive tract of the female. The sperm are then carried, either by their own swimming or by muscular contractions of the reproductive tract, to the region of the oviduct where fertilization occurs.

Fertilization

Strictly speaking, the gametes individually are not viable reproductive units—except in those cases such as the rotifers, aphids, and bees in which some of the eggs normally develop without activation by a sperm (a phenomenon that has been termed *parthenogenesis*). It is much more generally true, however, that the gametes must combine to form a zygote before development can proceed.

The interactions between gametes after they have been brought into close association have been most effectively studied in marine invertebrates, particularly the sea urchins and starfishes among the echinoderms, which can be induced to spawn in a dish of sea water in the laboratory. Under natural conditions these organisms reproduce seasonally. Simultaneous spawning of males and females is achieved in many forms by what appears to be a reflex response to the presence of spawn in the environment. Thus when one individual releases its gametes, all other individuals in the vicinity do likewise so that free eggs and sperm are simultaneously abundant in the surrounding water. When suspensions of eggs and sperm are mixed with each other in the laboratory, it is immediately apparent that the sperm stick to the egg whenever they contact it. In a very short time the gelatinous material (the *jelly coat*) which characteristically surrounds the echinoderm egg may have hundreds of sperm adhering to it, while those that have failed to contact an egg still swim about randomly in the vicinity.

The first step in sorting out the elements of this interaction was made by R. S. Lillie in 1913 when he analyzed the effects on the sperm of egg water—sea water in which a substantial number of eggs have been allowed to stand without being fertilized. When egg water was decanted from the eggs and mixed with a suspension of sperm, the suspension promptly agglutinated to form small clumps of immobilized sperm (Fig. 4-8). Although the inability of agglutinated sperm to

Fig. 4-8. Echinoderm sperm agglutinated by egg water. (From A. Tyler, in *Analysis of Development*, B. Willier, P. Weiss, and V. Hamburger, eds., Saunders, 1955, p. 187.)

fertilize eggs did not make this seem like a very promising beginning, the specificity of the reaction was highly suggestive. Thus egg water prepared from a particular species of eggs effectively agglutinated sperm of the same species, but much less readily agglutinated the sperm of other species with which they were normally unable to form hybrids.

Chemical fractionation and analyses have since demonstrated that the active agent in egg water is a fairly large protein with carbohydrate conjugants. Nearly pure preparations of this substance, *fertilizin,* have now been obtained by exposing sea urchin eggs to conditions that dissolve the jelly coat but appear to leave the egg otherwise unscathed. Indeed, the jelly coat undergoes a gradual dissolution in normal sea water, and it is this process that gives rise to the soluble fertilizin in egg water.

The adsorption of the sperm to the jelly coat presumably results from the direct combination of the sperm with an insoluble form of fertilizin that comprises the jelly coat. The agglutination of sperm by the soluble form of fertilizin may indicate that fertilizin is divalent with regard to the sperm: it has been proposed that a single molecule combines with two sperm cells, and that many molecules simultaneously acting in this manner have sufficient bonding strength to hold the cells firmly together. (The concentration of soluble fertilizin in sea water during natural spawning is too low to act as an agglutinin and therefore as a deterrent to fertilization.)

The proposal that fertilizin combines chemically with the sperm was confirmed when Lillie was able to demonstrate that a substance able to neutralize the effects of egg water can be extracted from sperm. Egg water that has been mixed with a sufficient amount of a sperm extract is no longer able to agglutinate sperm. Furthermore, when the sperm extract is added to a suspension of eggs, it agglutinates them in a manner quite analogous to the agglutination of sperm by egg water. The substance in sperm extracts that is responsible for this reaction has been shown to have the properties of a relatively small protein molecule, and has been called *antifertilizin.* The extraction procedures, one of which includes freezing and thawing the sperm in sea water and then discarding the insoluble carcasses, prevent a sure identification of the location of antifertilizin in the sperm. However, if its function is to attach the sperm to the jelly coat, it must be located at least in part on the surface of the sperm cell.

The story of fertilizin and antifertilizin has been worked out primarily for the eggs and sperm of sea urchins and a few other invertebrates. These have several uniquely helpful features, an especially important one being the ease with which they yield fertilizin for extraction and the discreteness of its localization in the jelly coat. The surface layers of other eggs vary greatly from that of the sea urchin. In some there is no obvious jelly coat, and in others it is present but not readily solubilized. As a consequence, substances analogous to fertilizin and antifertilizin are not always readily identified. The problem of sperm attachment is so general, however, that analogous mechanisms must be assumed wherever fertilization is achieved by a free-swimming gamete.

Sperm from a variety of animals also contain hydrolytic enzymes that can solubilize the membranes enveloping the eggs. A particularly clear example is the enzyme extracted from mammalian semen which can hydrolyze hyaluronic acid, a component of the cementing substances that hold the follicle cells together in an envelope around the egg.

Once the sperm is attached to the surface of the egg, it is still faced with the problem of entering the cytoplasm. In mammals and sea urchins the sperm appear to force their way by swimming actions through the envelopes weakened by lytic enzymes. In many forms one function of fertilizin appears to be to trigger a transformation in the acrosome (Fig. 4-9). In the few sperm which have been adequately studied the acrosomal vesicle opens to the outside of the sperm by fusing with the cell membrane. Simultaneously the contents of the acrosome are released to the environment, this being very probably

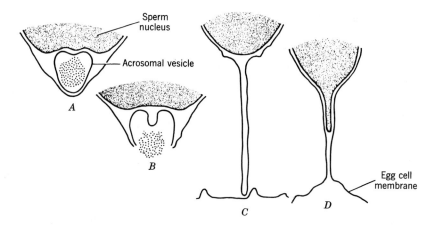

Fig. 4-9. The acrosome reaction in *Saccoglossus.* The cell membrane and the membrane of the acrosomal vesicle have fused in *B,* resulting in the release of the contents of the vesicle. In *D* the newly formed acrosomal tubule has fused with the egg cell membrane, and the sperm nucleus has begun to move into the egg. (From A. L. Colwin and L. H. Colwin, *Journal of Cell Biology,* **19,** 496 (1963).

the manner in which the sperm liberates its hydrolytic enzymes. The membrane that used to surround the vesicle is then transformed in probably a few tenths of a second into a fine tubule which is long enough to cross the jelly coat and fuse with the cell membrane of the egg. In addition to effectively informing the egg that a sperm has arrived, the reaction results in the production of a continuous membrane around the sperm and the egg. Although the mechanics of subsequent events are poorly understood, the nucleus and sometimes the mitochondria, basal body, and even the tail of the sperm move through the tubule into the egg cytoplasm. Whatever the mechanism, the end result is a fusion of the two cells to form a single, temporarily binucleate cell. Once the meiotic divisions of the egg have been completed (shedding of the eggs or sperm entry frequently triggers these), sperm and egg nuclei move toward each other and fuse, thus restoring the diploid condition and forming the *zygote* which is then able to commence development into a multicellular organism.

Gamete Formation and Fertilization in Angiosperms

The steps of gamete formation and fertilization described for animals bear very little resemblance to the analogous procedures in plants, despite the fact that both groups conform to the general statements about reproduction cited in the introduction of this chapter. Reproduction in the plant kingdom exhibits an astonishing diversity, the beginnings of which were indicated in the reproduction and sexual fusion of the unicellular algae (p. 64). In this section the flowering plants are used as the principle example, and some of the major departures from this pattern are then indicated.

The angiosperms are one of the groups of organisms in which reproduction and early development are associated with the sexual fusion of gametes. All three processes occur within the complex of organs that comprise the flower. In most angiosperms the flower consists of a central axis, or receptacle, on which several whorls of appendages are mounted (Fig. 4-10). Although the number and configuration of the floral appendages vary greatly among different species, they are usually arranged according to the following scheme. The appendages most basally placed on the receptacle are a set of *sepals*, which cover the flower bud before it has opened. More apically situated is a set of *petals*. Either the sepals or the petals, usually the latter, form the familiar colorful parts that characterize the insect-pollinated flower. Next is a set of *stamens*, each of which bears at its tip an *anther*, in which the pollen is formed. The last and most apical appendages are the *carpels*. Each carpel is differentiated into an *ovary* and a *style*, the

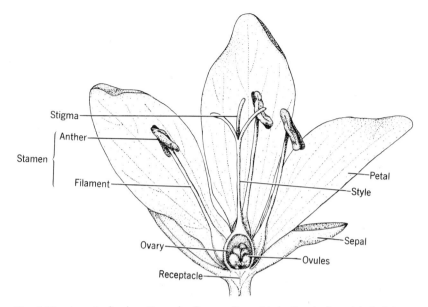

Stigma

Anther

Stamen

Filament

Petal

Style

Ovary

Receptacle

Sepal

Ovules

Fig. 4-10. Longitudinal section of a flower. (From V. A. Greulach and J. E. Adams, *Plants: An Introduction to Modern Botany,* Wiley, 1962, p. 169.)

latter being the sterile part to whose distal end the pollen grains attach prior to fertilization. In many instances the carpels are fused with each other, forming a single ovary and style of compound origin.

The developmental transformations most directly concerned with the genesis of progeny occur within the anther and the ovary. The first such transformation is the production of pollen grains, for which the lilies provide a thoroughly analyzed example. The lily anther is divided into four elongate lobes (Fig. 4-11). The *microsporocytes,* the cells whose meiotic products ultimately give rise to the pollen, are arranged as several columns of cells in the center of each lobe. Surrounding these is a discrete layer of cells, the *tapetum;* the tapetum is surrounded by various additionel layers that need not be specified here. As the anther grows, a chamber is formed within the tapetum. The microsporocytes become suspended in the chamber in a viscous fluid presumably secreted by the surrounding tapetal cells. At this stage all of the cells in the anther contain a diploid set of chromosomes. Prior to the opening of the flower, however, the microsporocytes undergo meiosis, each forming a tetrad of haploid cells, the *microspores,* which remain for a time in direct association within the cell wall of the microsporocyte (Fig. 4-11c-d). When the cell wall ruptures, the tetrads disaggregate and the individual microspores, while still suspended in the chamber, transform into *pollen grains.* The transformation consists of

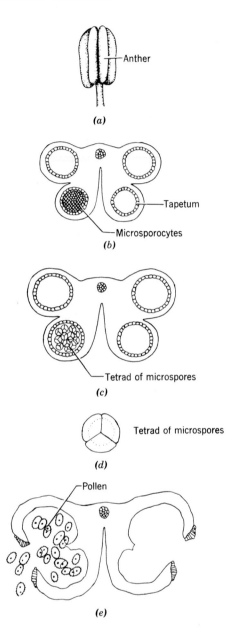

Fig. 4-11. Development of pollen in the anther. (From V. A. Greulach and J. E. Adams, *Plants: An Introduction to Modern Botany*, Wiley, 1962, p. 448.)

an enlargement of the cell followed by the formation of an unusually thick and highly ornamented cell wall. At some time before the liberation of the pollen grain from the anther, the nucleus undergoes mitosis, at maturity forming a 2-celled pollen grain (Fig. 4-12*a-d*).

When the flower opens, the wall of the anther splits and folds back, exposing the mature pollen grains to the wind or the insects (or other animals such as bats and hummingbirds in certain special cases) which may bear them to another flower. Enough pollen grains are liberated so that any female flowers produced in the vicinity are apt to be pollinated.

The structure and activity of the ovary are somewhat more complicated. A cross section of the lily ovary taken before pollination reveals three chambers, one contributed by each of the three carpels which fused to form a common ovary and style (Fig. 4-13). The ovarian section of a carpel consists of a fairly thick wall of parenchyma tissue in which is embedded a number of vascular bundles. Attached in two rows along the inner surface of the wall of each carpel is a series

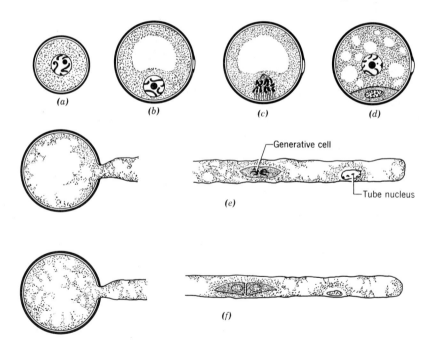

Fig. 4-12. Development and germination of the pollen grain. The generative cell formed by the mitotic division shown in c, divides again (e) to produce two gametes (f). (From F. Maheshwari, *An Introduction to the Embryology of Angiosperms*, McGraw-Hill, 1950, p. 155.)

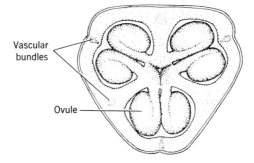

Fig. 4-13. Cross section of the ovary of a lily. (From V. A. Greulach and J. E. Adams, *Plants: An Introduction to Modern Botany,* Wiley, 1962, p. 170.)

of *ovules*, which bear the germinal tissue. As in the anther, and elsewhere in the plant, all cells in the ovule are at this stage diploid. However, a single cell, the *macrosporocyte* located near the tip of the ovule, is destined to undergo meiosis, forming four haploid *macrospores* (Fig. 4-14*b–d*).

The succeeding events vary a good deal among the different plants. Since *Lilium* is in some regards an exceptional case, it will be prudent at this point to turn to a more general plan. In many plants three of the macrospores disintegrate, and all subsequent development is due to the activities of the single remaining haploid cell (Fig. 4-14*e–f*). The nucleus of this cell then initiates mitosis. The number of divisions varies with the species, but in many cases there are three, yielding a total of eight haploid nuclei. All eight nuclei lie for a time in a common cytoplasm, forming a structure termed the embryo sac which in the mature flower can be seen embedded in the tissues of the ovule. Cell wall formation then occurs, leading to the configuration seen in Fig. 4-14*j*. The significance of five of these cells is not clear, for they take no obvious part in the subsequent formation of the seed. Of the re-remaining three, one is the female gamete. The other two play a role in the formation of the seed which will be considered in the next section. (In *Lilium* all four macrospore nuclei undergo mitosis, and the embryo sac ultimately contains eight nuclei—four haploid, and four triploid nuclei formed by the fusion of some of the mitotic products.) During the life history of the plant the binucleate pollen grain and the embryo sac containing eight haploid nuclei are comparable phases of the two sexes. The embryo sac lives in coddled privacy, compared with the teems of pollen grains produced in an anther; but this simply reflects the differences in their roles as agents of sexual fusion.

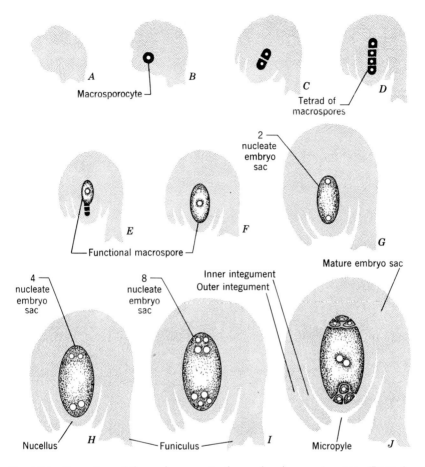

Fig. 4-14.   Formation of the embryo sac in the ovule of an angiosperm. (From A. S. Foster and E. M. Gifford, *Comparative Morphology of the Vascular Plants,* Freeman, 1959, p. 503.)

When a pollen grain lodges on the end of the style of an opened flower, it germinates. A tube grows out of the cell wall and through the tissues of the style and ovary to the embryo sac. The tube nucleus (Fig. 4-12*e*), which is presumed to govern in some manner the synthetic activities of the germinating tube, lies close to the growing tip. The generative cell enters the germinating tube behind the tube nucleus and at some time during germination undergoes mitosis to form two haploid gametes. Thus a total of three haploid cells are ultimately present in the pollen tube (Fig. 4-12*f*). Within a day or two the pollen tube finds its way to the embryo sac (Fig. 4-15*a*). When it actually

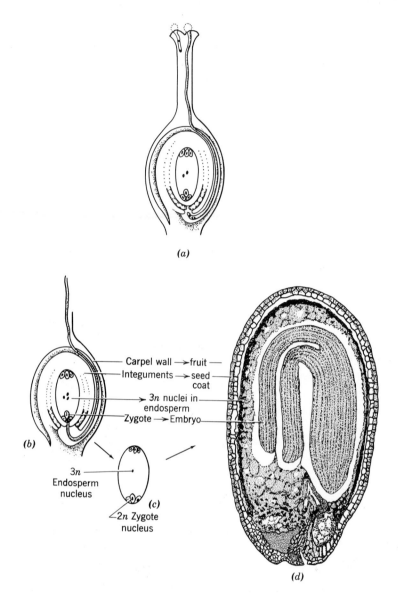

Fig. 4-15. Fertilization and seed formation in an angiosperm. *(a)* Pollen tube approaching the embryo sac. The generative cell (Fig. 4-12) has by this time divided to form two gamete nuclei, so the pollen tube is now trinucleate. *(b)* Entry of the two gamete nuclei, one of which fuses with the female gamete to form the zygote, while the second fuses with two female nuclei to form the triploid endosperm nucleus. *(c)* Embryo sac at the conclusion of fertilization. *(d)* Formation of the seed. The carpel wall forms the fruit, the integuments of the ovule form the seed coat, while the zygote develops into the embryo. (a from V. A. Greulach and J. E. Adams, *Plants: An Introduction to Modern Botany,* Wiley, 1962, p. 448; d from A. S. Foster and E. M. Gifford, *Comparative Morphology of the Vascular Plants,* Freeman, 1959, p. 526.)

120

contacts the embryo sac, the two gamete cells which had arisen by mitosis during the germination of the tube migrate directly into the cytoplasm of the embryo sac (Fig. 4-15b–c). Fertilization is achieved when one of these fuses with the female gamete nucleus. The resulting zygote is destined to form the embryo and ultimately the independent plant. The second pollen nucleus fuses with two of the haploid nuclei in the center of the embryo sac, forming a single triploid nucleus that later becomes involved in the formation of the endosperm (p. 122). This is an unusual event which has no counterpart in the sexual fusion and development of organisms other than angiosperms.

It should be noted that many pollen grains may lodge on the tip of the style, and sections of the style may disclose large numbers of germinating pollen tubes. Thus the five hundred to a thousand ovules in a lily ovary may all be fertilized more or less simultaneously, and may transform into a corresponding number of seeds.

Variations on this theme have significant consequences for population genetics. They involve mechanisms which assure that fertilization will occur only between flowers borne on different plants or within a single flower, as the case may be. For instance, cross-pollination is assured in *dioecious* plants, in which one individual is either male or female and which thus produce either stamenate or pistillate flowers, but not both. The Ginkgo and many hollies are examples of this pattern. The same result can be achieved in *monoecious* species by very different means. There are self-sterility genes in tobacco plants that prevent pollen landing on the stigma of flowers from the same or genetically identical plants from germinating at a rapid enough rate to reach the embryo sac before the flower has withered. Such mechanisms will, of course, be effective in wind- or insect-pollinated species. In a few insect-pollinated plants the flower is constructed so that an insect coming to feed on nectar will be dusted with pollen in such a position that it is only apt to contact the stigma on differently constructed flowers of other plants. At the opposite extreme are the closed flowers like those of sweet peas, in which self-pollination is assured by means of physical barriers to the entry of outside pollen. Finally, many plants can be cross-pollinated or self-pollinated with equal facility.

There are, then, specific situations in which natural selection encourages genetic interchange and therefore a high rate of adaptation to changing environments. On the other hand, the stability resulting from a low rate of genetic interchange is encouraged in other species. In the former case any of a variety of steps in the reproductive mechanism can be manipulated to assure cross-pollination.

The Formation of Seeds

The physiological activities of the flower, which so far have been directed toward abetting the differentiation of gametes and sexual fusion, now become geared to the formation of seeds and fruit. The petals, sepals, and stamens wither. The wall of the ovary grows to form the fruit (which may be a fleshy structure such as an apple or a banana or simply a casing such as the seed pod of a pea or a lily), and within the ovary the ovules grow into seeds (Fig. 4-15b–d).

When it is fully formed, the seed is encased in a tough jacket of cells—the seed coat—formed by the outer layers of ovular cells. Its development entails (1) the proliferation and enlargement of these cells to accommodate the growth of the tissues that they enclose, and (2) when growth has been completed, the production of thickened cell walls by the individual cells.

The embryo and endosperm lying within the seed coat are formed by cells whose nuclei are mitotically derived from the triploid and diploid zygote nuclei. The triploid nucleus gives rise to the endosperm, a tissue containing deposits of proteins, starch, and oils. (It is this tissue that makes cereal grains an important source of carbohydrate and protein in human nutrition). Soon after it has been formed, the triploid nucleus commences mitotic activity. Each of the resulting nuclei eventually becomes encased in a cell wall, along with some of the cytoplasm of the embryo sac, but in some cases up to ten successive cycles of nuclear division may occur before cell wall formation begins. The entire mass of triploid cells continues to grow until it has become hundreds or thousands of times more massive than the original embryo sac, and has received a substantial reservoir of nutrients from the vegetative parts of the plant.

The embryo itself develops from the diploid zygote nucleus and the part of the cytoplasm of the embryo sac that becomes separated off with the nucleus to form a cell. We shall extend our discussion of the development of the embryo in Chapter 5. The point here is that disengagement of the progeny from the parent does not occur until the conclusion of seed formation.

DIVERSITY IN REPRODUCTIVE CYCLES

Considered in the abstract, the primary difference between the events just described for angiosperms and the corresponding events in animal reproduction is the intervention of a short period of mitotic activity subsequent to meiosis and prior to fertilization. The pollen grain and embryo sac containing several haploid nuclei have no counterpart in the life history of animals, in which meiosis signals the onset of the differentiation of the unicellular gametes and fertilization ensues directly.

The haploid generation plays a much more prominent role in many plants than in the angiosperms. Among mosses, for instance, the tables are turned entirely. The free-living, leafy shoot consists of haploid cells numbering in the thousands or millions, and the diploid generation is the brown, spore-forming structure that grows out of the tip of the leafy shoot and depends entirely on the tip for its nutrition. Despite this difference, there is a common pattern to the life cycle of angiosperms and mosses. Some of the cells of the multicellular, haploid individual differentiate into gametes. The male gametes are then conveyed to the female. (In the mosses they swim of their own accord in a film of water that covers the plant in moist seasons.) After fertilization the zygote enters a period of mitotic activity, which yields a multicellular generation. Sporocytes in the fruiting structure of the diploid generation then initiate meiosis, and the meiotic products in turn germinate to produce a multicellular haploid generation (Fig. 4-16b).

Superimposed on these basic similarities between the mosses and flowering plants are differences in the developmental potentialities of the spores and zygotes (the spore forms a pollen grain or embryo sac in one case and a leafy shoot in the other) as well as in the time at which reproduction occurs in the more literal sense of physical disengagement from the parent.

Not all plants conform to the pattern of alternating haploid and diploid generations that prevail in the mosses, angiosperms, and other leafy terrestrial plants. Like the animals, a few of the brown algae, such as *Fucus*, have no haploid generation whatsoever. Meiosis is followed directly by the differentiation of gametes and fertilization, as in animals. Some of the green algae, such as *Spirogyra*, whose life cycle is considered in another connection below, have no diploid generation; fertilization is followed by meiosis, with no intervening mitotic activity. And in other groups of algae and fungi, spores differentiate from mitotic products. When this occurs, the plant can have several successive generations of diploid and haploid individuals. Thus we may trace any route indicated by arrows in Fig. 4-16a and be sure that some plant exhibits that particular sequence. In few if any instances are there any clues to the strategic advantages of one

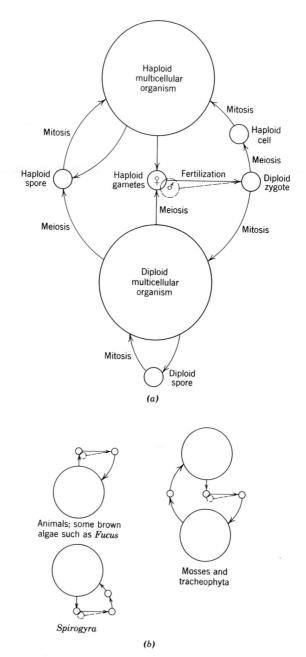

Fig. 4-16. (a) Composite diagram of the reproductive cycles of multicellular organisms. The small circles represent the types of reproductive cells produced by haploid and diploid organisms. (b) Some examples of how the reproductive cycles of individual organisms fit into the composite diagram.

124

pattern over another. The degree of diversity in reproductive and sexual cycles is simply a fact of botanical life.

The Relations Between Reproduction and Sexual Phenomena

Reproduction and sexual fusion are two discrete functions in microorganisms. Vegetative reproduction, budding, and asexual spore formation among multicellular plants reaffirm the fact that reproduction can occur independently of sexual fusion. When sexual fusion does take place in a multicellular organism, it generally occurs in tandem with reproduction—for it most frequently involves haploid cells, which will dissociate from the parent organism. An example may provide some clues to why this association between reproduction and sexual fusion should be so ubiquitous. The most significant outcome of the analysis will be to show that this arrangement prevents the formation of genetically heterogeneous individuals, which are as a consequence extremely rare in natural biological systems.

The filamentous green alga, *Spirogyra*, is induced to initiate sexual fusion toward the end of its growing season whenever two filaments lie closely parallel to each other (Fig. 4-17). Conjugation bridges formed between adjoining cells transform the two filaments into a structure that resembles a ladder. The protoplasts of the cells in both filaments shrink away from their cell walls; and then all of the protoplasts from one filament migrate across the conjugation bridges and fuse with those within their respective conjugant cells. The nuclei also fuse, and the resulting zygote produces a thick cell wall around itself, forming a tough and durable form of the organism, which has thus been termed a *zygospore*. The zygospore is liberated from the maternal cell wall when the latter eventually decomposes. Before germination at the outset of the next growing season, the diploid nucleus undergoes meiosis, producing four haploid nuclei. An extremely significant event reminiscent of the fate of the meiotic products in the embryo sac of most angiosperms then occurs: three of the four nuclei degenerate. Thus the nuclei of the filament that germinates from the spore are all the mitotic products of a single haploid nucleus (Fig. 4-18).

In no other multicellular organism does sexual fusion simultaneously involve all cells of the organism; in most cases the morphology of the organism is simply not consistent with such a feat. However, even in *Spirogyra* where interchange between all cells can and does occur, subsequent events assure that meiosis, a process that transforms a single diploid cell into four genetically different haploid cells (Stern and Nanney, Chap. 2), does not lead to the formation of genetically hetero-

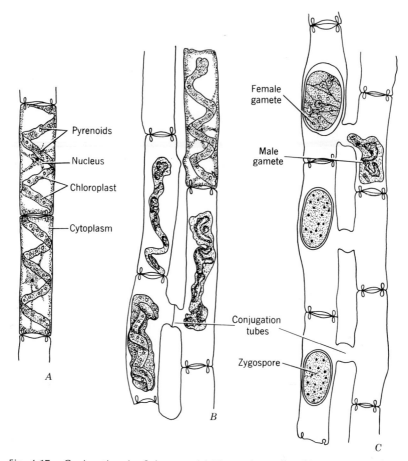

Fig. 4-17.   Conjugation in *Spirogyra*. *(a)* Vegetative cells. *(b)* Formation of conjugation tubes and condensation of protoplasts. *(c)* Migration of a male gamete
(top) and formation of zygospores. (From R. M. Holman and W. W. Robbins,
Elements of Botany, Wiley, 1940, p. 233.)

geneous filaments. One step in leading to this result is the separation of
zygotes from each other. If the meiotic products of several zygotes co-
operated in the further growth of the filament, the result would be a filament of cells that were correspondingly diverse in their genotypes. The
same would be true if all four meiotic products from a single zygote
contributed to the germinating filament. As it is, only one nucleus is
involved in the formation of a new filament, and since this divides
mitotically, there is assurance that a filament of *Spirogyra* always
consists of genetically similar cells.

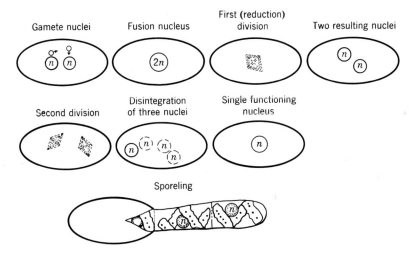

Fig. 4-18. Fertilization, meiosis and germination in the zygospore of *Spirogyra*. (From R. M. Holman and W. W. Robbins, *Elements of Botany*, Wiley, 1940, p. 235.)

This is not a special case. Reexamination of the reproductive cycles of animals, angiosperms, and mosses will indicate that here also meiosis, fertilization, and reproduction are so arranged that the individual organism consists of the mitotic descendants of a single cell. In every case meiosis is followed either by the death of all but one of the four meiotic products or by their disaggregation to form individual reproductive cells. (Exceptions are the embryo sacs of *Lilium* and several other flowering plants to which all four of the meiotic products of the megasporocyte contribute nuclei (p. 118). However, this diversity applies only to the nutritive portion of the seed; the cells of the seedling that ultimately emerges are the mitotic products of a single diploid zygote nucleus.)

This does not mean that genetically dissimilar cells cannot cooperate in the formation of a single organism. Syncytial fungal hyphae (p. 94) grown under crowded conditions can fuse with each other, leading to a condition in which their nuclei freely intermix in a common cytoplasm; and in some multicellular organisms genetically ambiguous individuals can be obtained experimentally with the assistance of grafting. The multicellular organism is in general the expression of the developmental potentialities of a single cell, which has multiplied mitotically, despite the fact that meiosis, fertilization, and reproduction could conceivably be arranged (as they are in the embryo sac of *Lilium*) to achieve a very different result. A comparison of an individual's right and left hands, or ears, or feet, or between identical twins demonstrates the level of phenotypic similarity that results from the developmental activities of mitotically derived cells.

This arrangement has fundamental consequences for population biology and evolution. Every feature of the multicellular organism is the developmental outcome of a single haploid or diploid complement of genes, rather than a haphazard combination of several genotypes. Thus the success or failure of the individual organism is an *unambiguous result* in the testing ground of natural selection. The simplicity of natural selection as a theory and its effectiveness as a process depend in no small measure on the arrangement of the reproductive cycles of multicellular organisms to favor the development of genetically homogeneous individuals.

THE NUTRITION OF REPRODUCTION

In a very real sense reproduction is not completed until the progeny are competent to function as independent organisms. In some organisms this ability is already possessed by the progeny when they become physically dissociated from their parent. For example, the spores produced by mosses and ferns are able to carry on photosynthesis and to absorb water and mineral nutrients as soon as they germinate. And a germinating fungal spore is as adept as a mature hypha at absorbing organic nutrients from its environment.

On the other hand, seed plants and most animals largely depend on a maternal source of nutrients for their early stages of development. Such organisms are able to produce relatively fewer progeny than spore-forming organisms, but the chances of success for any given offspring are commensurately greater. These are, then, two very different strategies for successful reproduction.

Maternal provisions for nourishing the progeny take several different forms. A common procedure among animals is to charge the cytoplasm of the egg with nutrients in the form of yolk. The formation of a placenta between the embryo and its mother is typical among mammals and seed plants, and occurs sporadically in other groups of organisms. The placenta is a zone in which there is a direct association between the cells of the embryo and the maternal organism, and across which a generous exchange of nutrients and metabolic products can occur. In the mosses the diploid sporophyte that develops from the zygote remains parasitic on its maternal parent throughout its life.

A third form of maternal (and in some cases paternal) care consists in bringing food to the offspring (or vice versa). In its crudest form this phenomenon is illustrated by a moth or butterfly that, in addition to supplying the cytoplasm of its eggs with a good supply of yolk, finishes its responsibility by seeking out an appropriate food plant and laying its eggs there. Many mammals, birds, and insects (especially the ants, bees, and wasps) provide more indulgent care. When it has left the uterus, the infant mammal temporarily feeds from the mammary gland. Even when it has acquired teeth and other refinements of its digestive apparatus and is able to take the same sort of food as its parents, it may not have become competent to forage for itself. Such patterns have led to the suggestion that complex societies (wherever they occur in the animal kingdom) had their evolutionary beginnings in the phenomenon of parental care, which brought different individuals together in a closely dependent relationship.

When the developing organism is ready to change from one mode of nutrition to the next, it already possesses the new anatomy and physiological abilities required of it. At no time can it afford to be incompetent to cope with the particular environmental conditions with which the members of its species customarily contend at that stage of development. The concept that a new-born baby is a helpless creature is hopelessly incorrect. A baby is fully competent to nurse, to breathe, and to coerce its parents into catering to its every need. A parent of one of these engaging tyrants soon becomes aware that reproduction is not really consummated until the offspring leave home.

THE DISSEMINATION OF PROGENY

For most organisms reproduction is not simply a matter of providing a new organism to take the place of an aged parent. It has very much the spirit of pushing on to new frontiers. This is particularly striking in the sessile plants, where wind-borne spores and seeds are a conspicuous feature. Nowhere are they more pronounced than in the fungi. The mode of feeding in fungi which has led to the body plan of the hypha with its invasive growth habits (Chapter 3) results in the organism's being literally buried in its food. When the time comes for spore formation, however, the hypha emerges from seclusion by forming filaments, which grow out of the substratum and into the air (or the surrounding water in aquatic forms) and transform into fruiting bodies at their tips. Mushrooms, puff balls, and the mold on the surface of spoiling food all illustrate this emergence from seclusion occasioned by the formation of aerial spores. Like the bacterial spores (Chapter 2) these spores mainly rely on chance to be deposited in circumstances favoring germination, but they are so prolifically produced that there is a good chance that at least some will make their way successfully.

The coincidence of dispersion and reproduction is also seen in many marine animals that are either sessile or relatively immobile. Here, as in the sea urchin described earlier, gametes are released to the environment, where fertilization and early development proceed. In many forms a motile larva is produced which may swim and feed for a considerable period of time as a pelagic organism before finally metamorphosing to a sessile adult.

The wholesale broadcasting of progeny in sessile plants and animals has several interesting consequences. One or more of these may be responsible for the selective advantages which have led to the adoption of prolific modes of reproduction and dispersion. For the fungi, in particular, dispersion is the predominant mechanism for finding food, as it is for the bacteria. This explanation seems particularly relevant to organisms such as the slime molds which can be induced to initiate fruiting by the exhaustion of their food supply. A second consequence is that the progeny, since they are apt to settle down at great distances, are less apt to be in direct competition with the parent organism. A third outcome is that the species continually invades "marginal" regions—areas beyond the limits of its current distribution, which are therefore less apt to be characterized by the specific physical and biotic features to which the species is adapted. Though a risky enterprise for the individual adventurer, this continual probing makes the sessile species as a whole responsive to the kinds of geographical shifts in its ideal environment which are known to have occurred in the course of geological history.

5

Development

At the outset of Chapter 4 we noted that reproduction gives rise to individuals that are of necessity smaller and structurally simpler than their parents, and that each offspring then launches on a program of development. In the process of development both an increase in mass and the elaboration of new structures are achieved. An understanding of these changes can be sought in terms of cellular activities, including the mitotic division, growth, migration, and differentiation of cells— and the cells must engage in these activities cooperatively, rather than independently. We shall begin our examination with the most obvious change—the increase in size—and then proceed to the subtler problems of structural transformations and developmental control mechanisms.

GROWTH AS AN INCREASE IN SIZE

The term growth is used here in its conventional sense as an increase in size. As such, the growth of an organism can be measured by weighing, by marking off a linear dimension such as height, by counting the number of cells, by determining the amount of protein or nucleic acid contained, or by specifying any other quantifiable index of changes in size with time. All of these measures increase in a developing organism, but not necessarily simultaneously. Hence we must specify the particular measure employed for each case under discussion.

When the weight of an organism is plotted as a function of its age, a result such as that shown in Fig. 5-1 is frequently obtained. The graph, based on data obtained for the growth of maize, shows a relatively

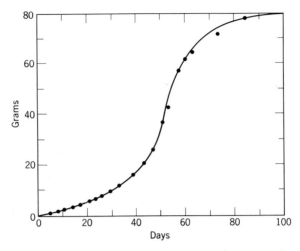

Fig. 5-1.   Growth in weight of maize. (From D. W. Thompson, *On Growth and Form*, 2nd ed., Cambridge, 1951, p. 116.)

slow increase in the weight of very young plants. This is followed by a period of rapid growth, then by a marked deceleration terminating in a constant size (or even diminishing size in periods of senility). The same general pattern of growth is exhibited by many other multicellular organisms, despite wide variations in the form and duration of their development.

A few of these variations are worth considering. Maize is an annual plant that sows its seeds and dies at the end of a single growing season. In a woody plant that lives through a number of discrete growing seasons, we would expect a periodic increase in weight leading to a growth curve shaped like a staircase. If the curve were smoothed out by measuring the weight of the plant just once a year—say, in October, at the conclusion of the growing season—the curve would show many of the same features as the curve for maize, although the time span of the total process would be very much greater. The woody plant, despite the unlimited growth potential of its individual apical meristems (pp. 138–149), may ultimately approach a limiting size. This is the point at which leaf fall, the death of shaded branches, and the shedding of bark equal or exceed the formation of new tissue.

As with plants having seasonal growth, the growth curves of animals frequently reflect crises or special events in the life of the organism. A silkworm interrupts the general progress in its growth at the time of molting; it stops feeding, sheds its old cuticle, and makes a new one. A substantial loss in weight occurs when it undergoes metamorphosis. The caterpillar again stops feeding, spins a cocoon, and undergoes several weeks of development, first into a pupa and then into a moth. During this period it may lose 50% or more of its larval weight. In many mammals, including man, the acceleration phase of growth is largely intrauterine; and deceleration begins well before birth. In addition, the smooth character of the growth curve is secondarily disturbed. Either a decrease or a temporary standstill occurs in the weight of mice at birth, at the time of weaning, and frequently at puberty (Fig. 5-2). Except for such irregularities, however, many multicellular organisms appear to follow a growth curve substantially similar to that of maize.

The form of such growth curves is analogous to that of a population of microorganisms. A bacterium presented with an environment suitable for its growth and reproduction will grow and divide, and its progeny will grow and divide, in such a way that each successive generation has approximately the same duration; that is, the time required between divisions will remain constant as long as there is an abundant supply of nutrients. The rate at which new bacteria are formed will thus be proportional to the number of bacteria already present. Expressed mathematically,

$$\frac{dn}{dt} = an \tag{1}$$

where n is the number of bacteria present in the culture at time t and a is a constant. The differential term dn/dt is the rate of change of n with time, or the growth rate of the culture. The form of such a hypothetical growth curve can be seen by transposing equation (1)

$$\frac{dn}{n} = a\, dt$$

and integrating to yield

$$\ln n = at + b \tag{2}$$

in which b is a constant of integration. If the logarithm (to any base) of the number of bacteria is plotted as a function of time, a straight line is obtained (Fig. 5-3), the slope of which is a measure of the constant a. The ease with which a can be measured has made it a particularly useful term in studies of growth. Because, according to equation (1), a represents the growth rate divided by the size of the growing system, it is conventionally called the relative growth rate.

The growth curve of a multicellular organism can similarly be plotted as a semilogarithmic function. When this is done the accelera-

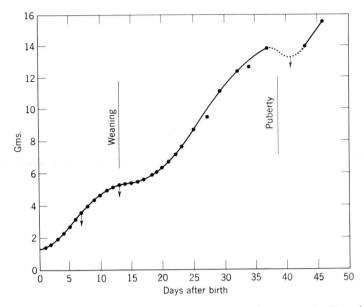

Fig. 5-2. Growth in weight of a mouse. (From D. W. Thompson, *On Growth and Form*, 2nd ed., Cambridge, 1951, p. 161.)

tion phase of growth appears in some cases to form a straight line, just as it does in the growth of a bacterial population. A multicellular organism is, after all, a clone of cells that might grow in exponential fashion whenever differentiation has not affected the growth rate of the individual cells. A good example is the period of cleavage in a frog's egg. Here the organism grows at the expense of its yolk, and since the yolk cannot be separately weighed, it is inconvenient to determine the size of the embryo. Nevertheless, a linear relationship such as that shown in Fig. 5-3 is obtained when the logarithm of the number of cells is plotted as a function of time since fertilization. In other words, the rate of cell formation is proportional to the number of cells present in the organism and, accordingly, to the amount of machinery available for making new cells.

Even when some cells cease to grow, so that the growth curve is no longer linear on a semilogarithmic plot, the same general explanation can account for the acceleration phase of growth. In maize plants, as we shall see shortly, some cells are incapable of producing new cells. We can readily see that the growth rate might be determined, however, by the rate at which the plant can feed itself, and that this in turn depends on the number of leaves and roots which it already possesses.

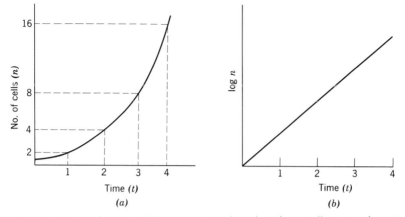

Fig. 5-3. Growth of a unicellular organism plotted arithmetically (a) and semi-logarithmically (b).

Thus we are proposing that the increase in the arithmetic growth rate in the early stages of development results from the fact that the growing organism gradually increases the amount of machinery available for feeding and growth. But what about the decrease in the growth rate that occurs when the organism approaches maturity? A similar deceleration also occurs in the bacterial culture. After a period of exponential growth, the rate of increase in the number of cells begins to decline and eventually comes to a stop. There are several possible causes for this. One is that the amount of food available in the culture begins to be exhausted. A second is that the metabolic products of the bacteria which accumulate in the culture medium may inhibit further growth. The first possibility can hardly be applied to the cessation of growth in the multicellular organism, because cessation occurs very often under environmental conditions that are optimal for feeding. A six-foot, eighteen-year-old boy cannot be induced to grow to seven or eight feet by increasing the size of his meals. Although there is a possibility that growth is to some extent limited by the metabolic products of the organism, there is a more important limitation — the intervention of cellular differentiation. Just as the acceleration phase of the growth curve of a multicellular organism can be explained in terms of the progressive addition of synthetic and feeding machinery to the system, the phase of deceleration can be explained in terms of the differentiation of cells for special functions and their consequent cessation of growth. This proposal is particularly convincing in such cases as the cells of striated muscle, which differentiate at a fairly early stage of development in animals and rarely if ever undergo mitosis. Further growth in a striated muscle is largely a matter of cell enlargement; but there is a limit to the enlargement that can be achieved in this way. Since wounding the organism may induce the adjacent muscle cells to undergo mitosis, the capacity to grow is not necessarily lost irrevocably by these cells during their differentiation.

There is a second category of cells in which differentiation is so extreme that it renders them inviable. The vascular cells of the flowering plants and the erythrocytes and keratinized epidermal cells of mammals are examples. All of these cell types lose their nuclei, and the tracheids and vessels of xylem and the keratinized cells of mammals also lose a functional cytoplasm. The phenomenon can also be seen at higher levels of organization. The cessation of growth in maize is marked by the initiation of flowering. The apex of the shoot, which had heretofore produced the stem and a succession of leaves, now produces flowers; and growth (except for seed formation) ceases entirely when the flower is completed.

By proposing that the machinery of growth tends to decline with age, we do not imply that cell division necessarily ceases altogether. This is clearly not the case in woody plants, and even many animals that have stopped growing show cell turnover, some cells dying and being replaced by the mitotic progeny of other cells. Certain cell types specialize in this renewal pattern: the functional life of cells that lose their nuclei during differentiation is much shorter than the total life span of the organism. (The human erythrocyte, for instance, has a life span of about 120 days.) Generally these dying cells are replaced by new ones derived from a special site of proliferation. Epidermal cells in mammals are replaced by a layer of mitotic cells lying on the inner side of the epidermis (Fig. 5-4). Under normal circumstances the progeny of these cells have no fate other than to become keratinized and gradually exposed to the surface as the overlying layers are worn away. Erythrocytes in mammals are produced by the progeny of cells that lie in the bone marrow. The cambium in woody plants, as an additional example, is examined in some detail on p. 149, and a most striking case of cellular turnover in the freshwater coelenterate, *Hydra,* is described on p. 88. There is a continuous variation among animals, from those such as *Hydra* which turn over their entire cell population regularly, to those such as the rotifers and nematodes which establish a fixed, small number of cells during development and retain them for the rest of their lives. Higher plants, especially perennials, predominantly follow the *Hydra* model; as we shall see, the living cell population in any given season is totally new in a woody plant.

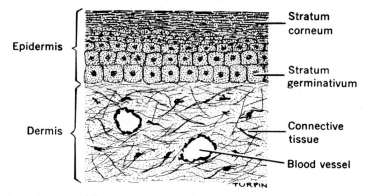

Fig. 5-4.   Diagram of the structure of vertebrate skin. Mitotic activity in the epidermis is confined to the *stratum germinativum*. (From T. W. Torrey, *Morphogenesis in Vertebrates*, Wiley, 1962, p. 181.)

DIFFERENTIAL GROWTH

Growth is more than simply a device for increasing the mass of the organism; it is intimately associated with several other aspects of development. It serves a direct function in molding the shape of the organism. This function is a consequence of what we will term *differential growth*—an unequal growth which leads to a greater increase in one linear dimension than another, and consequently results in a change in shape. As an extreme example, a sphere growing entirely in one dimension would result in an elongated cylinder. If it grew in two dimensions, a flat sheet would result, and if it grew equally in three dimensions, an enlarged sphere would result. These three situations are approximated in special instances: the germination of a spore to form a filamentous alga or fungus illustrates the first, the formation of a leaf from the leaf primordium approximates the second (although the starting point is not strictly spherical), and the growth of a spherical colony of *Volvox* approximates the third.

The role of growth in shaping the organism is explored in the next several pages; we will take for our example the development of flowering plants. Many aspects of the description will be applicable to other vascular plants, and several general problems that arise will pertain to all multicellular organisms. The description begins with the formation of the embryo in a seed—the point at which the description of reproduction in flowering plants was terminated (p. 122).

By the time the seed has matured enough to be dropped by the parent plant, the embryo has already developed sufficiently to exhibit some of the basic structure of a flowering plant. It may be described as a cylindrical axis to which appendages, in the form of one or two cotyledons, are attached at one end (Fig. 5-5). The cotyledons are fleshy structures containing substantial amounts of food reserves. (In some seeds, peas and beans, for instance, the cotyledons usurp the function of food storage, and there is little if any endosperm left in the mature seed.) The arrangement of cotyledons as appendages on the central axis and their transformation into active photosynthetic organs during the germination of the seed show that they can be regarded as modified leaves.

As the seed nears maturity, a zone of cell division termed an *apical meristem* develops at each end of the cylindrical axis. The apical meristem located between the cotyledons will form the shoot, consisting of stem and leaves, whereas that at the opposite end of the cylinder will form the root.

The growth of the plant after the seed has begun to germinate can be divided into three separate problems, which will be considered here in turn. The first of these is the elongation of the root and the stem, or *primary growth*. Second is the problem of growth in thickness, or *secondary growth*, which occurs most familiarly in woody plants. Finally, we will consider the formation of *lateral* structures—leaves, branches, and the floral appendages.

Primary Growth in the Root

Elongation in flowering plants is achieved primarily by the formation and growth of cells near the tip of the root and stem. This mode of elongation, known as *apical growth,* is to be distinguished from the generalized growth responsible for elongation in many filamentous algae, such as *Spirogyra,* and *Oedogonium,* in which all cells along the length of the filament are capable of growth and division. As

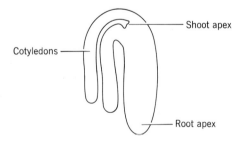

Fig. 5-5. Diagram of a longitudinal section of a dicot embryo.

will be noted shortly, an additional form of elongation called *inter-calary* growth is characterized by growth zones located at definite points along the length of the stem.

The occurrence of apical growth can be demonstrated by marking procedures. A growing root, for instance, is marked in some manner that will not damage its tissues—such as sprinkling it with carbon particles—and measurements of the distances between successive marks are taken at various intervals. In mature regions of the root the distances between marks do not change. Toward the apex the distances increase for a time and then become constant. Farther into the apical area the marks widen for longer periods and to a greater degree (Fig. 5-6). Assuming that the carbon particles still adhere to the epidermal cells which they initially contacted, the increasing distances must reflect the elongation of the tissues lying in the intervals between particles.

The cellular processes involved in the growth of the intervals can be surmised in a root tip that has been killed, sectioned, appropriately stained, and examined microscopically (Fig. 5-7). Near the tip of the root is a region of relatively small cells. Some of them contain mitotic figures, and therefore must have been in the process of mitosis at the time the root was killed. Since actively dividing cells must spend a good deal of time undergoing synthetic activities during the interphase (Stern & Nanney, Chap. 17), it is probable that most of the cells in this region which were not in the act of dividing were nevertheless involved in the synthesis and enlargement that are prerequisite to mitosis. This region is the *apical meristem;* it is often confined to the terminal millimeter of the root, and may be less than a quarter of a millimeter long.

The apical meristem is delimited, both apically and basally, by tissues in which mitotic activity cannot be detected. (At the microscopic level the apical meristem of a root, despite its name, is actually located 100 μ or so from the tip of the root.) The apical zone of nonmitotic cells, the root cap, consists of parenchyma cells, which facilitate the pushing of the root through the soil by secreting mucilaginous substances. The expansion of the root against the resisting soil causes the surface cells of the root cap to be abraded, and this loss is compensated for by the continuous addition of cells to the root cap from the apical meristem.

All others tissues of the root are laid down on the basal side of the apical meristem. These cells continue to elongate for a time after they have ceased dividing; the outcome is a central column of prospective vascular cells surrounded by a cortex of parenchyma cells.

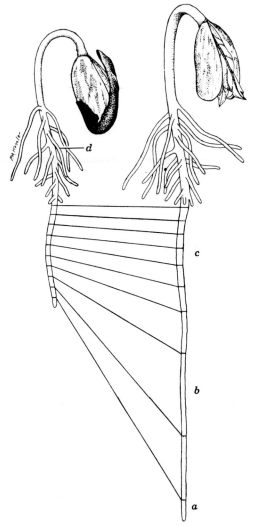

Fig. 5-6.   Elongation of root tip. (From V. A. Greulach and J. E. Adams, *An Introduction to Modern Botany*, Wiley, 1962, p. 163.)

This in turn is surrounded by a layer of flattened cells, the epidermis, which lies at the surface of the root.

The elongation of the root revealed by marking experiments is thus due to a combination of cell growth and division in the apical meristem and cell elongation without division basal to the meristem. This does not conclude the process of root formation, however; yet to be formed are the several definitive types of cells that are charac-

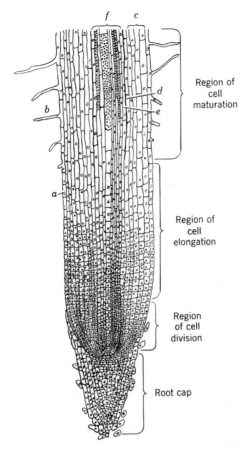

Region of
cell
maturation

Region of
cell
elongation

Region
of cell
division

Root cap

Fig. 5-7. Longitudinal section of a young root of barley. *a,* epidermis; *b,* root hair (a protuberance from an epidermal cell); *c,* cortex; *d,* endodermis; *e,* pericycle; *f,* differentiating conducting tissues of stele. (From H. J. Fuller and O. Tippo, *College Botany,* Holt, 1949, p. 171.)

teristic of a root and enable it to absorb materials from its environment and transport them to the stem. Before describing the course of cellular differentiation, however, we should look at the implications of the root's growth pattern for an individual cell which is formed in the apical meristem.

The essence of apical growth is that only the cells that remain in a limited region of the root tip continue to divide. A cell and its progeny are apt to be found at progressively greater distances from the apex due to the growth of intervening cells. When the distance has become great enough, the cell terminates its mitotic activity and much of the synthetic activity which accompanies it, and enters into a period of elongation. Overall, the apical meristem loses cells as rapidly as it produces them, so that the meristem remains relatively constant in size. At this point, we can only speculate that there must be local environmental conditions in the root tip which account for this conversion in the activities of individual cells.

In recent years it has been possible to describe the elongation of the root tip in quantitative terms. Root tips are marked in the way described above; employing photographic procedures, continuous records of the displacement of individual marks from the apex are made. A series of lines can be drawn (Fig. 5-8) representing the distance of each mark from the apex as a function of time. A vertical line is drawn through these lines at

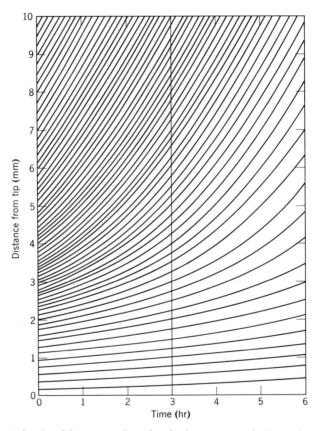

Fig. 5-8.   A family of lines recording the displacement marks from the tip of the root in maize. The slope of each line where it intersects the vertical line ($t = 3$ hrs.) is plotted in Fig. 5-9. (Tracing courtesy of R. O. Erickson.)

any arbitrarily selected value of t, and the slope of each line at the point of intersection is measured. Data are thus obtained for plotting the rate of displacement of a mark from the apex (dX/dt) as a function of its distance from the apex (Fig. 5-9). From the manner in which it is obtained, it should be apparent that dX/dt is the rate of elongation of that part of the root between the point X and the apex of the root. In morphological terms dX is that infinitesimal increment that has occurred in this length of the root in the time interval dt. All of the cells between 0 (the tip of the root) and X contribute to the increment.

Of greater significance might be the question: how fast are the cells elongating at each successive point along the length of the root tip, and how frequently does each cell undergo mitosis? Ideally, we would need to identify each successive cell along the length of the root. Although this particular feat is not yet possible, a useful approximation can be made by measuring the slope at each point of the curve in Fig. 5-9. The resulting term, $d(dX/dt)/dX$, is the rate at which growth changes with distance from the apex. In morphological terms it is the relative rate of elongation (recall, from p. 133, that the relative growth rate is the growth rate divided by the size of the system) of a very short piece of root, dX. The relative elemental rate of elongation, as this term has been called, is plotted as a function of X in Fig. 5-10. The point at which cells in the root tip are elongating at the fastest rate is located approximately 4 mm from the apex of the root in corn seedlings.

A parallel set of considerations, which we will not derive here, has indicated that the fastest rate of cell division $(dn/n\ dt)$ in the root of the corn seedling occurs at 1.5 mm from the apex (Fig. 5-11). Thus we can say that cells originating near the root apex, as well as their progeny, progressively increase their rate of cell division until they are 1.5 mm from

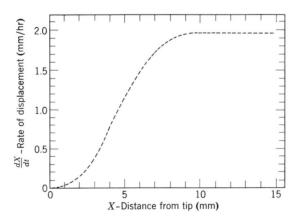

Fig. 5-9.   Rate of displacement of marks from the tip of a corn root. (From R. O. Erickson and K. Sax, *Proc. Amer. Phil. Soc.,* **100,** 494 (1956).)

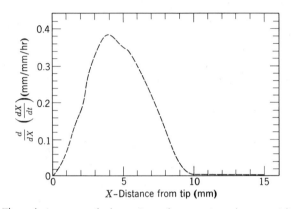

Fig. 5-10.   The relative rate of elongation of successive elements (dX) of a corn root. (From R. O. Erickson and K. Sax, *Proc. Amer. Phil. Soc.*, **100**, 495 (1956).)

the apex and cease dividing entirely by the time they are 3 mm from the tip. They continue elongating at an increasing rate, however, until they are 4 mm from the tip, and finally cease growing entirely at about 10 mm from the tip.

A precise description of growth is fundamental to the analysis of the physiological factors that control the rates of cell division and enlargement. Having demonstrated the fact that cell division reaches its fastest rate 1.5 mm from the root tip, and ceases entirely farther up the root, we would then like to identify the responsible physiological factors. From the point of view of understanding how differential growth shapes the organism, there have been no effective analyses of such questions. As we will see, however, this is a very general problem that arises in the development of all multicellular organisms, and one whose solution in any specific case will be a major accomplishment.

Differentiation of Subapical Cells. Wherever cells are yielded by growth, they do not serve simply as indifferent contributions to the total mass, but invariably participate discretely in the differentiation of structures and in the functioning of the organism. The growth that is accompanied by cell division must be considered a source of the raw materials for differentiation.

In primary root development a cell that has been left behind on the basal side of the apical meristem soon begins to show microscopic evidence of differentiation. Characteristically, the quality of its subsequent transformation is in harmony with its position. Thus for example certain epidermal cells, the root hair cells, each produce

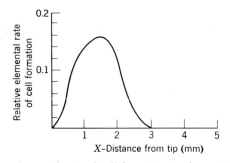

Fig. 5-11.   Relative elemental rate of cell formation in the root tip of maize.

a lateral process which projects into the surrounding soil and functions in the uptake of water and salts (Fig. 5-7). The cells of the cortex, in gymnosperms and dicots, remain as parenchyma cells with thin walls, large central vacuoles, and conspicuous intercellular spaces (Fig. 5-12). The inner side of the cortex is delimited by a single layer of cells in which the cell wall becomes thickened in localized regions by deposits of lignin and waxy materials. The endodermis, as this structure is called, forms a cylinder of cells separating an outer cylinder of cortex from an inner core of vascular tissue.

The most striking transformations are undergone by the vascular elements, the cells of the xylem and phloem. Since the details of the transformations of individual cells of the phloem and xylem are described in connection with differentiation (p. 176), our present concern is only with the arrangement of these cells in the primary root.

The first vascular cells to differentiate are the phloem cells which appear in bundles lying just inside the endodermis. Slightly farther up the root, bundles of xylem cells are formed by the elongate cells lying between the phloem strands. The initial strands of phloem and xylem differentiate before the elongation of the surrounding cells has been completed. With further elongation of the root tip, these cells become greatly attenuated, and their functions are finally taken over by neighboring cells that continued division and elongation until a later time. Ultimately, most of the cells central to the initial strands differentiate into xylem cells.

The structure resulting from primary growth in the root thus consists of a central core of xylem surrounded by a series of cylinders of other types of cells. In woody plants, which later undergo secondary growth, the layer of cells immediately adjacent to the xylem becomes the cambium, whose activities are discussed in the next section. Surrounding this is the phloem and then, successively, a layer of parenchyma cells (the pericycle), the endodermis, the cortex, and finally

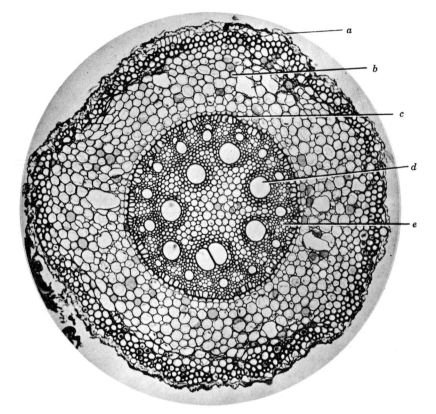

Fig. 5-12. Corn root, cross section. *a,* Epidermis; *b,* cortex; *c,* endodermis; *d,* primary xylem; *e,* primary phloem. (Copyright, General Biological Supply House, Inc., Chicago.)

the epidermis. The whole complex of tissues, when finally differentiated, can function (as described on p. 233) in the uptake and transport of water and minerals from the soil to the shoot and of photosynthetic products from the shoot to the growing apex of the root.

Stem Elongation. The mechanism of elongation of the stem is basically similar to that of the root, but is complicated by the simultaneous formation of leaves. The distribution of dividing cells, in particular, is influenced by the process of leaf formation. Cell divisions occur not only at the apex (there is no counterpart of the root cap in the stem apex), but also at the base of each growing leaf, so that the shoot apex may contain a series of zones of cell division, separated from each other by more mature areas of differentiation. (The stem at the point of attachment of a leaf is termed the *node,*

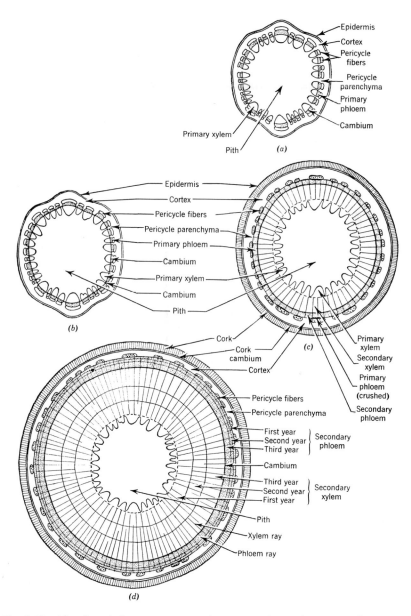

Fig. 5-13. The dicotyledonous stem seen in cross section at four successive stages of development. *(a)* Fully differentiated primary stem. *(b)* Origin of the cambium. *(c)* After one year of secondary growth. *(d)* After three years of secondary growth. (From R. M. Holman and W. W. Robbins, *Elements of Botany*, Wiley, 1940, p. 64.)

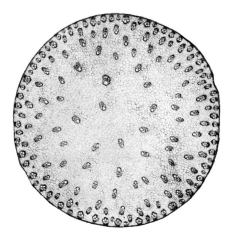

Fig. 5-14. Cross section of the stem of a monocot. (From R. M. Holman and W. W. Robbins, *Elements of Botany,* Wiley, 1940, p. 78.)

and that between nodes is the *internode;* see Fig. 5-18.) Despite the differences in distribution of these activities, the individual cells of the stem and root apices go through a comparable sequence of activities, beginning with their origin during mitosis and ending with the completion of differentiation.

The arrangement of the vascular tissue of a stem after the completion of primary growth differs somewhat from that of the root. In the dicots and gymnosperms the vascular bundles have a cylindrical arrangement around a central pith of parenchyma tissue (Fig. 5-13A), whereas in the monocots the bundles are scattered throughout the stem in a matrix of parenchyma cells (Fig. 5-14). Each bundle consists of both xylem and phloem cells, the latter always lying toward the outside of the stem from the former.

The tissues surrounding the vascular region of the stem may be organized very much as in the root. In such cases they consist of a cortex several cells thick, with an epidermis at the surface. In many monocots, on the other hand, the cortex is altogether absent, and the outermost vascular bundles lie adjacent to the epidermis.

Apical meristems and the associated zones of elongation and differentiation are responsible, with minor modifications, for the development of roots and stems in all vascular plants. One of the most striking features of this arrangement is its potential for unlimited growth. Except for the limitation imposed by the distances over which transport of materials can occur between expanding systems of roots and leaves, the root and the stem could conceivably continue their linear elongation indefinitely. (Indeed, when apical growth zones are isolated in culture they do show evidence of an ability to grow indefinitely.)

Apical growth also occurs in the multicellular fungi, where it abets their invasive growth habits, and in some of the multicellular algae, such as *Fucus*. But apical growth zones, with their self-perpetuating embryonic character, have no counterpart in the development of most animals. The regions of cell division occurring in animals are generally responsible for the production of one or a few types of cells— (p. 136) not for the whole complex of cell types constituting the organism. The most conspicuous exceptions to this are the growth zone of *Hydra* (p. 88), and those such as the apex of the stolon (p. 102) which is responsible for hydroid colony formation. The apical meristem is preeminently a characteristic of the sedentary plant, which depends on invasive growth to assure itself of an adequate supply of nutrients.

Secondary Growth

The structures laid down by apical growth do not always possess the definitive girth of the root or stem. A subsequent increase in thickness can occur which is entirely independent of elongation. *Secondary growth* occurs most obviously in woody plants; some trees continue to increase the diameter of their trunk and roots for hundreds of years. However, even annual plants and herbaceous plants whose aerial parts wither each year may exhibit some secondary thickening after elongation has stopped.

Secondary growth in woody plants is primarily accomplished by the cambium, a layer of meristematic cells lying between the xylem and the phloem. In the stem the cambium is at first confined to the vascular bundles. These separate strips are converted to a continuous cylinder of cambium by the resumption of meristematic activity in a sheet of cells located in the parenchyma tissue lying between the vascular bundles (Figs. 5-13b and 5-15).

In a cross section of a stem or root the cells of the cambium appear small relative to the highly differentiated cells of the xylem and phloem. In longitudinal sections cut tangential to the cambial layer, they present a very different aspect (Figs. 5-16). Some cambial cells are then seen to be exceedingly long, while others, occurring in clusters between the elongate cells, are approximately isodiametric. The latter cells give rise to the radial sheets of parenchyma tissue that occur in mature xylem and phloem (p. 180), while most of the progeny of the elongate cells become fibers and vascular cells.

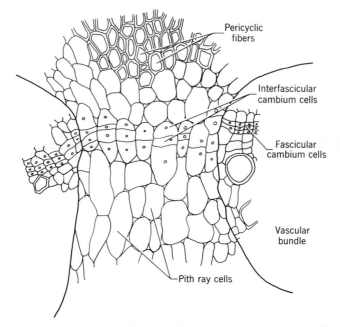

Fig. 5-15. Cambium arising in the parenchyma between vascular bundles in the stem of a dicot. (From R. M. Holman and W. W. Robbins, *Elements of Botany,* Wiley, 1940, p. 66.)

The geometry of the elongate cells, which may be anywhere from five to a hundred times as long as they are wide, raises special problems at the time of cell division. Most of them divide in the tangential plane along their longitudinal axes so that each daughter cell is just as long as the parent cell but (at the outset) only half as wide. In other instances mitosis divides the cell approximately transversely to its long axis, yielding daughter cells half as long as the parent cell; a period of elongation then ensues in which the daughter cells grow intrusively between neighboring cells until they have approximately restored their initial length.

As the girth of the stem or root increases in succeeding years, the cambial layer must itself grow in order to remain a continuous cylinder around the increasingly massive xylem. Such growth results from the production of daughter cells which lie in a plane tangential to the perimeter of the cambial cylinder. In most divisions of cambial cells, however, one daughter cell remains in the cambium and the second lies either more centrally in the zone of cells which differentiate into xylem or more peripherally in a layer of prospective phloem

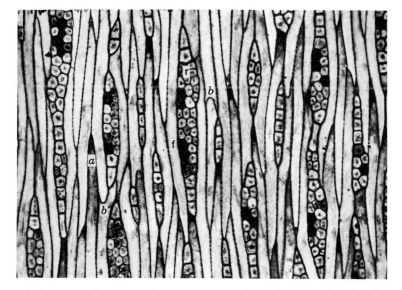

Fig. 5-16. Tangential section in the cambium of a walnut showing the clusters of isodiametric cells (ray initials) lying among elongate cells (fusiform initials). (From K. Esau, *Plant Anatomy,* Wiley ,1953, p. 634.)

cells. The course of differentiation of these cells is described on p. 176.

The Development of Laterals. The growth of the vascular land plant has so far been discussed as though it were simply one root and one stem growing in opposite directions from each other. To bring the picture closer to reality, some appendages must now be added. Roots and stems generally exhibit some degree of branching. The stems also bear appendages in the form of leaves and floral parts. The development of each of these laterals is a complex story, especially with regard to the diversity in their formation among various species of plants. Only the beginnings will be discussed here.

In dicots and gymnosperms lateral roots are formed in regions of the root which have completed their primary growth. A group of the parenchyma cells that lie between the phloem and the endodermis of the primary root resumes growth and cell division (Fig. 5-17). The resulting bud of cells expands and finally breaks through the cortex and epidermis. Subsequently, the bud behaves exactly like a root tip engaged in primary growth. Since the root bud is formed next to the vascular tissue, functional connections of its xylem and phloem with those of the parent root are achieved by appropriate differentiations of the newly formed cells. In woody plants the cambium of the branch also becomes continuous with that of the main

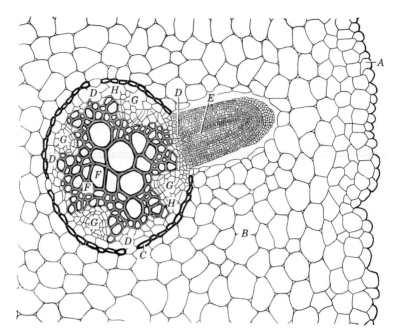

Fig. 5-17. The origin of a branch root from parenchyma cells (the pericycle) lying within the endodermis. *A*, epidermis; *B*, cortex; *C*, endodermis; *D*, pericycle; *E*, branch root originating from pericycle; *F*, xylem; *G*, phloem. (From H. J. Fuller and O. Tippo, *College Botany*, Holt, 1949, p. 174.)

root, and thus the production of secondary xylem and phloem is closely coordinated with that of the main root.

The production of laterals in the shoot is quite different because the primordia of leaves and the buds of lateral branches are laid down at the apex during primary growth. The earliest primordia of the leaves are visible as slight protuberances within a short distance of the apex (Fig. 5-18). The leaf buttress, as the protuberance is called, is formed by the growth and division of epidermal and subepidermal cells frequently lying within a few cell diameters of the center of the apex. The leaf is formed by an upward growth of the buttress, further growth of the apex having laid down more cells (which will form the tissues of the internode) between itself and the buttress.

Two very general problems are posed by the production of leaves. One concerns the factors that determine where they will be formed. Nearly every species of plant has a fairly precise arrangement of leaves. They may be in pairs, with each leaf on the opposite side of the stem from its partner, and with each successive pair arranged on the stem at a 90° angle to its predecessor. More often, the leaves are helically arranged with a more or less constant angle of divergence from each other. The factors that control

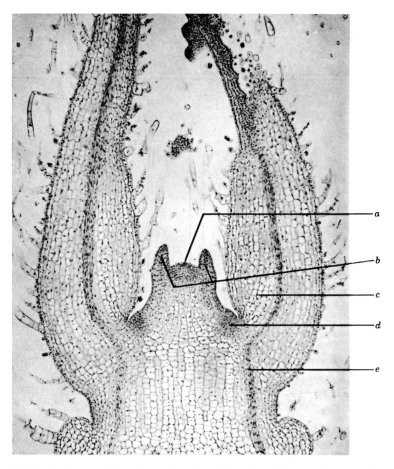

Fig. 5-18. Median longitudinal section of a *Coleus* shoot tip. *a,* Apical meristem, *b,* leaf primordia at first node; *c,* young leaf at third node; *d,* lateral bud primordium in axil of young leaf; *e,* provascular strand. (Copyright, General Biological Supply House, Inc., Chicago.) (From V. A. Greulach and J. E. Adams, *An Introduction to Modern Botany,* Wiley, 1962, p. 128.)

the point of origin of the leaf primordia have been the subject of many investigations. Whatever their nature, it is apparent that they operate in the apex by determining which cells will initiate lateral growth to produce the buttress. One possibility is that the apical cells themselves "remember" where and when the last leaf primordium was laid down, and direct a new one to be formed in an appropriate position. A second possibility is that the most recently established primordia influence the site of the new buttress.

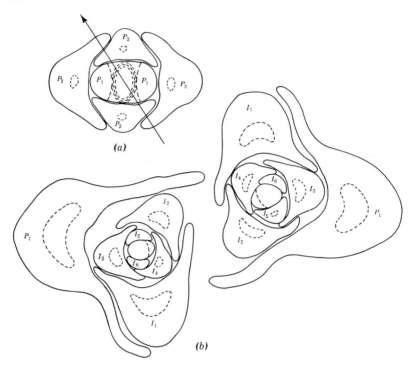

Fig. 5-19. Transverse section through the shoot apex of *Epilobium.* (a) The normal leaf arrangement with an arrow indicating the plane of the experimental cut. P_1, P_2, and P_3 are pairs of leaves present at the time of the operation. *(b)* I_1, I_2, etc., are the leaves produced subsequent to the cut. (From M. Snow and R. Snow, *Phil. Trans. Roy. Soc. London,* Ser B, **225,** 66 (1935).)

One of the most suggestive experiments favoring this view entailed cutting the shoot apex of *Epilobium,* which normally has opposite leaves, so that the apical meristem and one of the most recent leaf primordia were isolated from the second member of the pair. The altered apex continued to grow, but the new leaf primordia were now spirally arranged on the shoot (Fig. 5-19). The initial absence of one of the leaf primordia thus led to a self-perpetuating alteration, which clearly implicated the leaf primordia themselves as important agents in determining the site of new primordia.

The second major problem in leaf formation concerns the mechanisms which transform a small bump on the surface of the shoot apex, a few dozen microns in diameter, into a leaf—a flattened structure with a surface area of many square centimeters. The initial step in this direction is the upward growth of a finger-like projection from the buttress. For a time the outgrowth has an apical zone of growth and cell division, but very shortly cell divisions can be detected along its entire length. Most of this structure will ultimately form the axis of the leaf, differentiating into the petiole and the midrib. The blade of the leaf is formed from columns of cells lying on each side of the finger-like projection which, having resumed meristematic activity, grow laterally out from the differentiating midrib. The subsequent enlargement, shaping, and cellular differentiation that yield the final structure of the leaf will not be pursued in detail here. In principle they entail the same cellular mechanisms of development already described for the stem, but differing in their timing and location.

Lateral buds capable of forming branches arise in the nodes shortly after and just apical to the leaf primordium. Such buds are formed by the growth of the superficial layers of cells to form a small protrusion between the stem and the base of the leaf. Once established, a lateral bud may remain dormant for a considerable period of time. Hormonal control mechanisms (p. 259) can release it from its dormancy, however, so that its development is indistinguishable from primary growth as already described for the shoot apex.

Finally, some comments must be made on the formation of the flower. Like a leafy shoot, a flower consists of a central axis bearing lateral appendages that it supports and nourishes. It is formed by an apical meristem which lays down the primordia of the appendages as it goes. Indeed, the floral apex originates from either a shoot apex or a lateral bud, both of which under other conditions have the ability to form a stem with leaves. (The transformation of a shoot apex into a floral apex occurs under the influence of hormonal control mechanisms described in Chapter 7.)

There are several basic differences between the activities of these two apical growth zones. The floral appendages, as has been noted, are often arranged as a series of whorls (although some are placed helically, like leaves). Morphogenesis takes a different form in each whorl, forming the sepals, petals, stamens, and carpels in turn, rather than identical photosynthetic organs at all levels. Finally, the floral apex, unlike the shoot apex, has limited potentialities for growth. Rather than growing indeterminately, laying down the primordia of leaves and lateral buds for an indefinite period of time, the floral apex ceases growing once the final whorl of appendages, the carpels, has been formed. The basic philosophy of the floral apex seems to be that the plant should reproduce and then die; indeed, this is precisely what the annual plant does. Perennial and woody plants are rescued from the same fate either by producing flowers exclusively from lateral buds, or by regenerating leafy shoots the following year from lateral or adventitious buds.

It should be clear from this account that the elongation of roots and stems, secondary growth, and the formation of branches, leaves, and flowers all depend on the same basic processes—the growth, division, and differentiation of cells. The fact that different populations of cells can utilize the same basic mechanisms to yield such very different but precisely formed end products makes it necessary to postulate that the rate and direction of growth of each cell in the population are carefully regulated. The unvarying harmony between the growth of the cell and its position in the organism strongly suggests that a certain amount of control is exercised through relations with neighbors. With the singular exception of the control of some aspects of growth by hormonal mechanisms (p. 259), a general explanation of the mechanism of control of differential growth has not yet been offered; this problem remains one of the primary challenges in studies of the development of multicellular organisms.

MORPHOGENETIC MOVEMENTS

Differential growth is only one of two mechanisms that can cause changes in form. The migration of cells also can be an important factor in molding the shape of organisms. Morphogenetic movements, as these activities have been termed, are a universal component of the early stages of development in animals. Except for a few vivid examples among the algae and cellular slime molds, they do not occur in plants, where the cell wall in general militates against motility.

There are instances in which either morphogenetic movements or differential growth accounts completely for changes in form. We have just described differential growth in the absence of morphogenetic movements in flowering plants. In the cellular slime molds (p. 72), after cessation of feeding, the fruiting bodies are formed by morphogenetic movements largely in the absence of growth. Movements such as these are capable of generating form quite precisely. The structure of the end product is sufficiently stereotyped that interspecific differences in the structure of the fruiting body can be used to identify the species of slime mold (Fig. 5-20).

Morphogenetic movements are much more complicated in the animal embryo because they are not as clearly separated from growth; many embryos increase substantially in mass during their period of formative movements. In addition, the cellular differentiations that accompany the movements, rather than giving rise to two kinds of cells, give rise to many kinds, and the movements of cells are correspondingly complex.

Before discussing this case further, it is necessary to set the stage by describing some of the events subsequent to fertilization of the egg (p. 114). The zygote, which in animals is extraordinarily large for a single cell, initiates a series of mitotic divisions that restore

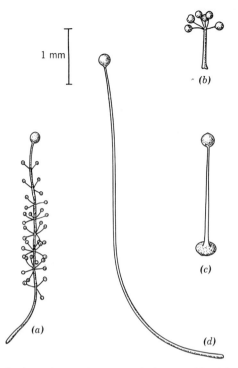

1 mm

(b)

(c)

(a)

(d)

Fig. 5-20.   Fruiting bodies of several species of slime molds. *(a) Polysphondilium pallidum, (b) Dictyostelium polycephalum, (c) D. discoideum, (d) D. mucoroides.* (From J. T. Bonner, *The Cellular Slime Molds,* Princeton, 1959, p. 20.)

it to the status of a multicellular organism. In general, the total mass of the system remains essentially constant during this period; the result is a progressive reduction in the size of the cells. For this reason the process is often called *cleavage.*

The geometry of cell division in the zygote varies with the amount and distribution of the yolk. In a relatively yolk-free egg, such as that of a mammal or a sea urchin, the first mitotic division cleaves the egg into two halves, and subsequent divisions follow the same pattern. The cleavages thus lead to a muticellular aggregate, the *blastula,* which generally retains the over-all shape of the uncleaved egg. A cavity, the *blastocoele,* lies at the center of the blastula, so that it is in fact a hollow sphere with a wall from one to several cells thick (Fig. 5-21*a-b*).

In eggs containing large masses of yolk, such as those of birds or fish, the cytoplasm gathers on one side of the yolk and divides to form a superficial cap of cells without even beginning to cleave the

yolk mass. The flattened cap on the surface of the yolk is designated
as the *blastoderm* (Fig. 5-21 *c-d*). It is the developmental equivalent
of the blastula, differing significantly only because it is encumbered
with a larger mass of yolk.

There then ensues a period of rearrangement in which the cells
of the blastula or blastoderm begin to form an embryo. As a formative process occurring in the three dimensions of space and the fourth
dimension of time, the cellular movements that shape the embryo
are peculiarly unadaptable to description within the two-dimensional
limitations of a page. In a few of the animals whose embryos develop from blastulae, the early stages of the process are relatively
clear, however, and it will suffice for the present purpose to generalize
from an example. It is convenient to divide the over-all process
into two periods: first, the transformation of the blastula into a gastrula, and then of the gastrula into an embryo.

Gastrula Formation

The blastula of *Amphioxus* consists of a hollow sphere of cells with
a wall one cell thick enclosing a relatively large blastocoele. Gastrula

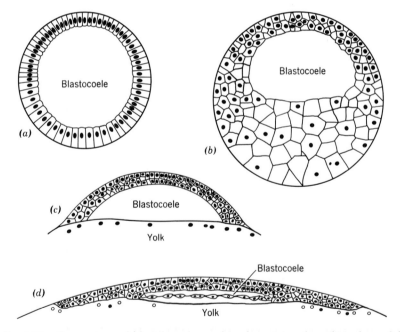

Fig. 5-21. Comparison of blastulae of an echinoderm *(a)*, a frog *(b)*, a bony fish
(c), and a bird *(d)*. (From B. I. Balinsky, *An Introduction to Embryology*, Saunders,
1960, p. 85.)

formation begins when one side of the blastula flattens and then bends inward, forming a pocket which intrudes into the blastocoele (Fig. 5-22). This process continues until the blastula has been converted into a spherical *gastrula*, a hollow structure with a wall consisting of two layers of cells. In this particular case the blastocoele is completely obliterated, and is replaced by a new cavity which connects with the exterior via an opening, the *blastopore*. The cells that remain on the outside of the gastrula, covering its entire surface, are derived from cells that initially covered only half (or less) of the surface of the blastula. Two basic types of movements thus occur during gastrulation: some cells move to the interior where they form the inner tissues of the embryo, and others spread out to cover the surface. It is interesting that the outer layer of cells in most animals never loses this ability to spread. One of the key features of wound healing in animals is an ability of the epidermis to spread out over the underlying exposed tissues until the gap has been completely covered.

The cells that invade the blastocoele and form the inner layer of the gastrula very soon subdivide, so that the animal comes to consist of three concentric layers of cells. The outer layer is the *ectoderm*, which will develop into the epidermis and nervous system. The inner layer, which will form the lining of the digestive tube and associated glands, is the *endoderm*. The remaining cells form all of the muscular,

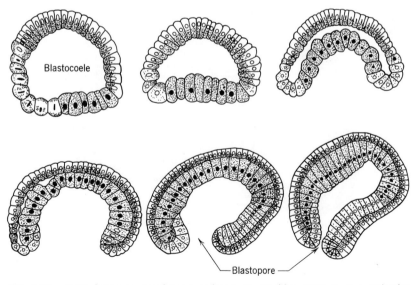

Fig. 5-22. Gastrulation in *Amphioxus*. (After E. G. Conklin, 1932, in B. I. Balinsky, *An Introduction to Embryology*, Saunders, 1960, p. 128.)

vascular, and supporting tissues lying between the ectoderm and the endoderm, and are designated as the *mesoderm*. The distinction between these three layers can be made at some stage of development in all major groups of multicellular animals except the coelenterates, in which the mesoderm may be greatly reduced or altogether absent. The origin of the three germ layers by morphogenetic movements from a blastula or blastoderm and the many parallels in their subsequent development are remarkably general considering the diversity of the adult types that are ultimately produced.

Embryo Formation

The formation of the gastrula is only a mid-point in the period of morphogenetic movements, for folding and shifting activities continue until an embryo is produced whose structure foreshadows much of the morphology of the mature organism. In the vertebrate, used here as an example, the culminating stage of the period of morphogenetic movements is depicted in Fig. 5-23.

The vertebrate embryo is basically cylindrical. It is covered by an outer jacket of *epidermis*, which will be perforated by a *mouth* and an *anus* at either end. Connecting the mouth and anus through the middle of the embryo is the *gut*. Dorsal to the gut is a rod of cells, the *notochord*, and dorsal to the notochord is another tubular structure,

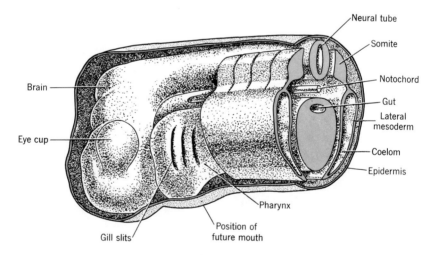

Fig. 5-23. The structure of the vertebrate embryo. Only the anterior half is shown. The epidermis is removed from the left side to expose internal structures. (From C. H. Waddington, *Principles of Embryology*, George Allen and Unwin, 1956, p. 7.)

the *neural tube*, which will form much of the nervous system. On either side of the neural tube and notochord are a series of blocks of cells, the *somites*. A double sheet of cells, the lateral plate, extends laterally and ventrally from the two rows of somites, around both sides of the gut, meeting along the ventral mid-line. The next question to be considered is how an embryo with this structure can be formed by the concentric layers of cells comprising the gastrula.

One of the earliest steps in the transformation is the division of the ectoderm into two parts, the epidermis and the neural tube. In most vertebrates the first signs of the formation of the neural tube occur when the ectodermal cells lying in the prospective mid-line of the embryo change from cuboidal epithelial cells to columnar cells (Fig. 5-24). The resulting thickened plate of cells then bends inward to form a groove; a tubular

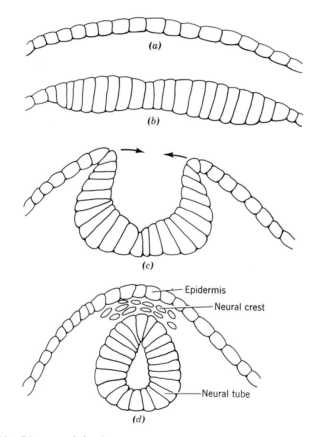

Fig. 5-24. Diagram of the formation of the neural tube from the epidermis in a vertebrate embryo. (Adapted from B. S. Balinsky, *An Introduction to Embryology*, 1960, Saunders, Philadelphia, p. 143.)

structure lying beneath the surface of the epidermis is formed when the edges of the groove bend toward each other and fuse. Finally, the tube separates from the prospective epidermal cells which have closed over the surface of the embryo behind it. As this occurs, a group of cells that connects the neural tube with the epidermis separates from both structures, and comes to lie on each side of the neural tube. These cells, which comprise the neural crest, participate with the neural tube in the subsequent differentiation of the nervous system.

When fully formed, the neural tube is an elongate structure running the full length of the embryo on its dorsal side. It is subdivided along its length into two morphologically distinct regions. For much of its length it is a fairly narrow structure, which will become the spinal cord. At its anterior end, however, it is greatly expanded with a large central canal. This region of the neural tube will form the brain (see Fig. 5-23).

By the time the neural tube has separated from the epidermis, the layers of cells representing the endoderm and mesoderm have also become subdivided into a series of discrete components. In the head, which is primarily occupied by the prospective brain, the mesoderm is poorly represented. In the posterior part of the head and throughout the rest of the length of the body, however, it is much more prominent. The notochord, somites, and lateral plate are all subdivisions of the mesoderm. Little can be said at this point concerning the mechanisms of their origin beyond the descriptive fact that the mesoderm, which comes through the blastopore as a continuous sheet of cells, then breaks up into discrete blocks of tissue with the configuration shown in Figs. 5-25 and 5-23.

Of these, the notochord has a transitory existence in the vertebrate embryo. In other groups of the phylum *Chordata* it serves the function of a skeletal rod. As will be noted shortly, this function is assumed at later stages of development in the vertebrates by the adjacent cells of the somites, which produce the vertebral column around the neural tube and notochord. The

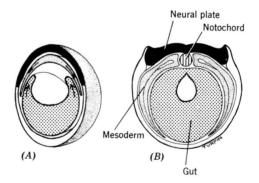

Fig. 5-25. The separation of the endoderm from the mesoderm in a frog embryo and beginning of the subsequent subdivision of the mesoderm. (From T. W. Torrey, *Morphogenesis of the Vertebrates,* Wiley, 1962, p. 114.)

notochord is obliterated in the process of vertebra formation, but during its presence it plays a critical role in the genesis of the vertebrate axis (p. 188).

The lateral-most extension of the embryonic mesoderm, the lateral plate, splits into two parallel sheets shortly after it is formed. The coelom and other body cavities in which the viscera of the organism ultimately lie originate from the cavity between the sheets, while the cells on either side give rise, among other things, to the peritoneum and to the mesenteries which suspend the visceral organs in the body cavities.

A final problem in folding and shifting during embryo formation is the conversion of the endoderm into the lining of a tubular gut. In amphibians this is achieved shortly after the completion of gastrulation when the endoderm disengages itself from the mesoderm, temporarily forming the equivalent of a sheet of cells. The endoderm then folds over dorsally and forms a tube (Fig. 5-25). The blastodermally derived embryos of reptiles, birds and mammals are faced with the problem of forming not only a tubular gut, but also concentric layers of lateral plate and epidermis surrounding it. The three germ layers extending outward from the neural tube, notochord, and somites are essentially tucked under and around the sides of the embryo until they have met and fused ventrally, thereby separating the embryo from the yolk everywhere except for a narrow stalk (Fig. 5-26).

Extensive areas of the blastoderm remain outside of the embryo. These continue to fold and grow, forming a variety of extraembryonic membranes which, in birds and reptiles, function in excretion, gas exchange, and yolk digestion. In mammals, which possess no extraembryonic yolk, they invade the tissues of the uterus to form the placenta. The embryo remains attached to its extraembryonic membranes by a narrow stalk consisting of cells from all three germ layers. The stalk becomes the umbilical cord in the mammals, and continues in its function as a route of exchange between the embryo and the placenta until it is severed or dries up at birth.

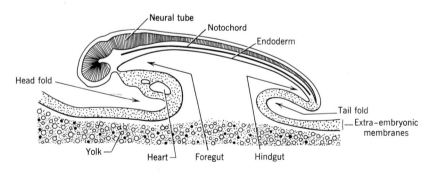

Fig. 5-26. Diagram showing the folding of the germ layers in a chick embryo to form a tubular embryo separated from the yolk mass. (From C. H. Waddington, *Principles of Embryology,* George Allen and Unwin, 1956, p. 252.)

Analysis of Morphogenetic Movements

The techniques employed in describing the morphogenetic movements of embryo formation and gastrulation deserve some comments. Observing the changes in form of the organism, as outlined in the previous sections, reveals the broad plan of the movements. But the origins of a cell, the route of its migration, and its final disposition could be more precisely determined if the cell could be observed in the course of its movements. Generally, the embryo is sufficiently opaque—and the cells so numerous and similar to each other—that direct observations of their movements cannot be achieved. Observation of the movements of labeled cells has thus proved invaluable. The earliest uses of this technique, such as the remarkable description by E. G. Conklin of morphogenetic movements in the tunicate, *Styela*, took advantage of natural markers. Yellow pigment granules become localized on one side of the *Styela* egg after fertilization. Their localization is retained up to the blastula stage when, as a consequence of the cleavages, they are contained in a discrete group of cells (Fig. 5-27). The yellow cells can then be traced during gastrulation, and Conklin was able to establish that they eventually form the muscles of the tail in the tadpole. (This was just one of

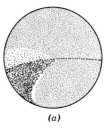

(a)

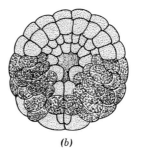

(b)

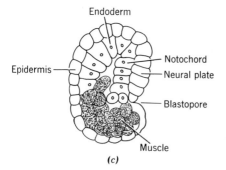

(c)

Fig. 5-27. Localization of the yellow pigment in Styela. *(a)* Lateral view of a fertilized egg. *(b)* Posterior view of an early gastrula. *(c)* Longitudinal section at the conclusion of gastrulation. The pigment-containing cells are now part of the mesoderm. (From C. H. Waddington, *Principles of Embryology,* George Allen and Unwin, 1956, p. 71.)

several markers in *Styela* that allowed a precise description of the developmental fate of every cell in the early cleavage stages.)

In the absence of natural markers, other eggs have been studied by means of dyes that will stain the cells of the blastula without interfering in their development. This feat was achieved in the amphibian blastula by Wilhelm Vogt, who in 1929 was able to publish maps indicating the origins in the blastula of every structure in the embryo (Figs. 5-28 and 5-29). By this device it has been possible to describe in remarkable detail not only the blastular origins of every structure in the embryo, but the precise route that each group of cells takes during the spreading and intrusive shifts of gastrulation and embryo formation.

Several problems are raised by descriptions of morphogenetic movements and the precision with which they proceed. Among these are

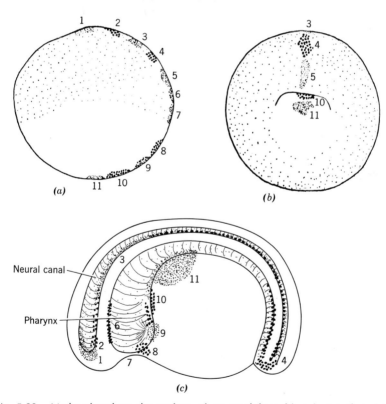

Fig. 5-28. Marks placed on the surface of an amphibian blastula (a), their later distribution on the surface of the gastrula (b), and in a dissected embryo (c). (From B. I. Balinsky, *An Introduction to Embryology*, Saunders, 1960, p. 135.)

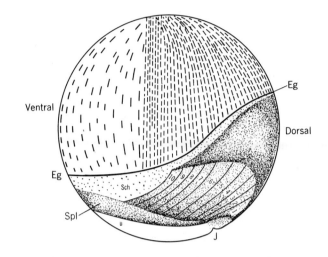

Fig. 5-29. Map of the presumptive regions of the urodele embryo, projected onto the surface of the blastula, as seen from the left side. Epidermis, sparse broken lines; neural plate, dense broken lines; notochord, dense dots; mesoderm, fine dots; endoderm, white. The future mesodermal segments are numbered. *Eg-Eg,* limit of invaginated region; *J,* site of first invagination; *Sch,* tail region; *Spl,* lateral plate mesoderm; *u,* position of future blastopore lip. (From H. Spemann, *Embryonic Induction and Development,* Yale, 1938, p. 12.)

the mechanisms of the movements, the factors that guide the cells as they progress toward their final location, and the circumstances that determine where they will finally settle down. The basic mechanisms of amoeboid movement exhibited by many types of animal cells are in some instances involved. This is the most likely possibility wherever cells migrate as physically independent units, as in the aggregation of slime molds. Even after aggregation, however, the movement of the slug and the climbing of the stalk appear to entail primarily the amoeboid movement of individual cells. The applicability of amoeboid movements to shifts that entail the coordinated movement of large populations of cells—for instance, the folding of the neural plate or the spreading of the ectoderm in animal embryos—is sometimes questioned. But there is as yet no conclusive evidence that a different mechanism is involved in such cases.

The question of what guides the cells to their final location and what determines where they will settle down has been dramatized by studies of cells experimentally separated from each other. One of the most startling findings has been the revelation that many aspects of the organism's expected final form can be achieved even when the initial position or the route of migration of the cells has been grossly disturbed. This was first demonstrated in sponges by H. V. Wilson in 1907. A suspension of disaggregated cells was obtained by squeezing a mature sponge through a fine mesh of silk cloth. The architecture of the sponge was completely disrupted and transformed into a suspension of viable cells in sea water. When the cells had settled to the bottom of the dish, they wandered about by amoeboid motion. On making a chance contact in the course of their wanderings, the cells adhered to each other and gradually built up multicellular aggregates containing several hundred or more cells. The significant point here is that at the conclusion of the reaggregation phase a sufficiently large group of cells could assume the pattern of cellular arrangement characteristic of a small sponge.

Embryonic cells in animals possess a similar ability to reaggregate and form a structure with some degree of morphological precision. This was demonstrated in a series of experiments by Johannes Holtfreter some forty years after Wilson's observations. In one of Holtfreter's experiments, two pieces of ectoderm were removed from an amphibian embryo in the early stages of neural tube formation. One piece was derived from the neural plate, the second from prospective epidermis. One of the pieces was stained with a dye, so that the individual cells could be identified with respect to their site of origin. The cells in both blocks were then disaggregated by exposure to a mildly alkaline environment. After thorough mixing, each group of cells was allowed to reaggregate by restoring it to an environment with a pH near neutrality. Within a few hours the randomly distributed cells had formed a compact sphere (Fig. 5-30); and within a day the two cell types had sorted out so that the prospective epidermal cells formed a spherical shell around an inner layer of prospective neural cells. The latter, in the meantime, had formed a hollow structure which might be interpreted as a fragment of a neural tube. When mesoderm cells were included in the reaggregating mass, these formed a layer of mesenchyme between the neural and epidermal cells. Here, as in many other experiments, different kinds of cells sorted themselves out. More significantly, they assumed positions relative to each other which corresponded to those they would assume in a normal embryo.

The mechanistic details of the process are not entirely obvious. The individual cells wander by amoeboid action through the aggregate, but it is not known whether their migration at the outset is randomly directed or oriented. It also seems likely that similar cells, on encountering one another in the mixed aggregate, adhere to each

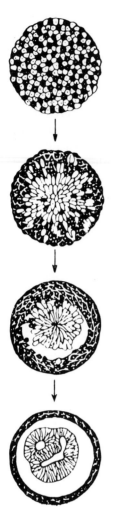

other in preference to the other cells present. But what accounts for the localization of epidermal cells at the surface, neural cells in the center, and mesenchyme cells between the two? This raises many questions. The important point for our purposes is that neural and epidermal cells do not need to rely on a specific initial arrangement or a specific route of migration in order to achieve their final relative positions. During their phase of migration they are effectively guided by unknown environmental cues to a place suitable for continuing their special routes of differentiation.

The orderly movements of cells during gastrulation and embryo formation occur under quite different circumstances from the sorting out of a random reaggregate. The rigid pattern of gastrulation reflects the fact that some degree of order already exists in the blastula, and that the movements largely entail blocks or sheets of cells rather than individual cells. An important consequence of the dynamics of gastrulation and embryo formation is that migrating cells are exposed in an orderly sequence to other layers of cells with which they have an opportunity to interact. We will return to some of the consequences of these interactions on p. 188.

DIFFERENTIATION

Fig. 5-30. Holtfreter's experiment demonstrating the sorting out of epidermal and neural plate cells that had been disaggregated and then mixed together. (From B. I. Balinsky, *An Introduction to Embryology*, Saunders, 1960, p. 158.)

Differentiation is a developmental pigeonhole into which a motley array of phenomena have at one time or another been placed. Like the word *growth*, it is a layman's term that has been adopted by developmental biologists and has at various times been given conflicting technical definitions. We shall adopt here the layman's understanding of the word—the intransitive verb, *to differentiate,* meaning to change from a homogeneous to a more heterogeneous condition. Accordingly cellular differentiation designates the process by which cells initially similar in appearance and behavior become very different from each other. The term also designates the increase in structural complexity at a higher level of organization—as, for example, when a plant embryo gradually forms the cotyledons and two apical growth zones, or when an animal blastula undergoes gastrulation and embryo formation. Confusion may arise from the mechanistic significance of the term. At the higher level of organization, differentiation is not brought about by any single mechanism. Differential growth, morphogenetic movements, or cellular differentiation (or any combination of these) might be involved, depending on the particular instance in question. *Differentiation* and *growth,* as used here, are everyday descriptive terms—with no special technical or mechanistic overtones unless appropriately modified.

Differentiation in the Vertebrate Embryo

We shall next describe the further development of several components of the vertebrate embryo. This is one of the richest sources of material for experimental studies of cellular differentiation and interactions. Specific cases will be studied, taking account of the concurrent differential growth and morphogenetic movements.

The Nervous System. The nervous system plays such a fundamental role in the integration of the mature animal, and promises to be the subject of such intensive research in the future, that its genesis in the embryo deserves special attention. The central nervous system— the brain and spinal cord—and many of the nerves that run from it to other organs of the body—are derived from the neural tube. Additional nerves and ganglia (the small masses of neural tissue which occur in the viscera and on each side of the spinal cord) are derived from the neural crest.

The central nervous system begins as a fairly simple tubular structure whose wall becomes, through folding and differential thickening, progressively more differentiated along its length, until it has assumed the intricate anatomy of a brain and spinal cord. The folding process is especially well illustrated by the development of the neural components of the eyes near the anterior end of the neural tube.

The eyes form as a pair of outpocketings, or *optic vesicles,* one on each side of the brain (Fig. 5-31), as soon as the latter structure

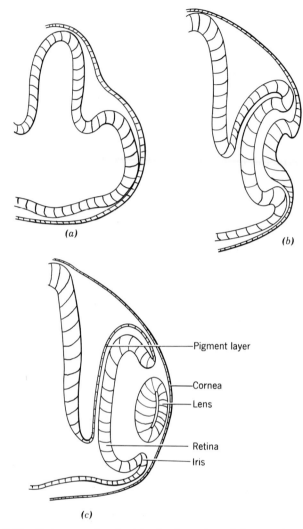

(a)

(b)

Pigment layer

Cornea

Lens

Retina

Iris

(c)

Fig. 5-31. Early stages involved in the formation of the vertebrate eye.

has separated from the epidermis. The growth of the two optic vesicles brings their outer surfaces into contact with the epidermis on the side of the head. Each vesicle then undergoes a second period of folding in which it is transformed from a balloon-shaped structure into something akin to a cup, with its open side facing the epidermis and its base attached to the brain by a tenuous stalk. Because of the way in which it is formed, the optic cup consists of two layers of cells. The layer that lines the cavity of the cup becomes the retina of the eye, its cells forming the photosensitive rods and cones (p. 307), as well as the neurons, which will at a later time relay nerve impulses from the light-sensitive elements to the brain. The outer layer of the cup subsequently transforms into a pigmented sheet (p. 307). The rim of the cup, where the two layers fold back on each other, is destined to become the iris—the derivative of the optic cup that is most readily visible when the eye is observed from the outside. Additional components are contributed to the eye by the surface ectoderm, which forms the lens and cornea, and by the mesoderm, which forms the outer sheath of connective tissue and the extrinsic muscles that move the eye. We will return to the problem of lens formation as an example of embryonic induction (p. 186).

In addition to outpocketings and foldings such as these, a key role in shaping the central nervous system is played by differential thickening of the wall of the neural tube. Growth in thickness of the spinal cord can be demonstrated by comparing the cross section of a newly formed neural tube in the trunk region of an embryo with the cross-section of a spinal cord at a later stage of development. Not only is the wall of the spinal cord a good deal thicker, but it also assumes a different shape, suggesting unequal growth (compare Fig. 5-24 with Fig. 7-32). Such inequalities are particularly pronounced in the brain, where localized regions of the neural tube give rise to massive structures such as the cerebral hemispheres and the cerebellum. It is not surprising that regions of the neural tube that are destined to become extremely thick have been found to contain a relatively high rate of mitotic activity. An important aspect of this proliferative function is that it is restricted to the cells that line the central canal of the neural tube, where a zone of cell division comparable to the meristems of plant development can be detected.

One of the most striking features of the differentiation of the nervous system is the production of the fiber tracts that traverse the length of the spinal cord and brain, establishing a network of functional connections between the various parts of the central nervous system. Fiber tracts of similar nature and composition comprise the peripheral nerves that connect the central nervous system with peripheral sense organs, muscles, and glands. The cellular mechanisms involved in generating the fiber tracts were first analyzed by R. G. Harrison in bits of embryonic neural tube that had been isolated in salt solutions and could be observed in the living state. Tenuous cytoplasmic processes can be observed in such preparations, arising from individual neural tube cells and growing out through the salt solution (Fig. 5-32). The tip of the process appears to crawl across

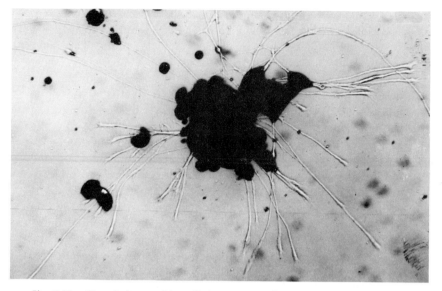

Fig. 5-32. Neural tissue with radiating nerve cell processes produced during 11 days' culture. The tissue was obtained from an amphibian embryo. (From M. C. Niu, in *14th Growth Symposium*, D. Rudnick, ed., Princeton, 1956, pp. 168–169.)

the substratum by a mechanism reminiscent of amoeboid movement. Rather than flowing into the "pseudopodium," as an amoeba would do, the main body of the nerve cell, including the nucleus, remains stationary and nourishes the outgrowth by feeding cytoplasm into it. In the embryo a single cell may put out a number of such processes varying in length from a few microns to several centimeters. Depending on the size of the animal at maturity, a process may ultimately be several meters long—sufficient to reach from an elephant's spinal cord to his foot, for instance.

Large populations of cells behaving in this manner give rise to the fiber tracts of the central nervous system. The absence of nuclei and the presence of relatively large amounts of lipid membranes produced around the fibers (p. 274) led to the designation of these regions as *white matter* in the brain and spinal cord. *Gray matter*, by contrast, is a term applied to the relatively nonfibrous regions of the central nervous system which contain nucleated cell bodies. Peripheral nerves are fiber tracts that connect the central nervous system with sensory and effector organs.

A host of problems are raised in connection with any individual nerve fiber which can be identified either in the central nervous system or in a peripheral nerve. At an anatomical level, where does the fiber terminate and where does its cell body lie? A physiologist must inquire about the consequences of a series of impulses running down its length. And the embryologist is concerned with the factors that caused the fiber to take this particular route during its growth and guided it to its final point of termination. It must suffice for the present to recognize that an essential aspect of a nerve cell's function is the nature of the structures on which it terminates. The way in which appropriate synaptic connections are established with sensory or effector organs, and with other neurons in the central nervous system, is one of the central problems in the differentiation of nerve cells—and in the integrative action of the nervous system. When the nervous system contains over a billion neurons, as it does in man, the problem is clearly very complex.

Mesodermal Development. Morphogenesis in the ectoderm and endoderm is largely achieved by the manipulation of entire epithelia, which fold and vesiculate, and grow and differentiate without ever losing their integrity as cohesive sheets of cells. The mesoderm of vertebrates is also formed initially as a sheet of cells, but it soon becomes subdivided into a series of discrete blocks (p. 160). Each block of cells to some degree retains its identity during subsequent development. For instance, the segmental somites are still clearly manifested in the swimming musculature of a fish, and the layer of lateral plate cells which lined the coelom of the embryo still lines the coelom of the adult. In addition, however, mesoderm cells can become transitory migrants that lose their adhesive properties, move individually away from their point of origin, and condense in other places within the embryo. The mesodermal cells that wander about in the interepithelial spaces of the embryo are collectively referred to as *mesenchyme.* By condensing and differentiating in appropriate fashion, they play an important role in the development of the vertebrate. They form the outer coating of the digestive tube and nervous system, and line the inner layer of the epidermis to form the dermis of the skin. In these sites the mesenchyme cells form layers of fibrous connective tissue, the capillary network of the vascular system and smooth muscle, especially around the digestive tube and many of the large blood vessels.

Among the more striking differentiations of the mesoderm is the formation of the skeletal system and the muscles that operate it from the somites and limb buds. The limb buds are formed when mesenchyme cells derived from the lateral plate condense and initiate heightened proliferation at four discrete points under the ectoderm (Fig. 5-33). The enlarging mass

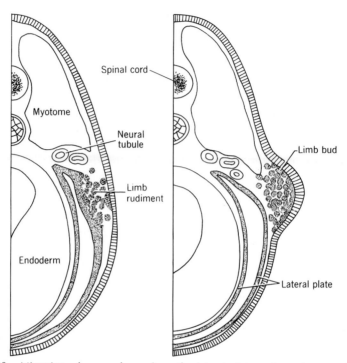

Fig. 5-33. Migration of mesenchyme from the lateral plate to form the mesoderm of the limb bud. (From B. I. Balinsky, *An Introduction to Embryology,* Saunders, 1960, p. 295.)

of mesenchyme with its cap of ectoderm protrudes from the surface of the embryo in the form of a bud that subsequently grows into an appendage—an arm, wing, fin, or leg.

One of the most prominent functions of the limb buds and the somites is the formation of the skeletal system. As would seem appropriate from their respective locations, the somites form the vertebral column and rib cage, while the mesenchyme of the limb buds forms the long bones of the appendages and the pectoral and pelvic girdles (shoulder and hip bones), which attach the limb to the vertebral column. The vertebral column arises when mesenchyme cells that migrate away from the inner side of the somites condense around the notochord and the ventral part of the spinal cord (Fig. 5-34). Similar condensations occur in the limb bud. In both, the cells comprising the aggregate adhere tightly to each other for a time and then commence the secretion of a matrix comprised of collagen fibers, chondroitin sulfate, and other substances. This complex of materials, called *cartilage,* has sufficient ability to withstand tension and compression without being greatly distorted. Thus it can serve as an effective skeletal material during the early period of the organism's growth. (At a later

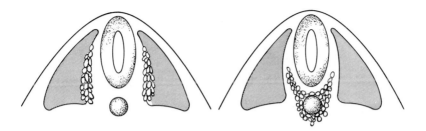

Fig. 5-34. Diagrammatic representation of the migration of somite cells to form a vertebra surrounding the notochord and neural tube.

stage, the cartilaginous matrix of the limbs and vertebral column is largely replaced in most vertebrates by bone, which possesses even stouter mechanical properties. Additional bone is laid down by the mesenchyme of the head to form the skull.)

Other components of the somites and the limb bud form the system of striated muscles that operate the skeleton. At the beginning of their transformation these cells become greatly elongated, and many of them fuse with each other to form syncytial fibers. During the course of elongation and fusion they synthesize the proteins myosin and actin whose properties account for the ability of muscle to contract (p. 316). During their subsequent growth the muscle fibers may attain lengths of 10 cm or more and a thickness of 10–100μ.

The many syncytial fibers that lie parallel to each other in a muscle are held tightly together by a connective tissue sheath. Additional connective tissue and blood vessels (all of which are products of differentiation of the mesoderm) lie between fibers throughout the mass of the muscle. Nerve processes growing out from cells in the central nervous system invade the muscle, forming motor end plates on the individual muscle fibers, and in some cases terminating in sensory structures. Finally, the muscle is attached at its ends either to a bone or to the surface of another muscle by its connective tissue sheath. The muscle, of course, accomplishes its work by shortening and thus pulling these two points of attachment toward each other.

Approximately 43 muscles and 29 bones are formed in the arm of a man. Their effectiveness in operating the appendage depends on each muscle's possessing appropriate points of attachment and being appropriately innervated. The precision with which the mature limb operates may depend partially on adjustments made in the central nervous system while the organism is learning to use its limbs. Although we do not presently know much about these adjustments, a precisely formed morphological pattern is surely prerequisite to them. And to achieve the pattern, we must postulate equally precise mechanisms of developmental correlation.

Cellular Differentiation in the Secondary Growth of Woody Plants

As a final example of cellular differentiation, we shall discuss the genesis of xylem and phloem from the cambium of woody plants. The xylem is produced to the inside of the cambium and the phloem to the outside; these tissues function primarily in conduction. Both tissues are composed of several type of cells, and it is the origin of these from the cambium which will now be considered.

The simultaneous occurrence of cellular differentiation with growth and morphogenetic movements in the animal embryo contrasts with the relative simplicity of its expression in secondary growth. Not only are morphogenetic movements totally absent, but—as in apical growth zones—meristematic activity and cellular differentiation are spatially separated from each other to a major extent. A cell produced by the cambium, after it is committed to either the phloem or xylem, may continue to grow and divide for a few generations; but its progeny finally cease dividing and begin to differentiate.

It will be recalled that there are two types of cambium cells, one of which is a good deal longer than the other. An elongate cell that has been added to the xylem may have one of several fates. If it transforms into a *fiber*, it first elongates to some extent, pushing its ends between neighboring cells as it grows. The occurrence of intrusive elongation is inferred primarily from the fact that mature fibers have a greater length than the cells of the cambium. (Unlike cellular elongation in the shoot or root apex, that accompanying secondary growth does not affect the overall length of the stem or root because it is intrusive.) Elongation is followed by a thickening of the cell wall, which in a fiber cell is sometimes so extreme that the cavity occupied by the cytoplasm is nearly obliterated (Fig. 5-35C). Finally, the cytoplasm in the fiber undergoes dissolution.

A thickening of the cell wall following growth is an important feature in the differentiation of many other plant cells. (The pollen grain is an example already cited.) The cell wall that is laid down in the course of growth is designated as the *primary* wall, and the one that appears after growth has ceased is the *secondary* wall. In fiber cells the secondary wall may attain a thickness ten times or more than that of the primary wall. The fibers undergoing this change in the xylem attain considerable tensile strength, and in the aggregate are major contributors to the mechanical strength of angiosperm wood.

The progeny of the elongate cambial cells also form the vascular cells. The most ubiquitous of these among the angiosperms and

Transverse section

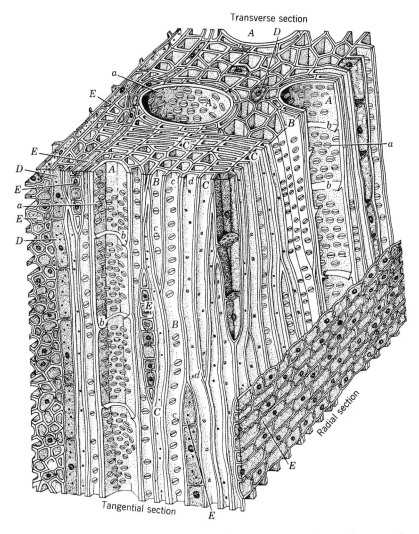

Fig. 5-35. A three-dimensional diagram of the structure of oak wood. *A,* vessels: *a,* pit in vessel walls; *b,* remnants of end walls of vessel elements. *B,* tracheids: *c,* pits in tracheid walls. *C,* wood fibers: *d,* pits in fiber walls. *D,* xylem parenchyma. *E,* vascular rays. (From H. J. Fuller and O. Tippo, *College Botany,* Holt, 1949, p. 216.)

gymnosperms is the *tracheid* (Fig. 5-35 *B*). Like the fiber, the tracheid is the transformation product of a single cell. It begins its differentiation with a period of enlargement that includes a substantial increase in girth, as well as intrusive elongation. It appears in cross sections considerably wider than a fiber. Enlargement is followed by a period

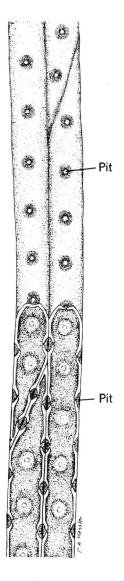

of secondary wall formation and finally by dissolution of the cytoplasm. The resulting thick-walled tubular structure is shaped very much like a pipe with pointed ends.

Some regions of the tracheid cell wall fail to take part in secondary wall formation. Instead, they remain at their initial thickness, and thus take on the appearance of pits in the cell wall (see Figs. 5-35 and 5-36). The arrangement and structure of the pits suggest that they are channels of communication between cells. Neighboring tracheids have their pits exactly adjacent to each other, forming what are termed *pit-pairs*. In addition, the primary cell walls which remain as the limiting membrane of the contiguous pits are abundantly perforated by minute pores providing continuity between the cavities of the adjacent tracheids. The perforations were previously occupied by the *plasmodesmata*—the cytoplasmic connectives that occur between neighboring protoplasts of all of the living cells in the plant.

The second type of vascular element in the xylem is formed by a longitudinal series of cells which transform into a much more extensive structure termed a *vessel*. While individual cells forming the vessel do not elongate like the tracheids and fiber-producing cells, they undergo a considerably greater increase in girth at the outset of their transformation. During the subsequent period of cell wall thickening the end walls between successive cells remain thin and ultimately disappear along with the cytoplasm. In this way the series of cell walls forming a vessel becomes a continuous tube (Fig. 5-35A). Vessels in some species of angiosperms have a diameter of up to a millimeter, and their length may vary from a few centimeters to several meters.

Fig. 5-36. A diagram of tracheids showing the structure of the pit-pairs. (From V. A. Greulach and J. E. Adams, *An Introduction to Modern Botany*, Wiley, 1962, p. 115.)

The walls of the vessels, like those of the tracheids, are pitted—especially when in contact with other vessels. Thus, while vessels are constructed primarily for transport along the length of the stem or root, there is also provision in their structure for lateral transport.

A final point concerning the differentiation of tracheids and vessels is the effects of climatic conditions. Vascular elements formed during good growing conditions have a significantly greater diameter than those produced during marginal conditions. In plants growing where there is an annual climatic cycle, the xylem consists of alternating rings of porous and compact wood, each set of rings representing the xylem added in a single year. A cross section of woody stem provides a cumulative record, expressed in the width of the annual rings, of the growing conditions that have prevailed throughout the life of the plant (Fig. 5-37).

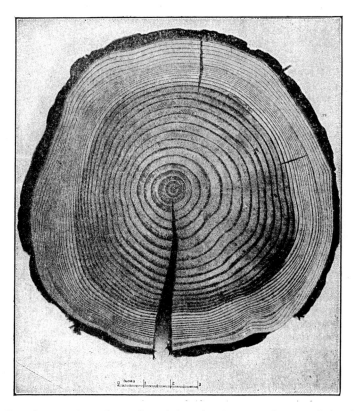

Fig. 5-37. Cross-section of a redwood log showing annual rings, dark-colored heartwood and light-colored sapwood. (From R. M. Holman and W. W. Robbins, *Elements of Botany,* Wiley, 1940, p. 70.)

The last cellular component of xylem to be considered here is the parenchyma tissue. Despite the fact that the vascular cells of the xylem are dead, conduction does not occur in the complete absence of living cells, for the tracheids and vessels in actively conducting wood are always embedded to some degree in living parenchyma. Xylem parenchyma is derived from two sources. It comes in part from the clusters of short cambial cells (the ray initials) described earlier. The parenchyma tissue laid down in both xylem and phloem by the proliferation of these cells has a radial arrangement, like the spokes of a wheel (see Figs. 5-35E, 5-38E, and 5-13c-d). Xylem parenchyma can also be derived from elongate cambium cells which, after being added to the xylem, have divided so as to form a longitudinal row of short cells (Fig. 5-35D). In both cases the parenchyma cells enlarge somewhat during their subsequent differentiation; but they never undergo extensive secondary wall formation, and they retain functional nuclei, cytoplasm and plasmodesmata for a period of years after their addition to the xylem.

Although a functional relationship of the xylem parenchyma to conduction has not been established, the widespread occurrence of parenchyma leaves little doubt that it plays a critical role in the economy of the organism. Before the parenchyma cells die, they secrete a variety of substances—oils, gums, tyloses—that impregnate the cell walls of the xylem and fill the cavities of the cells. The result is the formation of the heartwood, which, in commercial lumber, is much more resistant to decay than the sapwood which surrounds it (see Fig. 5-37).

Phloem is formed by the differentiation of the progeny of cambium cells, much as the xylem is formed. Fibers, parenchyma tissue, and conducting cells are all differentiated in the phloem; and in angiosperms, the vascular elements may be produced either from individual cells or by the cooperative action of a longitudinal series of cells.

The vascular components of phloem, like those of xylem, are derived from elongate cells that undergo further enlargement early in their differentiation. Although the secondary thickening of the cell wall is not as great as in the tracheids and vessels, pits are nevertheless formed at an early stage of differentiation. The perforations in the primary wall of one or several neighboring pits become greatly enlarged in subsequent stages of differentiation, and the walls of each perforation become lined with a poorly defined substance called *callose*. The resemblance of the perforations to the pores of a sieve has led to the designation of these cells as *sieve cells*, and the appropriate regions of the wall as sieve areas (Fig. 5-38H). The sieve

Transverse section

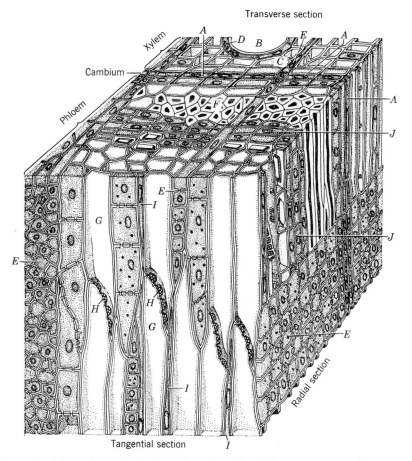

Tangential section

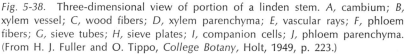

Fig. 5-38. Three-dimensional view of portion of a linden stem. *A*, cambium; *B*, xylem vessel; *C*, wood fibers; *D*, xylem parenchyma; *E*, vascular rays; *F*, phloem fibers; *G*, sieve tubes; *H*, sieve plates; *I*, companion cells; *J*, phloem parenchyma. (From H. J. Fuller and O. Tippo, *College Botany*, Holt, 1949, p. 223.)

areas may be generally distributed along the walls of a cell, wherever it is in contact with other sieve cells. In species where a longitudinal series of cells form a sieve tube analogous to the vessels of xylem, the sieve areas tend to be limited to the end walls between successive elements.

An additional point of contrast with the differentiation of xylem is that the vascular cells of the phloem retain their cytoplasm at the conclusion of differentiation. In the final stages of the transformation the nucleus disintegrates and the central vacuole becomes greatly enlarged. A thin layer of cytoplasm containing large amounts of what has been described as "slime" remains around the periphery of the cell and in the perforations of the sieve areas. The conduction of sugars, amino acids, and additional synthetic products thus occurs through living cytoplasm rather than through a tube formed only of the residual walls of dead cells. The anucleate cell with its vacuole and cytoplasm appears to remain otherwise intact for the duration of its life as an actively conducting vascular element (Chap. 6, p. 236).

As in the conducting elements of the xylem, sieve cells and sieve tubes are associated with parenchyma tissue. In certain angiosperms some of the parenchyma cells have such a close association with the sieve elements that they are regarded as *companion cells* (Fig. 5-38*I*). The association arises when a new phloem cell undergoes its final mitotic division and one of the two progeny commences its enlargement and differentiation into a sieve element. Its neighboring sister cell may undergo several additional divisions, forming a series of shorter cells lying adjacent to the elongate sieve element. The companion cells do not enlarge as much as the sieve element, and they are readily recognized in cross section as small nucleate cells with numerous plasmodesmata connecting them to their vascular sibling.

After one to several years the sieve cells and the accompanying parenchyma die. Unlike the xylem, which is trapped within the root or stem as a perpetual record of its growth, the eventual fate of the phloem is to peel off the surface as bark. It is easy to understand on mechanical grounds that this would be the fate of any tissue that lies outside the vascular cambium and has lost its capacity to grow in pace with the increasing volume of the secondary xylem and phloem. But some of the peripheral tissues do keep pace for a while. The epidermal and cortical tissues initially laid down in the primary root and stem may continue to increase their girth for as much as a year or more in some woody plants before they finally die and are sloughed off by the expanding secondary tissues. In woody plants there may also be a *cork cambium*, which arises periodically in the outer tissue of the stem—in the cortex at the outset and in the nucleated parenchyma cells of the phloem after the cortex has disappeared (see Fig. 5-13*c-d*).

The cork cambium is a layer of meristematic tissue which produces an insulating layer of cork cells surrounding the stem. (It was the structure of this material that led Robert Hooke to coin the term *cell*.) Because of its location, a given layer of cork cambium becomes increasingly separated from the functional vascular system by the accumulation of secondary phloem. As a consequence, it eventually dies and is replaced by a new layer of cork cambium formed by the resumption of meristematic activity in phloem parenchyma cells lying closer to the vascular cambium. The bark that peels off of the trunk of a tree may thus consist exclusively of phloem tissue or of a combination of phloem and cork. In some trees, as in the cork oak, the cork cambium is so prolific that the bark is composed almost exclusively of cork cells.

Finally, it should be noted that vascular, fibrous, and parenchyma cells such as those produced by the cambium can also arise, along with additional types of cells, in other places in the plant. They are generated along with *epidermal* and *collenchyma* cells (parenchyma-like cells with stiffened walls) at zones of differentiation in the shoot and root apices. In the developing leaf primordia they are formed along with leaf parenchyma cells containing chlorophyll and the epidermis with its stomata and guard cells. Wherever meristematic activity provides a source of cells, there appear to be mechanisms that assure that the components of xylem and phloem will differentiate and that their differentiation will occur in the appropriate spatial pattern.

THE CONTROL OF DIFFERENTIATION

As a first step in analyzing the origins of spatial precision in the development of multicellular organisms, it is necessary to explore the factors which govern the quality of cellular differentiation. How does it happen that a vascular cell produced on the outer side of the cambium becomes a sieve element, while one on the inner side becomes a tracheid? What determines whether a particular somite cell will become muscle, cartilage, or one of the components of connective tissue?

Broadly speaking, there are two categories of factors that can bias the quality of differentiation. On the one hand, we can assume that differentiation of cells is influenced by factors in their environment —factors sufficiently restricted in their distribution so that all cells are not equally exposed to them. On the other, it is reasonable to expect that the quality of differentiation can be controlled by intracellular factors that were unequally distributed during earlier cell divisions.

Applying these alternatives to a specific case, we wonder about the origins of the difference between a sieve cell and its sister that will give rise to companion cells. Is the difference between these two cells the consequence of a qualitatively unequal cell division, or is it induced by environmental factors that are so localized that the two cells are unequally exposed to them? Or is it possible that both types of mechanism are employed? While an answer cannot be offered for this particular case, both types of mechanisms have been found to operate in the development of multicellular organisms.

The cytoplasm of an unfertilized egg in an animal exhibits a number of inhomogeneities. This is illustrated by the eggs of many aquatic animals. The nucleus frequently lies near one side, the *animal* pole of the egg, while the heavier yolk settles toward the opposite *vegetal* pole. In many instances there are also obvious differences in pigmentation at the surface of the egg. The animal hemisphere of a frog's egg, for instance, is heavily pigmented with melanin granules which lie in the superficial cytoplasm or *cortex* of the egg, while the cortex of the vegetal hemisphere may be nearly free of such granules.

As cleavage occurs, differences such as these become segregated from each other by cell membranes, and even in the blastula they retain their same relative positions. A nucleus, of course, is present in every cell; but the cytoplasm of the cells in the animal hemisphere of a frog's egg tends to be relatively free of yolk, while the vegetal cells are laden with yolk and are consequently a good deal larger than animal hemisphere cells. The reverse distribution for melanin pigmentation is also maintained. With the onset of gastrulation the positions of these cells change drastically. In many groups of animals the yolk-free cells of the animal pole become the ectoderm, the cells near the vegetal pole become the endoderm, and those with intermediate characteristic around the equator of the blastula become mesoderm.

That the overt differences along the animal-vegetal axis of the egg are paralleled by meaningful differences for differentiation has been demonstrated in many kinds of eggs. The eggs of a sea urchin have been particularly revealing. Here the first two cleavages are meridional, yielding four cells that extend all the way from the animal pole to the vegetal pole. Hans Driesch demonstrated in 1891 that if these four cells are separated from each other, each can continue to develop into a reasonably normal sea urchin larva, although each, of course, has only one fourth the volume of an embryo developing from an intact egg (Fig. 5-39). The third cleavage, however, is equatorial. If the eight cells resulting from this cleavage are isolated from each other, their subsequent development is quite abnormal. In order to avoid the criticism that one eighth of the mass of the egg is too little to support normal development, the experiment can also be done by simply dividing the eight-cell system into two groups of four cells, one group from the animal half and the other from the vegetal half. The groups of cells from the vegetal half of the egg develop into embryos with very little ectoderm, while those from the animal half

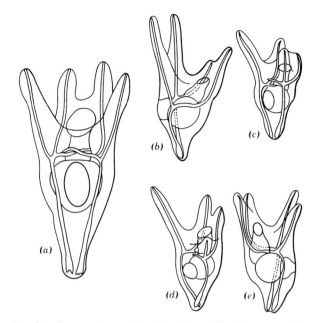

Fig. 5-39. Results of separation of the first four cells of a sea urchin's egg. *(a)* Normal larva. *(b)—(e)* Larvae of normal structure but diminished size, each developed from one of the cells of the four-cell stage. (From S. Horstadius and A. Wolsky, 1936, in B. I. Balinsky, *An Introduction to Embryology,* Saunders, 1960, p. 89.)

are deficient in endoderm. It is thus apparent that a significant differentiation has occurred along the animal-vegetal axis of the egg, even by the time of the third cleavage.

There is a good deal of variability among other animals in the results of separating the products of the first two meridional cleavages; in some cases even these show signs of differentiation. But the isolated products of the equatorial cleavage, if they can successfully continue their development, usually yield partial embryos. There seems to be little doubt that the earliest stages of differentiation in animal eggs entail a parceling out by cell divisions of cytoplasmic differences already established in the uncleaved egg.

That these differences are in fact cytoplasmic rather than the consequence of unequal nuclear divisions is suggested by experiments in which the distribution of nuclei has been disturbed. Although such experiments have been performed on a variety of animal eggs during the last sixty years (see review by L. Barth cited in the list of additional references), recent experiments with frog's eggs have been among the most decisive. The unfertilized egg is activated to develop parthenogenetically by puncturing it with a needle. The meiotic spindle, which then appears at the surface of the egg in preparation for first polar body formation, is removed with all the associated chromosomes, thus leaving the egg without a nucleus. It is then possible to inject through a fine glass needle one of the nuclei obtained from an egg that has already undergone cleavage. As the cells become smaller in the course of the cleavages, it becomes increasingly difficult to obtain a nucleus for microinjection without damaging it. Nevertheless, a large proportion of the nuclei taken from a blastula and from even more advanced stages will initiate mitosis when injected into an enucleated egg. Most of the eggs that successfully initiate cleavage after being injected with a blastula nucleus then proceed to develop into tadpoles that appear to be completely normal. [A different result may be obtained with gastrula nuclei, but this does not affect the present argument.]

Since nuclei from both animal and vegetal regions of the blastula behave in the same fashion, either they are functionally equivalent (and thus undifferentiated) or they quickly lose whatever specializations they may have previously achieved on introduction into the cytoplasm of the uncleaved egg. In either case, when these results are added to the fact that isolated blastomeres develop in very different ways and that these differences are often correlated with visible cytoplasmic gradients, it is apparent that the cytoplasm is the primary site of the differentiations parceled out during the early cleavages of an animal egg.

Turning now to the second category of factors controlling differentiation, the most clearly understood instances where factors external to the cell influence the quality of its differentiation come from experiments entailing surgical transplantations between animal embryos. The cases cited are examples of embryonic induction—alteration in the developmental history of cells in an embryo which are elicited by neighboring cells of another kind or history.

In the early stages of formation of the vertebrate eye (p. 170), the optic vesicle, an outpocketing that arises on each side of the neural tube, bulges laterally until it has contacted the overlying epidermis. The contacted epidermal cells promptly undergo a change in structure. At first they form a plate of cells that is distinctly thicker than the surrounding epidermis (Fig. 5-31). When the optic vesicle folds inward to form the optic cup, the plate of cells bends inward and separates from the epidermis in the form of a small, hollow sphere, the *lens vesicle*. The epidermis spreads and fuses to cover the surface from which the lens vesicle detached itself. The lens vesicle subsequently grows considerably and transforms into a transparent, refractile structure, which assists in focusing light on the retina.

Various experiments have revealed that some event occurring during the contact of the epidermis with the optic vesicle is responsible for the initiation of lens formation. One of the conclusive experiments was performed by Warren H. Lewis in 1905. It consisted of cutting the epidermis over the optic vesicle of a frog embryo so that it could be opened as a hinged flap before the two structures came into contact with each other (Fig. 5-40). Through the opening, Lewis inserted glass needles with which he cut the connection between the optic vesicle and the brain. The loosened optic vesicle was then pushed posteriorly between the epidermis and the mesoderm until it lay in the trunk region of the embryo. Finally, the flap of epidermis was laid back in place and allowed to heal with the surrounding epidermis.

There were two significant alterations in the development of embryos that had been treated in this fashion. In all cases in which the optic vesicle was completely removed from the head, the epidermis that would otherwise have been contacted by the optic vesicle failed to form a lens. This failure could not be attributed to surgical trauma, for a normal lens was frequently formed when all steps of the operation were performed *except* for the removal of the detached optic vesicle from its normal site in the head. Such results suggested that the formation of a lens from the epidermis is dependent upon proximity of the optic vesicle.

This suggestion was strongly reinforced by events which occurred in association with the dislocated optic vesicle in the trunk region. Here the optic vesicle continued its development to form an optic cup and a rudimentary eye—which, however, lacked a neural connection with the brain. When the optic cup was oriented so that

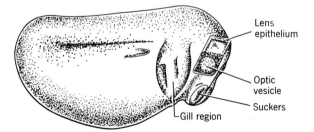

Fig. 5-40.   Exposure of the optic vesicle in a frog embryo. (From V. Hamburger, *A Manual of Experimental Embryology,* Univ. Chicago, 1942, p. 105.)

188 THE BIOLOGY OF ORGANISMS

its outer surface contacted the overlying epidermis, the cells in the latter layer formed a lens in a way not obviously different from normal lens formation in the head. These experiments proved unequivocally that the epidermis is stimulated to form a lens when brought into close association with the optic vesicle.

It was found later that in other species lens formation by the epidermis depends on association with the optic vesicle to differing degrees and that it also depends on such environmental factors as temperature. For instance, an incomplete lens may be formed in the absence of an optic vesicle. Nevertheless, the validity of Lewis' demonstration of what has been termed *embryonic induction* cannot be challenged. Developmental integrating mechanisms of the same general sort have now been demonstrated in many other instances in which an organ is formed by the cooperative action of cells from two different sources.

A more renowned case of embryonic induction was revealed by Spemann and Mangold in Germany about fifteen years after Lewis' experiments. The process here occurs during the formation of the gastrula. From the surface of an early amphibian gastrula Spemann and Mangold excised a block of cells that would shortly be expected to sink beneath the surface and form the dorsal part of the mesoderm —specifically, the notochord and the adjacent parts of the somites. The region where the prospective dorsal mesoderm is actually in the process of turning from the surface into the interior of the gastrula is termed the *dorsal lip* of the blastopore (Fig. 5-41).

The dorsal lip was transplanted by Spemann and Mangold to another early gastrula into the region that would be expected to form the ventral side of the embryo. In its new position it sank beneath the surface just as it would have in its site of origin. The surprising result was that the embryos that developed from this combination of graft and host exhibited varying degrees of twinning. They usually had two trunk regions, and frequently had two heads or two tails. In extreme cases they were two nearly complete embryos fused together by their ventral sides. Microscopic sections of such embryos revealed two notochords, two sets of somites, other mesodermal structures, and two neural tubes. One set of these structures, of course, could be interpreted as that which would normally have been produced by the host. The secondary set, however, consisted of dorsal structures that had been produced in association with the graft on the ventral side of the host.

Either of two interpretations could explain this result. One would be that the graft itself formed the secondary embryonic structures in

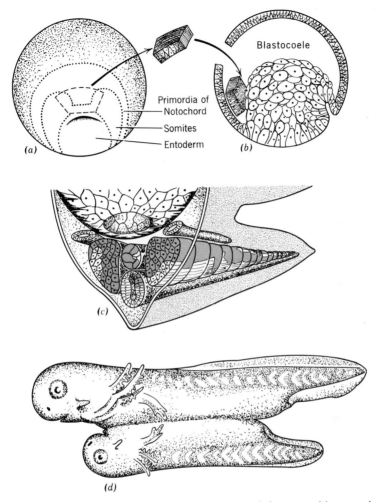

Blastocoele

Primordia of
—Notochord

—Somites

—Entoderm

(a)

(b)

(c)

(d)

Fig. 5-41. Diagram of the transplantation of a piece of the upper blastoporal lip into another gastrula *(a, b)* and the differentiation of the graft and associated tissues *(c, d)*. In *(c)* the tissues derived from the graft are shown in black, and the induced tissues in white. (From J. Holtfreter and V. Hamburger, in *Analysis of Development,* B. Willier, P. Weiss, and V. Hamburger, eds.) Saunders, 1955, p. 244.)

their entirety. The other would be that the graft formed some of the secondary structures, but that the adjacent tissues of the host were induced to form others. One of the essential features of Spemann and Mangold's experiments was that the graft came from a species whose cells were distinguishable by their color from the cells of the host. They observed that in the secondary embryo the notochord and adjacent regions of the somites were composed of grafted cells, and that sometimes cells from the graft were visible in the neural tube. But most of the neural tube and the lateral regions of the mesoderm were composed of cells contributed by the host. The underlying endoderm of the host had even folded upward to form a tubular gut. The cells of the host that surrounded the graft, therefore, must have been induced to cooperate with it in the formation of structures which they would otherwise never have formed. This experiment strongly indicates the presence of spatial integrating mechanisms whose function is to assure that in the normal embryo the notochord will lie in the center of the dorsal embryonic axis, with the neural tube lying directly over it, the digestive tube directly under it, and the somites on either side.

Transplantation experiments have thus demonstrated that the development of groups of cells can be profoundly altered by changing the identity of the cells with which they normally associate in the embryo. Considering the physical character of the problem, there are three ways in which a cell might influence its brethren. One would entail the secretion of substances analogous to hormones which can circulate in the organism and thus come in contact with other cells. But it is necessary to rule this device out as a significant agent of spatial coordination, because freely diffusing substances are simply too widespread. At the opposite extreme would be direct contact between cells, with the possibility that either contact *per se,* or the direct transfer of an "inducing agent" from one cell to the other, is the critical step in induction. Here, of course, all of the requirements of spatial integration are met. It is interesting to note that in plant cells, presuming that inductive interactions do in fact occur, the absence of intercellular spaces and the presence of plasmodesmata make this the only likely mode of communication between cells.

In the animal embryo a third possibility exists. While the interacting cells may be in close association, they need not actually contact each other. Instead, they may simply be close enough so that the inducing cells can in some manner alter the local environment of the responding cells. Close association without contact appears to be a sufficient condition for induction in several carefully analyzed cases in which filters of varying thickness and porosity have been inserted between inducing and responding cells.

An avenue of contemporary investigation into the mechanism of inductive interactions has been to establish culture systems that provide a suitable environment for the differentiation of small fragments of the embryo. In such simplified systems it is possible to control the cellular, chemical, and physical environment of a developing organ with a good deal of precision. There are thus good grounds for hoping that a textbook written ten or fifteen years from now may be able to include some definitive statements about the material basis of induction.

PATTERNING

From the fact that there is precision in the anatomy of the mature organism, it follows that there must be at least an equal degree of spatial precision in the mechanisms that control growth and differentiation. The discussion of the control of differentiation is concluded here with some observations on this problem, which we will refer to as the patterning of development.

Up to a point, the organism can rely on external cues to orient its growth and differentiation. This is the likely mechanism, for instance, for determining the direction of germination of many plant spores and zygotes. A classical example is the egg of the brown alga, *Fucus,* whose first visible differentiation entails the formation of a protuberance on one side (Fig. 5-42). Then the egg divides into two daughters. One of these contains the protuberance, which continues to elongate, forming the holdfast that will anchor the plant to the rocks. The other cell gives rise to the cells that will form the erect parts of the plant. It can be shown that the point at which holdfast formation will initiate is determined by asymmetric environmental conditions, the foremost of which is the direction of illumination. The holdfast grows out of the unilluminated side of the egg, while the illuminated side will form the erect parts of the plant. It is quite possible that external factors are responsible for orienting the initial differentiations of other reproductive cells, including the animal-vegetal differentiation of animal eggs. In these cases, of course, it is not the external environment but the ovarian environment that has a direct influence. These effects are especially likely in organisms such as the insects and the flowering plants in which the earliest differentiations within the reproductive cells have a consistent orientation with relation to the structure of the ovary. In the insect egg, for instance, the anterior-posterior axis of the embryo always parallels that of the ovary in which the egg was formed.

We could readily imagine that the external environment continues to participate in patterning the organism during its later development. Both light and gravity play key roles in orienting the growth of stems

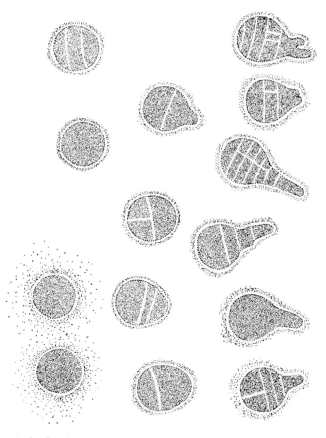

Fig. 5-42. Early development of *Fucus* eggs as figured by Thuret in 1854. Eggs surrounded by sperm in the lower left; rhizoid formation in the right-hand column. Subdivision into cells is seen in most of the eggs. (From G. Thuret, *Annales des Sciences Naturelles,* IV, 1854, Pl. 14.)

and roots (p. 259), although there is no substantial evidence that they control the locus of differentiation of specific cell types.

The external environment is also a patterning factor in the animal embryo; during morphogenetic movements prospective epidermal cells always take up a position at the surface of the embryo, while neural, mesodermal, and endodermal cells always move into the interior. But many of the cues controlling the location, the rate of growth, and the differentiation of cells during the later development of animals appear to be provided instead by interactions with neighboring cells, as we saw in the case of embryonic induction. A very real problem, then, faces us in understanding how a set of embryonic inductions can be organized, temporally and spatially, to guide the transformation of a mass of embryonic cells into the precise and intricate anatomy of an adult.

Perhaps the most helpful observation here is that complexity is built up gradually rather than appearing all at once. Thus the initial differences which have resulted either from asymmetric environmental cues or from unequal cell divisions can themselves serve as the emitters of cues for the patterning of subsequent differentiations. An instance of this has already been explored with lens induction. The optic vesicle is a structure whose formation by the ectoderm was elicited as a part of the response to neural induction during gastrulation. Once having been formed, however, it governs in turn the site at which still another region of the ectoderm will produce a lens. Thus the definitive anatomy of the organism is built up gradually during the period of development, under the guidance of a progressive sequence of inductions.

But there are also many parts of the embryo that exhibit some degree of autonomy in their development shortly after they have been formed—an autonomy such as that exhibited by the egg itself at an earlier stage of development. An example is the limb bud of a vertebrate which, as we have seen, consists of a cap of epidermis lying over an accumulation of mesenchyme cells derived from the lateral plate mesoderm (p. 174). The development of the limb bud is influenced to some degree, of course, by the rest of the embryo, as seems likely simply on the grounds that it always forms where a limb should be formed, and that the anterior, posterior, dorsal, and ventral sides of the resulting limb always coincide with those of the rest of the embryo. (There are also experimental confirmations of this proposal that we need not pursue here.)

Beyond these limitations, however, the limb bud exercises a significant degree of autonomy in patterning its own differentiation—in determining, for instance, where mesenchyme cells will condense to form the cartilaginous precursors of bones, where muscles will be formed, and where joints and digits will be positioned. This can be demonstrated by transplanting the early limb bud to other regions of the embryo where limbs normally do not form, or by explanting it to a culture medium. In these completely foreign circumstances, which could not be expected to provide normal patterning influences, the bud will nevertheless continue along a reasonably normal course of development. At the stage of development when transplantations yield these results, there is very little visible organization and differentiation within the limb bud beyond the distinction between epidermis and mesenchyme. The primitive organization of the limb bud is further illustrated by the fact that it can be divided into two parts; each of these in a suitable physical and nutrient environment will form a complete limb rather than a half limb. Or two limb buds may be fused with each other, and if their axes of orientation coincide they will form a single limb rather than two. Despite the lack of apparent differentiation, however, the early limb bud has already incorporated into its structure the necessary organization enabling it to develop into an appropriately oriented limb in the absence of additional patterning stimuli from surrounding tissues.

The development of the animal embryo seems mainly to consist of the progressive subdivision of the individual into more and more restricted areas, such as the limb bud, whose initial location and orientation are established by interactions with surrounding tissues but which then derive a certain amount of autonomy. A variety of terms have been proposed to designate this phenomenon. The regions of an embryo that are able to pattern themselves in the absence of additional external stimuli have been termed *fields*, and the process of self-organization that they undergo has been called *individuation*. These terms are readily abused, however, and we must be wary of using them as anything more than convenient words for designating experimentally demonstrated phenomena.

HEREDITY AND DEVELOPMENT

One of the basic observations that gave impetus to the study of heredity is that reproductive cells develop into reasonable facsimiles of the parent organism at comparable stages in its life history. Analysis of the inheritance of mutations has demonstrated that many aspects of the hereditary information which influences the specific configuration of development are incorporated in the structure of the chromosomes. Given the same cytoplasm, the same environmental conditions, and the same complement of other nuclear genes, the presence of a mutation results in a modification of the outcome of development. Indeed, it is the developmental effects of a mutation which give an indication of its presence.

The effects of a mutation in a developing system form a manifold problem that varies in character with the level of organization at which they are examined. An example is provided by the action of the human gene that causes the hereditary disease, sickle-cell anemia. At the level of the protein this gene varies from its alleles in causing a different amino acid sequence in the protein hemoglobin, different by only a single amino acid. In the heterozygous condition the erythrocyte contains a mixture of normal and sickle-cell hemoglobin. In the homozygous condition, which usually results in death, all of the hemoglobin is of the sickle-cell variety.

At the cell level of organization the gene affects the structure of the erythrocyte. This results from the fact that sickle-cell hemoglobin in the unoxygenated condition tends to form crystals, whereas normal hemoglobin remains in solution within the erythrocyte. The formation of crystals causes the distortion in shape of the erythrocyte, which has led to the name of the disease. At the whole-organism level the gene has several effects. One of these is a sharply reduced vigor, especially in homozygous individuals, resulting from the fact that sickle-cell hemoglobin is a less efficient carrier of oxygen. In addition, there is a less readily explained effect. Heterozygous individuals are more resistant to infection by the protozoan parasite which causes malaria.

It is now generally presumed that the cell and organism level effects of this and every other gene are exerted exclusively through the specific sequences of amino acids in the proteins whose synthesis they govern. A protein such as hemoglobin is a key constituent of the human body, and it is easy to imagine that a slight modification of its structure might have many unforeseen consequences at the higher levels of organization.

Although the sickle-cell gene has no obvious morphogenetic effects beyond the distortion of the erythrocyte, it is one of the few genes whose effects are well enough known at all three levels of organization so that contrasts can be made. There are many other morphogenetic genes, such as those causing extra digits and other morphological abnormalities, and the genes that affect the growth rates of organisms. Many genes have multiple effects on the morphology of the organism. For instance, there is a gene occurring in rats, which in the homozygous condition leads to a hypertrophy of many cartilaginous structures. The cartilages that line the nasal passages and the trachea (the air tube from the pharynx to the lungs) and those forming the ribs become excessively thick. One of the many consequences of these deformities is an impairment of breathing, which is usually lethal. The phenomenon has not been explained at the cell level, and is even more obscure at the molecular level of analysis. If the present concepts of genetics prove to be applicable to such cases, however, the diffuse and multiple effects of the mutant will all prove to be the consequence of an unusual form of a protein which has a key function or structural position in cartilage cells.

Another approach to development through genetics concerns, rather than differences between organisms that vary in their genotype, differences between cells that, in a single organism, have embarked on alternate courses of differentiation. Cells that have differentiated along different pathways—such as an erythrocyte and a muscle cell—contain some very different proteins. Both of these cells are mitotically derived from a common ancestor (which existed at an earlier cleavage stage). It is therefore reasonable to suppose that they have had, at least in their recent lineage, a common set of genes. But something has happened in the intervening time that has led to an excessive synthesis of hemoglobin in one case and of actin and myosin in the other. In short, it can be supposed that a different set of genes has been allowed to manifest itself in each case.

Not all cases of cellular differentiation fit obviously into this scheme. One of the differences between a tracheid and a fiber in xylem appears to depend on the diameter of the cell when secondary cell wall formation commences, and this in turn is a matter of the size attained by the central vacuole. Although this does not eliminate some fundamental difference at the level of protein synthesis, it emphasizes the fact that there are still many unanswered questions concerning the relations between genes and cellular differentiation. Nevertheless, enough cases are known of qualitative differences between the proteins of different cell types so that we must consider the manipulation of synthetic activities as a frequent and perhaps even a general characteristic of cellular differentiation.

That the factors which control differentiation do so by permitting certain genes to manifest themselves while suppressing the action of others has been confirmed in recent years by studies of the chromosomes in several groups of flies. These insects do most of their growing as larvae and then undergo metamorphosis—first into a pupa and then into an adult fly. An unusual feature of their larval growth is that many tissues grow exclusively by an increase in the size of cells that were produced by mitosis in the embryo. In the course of their growth the chromosomes in these cells duplicate many successive times, but in the absence of mitosis the duplicated strands are never separated from each other. Consequently, highly polytene chromosomes arise which consist of many parallel strands of DNA with some associated RNA and protein. Such chromosomes are uniquely visible with ordinary microscopic observation of cells which are not in the process of mitosis. These chromosomes have a banded appearance, and it has been shown in *Drosophila* and several other species of flies that genes can be localized with reference to the bands (Stern and Nanney, Chap. 19).

An interesting feature of the polytene chromosomes is that they often exhibit swellings or "puffs" at discrete points along their length. In every cell of a particular type at a particular stage of development the same points on the chromosome are in the swollen condition. In the course of development, however, some puffs may disappear and new ones arise. In different types of cells—mid-gut and salivary gland cells, for instance—completely different sequences of puffing patterns occur.

Based on such observations, it has been proposed that puffing is a morphological manifestation of the synthetic activities associated with a gene at that particular locus on the chromosome. According to this interpretation, the lack of similarity of puffing patterns between salivary and mid-gut chromosomes reflects the fact that different genes operate in cells that have taken alternate pathways of differentiation. Evidence in favor of this interpretation has been obtained from studies of a mutation that affects the salivary secretions of the fly, *Chironomus*. Located at the base of each salivary gland is a cluster of four cells that secrete a granular material into the saliva. Prior to secretion the granular component is visible in the form of droplets in the cytoplasm of these cells. In one species of *Chironomus* the four basal cells fail to synthesize the granules in detectable amounts. Analysis of the chromosomes has indicated that a puff normally present in the basal cells of species that produce the protein is absent from the chromosomes of the deficient species (Fig. 5-43). Furthermore, chromosomal mapping experiments (involving hybrids between one species which does and another which does not produce the protein secretion) have demonstrated that a gene governing the formation of the granules by the four basal salivary cells is indeed located in the region in which the correlated puff occurs.

This combination of observations makes it very likely that puffing is indeed a manifestation of gene action, and thus confirms the more general proposal that an important aspect of differentiation is a chromosomal response to developmental control mechanisms residing either in the extracellular environment (in the case of induction) or in the cytoplasm (in the case of differential cell divisions).

In concluding, we wish to explore two different aspects of the relationship between structural specificity at the molecular level and at the organismic level. The first of these comes directly out of the analysis of puffs just described. It is clear, at least to a first approximation, that the multicellular organism is a clone of genetically similar cells which are mitotically descended from a single celled zygote or spore. When the cells comprising a complex organism differentiate into a hundred types, each performing a set of metabolic spe-

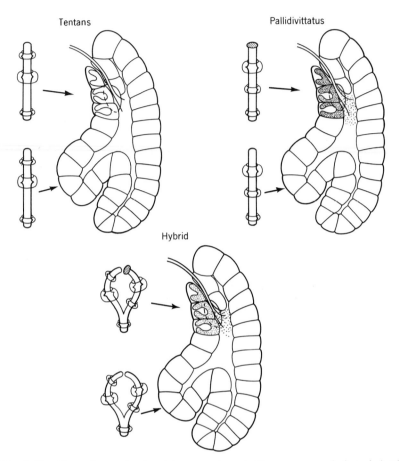

Fig. 5-43. The salivary glands of two species of *Chironomus* and their hybrid. The puffing pattern of the polytene fourth chromosome is indicated adjacent to each cell type. (From W. Beerman, in *American Zoologist,* **3,** no. 1, p. 29 (1963).)

cialties, the total informational load in the genome is enormously multiplied relative to that of a microorganism; each cell must contain all the information necessary for itself *and all other differentiated cell types as well.* Since it is engaged in only a small fraction of the total *special* biochemical syntheses of the whole organism, it requires very selective nuclear controls to insure that the appropriate loci are active and that a host of inappropriate ones are turned off. In addition, complex multicellular organisms have a developmental history that is critically dependent on cellular interaction and hence on the development of special sensitivities at particular times. So the control of the activities of genetic loci must be temporally as well as spatially precise. The microorganism has thus far been the crucial participant in the exciting new revelations about how genes act; though bacteria surely exhibit some repression mechanisms, it may take a metazoan or metaphytan cell to give us a full understanding of the ways in which genes may be controlled.

The second point involves a contrast between the way in which structural specificity is achieved at the molecular and organismic levels. The multicellular organism is a precisely ordered array of differentiated cells, just as the protein molecule is a precisely ordered array of different amino acids. Yet there is a fundamental difference in the mechanism of assembly of the two arrays. We now know that the synthesis of a specific protein consists of arranging chemically different amino acids on a template, following which they are bonded together. In sharp contrast, spatial precision in the organism often results from the differentiation of previously similar cells according to the location in which they already find themselves. Very clearly, the organizational strategies at the molecular level need not be imitated by those at the organism level, even though the same sort of genetic information must direct some aspects of the development of both.

6

Metabolism of Multicellular Organisms

In the 1930's it became possible for the first time to trace the biochemical fates of molecules after they had been taken into an organism. This method (as explained in Stern and Nanney) depended on the discovery that isotopes substituted into metabolically important compounds could act as tracers of the fate of those compounds in the organism. When various tissues taken from animals fed on such compounds were chemically fractionated, it was easy to show that the compounds had been moved around a good deal—that they had been broken down and recombined, often in a startlingly short time.

These early demonstrations convinced biologists that organisms and their parts were very much less static objects than they had previously thought them to be. It was realized that even the cells that preserve a constant form throughout life, like nerve or muscle cells, totally reconstitute most of their components from new molecules many times during their existence. Complex molecules are constantly being broken down into basic molecular units, and "pools" of these units exchange with all of the supposedly permanent structural elements of the organism. This "dynamic state of body constituents," as it was called by one of the pioneers in tracer measurement, extends even to simple molecules, where the supposedly unitary amino acids are found to exchange atoms and small chemical groups.

Therefore we cannot look upon the organism as something permanent in the sense that a crystalline structure (like a rock, or glass, or metal) is permanent. Instead, in December the organism may have a composition entirely different from the composition it had in May; it

200

has, like a whirlpool or an eddy in a stream, only the permanence of outline. The living organism is a vortex through which materials are being rotated at a fantastic rate.

As a first approximation this activity can be analyzed by measuring the influx and outflow of matter and energy. This is precisely what Lavoisier did in the 18th century by inserting a sugar-fed guinea pig into a calorimeter and measuring its heat and gas exchange. He demonstrated that the combustion of a mole of sugar by an animal yields the same amount of heat and carbon dioxide and requires the same amount of oxygen as when a mole of sugar is burned in a flame.

Metabolic mechanisms are of course one of the major concerns of cell biology, but at the organism level there is a set of problems unique to the multicellular state which require additional attention. In part these arise from the fact that organisms are differentiated systems with their different parts having different and interacting metabolisms; in other words, there is a significant amount of "cross-feeding" between the various kinds of cells and tissues. In addition one of the consequences of the large size attained by many multicellular organisms is its effect on the efficiency of exchange with the environment. How does the organism provide for the necessary exchange of matter and energy between the environment and a cell buried in the midst of its tissues? The latter in particular will be examined in considerable detail.

At the outset we will consider the problem of measuring the overall metabolism of the whole organism, for this is perhaps the most convenient indication of the demands it makes on its environment—of the material and energy requirements that must be satisfied in the course of its maintenance, development, and reproduction.

THE METABOLISM OF THE WHOLE ORGANISM

The problem of measuring metabolism in intact organisms meets with an uncomfortable array of technical difficulties. The first of these has to do with what the experimenter shall choose to measure. Among heterotrophic plants and animals the component cells may exhibit aerobic or anaerobic metabolism; thus the total metabolism is often a blend of both kinds. The simple (and most frequently used) method, that of measuring *oxygen consumption*, may lead to false conclusions. In photoautotrophic green plants the problem is even worse: the process of photosynthesis (which *utilizes* carbon dioxide and *produces* oxygen) is proceeding simultaneously with—and supplying the chemical starting materials for—energy-yielding metabolism. Since the latter, if it is aerobic, utilizes oxygen and produces carbon dioxide, one must halt photosynthesis or measure it independently in order to obtain a measurement of oxygen consumption.

Whole-organism metabolism must also be measured in a "closed system," in which the temperature, available atmosphere, products of metabolism, and food supplied are kept constant (or at least regulated). This is often technically difficult: a clever zoologist once solved the problem for an elephant—a rather small elephant—but no one has been quite enterprising enough to try it with an oak tree. Many measurements of this kind have been made on *parts* of organisms; but there is no guarantee that the parts are alike. In most cases, in fact, it is certain that they are not.

The methods used in determining over-all metabolism all involve the measurement of oxygen consumption, carbon dioxide production, or both, in a closed system. When oxygen consumption is to be measured, the organism is placed in a closed vessel containing an absorbent for carbon dioxide; thus the total change in volume of the system is due to oxygen uptake, which is measured with a manometric device, usually suspended in a constant-temperature bath. Many modifications of this basic apparatus have been devised to work with very small organisms or single cells, or to absorb oxygen and measure carbon dioxide output, etc. When plant material is used, paired measurements are usually made in light and in darkness; in a dark vessel, of course, respiratory metabolism may be measured without the occurrence of photosynthesis.

The results from a huge number of experiments reveal some generalities about the metabolism of whole organisms. The first of these is hardly a surprise: the most important determinant of metabolic rate (usually expressed as amount of oxygen consumed *per unit wet weight of tissue per hour*) is the level of growth or some other activity. Flying insects metabolize at a higher rate than sitting ones, for example; and with higher plants, which (as we have already pointed out) are in a kind of "permanently growing" state, the level of metabolism is proportional to the percentage of the total plant tissue engaged in active elongation. Embryonic plants respire much faster than do more mature ones.

In higher animals dramatic differences exist in metabolic rate between those animals (poikilotherms) whose temperature fluctuates with that of the environment, and those animals who expend energy to maintain a constant temperature (homoiotherms—the mammals and birds). Obviously, a significant additional metabolic "load" is assumed

with the heating function, and homoiothermic animals have much
higher metabolic rates than cold-blooded ones. For birds or mammals
a rigorous correlation exists between size and metabolic rate. In
general (see Fig. 6-1), the smallest birds and mammals have much
higher oxygen consumption per unit body weight than larger ones.
This correlation has an extremely simple basis. It must be remembered
(and we will have cause to refer back to this rather soon) that an
organism is a three-dimensional structure, and that as it increases
its linear dimensions its surface area will increase as the *square* of
the linear dimension and its volume as the *cube* of the dimension. To
illustrate: a cube of side one inch has a total surface area of 6

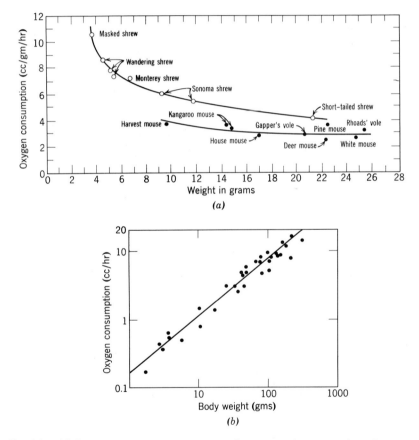

Fig. 6-1. (a) Oxygen consumption versus weight in several species of small mammals. (b) Oxygen consumption of individuals of a single species of crab *(Pugettia)*
as a function of body weight. (From C. L. Prosser et al., *Comparative Animal
Physiology,* 1st ed., Saunders, 1950.)

204 THE BIOLOGY OF ORGANISMS

inches^2, and a volume of one inch^3; if we double the side, the surface now becomes 24 square inches and the volume 8 cubic inches. Thus by doubling the linear dimensions, we have increased the surface by a factor of 4 (2^2) and the volume by a factor of 8 (2^3). Exactly this happens as organisms get bigger, even though they aren't cubes. Loss of heat to the environment is a surface-exchange phenomenon, depending on surface area; but heat production varies with the *mass* of tissue involved in producing it, and thus depends on volume. The bigger a homoiothermic animal is, the larger its heat production in relation to the surface which can radiate that heat away, and the less metabolic work (per unit weight) it must do in order to maintain its body temperature above that of the environment.

One interesting result is that the very smallest warm-blooded animals (shrews among mammals, and hummingbirds among birds) have such a huge metabolic burden that they have developed identical adaptations for reducing it. Both are capable of reducing their body temperatures to that of the environment during periods of inaction. They are thus spared the metabolic demands created by incessant heat loss. This process may have a desirable side effect. It appears that the small homoiotherms who live a fast-paced metabolic life usually pay for it with a quick demise. It seems that the small birds and mammals who put themselves on the metabolic shelf by allowing body temperature to drop periodically gain increased longevity; certain small bats, which cool down at night *and* hibernate all winter (during which time they are virtually inert metabolically), may have life spans of twenty-five years or more despite their small size and high metabolism when active.

The Differentiation of Metabolism

Although one can learn many things by studying oxygen consumption or carbon dioxide output from whole organisms, one also misses a great deal. As we have pointed out in Chapter 5, the cells of any multicellular organism become differentiated during development; this differentiation involves not merely the form and operational status of the cell, but its metabolic activities as well. The whole organism is a population of interacting, integrated, and individually specialized cells, between which all kinds of metabolic exchanges and "cross-feeding" occur. Measuring the metabolic rate of the organism as a whole tells us nothing about such events; it gives us only their arithmetic sum.

A very obvious example of such differentiation in metabolism is found in the higher plants. Chloroplast-containing cells are, of course, restricted mainly to the leaves; the total burden of photosynthesis falls upon only a fraction of the whole cell population. A given cell from the mesophyll of a leaf must be able to produce enough glucose from its photosynthetic activity to take care of its own needs and also to export an excess for the supply of nonphotosynthetic cells in the stem and roots. A root cell, for example, will use that glucose in the oxidative pathways which yield energy and will produce carbon dioxide from these reactions.

Similar exchanges of metabolites occur in animals. Muscle cells in a mammal, for example, have huge energy requirements because they are engaged in very rapid conversion of chemical energy into the mechanical energy involved in contraction. A muscle cell doing active work must rely largely on anaerobic metabolism for its energy production, and therefore produces large amounts of lactic acid (see the schemes for energy metabolism in Stern and Nanney, Chap. 7). Its demands for energy-rich compounds, furthermore, are extremely high. The muscle cell is supplied with glucose from the blood. Blood in turn is supplied with glucose from liver cells, which are specialized for storing it in the form of the polymer *glycogen*. When an actively working muscle cell accumulates lactic acid, much of it passes into the bloodstream and is returned to the liver, where it is resynthesized into glycogen once more. In other words, two differentiated cell types —the liver cell and the muscle cell—"swap" metabolic products in an arrangement that is obviously an efficient one for the whole organism.

These examples show that cells are as well differentiated in the kind of metabolism they practice as they are in their shape and size. The most important feature of this metabolic specialization is that it has been accompanied by the development of *dependence* of one cell type on another for some metabolic product. Thus the total metabolism of an organism is the product of a number of special and interlocked cellular metabolisms.

EXCHANGE WITH THE ENVIRONMENT

The Necessity for Exchange

The remainder of this chapter will be devoted to an analysis of the arrangements which the organism makes to link its individual cells to the sources of supply for metabolism; it is an obvious fact that a cell must be supplied with the wherewithal for each of the special metabolic functions it performs. One of the first consequences of multicellularity, however, is that some cells are inside and some outside; organisms don't generally consist of a flat double sheet of cells, though certain lower invertebrate animals and some aquatic plants approach this condition closely. The problem is complicated, as in the higher plants for example, where exchanging surfaces contact two radically different environments—the atmosphere and the soil. An important result of the third dimension in organisms is that interactions with the environment take place in two stages, the first of which is *exchange* between the environment and the boundary cells, and the second of which involves *transport* of energy and materials to other cells. Obviously, internal transport mechanisms can work only with what has already been absorbed by the cells that are in contact with the environment, and our first consideration will be of the process of exchange.

Energy Exchanges. The function of exchange and transport mechanisms in multicellular organisms is to provide each constituent cell with the appropriate conditions and materials for carrying on its activities. Although we tend usually to think about the exchange of materials, many of the important relations involve energy instead. For example, active metabolism on the part of cells produces large amounts of heat; and whether or not the organism regulates its temperature by holding it constant, an important process of energy exchange involves heat transfer. Some bacteria and blue-green algae can withstand remarkable temperature extremes, but most cells cannot; the protein constituents on which they depend for enzymatic activity as well as structural integrity maintain their native properties only within a fairly narrow range of "physiological" temperatures. The consequences of inadequate exchange are seen, for example, in the spathes (central, fleshy shoots) of plants related to the jack-in-the-pulpit, where metabolic heat can raise the surface temperature of the tissue to around 60°C—uncomfortably hot to the touch. Nor is the requirement for heat transfer restricted to allowances for heat *loss;* conservation of metabolic heat may be of critical importance in cold environments. Equally obvious is the importance of such energy exchanges as those involving light in photosynthetic plants, and the reception of a variety of forms of stimulus energy through sense organs. Although in the latter case energy does not directly reach and affect all cells of the organism, the information provided makes possible adjustments of the greatest importance between the whole organism and its environment (Chapter 7).

Material Exchanges. The external boundary of the organism is a transfer point for a variety of substances critical for the internal cells.

First, the internal cells require a variety of substances that can be lumped under the heading "food"—the molecular components which the cell requires for synthesis of its own macromolecules, and as substrates for oxidative, energy-yielding metabolism. Autotrophic organisms are able to synthesize these things from relatively simple precursors, but a heterotrophic organism must import them from the environment and must depend on external exchange to do so. Second, the internal aqueous medium is essential for the existence of cells, and its content of inorganic ions must be closely regulated. Finally, respiratory gases —oxygen and carbon dioxide—must also be exchanged; and various products of cellular metabolism must be gotten rid of, either because they are toxic or because they may pile up and prevent the continued progress of the reversible biochemical reaction which produced them.

Energy in various forms, as well as a host of different sorts of molecules, must thus be in constant flux across the surface of an organism. This flow is regulated by mechanisms which control the extent, the quality, and the rate of these exchanges between the organism and the world outside.

Cellular Arrangements for Exchange

Reference has been made earlier (p. 203) to the mathematical relationships which govern the relative increase of volume and surface as organisms become larger; increased size has as its inevitable consequence a *volume which becomes larger with respect to the surface.* The decrease in surface/volume ratio as the organism gets bigger means that it becomes harder and harder for surface exchange systems to keep up with the demands of the cells within. It is no surprise, therefore, to find that the chief characteristic of the cellular systems involved in exchange is an elaborate set of arrangements for the relative increase of surface area.

Respiratory Exchange. The problem of exchanging O_2 and CO_2 can be stated quite simply; the following analysis is borrowed partly from that by the late August Krogh, whose book *The Comparative Physiology of Respiration* is an elegant account of the problem for the student who wishes to go more deeply into it. All known respiratory exchanges take place by simple diffusion of the gases along concentration gradients (though it was once thought that "active" oxygen transport mechanisms existed, these have only been demonstrated in the special case of the fish swim-bladder, which is a hydrostatic and not a respiratory organ). The transfer of materials across a surface by diffusion depends on the concentration gradient, according to Fick's law:

$$\frac{ds}{dt} = -DA\frac{dc}{dx}$$

where A is the surface area and D the diffusion constant. In other words, the amount of substance s crossing the boundary in time t is proportional to the concentration gradient dc/dx across it.

Let us examine first the exchange of gases in water, where organisms originated. At standard atmospheric pressure (sea level) and at a temperature of 20°C, water will hold about 6.5 ml of oxygen per liter. The concentration of a gas in aqueous solution is often expressed as its *tension*, defined as the pressure of that gas in the atmosphere with which the solution is in *equilibrium*. In air at a standard pressure of 1 atmosphere (760 mm Hg), the *partial pressure* of oxygen is 155 mm Hg, and thus the oxygen tension of a thin layer of water in equilibrium with that air is also 155 mm Hg, or 0.2 atmospheres.

This is the amount of dissolved oxygen, or less, with which the aquatic organism must work. To define the limits of diffusion as a distribution process, we may imagine a small organism the shape of a sphere. For a spherical organism, assuming that it is using oxygen at a constant rate so as to maintain zero concentration at the center,

$$C_0 = \frac{Ar^2}{6D}$$

where C_0 is the concentration of oxygen at the surface of the sphere in atmospheres, A is the respiratory uptake in milliliters/gram/minute, r is the radius, and D is the diffusion coefficient for oxygen. Using the appropriate constants and assuming a reasonable respiration of 1/600 ml O_2/g/min, the concentration outside necessary to supply an organism of radius 1 cm would be 25 atmospheres. This is, of course, ridiculous; such concentrations are not available. If the radius were 1 mm instead, the required concentration would be 0.25 atm, very nearly what is available under the best circumstances. The conclusion is that for nearly spherical animals 1 mm would be the limiting radius allowing the use of unaided diffusion for respiratory supply. Of course, the sphere is the shape with the minimum surface area for a given volume; any departure from this will improve things, and thus a variety of small aquatic invertebrates with fairly slow metabolism manage to get along by diffusion alone.

It must be mentioned here that a crucial modification for improving this situation can be accomplished if the internal solution is moved with respect to the surface. If internal distribution is achieved by convection, the diffusion gradient across the surface can be maintained near its maximum value, and exchange will be very much more rapid. Calculations for such a mechanism suggest that the permissible radius for a spherical animal would go up tenfold. In fact, of course, there is no such limitation; this is partially due to the fact that metabolic rates drop with increasing size.

More important, however, is that organisms have developed special respiratory epithelia. These structures begin as rather simple extensions from, or pockets into, the body surface. Their main function is to increase surface area, and the structures that are termed *gills* in a variety of aquatic organisms are often elaborately branched or feathered. Although in simpler cases the gills merely supplement respiratory exchange through the general body surface, they take over the function entirely in many arthropods and fish, where the permeability of the rest of the surface is drastically reduced to conform to the demands of water regulation. Such gills are often marvelously efficient; where it has been possible to measure accurately the O_2 content of water on the way into and on the way out of gill chambers, oxygen utilization (the amount removed expressed as a percentage of the total present) may exceed 80 per cent. This process is made especially efficient in fishes, where the flow of water across the gills is opposite in direction to the flow of blood within them. With this countercurrent arrangement, the final saturation of blood is determined by the oxygen tension of the water entering the gills, not by that leaving them.

At first glance the adaptation of respiratory surfaces to handle oxygen and carbon dioxide *in air* appears to be a major task. But in fact the terrestrial organism has a number of advantages. Whereas 1 ml of O_2 is contained in 200 ml of water, the same amount of O_2 is available in 5 ml of air at sea level. Moreover, the diffusion rate of O_2 in air is 300,000 times that in water, so that quick mixing of air outside the absorptive epithelium is assured. Finally, the energetics of moving a gas as opposed to a liquid are favorably low, so that respiratory movements are more economical.

The major difficulty for respiratory surfaces in air is that the diffusion gradient for water is so strongly directed out that such epithelia represent a major avenue of water loss. It is for this reason that all lungs are internal structures. They may be provided with fresh, oxygen-rich air by diffusion (as in the "lungs" of various air-breathing snails and some crustaceans) or by active filling movements, called *ventilation*. These rate-control devices will be considered in a later section. The essential features of lungs are not very different from those of gills: they are enormous expansions of an exchanging surface. In mammals exchange takes place in a host of tiny pockets, the *alveoli;*

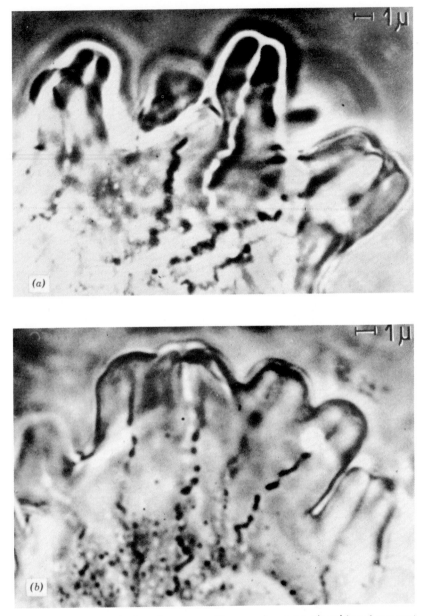

Fig. 6-2. Pinocytosis in Amoeba proteus. The amoebae were placed in a 1 per cent albumin solution; *(a)* and *(b)* are phase-contrast photomicrographs taken 35 seconds apart. Note that the vacuoles in *(b)* are formed along the pinocytosis channels seen in *(a)*. (Phase-contrast photomicrographs by D. M. Prescott, in H. Holter, *Internat. Rev. Cytol.* **8,** 48 (1959).)

these are blind endings of tubules (the bronchioles) that branch off from the bronchi. The total surface area available in the lungs of man has been estimated at nearly 200 square meters, and over two-thirds of this is covered with capillaries. Although oxygen enters the alveolus in the gaseous state, it goes into solution in a film of water overlying the alveolar epithelium, and thus the final act of exchange is accomplished *in solution*. Gills and lungs, then, are not fundamentally different; one of the two is merely inside out.

Nutritional Exchange. Although the absorption of food molecules from the environment by animals can (and does in the more primitive cases) involve the same surfaces as are used for respiratory gases, the problems are different because the molecules involved are very much larger. Heterotrophic organisms often obtain nutrition from large molecules (proteins, polysaccharides, fats) that challenge the absorptive capacities of the surface cells. In protists and some lower metazoans large molecules or particles are absorbed by being enfolded in a part of the cell membrane, which subsequently breaks off inside the cell as a kind of package (Fig. 6-2); this kind of absorption, which may be considered a fine form of particle ingestion into vacuoles, is called *pinocytosis* and may be of general importance in other cells. In sessile marine invertebrates a large part of the nutritional burden can be handled by the active absorption of small, energy-rich molecules in the environment; some marine invertebrates, for example, are able to accumulate glucose or amino acids in this way.

Heterotrophic plants such as the fungi cannot ingest a particle or molecule that is too large to penetrate the cell wall. These organisms rely not only on the absorption of small organic molecules from their environment, but also on products that they can obtain from the breakdown of the materials into which they grow. This is, of course, achieved by the secretion of hydrolytic enzymes, which have the ability to break down a wide variety of large molecules into organic monomers such as glucose and amino acids.

But most animals cannot get along by simply absorbing molecules out of their environment. Instead, they have evolved means of actively seeking or harvesting other organisms, and of ingesting them into an internal digestive tract. Internalization, of course, has a number of advantages: it concentrates both the food and the enzymes that digest it, and effectively immobilizes prey that could otherwise escape. These procedures have had profound consequences for both the behavior and anatomy of animals with regard to the problem of catching food and of mechanically processing, digesting, and absorbing it.

In coelenterates and flatworms the internal digestive tract is simply a blind pocket; but in all higher forms it is a continuous tube with openings at either end. Typically, it is longitudinally differentiated, like an assembly line, with functions occurring in sequence along its length and the structure varying appropriately. In a great variety of organisms the morphology of the digestive tract shows common features. All, for example, have vastly expanded surface areas; this involves not only length, which is usually increased through internal coiling, but also cross-sectional area. The latter is enlarged through foldings and/or internal projections (*villi*).

Most significantly, the process of exchange is universally dependent on the enzymatic secretions of special cells in the exchanging epithelium—in short, on glandular activity. Aside from the special processes of pinocytosis or phagocytosis, cells do not generally take in whole protein, polysaccharide, fat, or nucleic acid. Since these large molecules must be broken down to their basic components and then resynthesized into the specific macromolecules of the new owner, most heterotrophic organisms have arranged for the digestion to be handled *before* absorption. Unlike the heterotrophic plants and microorganisms, animals have evolved specialized cells, often organized into minute secretory systems, which produce and liberate a variety of enzymes to act on foodstuffs in the digestive tract (Chap. 3, p. 90). In addition, other secretory activity may accompany this; for example, mucous secretion is often necessary to lubricate the passage of materials along the tract, or acid secretion may be performed to regulate the pH of digestive fluids.

The basic biochemical action involved in the "digestion" of all food molecules is one of hydrolysis. The chemical bonds between amino acids in a protein, between nucleotides in a nucleic acid, between sugar residues in a polysaccharide, or between fatty acids and glycerol in a fat, can be broken with the simultaneous splitting of water so that a hydrogen atom is added to one fragment and a hydroxyl group to the other. This similarity is illustrated in Fig. 6-3. Such digestion is termed a *hydrolysis*. Hydrolyses can be performed without catalysis, but they take a long time. Under strongly acid conditions it would take many hours even at 100°C to accomplish the hydrolysis performed by the human stomach during a few minutes under only mildly acidic conditions at normal body temperature. The immensely greater rate of biological digestion, of course, is due to the action of catalysts. Hydrolytic enzymes, like the more familiar enzymes involved in cellular oxidations and reductions (see Stern and Nanney), are proteins. The digestive enzymes, however, differ from many oxidation-

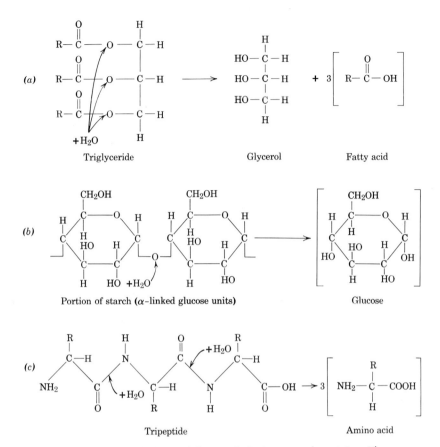

Fig. 6-3. Enzymatic hydrolysis of fats, carbohydrates, and proteins. The arrows indicate the bond to which a water molecule is added in each case.

reduction enzymes in that they have no obvious requirement for co-enzymes or heavy metal prosthetic groups.

In the mammalian digestive tract the only digestive action taken before the stomach occurs in the mouth, where salivary glands secrete lubricating fluid and also an *amylase* (the general term for starch-digesting enzymes). Much of the starch is broken down to two-unit sugars (disaccharides) by the action of this enzyme during and after chewing. In the stomach the clefts between folds of the gastric mucosa are studded with secretory cells. Two cell types are found: one type, the chief cell, produces the enzyme pepsin, a *protease*. The other, the parietal cell, secretes hydrochloric acid. This latter performance is especially remarkable since the concentration of HCl as it leaves the parietal cell is at least 0.1 Normal (corresponding to a pH of 1). Deleterious effects upon the producing cell itself are apparently avoided by having the acid secreted into a tiny canaliculus that penetrates the very cytoplasm of the parietal cell itself; the walls of the canaliculi, which alone are in contact with the acid after it becomes highly concentrated, appear resistant to it. Diluted by mixing with the gastric fluids, the HC1 provides a stomach pH of 1.5 to 2.5—strongly acid but near the optimum value for the activity of pepsin. The stomach also produces rennin, an enzyme specific for the hydrolysis of certain milk proteins, and a fat-digesting enzyme or *lipase*. The latter is probably not functional in adult mammals; the elaborate arrangements for the maintenance of low gastric pH indicate that the stomach is tailored specifically for protein hydrolysis by pepsin.

The intestinal epithelium also contains several types of secretory cells. Their presence individually is remarkably transitory: produced near the base of a villus, they secrete for a brief period and are eventually sloughed off at the top of the villus. This sequence produces a kind of parade of epithelial cells moving up the villus with continual replacement from below. Some enzymes active in hydrolyzing disaccharides, some peptidases (which act on short chains of amino acids liberated from proteins), amylase, and lipase have been identified as products of intestinal glands. Far more important in hydrolytic function, however, are enzymatic secretions of the pancreas. This large gland, connected to the digestive tract by a duct opening near the beginning of the small intestine, is composed of two types of glandular tissue. One kind, comprising the Islets of Langerhans, is concerned with the production of the hormone insulin. The other consists of small spheres of short tubular cells opening into a duct; these multicellular glands are called *acini*, and their individual ducts form the common pancreatic duct leading to the intestine. The acinar cells are responsible for the secretion of the proteases chymotrypsin and trypsin, carboxypeptidase; lipase, amylase, and enzymes responsible for the hydrolysis of nucleic acids. This secretion unquestionably carries the main burden of digestive hydrolysis.

This inventory of enzymes and their sites of production leaves a great many questions unanswered. Why should there be so many of one kind of enzyme—proteases, for example? Apparently proteins are sufficiently diverse that a number of points of attack are required. Chymotrypsin, for example, attacks the carboxyl end of peptide bonds involving the amino acids tyrosine, tryptophan, phenylalanine, and methionine; trypsin, on the other hand, cleaves those adjacent to arginine or lysine. Pepsin also cleaves bonds involving the phenyl containing amino acids tyrosine and phenylalanine, but on the amino side. Peptidases, which also hydrolyze peptide bonds, apparently cannot reach the interior of a long-chain protein, and so are restricted to action on the short-chain peptides produced from whole protein by pepsin, trypsin, and chymotrypsin. Even these are divided specifically into types which attack terminal amino acids and those that cleave the middle of a chain.

How are the cells that produce proteolytic enzymes spared from the action of their own secretions? The protease-synthesizing cells are not actually committing perpetual suicide: the enzymes they manufacture are initially produced in an inactive form (as so-called zymogens), and subsequently activated in a variety of ways. Pepsin is produced from inactive pepsinogen when the latter encounters the acidic environment of the gastric cavity; there is also an autocatalytic process involved, since pepsin can activate pepsinogen. It appears that this reactivation may involve the removal of a small (4000 MW) polypeptide that masks the active site of the enzyme. Trypsinogen from the pancreas is activated by an enzyme, *enterokinase,* produced in the small intestine; chymotrypsinogen is activated by trypsin. These mechanisms circumvent the embarrassing possibility that secretory products might destroy their parent cells.

Controlled and Selective Exchange

The preceding section has been concerned with a variety of cellular arrangements designed for facilitating (or preventing) the exchange of matter or energy between organism and environment. But organisms do more than merely provide a boundary that is adapted for commerce with the environment; in general, special regions of the body surface are especially equipped to control both the *rate* and the *quality* of exchange. The boundary between organism and environment not only allows exchange to take place, but often exercises elegant regulatory powers over what is exchanged and how fast.

Rate Controls. Systems for the exchange of respiratory gases in both plants and animals are subject to rate regulation; this generally takes the form of control over the extent of contact of the absorptive surface with the exchanged gas. The stomata of higher plants and the spiracles of insects, despite their totally independent origins and functions, show remarkably similar arrangements and control mechanisms.

STOMATA. These are the "pores" in plants through which water vapor exits and carbon dioxide enters. In most plants they are restricted to the lower surface of the leaves; they account for over 90% of the total gas exchange of the leaf, whose surface is otherwise covered by waxy secretions of the epidermal cells. A single stoma is elliptical in shape, with a length averaging only about 20μ. It is actually the space between two cells called *guard cells*. These contain chlorophyll, and are photosynthetic; but their main function is in the regulation of the stomatal opening, which forms the passageway from the atmosphere into the spongey and gas-filled interior of the leaf. If guard cells are observed microscopically while immersed in solutions of different osmotic pressures, it can be shown that the size of the opening depends upon the turgidity of the guard cells. In sugar solutions, for example, the guard cells would be expected to have a lower-than-normal internally directed osmotic gradient and thus to become relatively flaccid; under these conditions the stomatal opening is reduced. The same effect can be produced by depriving the plant of water and wilting it, or by puncturing the guard cells. The architecture of the guard cells is such that when they take on water and become turgid, their inner walls bow out and open the stoma; when, conversely, they lose turgidity, the walls relax against one another and close the stoma (Fig. 6-4).

Stomatal exchange means two things to the plant. First, it is the route through which carbon dioxide enters the leaf spaces and is made available for photosynthesis in mesophyll cells. Second, it is

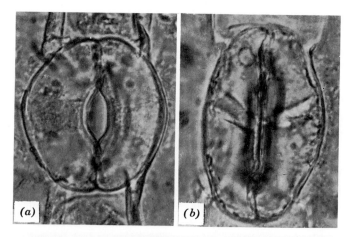

Fig. 6-4. Stomata of an onion leaf. (a) Partly open, guard cells turgid. (b) Closed. (From M. Shaw, *New Phytologist*, **53,** 344 (1954).)

the route to the exterior for water in the transpiration stream; (pp. 234–236). We may thus expect stomata to have an important influence on the rate of water uptake in roots. But since there may be occasional conflicts of interest between conserving water and obtaining CO_2 for photosynthesis, the matter of stomatal control is a complex one. In general, the stomata open in the daytime and close at night.

Both light and CO_2 can function in the control of stomatal opening. When illuminated, the leaf begins active photosynthesis, which reduces the concentration of CO_2 within the air spaces and inside the cells as well. The guard cells, though they photosynthesize slowly, probably drop in CO_2 content primarily as a result of their own photosynthesis rather than through the decrease in CO_2 concentration surrounding them. It appears that the decrease in CO_2 produced within the guard cell as a result of illumination is the direct cause of the turgidity increase; it was once thought that the manufacture of sugars by the heightened photosynthesis was responsible for increasing osmotic pressure, but the stomata open much too quickly for that. Furthermore, experimental reduction of CO_2 inside the leaf will duplicate the effect. Unfortunately, we have no idea of the way in which CO_2 increases guard cell turgidity.

The result of these mechanisms is that during daylight the demand of the plant for CO_2 to fix in photosynthesis is met by the freedom of diffusion provided through open stomata. At night, on the other hand, water loss is restricted by their closure. On extremely hot days the heating of leaves by radiation and the favorable circumstances for evaporation can produce a serious challenge to the plant's water balance. Under these circumstances the stomata act as a useful safety device. When water loss becomes serious enough to produce the beginnings of wilting, the guard cells themselves have been so reduced in turgor that the stomata close and limit all further water loss.

SPIRACLES. Insect spiracles form a similar passageway for gases; but here oxygen is moving in and carbon dioxide out. The opening valve is regulated by a tiny ring of muscle. Here, too, the loss of water vapor is a critical exchange factor—for terrestrial insects must conserve water. Though the spiracular muscle is controlled primarily by the activity of nerves running to it, one interesting parallel does exist with the stoma: the spiracle also may respond directly to a change in the partial pressure of carbon dioxide in the system of air spaces inside the organism. The spiracles in most insects are kept closed much of the time (for water conservation) by a steady barrage of impulses in the nerve fibers which innervate them. But if the internal concentration of CO_2 becomes too high, it forces relaxation of the muscle, overriding the mechanism which normally tends to keep it contracted.

RATE CONTROL IN OTHER RESPIRATORY SYSTEMS. In the lungs of mammals, respiratory exchange rate is regulated by the frequency with which the lungs are filled and emptied. The lung volume is controlled by muscles between the ribs (the intercostal muscles) and by the diaphragm; contraction of the former set of muscles elevates the ribs, and of the latter pulls the bottom of the chest cavity downward. The lungs inflate passively, following the volume changes of the thoracic cavity. In normal breathing at rest expiration is primarily a passive process, while inspiration involves active contraction of the muscles just mentioned. With each normal breath only about a tenth of the total air in the lungs is exchanged.

Both the rate of breathing (a process which is only partially under voluntary control) and its depth are regulated by the metabolic demands of the tissues. This is achieved in an interesting way. The nerves passing to the muscles operating breathing are controlled from a *respiratory center* in the medulla at the base of the brain. Cells in this area are extremely sensitive to the chemical composition of the blood that circulates through it. The result of stimulation is an increased rhythm of activity in the controlling nerves, which in turn increases breathing rate.

The critical question concerning the mechanism of this control is whether it is triggered by the depletion of oxygen in the blood or by an increase in carbon dioxide. The first answer was provided by some extremely ingenious though simple experiments, performed mainly by J. S. Haldane in England on himself: most of them involved the breathing of gas mixtures. An increase in the carbon dioxide present in alveoli of only 0.25% is sufficient to increase breathing by 100%, whereas rather large changes in the percentage of O_2 alone have little effect. The ability to hold one's breath, moreover, is very much increased by heavy voluntary breathing beforehand—a procedure which clears CO_2 out with residual air in the lungs but has little effect on the O_2 concentration. These and other experiments showed that high carbon dioxide rather than low oxygen is the primary trigger for accelerating respiratory rate. More recently, it has been shown that low O_2 can also stimulate increased breathing. But this effect is not a direct response of the medullary nervous center. Rather, chemical receptors in the arterial system respond to the lowered oxygen concentration in the blood and send nerve impulses to the respiratory center.

Rate control in other respiratory systems is achieved by a variety of means. Aquatic animals with gills often have means of altering the rate at which water flows over them; the higher this rate, the less the likelihood that the exchanging surface will be confronted with an environment partially depleted of oxygen, or partially saturated with CO_2. In some crustaceans a special set of appendages maintains currents of water through the gill chambers, and in many fish the flaps (opercula) covering the gills are equipped with muscles that enable them to pump water through the chamber beneath. In some other fish, however, these muscles are lacking, and the production of water currents across the gill surfaces depends simply on the fish's swimming constantly with the mouth open. This is true of the mackerel, for example. It seems probable that this odd state of affairs arose—and is economical—only because the mackerel feeds by filtering minute organisms out of the water; since he has to swim fast with his mouth open anyway, the additional fulfillment of respiratory requirements is simply a bonus.

Any exchange process across a surface depends on a gradient—that is, on the relative amounts of something inside and outside. The control mechanisms just considered are all concerned with the amount of something *outside;* in other words, with the rate at which something can be brought to the external surface. But such systems cannot work efficiently if, as soon as the exchange is completed, the exchanged material (or energy) simply piles up on the inside of the surface. The gradient tending to accumulate the exchanging substance will be cancelled in short order, and no further exchange can occur. Thus the operation of exchange depends heavily on the efficiency of internal transport systems in distributing the products of exchange.

There are innumerable examples that could be used to illustrate this principle; many of them properly belong in the next section, which deals with transport systems. In general, we find that exchanging surfaces are richly supplied with systems of transport; the blood supply of gills and lungs or of the skin and the vessel elements in plant roots are examples. Particularly in the circulatory systems of animals, the control systems for internal transport and those for exchange are closely linked. In mammalian respiration, increased heart rate accompanies acceleration of respiratory reflexes in order to handle the increased load. And one of the most important means of control over heat exchange in warm-blooded animals is by regulation of the transport system—here again, the blood. Smooth muscles in the walls of arterioles can control the diameter of these vessels, and thus regulate the amount of blood which is permitted to flow into a given region of skin. Usually, blood flow to the skin is regulated by these means so that it is relatively heavy under conditions in which a high level of heat exchange with the environment is desirable (e.g., during heavy exercise with its concomitant high heat production).

Behavioral Controls. In some situations the apparatus for controlling exchange is simply not competent to handle the load placed upon it. Many organisms present behavioral solutions to such circumstances. Small mammals, for example, have such high metabolic rates (p. 203) that their heat-loss systems would be severely stressed in a very hot environment. Most very small mammals, however, are either nocturnal, live in burrows, or both, and are thus protected from extremely high temperatures. Reptiles do not regulate their body temperature metabolically, but they are extremely careful about their choice of sunny or shady spots (depending on the time of day), and are able to exert remarkable control over their own temperature in this way. A similar problem is faced by homoiothermic animals whose developmental stages are not capable of temperature regulation. Most birds must incubate their eggs and in some cases the newly hatched young as well, since the offspring have inadequate metabolic machinery of their own. This behavioral control is carried further by the incubator birds of New Guinea, who avoid the necessity for personally incubating the eggs by constructing a huge mound of forest litter and laying their eggs in the middle of it. Inside these mounds fermenting bacteria and fungi acting on organic matter raise the temperature enormously, and it is controlled within appropriate limits by the parents— who methodically uncover and rebury the eggs each day, holding their temperature constant within 1°C.

Finally, it should be noted that in plants the equivalent of behavioral control of exchange systems is accomplished by the sensitivity of the growth apparatus to environmental influences. The most familiar instance of this, of course, is the phototropic growth of the shoot apex (pp. 260–261), which places the photosynthetic parts of the plant in a suitable position for the absorption of light energy.

Controlling the Quality of Exchange. Rate controls may be achieved by devices that admit the exchanged material to the absorbing surface only occasionally, by altering the rapidity of internal transport, or by behavioral changes in the organism's relation to the environment with which he is exchanging. Often, however, the organism is confronted with a number of things in his environment, some of which ought to be crossing the boundary and some of which should not. Here the problem is less one of rate control than of *quality* control: the exchanging surface must exert a selectivity over which things move in and what move out.

Nowhere is this problem of selective exchange more dominant than in the water relations of organisms. Most of the organisms in the world live in water; those that do not must conserve it, usually by regulating with care the extent to which it is lost. The importance of water to organisms, of course, is that their cells (and intercellular fluids) are largely water solutions. Water is important not so much for what it is as for what it contains: a majority of the important events in biological chemistry happen in aqueous solution. The exchange of water, then, really also means the exchange of everything which may be in solution in it: and this will include a variety of ions, small molecules important in nutrition, metabolic waste products, and so on. Over this host of materials the exchanging boundary of the organism must exert selective control, retaining some, eliminating others, absorbing some actively from the environment, and actively keeping still others *out*. And as these dissolved substances go, so goes water: for across all biological membranes (including the cell membranes that make up exchanging surfaces) *osmotic* forces are active, and thus the movement of water molecules across such membranes will be in the direction of the highest concentration of those solutes to which the membrane is less permeable than it is to water. The organism has a huge stake in the accurate regulation of water and dissolved materials. Upon it depends the well-being of every one of its constituent cells—for each cell must be in delicate equilibrium with the environment or, in animals especially, with the intercellular fluids that bathe it.

DEVICES AT THE CELLULAR LEVEL. The basic mechanism underlying selective regulation of absorption is common to many cells, but especially developed in those concerned with exchange. The mechanism really consists of two parts. First, cell membranes show "selective permeability"; that is, they are crossed more readily by some molecules than by others. All of them are highly permeable to water, but they differ markedly in their permeability to various ions and small molecules. We do not have in all cases ready explanations for these differences. Sometimes they can be interpreted on a size basis, as though the membrane had "pores" that let small things through but not larger things; sometimes differential solubility of a particular molecule in water and in the lipids that make up much of the cell membrane seems to be responsible, and in many cases it is anybody's guess. A second factor of even greater importance in selective absorption is *"active"* transport. This term is used to describe a process by which cells appear to break the laws of diffusion. In general, the net movement of molecules across any membrane that they can pass will be from the side of higher concentration to that of lower concentration; in other words, the molecules travel down a diffusion gradient. But many cells can accumulate ions or molecules—or prohibit their entry—against concentration gradients of 20:1 or higher. Of course, maintaining such a high concentration gradient requires energy—hence the term *active* for this kind of transport. Although details are not known for any case of active transport, one hypothesis is worth describing because it may help to remove some of the mysterious aura that surrounds the process. Suppose that a cell maintains (as indeed many cells do) a relatively low internal concentration of sodium ion (Na^+). This could be achieved by having the cell synthesize a molecule (say X) which combines reversibly with sodium, and which when so combined crosses the membrane more easily than either it or Na^+ crosses when uncombined. As long as the cell keeps making more X, there will be an outwardly directed diffusion gradient for Na^+X and the cell will lose sodium, even though uncombined sodium may be ten times as concentrated on the outside as on the inside. To make this work in the long run, we would have to arrange for the destruction of X outside the cell, but a reasonable postulate could be devised for this. The expenditure of energy which the cell would have to make to accomplish this hypothetical active transport is represented by the work of synthesizing X.

UPTAKE OF IONS BY PLANT ROOTS. Except for the exchanges of respiratory gases and water vapor through the leaves, vascular land plants depend on the relationship between their root system and the soil for their entire commerce with the environment. The roots form the only avenue for the entry of water and for the dissolved mineral nutrients required for a variety of cellular processes.

Uptake in plant roots is an enterprise participated in by a number of epidermal cells, the developmental anatomy of which has been described on pp. 138–146. The root system of a higher plant taken together presents an enormous surface area; over 90 per cent of this is accounted for by root hairs, which are projections of the epidermal cells present in a region just behind the growing zone. These small expansions are in direct contact with water held in the matrix of the soil; together with the growing tip of the root, they carry responsibility for the processes of water and mineral ion exchange. As the root grows, the hair zone is progressively advanced into less-depleted soil regions.

The epidermal cells of plant roots are capable of some impressive feats of active transport. In general, they are able to accumulate potassium ions (K^+) to a considerable extent; in addition, they actively *exclude* Na^+ against a concentration gradient that would normally force its entry. Other ions are actively accumulated as well in certain plants; and the halophytes (plants existing in very salty environments) seem to accumulate sodium as well as potassium. Selectivity in the uptake of negative ions is also shown.

The active and selective accumulation of particular ion species is important to the plant's economy in two ways. First, certain minerals are required as specific participants in cellular reactions, and selective absorption mechanisms must be practiced to fill this need. Second, and perhaps more important, the plant must concentrate water from its environment and supply it to the cells—both to maintain the water balance of their cytoplasms and to utilize in photosynthesis. Most cells cannot actively transport water, mainly because their cell membranes are much too permeable to it. (Contractile vacuoles may be an exception to this.) Instead, water must be moved by indirect means, the most effective of which involves the production of an osmotic gradient into the cell by concentration of solute within it. This is exactly what is done by the epidermal root cells of plants. The active accumulation of ions creates a higher concentration of solute within the cells. Water subsequently enters, driven by the osmotic pressure difference created by solute accumulation.

Of course, the subsequent history of movement of the water and ions carried in it involves the participation of other cells; ultimately the water must be conveyed to the xylem (pp. 234–236) for upward movement in the transportation stream. It will be recalled from Chap. 5 that the arrangement of xylem and phloem in the root is different than in the stem: in particular, xylem elements are distributed in the form of a cross, the arms of which extend peripherally toward the surface of the root, and thus offer direct access to water entering the epidermal cells. Nevertheless, in order to get into the upward-conducting xylem elements water must pass across several cells. This is accomplished through a series of osmotic relationships between the cells of a given layer in the root and their neighbors on either side.

A minor digression is necessary to explain this series of osmotic movements. Animal physiologists are accustomed to thinking of osmotic forces as causing changes in cellular *volume;* since such changes soon cause rupturing of cell membranes, the osmotic relations between animal cells and the fluid surrounding them are usually carefully regulated. An important outcome of the enclosure of plant cells in cellulose walls, however, is that the osmotic entry of water acts against a constant volume, and hence produces a hydrostatic pressure change. Thus it is not at all unusual for a plant cell—which is reasonably well-exposed to water, either in the xylem or the outside environment—to show positive internal pressures of 100 pounds per square inch. This positive hydrostatic pressure is required to balance the tendency of water to enter the cell; thus plant cells are generally turgid when in osmotic equilibrium. This fact is of crucial importance to the mechanical rigidity of nonwoody parts of plants such as leaves and young stems. It is also critical in the movement of water. As water is lost from the cell, whether by evaporation or other means, the cell becomes less turgid; the osmotic force driving water inward is opposed by a lower hydrostatic pressure, and water will be drawn in. Reduction of pressure in the xylem caused by evaporation in the leaves can cause water to enter the root xylem from neighboring cells; in turn, the reduction in turgor pressure there draws water in from more peripheral epidermal cells, and this eventually facilitates osmotic entry of water from the soil. From here on, the history of water movement is one of internal transport (discussed in the next section).

Like plants, animals must regulate the volume and ionic composition of their body fluids. In many animals these functions are handled by the very same exchanging surfaces already specialized for the transfer of respiratory gases to and from the aquatic environment. In the simplest case the whole body surface is involved; often it is the cells of the gill epithelium. Most marine invertebrates engage in little transfer of water with their environment and maintain internal osmotic pressures close to that of sea water. But despite this, they often show active uptake of certain ions (e.g., potassium), and can eliminate others (e.g., sulfate, magnesium) so as to hold them at values several times less than those found in sea water.

THE KIDNEY. A variety of specialized cellular systems for serving the water-balance requirement have arisen. These begin with simple tubes connecting the body cavity with the external environment, often equipped with cilia; the general function of such channels is for water elimination, but they frequently do not accomplish a net loss of water. The channels are often tortuous and complex, allowing for reabsorption from, and secretion into, the fluid that is on its way out.

Their existence allows the organism to maintain a tight control over the concentration of body fluids, whether the material eventually secreted is more concentrated or less concentrated in the organism than outside.

The most complex structures of this general kind are the kidneys of vertebrates. Although we tend to think of kidneys as primarily functioning in the elimination of metabolic waste, no concept could be more misleading. The kidney arose as a water-balance organ, and this is still its primary function. Metabolic waste products, of course, use this existing pathway of fluid themselves; but this is best looked upon as a useful by-product of the kidney's primary job.

The most interesting aspect of kidney function is that it makes some complex and successful uses of multicellular organization. Unlike the relatively independent transport actions of root epidermal cells or gill epithelial cells, the kidney presents some elegantly complex cell interactions in the achievement of ionic regulation.

The kidney's primary concern is the regulation of the composition and volume of the blood; the latter, in turn, will determine that of the extracellular fluid and of the cells it bathes. The major departure in the operation of the kidney from that of more primitive systems is that it processes the entire circulating fluid of the organism very frequently: in short, the accuracy of its regulation depends on the fact that it virtually reconstitutes the circulating fluid of the organism from "scratch" at frequent intervals.

The kidney is a large structure, composed (in man) of about a million basically similar units. Each is called a *nephron:* it consists (Fig. 6-5) of a capsule and a tortuously winding tubule that (in mammals and birds) has a relatively straight loop in the middle. These tubules join into collecting ducts, which in turn form the *ureter,* the major urinary duct leaving the kidney which passes urine to the bladder for storage and eventual elimination. The nephrons are associated with one another in such a way that the capsules and associated convoluted tubules are located in the exterior *cortex* of the kidney, whereas the straight segments of the nephrons and the collecting ducts form the inner layer or *medulla.*

The kidney as a whole receives an extremely rich blood flow from the renal artery. Divisions of this artery called *afferent arterioles* pass into each of the nephron capsules, where they form a complex tuft of twisted capillaries, the *glomerulus.* The capillaries reform into an *efferent arteriole* which leaves the capsule. The efferent arteriole then makes a second pass at the nephron, forming a capillary bed *around the tubule.*

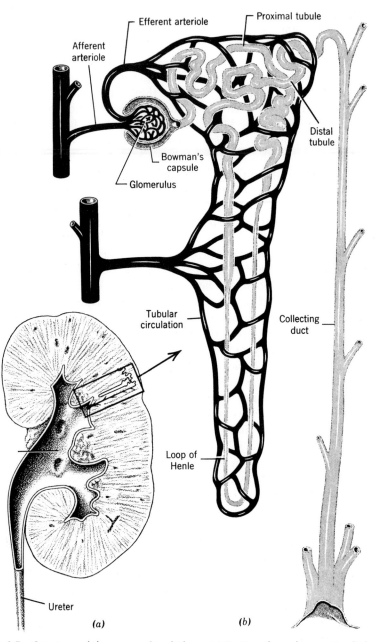

Fig. 6-5.   Structure of the mammalian kidney. (a) Section through an entire kidney, with a single nephron indicated in black; (b) enlarged view of the nephron. (From H. W. Smith, *Scientific American,* **188,** 40 (1953).)

We thus know that blood enters and leaves the kidney, and that urine is formed there. The concentration of the urine varies with the species of vertebrate, and seems to have a great deal to do with the amount of water conservation which the environment dictates. We know, too, that in other respects the urine differs from body fluids— that it contains more of some dissolved substances and less of others. These facts were all appreciated a great many years ago. Now we are in a position to answer several more complex questions about the kidney's function. This will be done in some detail because the kidney is a wonderful case study, both as an example of the strategy of experimental physiology and in its own right as a device for regulating selective exchange between organism and environment. Perhaps better than any other system, the kidney demonstrates the contributions of two kinds of experimental approaches: first, the application of special and ingenious methods of analysis, and second, comparative physiology, which makes use of the "ready-made" experimental situations provided by animals whose environments make their requirements—and therefore their physiological adjustments—special in some way. The operation of the kidney has thus come to be understood both through the "general" and the "comparative" approach.

1. How is urine formed? It is obviously necessary to know the initial process by which body fluids get from the blood into the tubular system that composes the nephron. It was clear to William Bowman, who first described the structure of the nephric capsule over a hundred years ago, that the capsule acted as a filter across which urine was produced from blood flowing through the capillary glomerules. He supposed that this filtration was achieved through "secretory activity" on the part of the capsular cells. Later, however, it was proposed that the glomerlus and capsule acted as a mechanical filter, the pressure for which was supplied by the flowing blood driven by the heart. This idea was supported by the first applications of an ingenious method of microanalysis. Tiny glass tubes or cannulae were inserted into the glomeruli of frogs and were used to remove samples of the fluid filtered there. Analysis of these samples —and similar ones subsequently made on other species—revealed that the fluid which passes across the glomerular wall and into the proximal tubule is an *ultrafiltrate* of blood plasma: that is, it contains *all* of the substances found in plasma which are smaller than protein molecules. Thus proteins and red blood cells are retained by the filter, but all smaller molecules pass through it. The rate of this action can be measured by a technique developed by H. W. Smith. It involves the use of a plant carbohydrate, *inulin*, which is filtered by the glomerulus

but (since it is a very large molecule) is not affected by tubular events thereafter; we can inject this substance into the blood until it reaches a certain concentration, and then measure its proportion in the urine. The amount of blood filtered by both kidneys can thus be calculated. In man it reaches the remarkable value of 180 quarts a day.

2. How is *retention* of water and solutes accomplished? The very size of the filtration figure makes this next question a crucial one. Although 180 quarts of fluid are filtered through the glomeruli per day in man, it is fairly obvious that we excrete but a very small fraction of that amount. Evidently, water is reabsorbed between the process of filtration and final excretion, and this process takes place in the tubules. The kidney tubule is a simple layer of epithelial cells, which are capable of active transport and move an astonishing variety of materials between the tubular fluid and the capillary circulation surrounding them on the outside. Not only is over 98% of the water reabsorbed from tubular urine, but most salts, all of the glucose, most amino acids, vitamins, and a host of other important substances find their way back into the circulation and are thus conserved.

Various experiments have revealed that in birds and mammals the great bulk of this absorption takes place in the proximal convoluted tubule—the part of the tubule which immediately follows the capsule. As with the plant root epidermal cell, the transport of water itself is not "active". Solutes, especially sodium, are actively reabsorbed by cells of the proximal tubule; as the concentration of solutes in these cells increases, water tends to enter by osmosis. In this way both water and dissolved substances are removed from tubular fluid. But the *total concentration* of dissolved substances in the urine is not changed in the proximal tubule. We know this through evidence from still another ingenious technique, called the "stop-flow" method. If the ureter of an experimental animal is blocked, tubular flow may be prevented for a period of time. Sudden removal of this block will release fluid from all the nephrons; the fluid emerging first will be from the collecting ducts, and the last to come out will be from the proximal tubules. Because of the pressure built up in the plugged system, fluid from the proximal region of the nephron is little changed by its passage through distal parts, and thus an experimental analysis of the fluid from each stage in the nephron is possible. Results from stop-flow procedures show clearly that blood plasma and proximal tubular fluid have the same total solute concentration, and hence the same osmotic pressure. They are thus termed *isotonic*.

3. Comparative studies of nephric function. Inspection of a variety of different kinds of vertebrate animals has contributed greatly to our knowledge of which parts of the nephron do what. The kidney, as we have emphasized before, is a water-balance organ; and vertebrates occupy a variety of environments which present different demands for water conservation. In fresh water the total solute concentration is lower than that of the blood, so that water constantly tends to enter organisms that live in it. Sea water, on the other hand, can be regarded as a "physiologically dry" environment, since it is equal to or greater than the blood of most marine vertebrates in osmotic pressure. Terrestrial organisms are not in contact with water and must drink it or derive it metabolically from foods, and so they too are confronted with a conservation problem.

A simple anatomical inspection of the nephrons of different vertebrates living in these situations tells us a great deal about function. Marine bony fish, for example, are able to drink sea water and excrete much of its salts through the gills; but they still must conserve water and therefore possess reduced glomeruli. Some of them have even disposed of glomeruli altogether. These marine fish therefore save water by pumping less of it. Freshwater fish and amphibians, on the other hand, are perpetually flooded with water; they possess large, active glomeruli. Since there is no requirement for water reabsorption in these animals, no segment specialized for that purpose is present in their nephrons—though *salt* conservation through reabsorption is practiced.

Among vertebrates birds and mammals are unique in their ability to excrete a urine which is *more concentrated than the blood*. This ability is associated with an elongated "thin segment" of nephron, called Henle's loop, interposed between proximal and distal tubules. These structures loop out into the medulla of the kidney and back; the nephron then once again doubles back on itself, and collecting ducts pass the loop on their way to the center of the medulla. Apparently, the action of Henle's loop is actually to reabsorb more sodium from the urine passing through it; temporarily, the urine is thus made less concentrated than blood plasma. But the effect of this additional solute reabsorption is to make the intercellular fluids of the renal medulla more concentrated. Thus (under some conditions) water will be withdrawn osmotically from the collecting ducts that pass back through this region, and in this way the final urine can be made more concentrated than the blood plasma from which it was originally filtered. The secret of the system is that channels flowing in opposite directions are exchanging material and thus influencing one another. Such *countercurrent exchange* systems are often encountered in biology (p. 209); often, energy (i.e., heat) is exchanged instead of material.

So far our emphasis has been that the vertebrate kidney regulates body-fluid volume and concentration by filtering blood and then selectively reabsorbing much of the water and dissolved material. There is no question that in its evolutionary history the kidney was originally a water-balance organ. But animals also use their kidneys to eliminate toxic metabolic products. The nephron must therefore have the capacity for total excretion of certain kinds of molecules, which means that it must do more than simply filter them. This is achieved through a different kind of active transport process—one of forcible excretion, even against a concentration gradient. One molecule treated in this way is para-amino hippuric acid (PAH). When this substance is injected into the blood, all of it is removed in the urine. This fact provides physiologists with a convenient way of measuring blood flow through the kidney. If the concentration of PAH in the blood is known, its rate of appearance in the urine can be used to calculate directly the amount of blood passing through the kidney per unit time. The site of active excretion is the proximal tubule.

Aside from its experimental convenience, PAH is not a particularly important molecule. But a group of very important substances indeed turn out to be handled in exactly the same way; these are nitrogenous excretory products derived ultimately from ammonia (NH_3). In a variety of cellular metabolic processes involving purines and pyrimidines ("nitrogen bases") as well as amino acids, such products are ultimately released from cells. The specific final form in which they are excreted depends on the kind of organism and, in particular, on the water available to it. Most marine invertebrates, which are isotonic with the water in which they live, and freshwater invertebrates, which are osmotically superior to their environment, are able to maintain a high level of fluid exchange between inside and outside. Both are able to flood out toxic waste products in very dilute solution, and the ammonia can therefore be disposed of directly. Since marine fish must conserve water, they could not possibly dilute a waste product to this extent. They convert their ammonia to trimethylamine $[(CH_3)_3N]$, which is less toxic. Most mammals produce urea (Fig. 6-6) as an end-product of nitrogen metabolism; this substance is less toxic than ammonia and is actively secreted by the proximal tubule, so that its final concentration in urine is very high. Of all urea-producing vertebrates, only one group—the marine sharks—has adopted

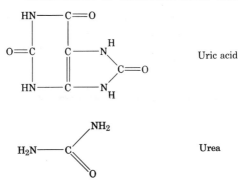

Fig. 6-6.   Structural formulae for uric acid and urea.

a means of handling urea other than total excretion. Sharks tolerate a very high concentration of urea in the blood, utilizing it to raise the internal osmotic pressure to a level considerably higher than that of the sea water. They are the only animals to have evolved a means of attaining osmotic superiority over the ocean. Reptiles and birds, perhaps the champion water conservers of the entire animal world, produce (in common with insects) still another nitrogenous waste product. This is uric acid (Fig. 6-6), an extremely insoluble compound; it is concentrated by active secretion into the tubule, where it finally crystallizes out. Water can then be reabsorbed until the uric acid is virtually a paste, whereupon it is excreted. This substance (though not regarded with affection by lovers of park statuary) can accumulate into fertilizer deposits of considerable economic importance wherever birds are thoughtful enough to nest in large colonies.

It should be noted that neither water balance nor nitrogen excretion is a major problem for most plants. The former problem is virtually eliminated by the tolerance of osmotic swelling provided by the cell wall. Nitrogen excretion is a problem primarily for animals, most of which feed on protein-rich diets containing far more amino acids than they require for their own growth. As in the case of bacteria feeding on amino acids (Chap. 2) excess amino acids can be degraded as an energy source, and it is the products of degradation that give rise to the problem of nitrogen excretion. Most plants, on the other hand, require ammonium salts or some other inorganic nitrogen salt as a source of nitrogen for the synthesis of proteins and are not apt to use these hard-won proteins as energy sources. It is sometimes said that plants are preeminently machines that metabolize carbohydrates, whereas animals are primarily protein metabolizers. An overstatement in the qualitative sense, this notion has some merit as a quantitative comparison; it helps to account for the different ways in which the two groups handle exchange with the environment.

An additional difference is seen in the tendency of some plants, particularly the woody plants, to deposit nitrogenous compounds such as the lignins and alkaloids in the xylem of the heartwood that no longer serves as conducting tissue. Whether this can be considered as the deposition of excretory products is not clear, but these compounds certainly serve ancillary functions in strengthening the heartwood and making it more resistant to decay.

INTERNAL TRANSPORT

The Size Problem

Reference has already been made, in connection with exchange processes (p. 203), to the problem of increasing size that confronts multicellular organisms. The same limits are imposed on transport systems. Diffusion, though an adequate means of distribution to nearby points, cannot keep pace with the demands of a large and active cell mass when the distances involved are large. Thus multicellular organisms have evolved transport mechanisms that rely, not on the movement of molecules within a solution, but on the more efficient system of mass flow of the entire solution itself—in other words, on *convection*.

Cellular Transport Systems

Some organisms, especially some invertebrate animals, have based an entire transport system on a mechanism of cellular transport that has great general significance. These organisms are too large to rely on diffusion for the supply of nutrients to their constituent cells, but they lack the means for systematic circulation of body fluids. The body cavity of a coelenterate, for example, is lined with an absorptive epithelium. Among the cells composing this layer are some whose location there is only temporary. These wandering cells, which have a variable shape and move by pseudopodia, are called *amoebocytes*. They engulf small particles of food and then detach from the epithelium, moving elsewhere and passing on the proceeds to cells in other locations. During this time much of the actual chemical breakdown of food molecules occurs, and digestion in such animals is largely intracellular.

Liquid-Phase Transport Systems

Generally the remarkable properties of water as a "universal solvent" suffice for the job of transporting sufficient quantities of substances (respiratory gases, dissolved food molecules, etc.) to fill the demands of the cells at long distances from the exchange surfaces of multicellular organisms. When demands for a particular substance are especially high, however, such transport systems can rely on the added efficiency of special carrier compounds, which enable the circulating medium to transport more material per unit volume than it could hold in simple solution. (Such a carrier is the protein hemoglobin, which transports loosely combined oxygen in the circulatory systems of many animals.) In either case, it is necessary to have a route of transport and a mechanism for pumping the aqueous solution. We will consider a number of examples, beginning with the transport mechanisms of vascular plants.

Transport Systems in Vascular Plants. The magnitude of the transport problems faced by organisms is probably nowhere more obvious than in vascular land plants; not only are some of them immense, but there is an unparalleled segregation in space of different metabolic functions. All of the water and dissolved mineral substances necessary for the growth and maintenance of, say, an oak tree must enter through the deeper portions of the roots—though the entire production of energy-rich organic compounds takes place in the leaves. Each site thus depends in a crucial way on the other; yet they may be hundreds of feet apart.

Generally the transport of elaborated organic materials on the one hand, and of salts and water on the other, take place in two separate conduction systems, the *xylem* and the *phloem,* whose development and anatomy were discussed in Chapter 5 (p. 176–183). Normally, xylem transports water and dissolved salts up the stem, from roots to leaves, while phloem is involved with the downward transport of a rich solution of carbohydrates (largely sucrose) produced as the result of photosynthetic activity in leaves. There are exceptions: organic substances must at times move upward through phloem from leaves to immature parts, especially fruits, which are higher on the stem; and sugars sometimes appear in xylem vessels, the most celebrated instance being that maple sap is actually tapped from xylem, not phloem. As far as is known, however, xylem conduction always is upward, whereas that in phloem may be up but is usually down.

THE TRANSPIRATION SYSTEM:XYLEM. It will be recalled that the xylem of plants is composed of several cell types, of which those concerned with conduction are the cylindrical tracheids and vessel elements. In mature and functional xylem these cells have lost their protoplasm but retained their wall structure. Tracheids (Fig. 6-7), which are

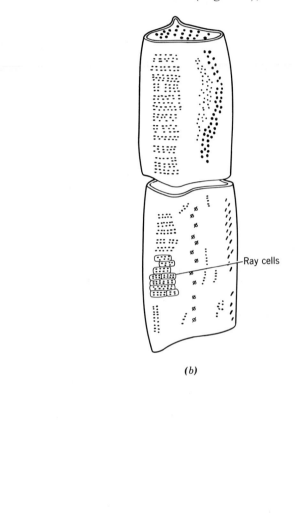

(b)

(a)

Fig. 6-7.   Vessel elements in xylem. (a) Xylem of tulip tree, Liriodendron. (b) Xylem of oak, Quercus. (From K. Esau, The Anatomy of Seed Plants, Wiley, 1960, pp. 79, 81.)

the main conducting elements of conifers, are basically "single" in structure; but the vessels of angiosperms usually occur in long lines, end-to-end, with the original end-walls lost so that they form pipes which may be many meters in length. In both cases there is a continuous sequence of conducting cells from the zone of root hairs near the root tip to the meshwork of veins embedded in the parenchyma of the leaves.

In a tall tree this is a long route for water and dissolved nutrients to take; and the fact that it is accomplished against gravity has made the ascent of sap in xylem a fascinating problem with a very long experimental history. In fact, most of the significant observations on this remarkable phenomenon were made well before the twentieth century. One of these was that the stems of some species of plants with their root system intact exude sap upward. If a tube is attached to the stem, the pressure created in the roots can be measured by the height to which fluid can be raised. Pressures of several atmospheres have been reported in such experiments. The basis for such a *root pressure* was made clear in the section on absorption mechanisms. Water is driven into the epidermal root cell osmotically; the sequence of turgor pressure increases would be expected to force water into the xylem channels and thence upwards. The difficulty is that in many plants, including reasonably tall ones, significant root pressures cannot be demonstrated. And even where they are found, there is doubt that they play an important role in the ascent of sap.

The second observation is that actively transpiring branches or tops of plants are able to *pull* a column of water upward; a common household repetition of this experiment is the uptake of dye by cut flowers placed in a vase of dyed water. The forces developed by this mechanism are considerable: some transpiring branches are able to raise a column of mercury to heights of over a meter. This phenomenon is now widely held to be the crucial one in driving the transpiration stream upward in plants. The "cohesion-tension" theory includes the following features. (1) Water is lost from the leaves, primarily through the open stomata, by evaporation; the water-depleted cells then exert an increased inward *osmotic* pressure on the water in xylem elements in the leaves. (2) Water is thus withdrawn from the top of the xylem columns, creating a negative pressure or *tension* in the column, which is transmitted to the surrounding cells in the root. (3) These cells, in turn, lose water to the negative xylem pressure and gain it osmotically from the outside. Thus the transpiration stream is believed to be driven not by pushing but by pulling; the critical event is water loss from the leaves, not absorption in roots. The stomata (pp. 216–217) play the major role in regulating transpiration rate.

It must be noted that the force which moves the water upward is *not* "suction"; even a perfect vacuum cannot raise water higher than 32 feet. The forces of cohesion are the attractive forces that bind water molecules to each other and to the stem; thus it is essential that the column *not* be broken by air, since the attractive forces between gas molecules are negligible compared to those between molecules in a liquid. It has never been proven that the columns are unbroken by gas; in fact, it is thought by some that they are, and that the cohesion theory must therefore be incorrect. Nor has a satisfactory direct measurement of tension in a "normal" and unbroken xylem column been made. It is clear, however, that the pressure inside xylem in trees is less than 1 atmosphere, and that the system is therefore not driven by root absorption. At present, the cohesion-tension theory is the most satisfactory explanation.

TRANSLOCATION OF ORGANIC MATERIALS. It was established long ago, initially through some ingenious experiments performed by the great Italian biologist Malpighi in the seventeenth century, that the outer layer of conducting tissue in trees (the phloem) is responsible for the downward transport of materials produced in the leaves. The experiment is a simple one. A ring is cut into the bark around the stem or a branch, so that the externally located phloem is cut but the xylem layer is not interrupted. Gradually, organic materials accumulate *above* the ring but are depleted below it, showing that a downward pathway has been intercepted. If the cut is made deeper, into the sapwood of the tree so as to cut the xylem also, the leaves above the cut quickly wilt, showing that an upward route for water has been severed in addition. More recent evidence, using radioactive labeling of photosynthetic products with $C^{14}O_2$, has confirmed the old conclusion that they travel in phloem cells.

Phloem, like xylem, is composed of several types of cells derived from the cambium. The elements of primary concern in the translocation process are *sieve cells* or *sieve-tube elements*—the latter differing from the former in that they are joined together in a compound tube of considerable length. Sieve cells are found in coniferous trees, and probably are the evolutionary precursors of the more highly specialized sieve-tube elements found in angiosperms. The general structure of sieve-tube elements is shown in Fig. 6-8. A most important feature is that these cells (though they do not possess nuclei when mature) are, unlike xylem elements, "alive" and contain cytoplasm. Each element is usually accompanied by smaller phloem companion cells. The connections between elements are of particular interest: the

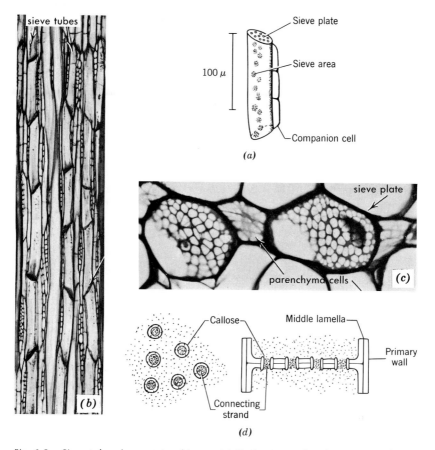

Fig. 6-8. Sieve-tube elements in phloem. (a) Single sieve-tube element in *Robinia*. (b) Tangential section through phloem of *Campsis*. (c) Sieve plates of *Cucurbita*. (d) A sieve plate system (diagrammatic). (From K. Esau, *The Anatomy of Seed Plants*, Wiley, 1960, p. 123, 126, 127, 124.)

end walls are pitted, forming a sieve plate dividing off the two elements. Through these pits the adjacent sieve-tube elements are connected by protoplasmic strands, which can be interpreted as greatly enlarged plasmadesmata.

The efficiency with which carbohydrates derived from photosynthesis can move along these channels is perhaps best illustrated in some plants which store these products (e.g., starch) in their roots or in fruits. In pumpkins the peak dry weight gain per hour is nearly 2 g. The approximate concentration of carbohydrate in a sample of phloem fluid can be measured, and sensible estimates of the total cross-sectional area of the sieve tubes determined. Such a calculation reveals that the amount of material accumulated in a potato, for example, requires rates of movement of sugars in the phloem which are many thousands of times faster than known diffusion rates. Apparently, we must look for a different explanation.

Although this issue has not been completely resolved, the most reasonable explanation of movement in phloem is that it is achieved through a kind of mass flow, driven by pressure, in which both solvent (water) and solute (sugars) move through the channel together. This system is entirely different from diffusion, in which solute molecules distribute themselves in a stationary solvent. The driving force for this movement comes from the active secretion of sugars into the phloem elements in the leaves. Phloem fluid from leaves or upper stems may contain 30% sucrose; in the lower stems or roots the concentration of sucrose is much lower. The high internal concentration of sugar in the upper phloem will cause water to enter these elements osmotically, producing a powerful positive pressure capable of moving the whole fluid column downward. In those cases where sugar concentrations in the phloem elements are higher at a point lower on the stem, the driving force will be upward. This probably explains the fact that phloem transport may be upward, as, for example, in the transfer of sugar to fruits located high in a tree. One argument brought against the mass-flow theory is that bidirectional transport between two points has been shown to occur simultaneously. This would be damaging evidence indeed if the same set of elements were involved in both directions of movement; but this has *not* been shown, and it is perfectly reasonable to suppose that *adjacent* sieve channels might conduct in opposite directions.

Recent evidence supporting the mass-flow theory has been produced by experiments that take advantage of natural syringes for sampling phloem fluid. Previously it had been necessary to obtain such fluid by cutting into the conducting tissue; but under these circumstances the phloem cells are damaged and the fluid may be contaminated by contact with other tissues. Certain aphids, however, feed on phloem tissue by inserting a proboscis composed of separate stylets into a single sieve tube element. (Fig. 6-9). By detaching the aphid from its beak and substituting a fine capillary, the experimenter can sample the fluid. The exudation of sugar solutions from the aphid stylets shows that the fluid within the phloem elements really is under pressure. Furthermore, studies on such exudates have revealed that the sucrose concentration does in fact decrease downward in the system. The only current argument against the mass-flow theory

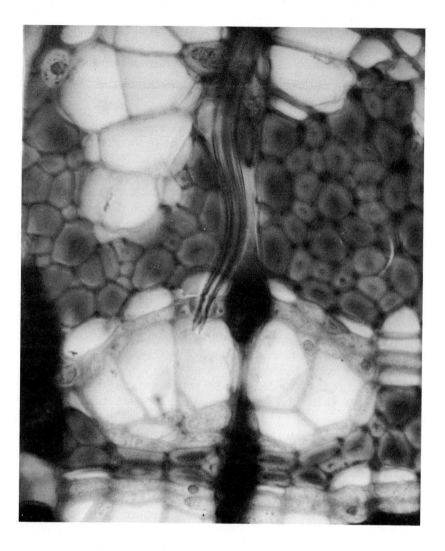

Fig. 6-9. Penetration of a single sieve element by the stylets of an aphid. ×540. (From M. Zimmerman, *Science,* 134, 76 (1961).)

proposes that the sieve plates may not be sufficiently porous to allow mass movement at the observed rates. Until it is proven that the perforations are really "plugged," however, it remains the most likely explanation of the movement of photosynthetic products from leaves to other structures in the stem.

Circulatory Systems in Animals. One of the most important differences between plants and animals reflects the basic way in which their tissues are put together: animal tissues, consisting of cells unconfined by cellulose walls, are permeated by relatively large areas of free space. The more organized into tissue and organ systems an animal becomes, the larger and more systematically these "extracellular spaces" are. In plants the major moving fluid systems are confined within cellular elements of xylem and phloem. But in animals blood and other circulating fluids are extracellular in location.

With a permissible use of imagination, one can trace the probable evolutionary history of these extracellular fluids. In lower invertebrates the major space is the primitive gut or archenteron; it and the more confined gaps between cells in the tissue layers are bathed essentially in the external medium, usually sea water. With the development of a true coelomic space between tissues of the gut and the body wall, however, a new compartment originated which could be kept out of communication with the external environment—unlike the gut, which must always be open for business in connection with nutrient exchange processes. These coelomic cavities connect freely with the smaller spaces between tissue cells; and the fluids within can now be made to differ markedly in composition from those of the surrounding environment, providing a sort of buffer between the cells and the external medium. Exchange, of course, thereby becomes for the most part a two-step process, with the extracellular fluids acting as intermediary. But at the same time, the opportunity arises for facilitating exchange by *moving* the extracellular fluids—both with respect to the external medium and the internal cells served. Such a movement hastens exchange by insuring that both saturated and depleted fluids are continually replaced at their respective points of equilibration. A separate and mobile internal fluid compartment also confers other advantages: it can be subjected to regulation, and provides a sort of portable environment for the animal's cells which frees them from many obligations of self protection. The importance of this was classically expressed in Claude Bernard's dictum: "La fixité de la milieu intérieur c'est la condition de la vie libre" (The stability of the internal environment is the condition for a free life).

Originally, movement of the extracellular fluid compartment was achieved by generalized body muscles in the course of their use for other purposes. In some organisms, however, special muscular pumps for the purpose evolved; these are found in most higher invertebrates and all vertebrates. In the simplest case the heart serves merely to slosh the fluids around. But in arthropods and some other invertebrates vessels are employed to conduct the fluid from the heart to specific tissues or exchanging surfaces. The fluids are free to return through body spaces to the heart, and the system is thus an *open* one in which no distinction can be made between the fluid within the vessels and that without. The final step was taken with the addition of a new fluid compartment by enclosure of a special circulating medium entirely within vessels. Such completely *closed* circulatory systems, characteristic of all vertebrates and a few invertebrates, permit the retention of special cell types, proteins, etc., that differentiate blood from the extracellular fluid proper. The circulatory system of a vertebrate animal serves as the highway for a remarkably diverse commerce. Blood carries oxygen to cells and transports carbon dioxide away from them; it supplies glucose and other nutrients and withdraws nitrogen wastes; transports a variety of hormones; carries phagocytic cells from place to place; serves as a vehicle for countless types of antibodies; and controls temperature. In the following general account of animal circulatory systems, we refer for the most part to the closed circulation characteristic of vertebrates.

THE DYNAMICS OF CIRCULATION. In any closed circulatory system, the exchange occurs exclusively in the meshwork of capillaries that permeates the living tissues of the organism. The rest of the system, including the heart and major vessels, is devoted to pumping and routing the blood. Even cells in the walls of these structures must rely on a capillary meshwork that is fed blood from collateral blood vessels, rather than from the lumen of the heart and blood vessels themselves. The capillaries of a mammal constitute a remarkable organ system: their total length is over 50,000 miles in man, and they reach within rapid diffusing distance of every cell. They differ in structure from arteries and veins, the major vessels leading from and to the heart respectively. Arteries have reasonably thick walls consisting primarily of smooth muscle surrounded by a connective tissue sheet; the walls of veins largely lack the muscle layer and are thus substantially thinner (Fig. 6-10). Capillaries are the most reduced of all, their walls consisting merely of a delicately fitted masonry of thin endothelial cells which is continuous with the endothelial lining of the arteries and veins. They are so small, usually 15μ or less in diameter, that red blood cells are in close contact with the walls (and may even get stuck temporarily) as they are moved along. The capillary wall is selectively permeable: water and all dissolved small molecules flow readily through it, but it restricts (though not always completely) the passage of protein molecules and

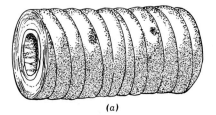

(a)

(b)

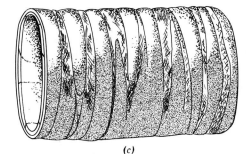

(c)

Fig. 6-10.   Structure of the walls of blood vessels. The capillary (b) consists of only a single layer of endothelial cells. A similar endothelium in the vein (c) is surrounded by fibrous tissue and a thin muscle layer, whereas in the artery (a) it is sheathed by layers of muscle and fibrous tissues. (From B. Zweifach, Sci. Amer., **200,** 54–60, (1959).)

of blood cells. If diffusion or pressure gradients exist, the small molecules in blood plasma may move into or out of the extracellular fluids, while proteins and cellular components of the blood are retained within the blood vessels. To provide intimate commerce with individual cells, the capillary system has an intricate microanatomy within each tissue. Capillaries in a muscle run parallel to fiber bundles with occasional cross connections (Fig. 6-11). In the nervous system, there is frequently a delicate tracery of capillary loops surrounding the cell bodies of neurons; and in other tissues complex crossing arrangements insure that every cell is within close range of one or more capillary lines.

This complex apparatus is served by a pump, the heart; blood flows to the capillary system through arteries and returns in veins (but in open systems through spaces or sinuses in the tissues). Since one of

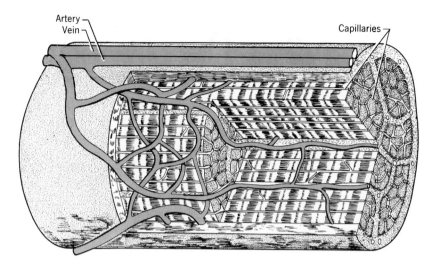

Artery
Vein
Capillaries

Fig. 6-11. Invasion of a single muscle fiber by capillaries, which form a parallel, cross-connected network among the individual fibrils. (From B. Zweifach, *Sci. Amer.,* **200,** 54–60, (1959).)

the major functions of a circulatory system is to provide for the exchange of oxygen and carbon dioxide, the blood must at some time pass through a capillary network located at an exchanging surface. We cannot explore in any detail the comparative anatomy of vertebrate circulatory systems, but it is worth noting two basic kinds of plan for the circuit between exchanging areas and tissue cells. In fish the circulatory system operates essentially as a one-cycle system. Blood enters the heart from systemic veins and is pumped into an arterial system leading to the gills. There it becomes oxygenated and gives up carbon dioxide in an exchanging capillary system, and enters another set of arterial vessels which conduct it to the tissues. From there, it returns in systemic veins to the heart once more. In the quasi-terrestrial amphibia, however, a portion of the blood is sent to the lungs and skin for oxygenation and a portion in systemic arteries to the tissues; a partial division of the heart results in only incomplete separation of oxygenated and depleted blood. Thus the beginnings of a two-cycle system appear, but the phases are not fully separated. In mammals and birds they are discrete phases: the heart is fully divided into two halves, one receiving blood from the tissues and pumping it to the lungs for oxygenation, the other receiving oxygenated blood from the lungs and conveying it to the tissues.

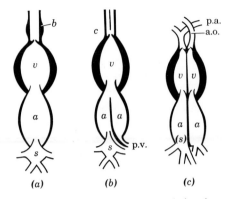

Fig. 6-12. Evolution of the heart. The arrangement of chambers is shown diagrammatically for (a) a fish; (b) an amphibian; and (c) a mammal. a, atrium; v, ventricle; b, bulbus arteriosus; s, sinus venosus; pa, pulmonary artery; pv, pulmonary vein; ao, aorta. (After Kingsley.)

The flow of blood through this vessel system is dependent on hydrostatic pressure supplied by the contraction of heart muscle. The mammalian heart consists of a pair of ventricles pumping directly into the arterial system, and a pair of auricles that receive venous blood. The ventricles are thicker walled and more muscular, providing the major source of pressure for the system; the auricles are employed mainly to pump blood through one-way valves into the ventricles. Ventricular muscles are arranged in spiral sheets; since they contract from the front backward, they actually wring blood out into the arterial tree. In detailed structure heart muscle differs from other striated muscles in that the fibers form a branching, anastomosing system in which the fibers may be regarded as essentially continuous. Though divided at points by disc-like discontinuities (the intercalated discs, see Fig. 7-27), heart muscle fibers conduct excitation and hence contraction freely from one point to another, and thus the heart behaves as a unit in contraction.

One of the easiest physiological experiments is to excise a frog's heart and place it in a Ringer's solution designed to duplicate its normal ionic environment. It keeps beating at an essentially normal frequency, often for hours. Although the heart is normally supplied with nerves from the autonomic nervous system, these clearly are not required for the normal initiation of its beat; the rhythm of contraction arises in the heart muscle itself. Such hearts are called *myogenic;* the hearts of some invertebrates (including arthropods) depend instead on a small intrinsic network of a dozen or so nerve cells for the initiation of contraction, and hence are called *neurogenic.*

We can get some clue to the place of origin of the heartbeat by two means: first, exploring with electrodes to find the locus of the earliest electrical activity that must precede contraction; and second, comparing mammalian hearts with those of lower vertebrates. The first experiment indicates that the earliest region of excitation is located in the right auricle (or atrium) of the mammalian heart. In a fish heart, in which atrium and ventricle are undivided, the anatomical arrangement resembles a segmented tube more than a compressed, rounder structure. The first "segment" is a coalescence of veins, the *sinus venosus*; the second is the atrium, the third the ventricle, the fourth the beginning of the aorta. The tube contracts from front to back, that is, the beat is initiated in the sinus venosus. Other evidence indicates that the sinus venosus of lower vertebrates has been amalgamated into the right atrium of higher vertebrates; it has still retained its function as the leader or pacemaker in heart contraction, and is now called the *sinus node*.

When blood is forced out of the ventricle into the arterial system, it is pushed with considerable force. The hydrostatic pressure exerted on the walls of the aorta (the exiting arterial trunk) in man is normally 120 mm of mercury at the peak of the ventricular contraction (systole) and 80 mm. Hg when the ventricles are relaxed and filling passively (diastole). This difference is felt as the "pulse." Fluid under pressure in any system of filled pipes, of course, encounters a frictional resistance from its movement past their walls (if this were not true, oil could be piped from Texas to Massachusetts by one small pumping station). The pressure drops to about 60/40 mm Hg in smaller arteries, to 40 mm Hg at the small arterioles, to 15 mm Hg at the venous ends of the capillaries, and below 10 mm Hg in some of the major veins. The pulse drops out and usually cannot be detected in capillaries. The low venous pressure is assisted in returning blood to the heart against gravity by the action of skeletal muscles against the thin-walled veins, which occurs in the course of the normal movements of the individual. One-way valves in the vein make this a "lock" system in which external pressure squeezes blood up above the next valve, where it is held.

Pressure also plays another important role. In the capillary it tends to drive fluids out through the permeable walls into the surrounding extracellular fluids. If only this outward hydrostatic pressure existed, the circulation would lose volume rapidly, but a compensating inward pressure is supplied osmotically. The capillary wall is impermeable to proteins; plasma, containing a large concentration of proteins, exerts an inward osmotic pressure (*colloid osmotic pressure*) across the wall. This value is intermediate between the hydrostatic pressure extremes

for "arterial" and "venous" capillaries respectively, and thus net exchange between blood and extracellular fluid will usually be outward
in arterial capillaries (where hydrostatic pressure exceeds osmotic
pressure) and inward in venous capillaries (where osmotic pressure is
greater). This hypothesis, originated by the British physiologist Starling,
was ingeniously confirmed by experiments like that shown in Fig. 6-13.
The capillary was compressed, and its internal pressure was measured.
At the same time the rate of flow into it (absorption) or out of it (filtration) was measured by the rate of flow of red blood cells away from or
toward the compression point.

These designations arterial and venous originally referred to the two
ends of one capillary. It is now understood that many capillaries in a
tissue at any given time are made inactive by constriction at the
arteriolar ends; such capillaries are venous in terms of pressure, and
open ones are arterial. In this way blood plasma, while retaining its
assortment of special proteins and cellular elements, is permitted to
engage in wholesale exchange with the fluids that directly bathe the
cells. It is probably true, nevertheless, that the straightforward diffusion
of such molecules as glucose and urea is a more important force in their

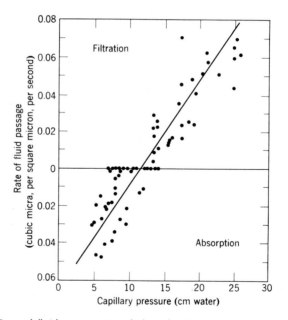

Fig. 6-13.   Rate of fluid passage into (below the line) and out of (above the line)
a capillary, as a function of the hydrostatic capillary pressure. Determined by
Landis using the technique described in the text. (From E. M. Landis, Am. J.
Physiol., **82**, 217–238 (1927).)

distribution between plasma and tissue than their *mass* transport in an osmotically or mechanically shifted volume of solvent.

TRANSPORT OF RESPIRATORY GASES. One of the critical functions of many circulatory systems is the transport of oxygen to tissue cells and of carbon dioxide away from them. The first requirement is that the system be composed of a fluid in which both gases are soluble (water qualifies), and that the fluid move sufficiently with respect to cells and exchange regions that maximum gradients for equilibration are always available. In other words, an ordinary aqueous solution such as blood plasma or coelomic fluid will do *if* the demands of the tissues do not exceed the capacity of the solution to hold enough O_2 or CO_2 in solution. Demand, of course, depends on two factors: the volume of cells being served and their level of metabolic activity. In most large, active, complex animals the oxygen-carrying capacity of blood is boosted tremendously by the use of special protein carriers that combine with oxygen. The solubility of oxygen in blood plasma is about 0.3 volumes per cent at 37°C; the presence of hemoglobin, the protein carrier in mammalian red blood cells, boosts this to about 20 volumes per cent. Some lower invertebrates get along without blood pigments; more surprisingly, a few vertebrates do too. Several kinds of antarctic fish have "red" blood cells that lack hemoglobin entirely; all of the oxygen transported is carried in physical solution in the plasma. They manage to get away with this because water holds more oxygen in solution at low temperatures, while at the same time metabolic demands of the tissues are considerably lowered.

The oxygen carrier of all other vertebrates is hemoglobin; it is a protein with a molecular weight of 68,000, bound to one or more molecules of the iron prophyrin class (*heme*) (Fig. 6-14). It is thus

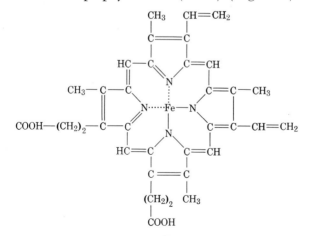

Fig. 6-14. Structure of heme, the prosthetic group of hemoglobin.

chemically related to the cytochrome pigments so important in cellular oxidations (Stern and Nanney, Chap. 8). The protein component (globin) varies from species to species as most proteins do, though in higher vertebrates there are always four heme groups per protein molecule. The very primitive cyclostomes (lampreys, etc.) have a protein of about a quarter the molecular weight and containing only a single heme. So does *myoglobin*, a related pigment of mammalian muscle. Thus there seems to be something important about the submultiple molecular weight value of 17,000 and its association with the heme group: indeed, vertebrate hemoglobin proteins break up rather easily into two chains of 34,000 MW, and secondarily into 17,000 MW fragments with 1 heme each. The heme groups are probably located at surface sites, bound through the iron atom to the amino acid histidine.

The red blood cells (erythrocytes) in which vertebrate hemoglobins are carried are highly specialized cells which, when mature, are little more than sacks of pigment; those of mammals even lose their nuclei. They are produced by special tissues—primarily bone marrow in adult mammals—and have a fairly short life in the circulation (about 100 days in man). Thus the replacement demands are little short of fantastic: something like 2 million new red blood cells are produced *per second* in man.

The respiratory pigments have probably evolved several times; many invertebrates have hemoglobins with a similar heme, but attached to proteins with molecular weights of over a million. These large molecules are free in the circulatory fluid, rather than being enclosed in cells. Some annelid worms possess chlorocruorin, an iron-containing green pigment with a porphyrin different from that of hemoglobin. There are two other pigments of importance in invertebrates in which the metal is attached directly to the protein. In hemocyanin, the blue respiratory pigment found in many molluscs and arthopods, the metal is copper, while in hemerythrin (found in a few annelids and other invertebrates) it is iron. The former pigment is always free in solution, the latter always contained in blood cells.

COMBINATION OF OXYGEN WITH RESPIRATORY PIGMENTS. The important feature of any of the carrier proteins is their ability to combine *reversibly* with oxygen, loading it at exchanging surfaces where the oxygen concentration is relatively high and unloading it freely in the tissues where it is low. The nature of this combination is often misunderstood. Oxygen does bind to the heme groups of hemoglobin, but the hemoglobin does not become oxidized: the iron is in the ferrous (Fe^{++}) condition whether or not it is combined with oxygen, and so electrons are neither lost nor gained. This loose covalent association between a heme group and a molecule of oxygen depends on the presence of the protein; heme groups alone do not combine in this way. It also depends, of course, on the amount of available oxygen—that is, on the partial pressure of oxygen at which the measurement is made—and on the oxygen affinity of the respiratory pigment (some hemoglobins are more avid combiners than others). Such measurements are usually made spectroscopically. The absorption spectrum of reduced hemoglobin has a large absorption band at short wavelengths (the Soret band) and a low secondary maximum in the middle of the spectrum. When the hemoglobin is oxygenated, a pair of intensified bands appears in the middle instead, and the change can be followed by measuring the altered absorption. The percentage of hemoglobin combined with oxygen, plotted against oxygen tension, is the *oxygen equilibrium curve.*

The maximum amount of oxygen which can be carried is very different in different organisms: human hemoglobin carries 20 volumes per cent at saturation, whereas that of a mudflat worm, *Arenicola,* carries only 7 volumes per cent. In general, active animals have much higher carrying capacities than sessile or sedentary ones with lower metabolic rates, and other environmental correlations can be found as well; high-altitude mammals and diving mammals (like the seal) have even higher carrying capacities than man. Second, the form of the oxygen equilibrium curve may differ: for *Arenicola,* the curve has its region of most rapid change at very low oxygen tensions, saturating at values of only 8–10 mm Hg. This high-affinity pigment is very useful to its owner, which must load oxygen at the very low partial pressures found underneath tidal mud and must unload it at tissue tensions just a little lower. It would be no good at all to a mammal, however, because it would never surrender its oxygen at the oxygen tensions normally found in mammalian tissues.

The curve for mammalian hemoglobin is sigmoid in shape, though we might have expected it to be a simple hyperbola of some sort. The complexity of form is due to interactions between the heme groups, such that the combination of an oxygen molecule with one heme group on a globin makes it likelier that an oxygen molecule will combine with the second, third, or fourth. Pigments (like myoglobin) with only one heme per globin actually do have hyperbolic equilibrium curves. The important feature of the hemoglobin curve is that it becomes almost completely saturated at oxygen tensions characteristic of lung alveoli (about 100 mm of Hg, a little below the partial pressure of atmospheric oxygen); and that it unloads a substantial amount of this oxygen at tissue tensions (which may range between 5 to 30 mm Hg in different capillary systems).

The affinity of blood pigments for oxygen is affected by other factors;

among the most important of these is the pH of blood. When CO_2, produced through the metabolic activity of cells, enters blood in the capillaries, much of it forms carbonic acid (H_2CO_3), the dissociation of which lowers the pH of the blood somewhat. Human hemoglobin and many others show a reduced oxygen affinity with increased H^+ ion concentration, and the shift of the equilibrium curve is called the *Bohr Effect*. It actually facilitates the transport function, since the drop in pH occasioned by the addition of O_2 in the tissues causes the blood to release more oxygen than it otherwise would. Conversely, the loss of CO_2 in the lungs increases oxygen affinity once again at the loading site.

TRANSPORT OF CARBON DIOXIDE. Blood carries much more carbon dioxide than it should: up to 60 volumes per cent compared to the value of 2.5 which would be expected to enter physical solution on the basis of the partial pressures of CO_2 encountered by blood. Clearly most of the CO_2 is not in solution, nor is much of it transported by protein carriers (hemoglobin does combine with a little). By far the major portion is in the form of bicarbonate ion (HCO_3^-) in combination with various cations. The combination of CO_2 with water to form H_2CO_3 is normally very slow; but vertebrate red cells contain an enzyme, carbonic anhydrase, which catalyzes this reaction; thus virtually all of the bicarbonate ion is formed in the red cell, according to the over-all equation:

$$H_2O + CO_2 \underset{\text{anhydrase}}{\overset{\text{carbonic}}{\rightleftharpoons}} H_2CO_3 \rightleftharpoons H^+ + HCO_3^-$$

As the bicarbonate ions so produced move out of the red cell along their concentration gradient, Cl^- ions exchange with them. There remains the problem of the H^+ ions produced in the dissociation, which represent a potentially very serious drop in pH. This pH change is restricted by an extremely effective buffer system involving hemoglobin. When uncombined with oxygen, hemoglobin is weakly acidic, represented as HHb; $HHbO_2$, oxygenated hemoglobin, dissociates H^+ ions more readily. These different acidic strengths of hemoglobin very nearly balance the gain and loss of H^+ ions from carbonic acid. Thus in the tissues where H_2CO_3 is produced, the increased H^+ concentration resulting is counter-balanced by the association of H^+ with hemoglobin which has been transformed into a weaker acid by its loss of oxygen; and in the lungs the decrease in H^+ concentration (due to the conversion of H_2CO_3 to H_2O and CO_2) is balanced by the greater dissociation of HHb resulting from oxygenation. The essential condition of a buffer system—the coexistence of two acids and the affiliation of H^+ ions with the weaker—are fulfilled because of the variation in acidic strength shown by hemoglobin.

Despite the fact that the respiratory gases O_2 and CO_2 are transported in quite different ways, the carrier mechanisms for both interact—the addition of CO_2 facilitating unloading of oxygen, and the combination of oxygen with hemoglobin affecting its dissociation constant so as to provide buffering capacity for the acidity due to added CO_2.

THE CONTROL OF THE CIRCULATION. Several problems are inherent in the regulation of circulatory flow. First, the potential volume of capillaries is much larger than the total blood volume. Second, tissues differ from time to time in their demands for oxygen and nutrients. Clearly, the organism as a whole cannot afford to oversupply one region at the expense of another, and thus blood distribution must be carefully controlled over a rather wide range. This is an impressive but by no means isolated instance of the kind of integrative regulation that must be provided for every sort of function at the organism level.

It is possible to regulate the flow of fluid being pumped through a system of pipes in three different ways. Either the rate at which the pump works or the volume pumped with each stroke can be changed, or the pipes can be arranged so that their relative diameters can be changed, thereby altering the distribution of fluid flow through each set. The vertebrate circulatory system uses all three kinds of controls.

The heart, though it can beat in isolation, is nevertheless served by nerves from two different sources. One is part of a cranial nerve, the vagus, which comes from a center in the hindbrain; the other source is the sympathetic system. Stimulation of the vagus nerve causes inhibition or slowing of the heartbeat; in the 1920's an ingenious experiment by Otto Loewi (p. 325) established that this effect is caused by the release of a chemical mediator, since found to be acetylcholine. Sympathetic nerve stimulation, on the other hand, accelerates the rate of beating. Both these sets of regulatory neurons are controlled from centers in the hindbrain: stimulation of specific regions there can evoke cardio-acceleration or cardioinhibition.

In addition, however, the heart is able to adjust its performance in terms of the quantity of blood returned through the veins. When filling of the ventricles during systole is rapid and extensive, the contraction is more powerful than if filling is modest. This phenomenon, called Starling's law after its discoverer, insures that the stroke volume keeps up with venous return, though in the intact animal it is often overridden and obscured by the neural control systems.

The smooth muscles that coat arteries and arterioles receive a nervous supply also. The best-defined elements of this supply are sympathetic neurons which, when stimulated, cause contraction of arteriolar smooth muscle, and hence restrict by *vasoconstriction* the flow of blood through that portion of the system. Local dilation of such vessels can also be accomplished by certain parasympathetic motor nerves and by local sensory nerve activity. Vasomotor mechanisms are centrally controlled by areas in the hindbrain, just as heart rate is; and lesions in specific regions can produce dilation of peripheral vessels (and a consequent drop in blood pressure) by interrupting the continuous flux of activity that usually characterizes vasoconstrictor neurons.

What sorts of signals from the circulation bring these integrative systems into play? Basically, they are of two types: chemical, having to do with the oxygen or carbon dioxide content of the blood, and mechanical, concerned with blood pressure. Sensory endings in the aorta and in the carotid arteries respond with increased discharge to increases in blood pressure, and the integrated responses is a decrease in heart rate and vasodilation, especially of the capillaries in the viscera; in this way the pressure is taken off. Conversely, their "spontaneous" frequency can drop when blood pressure decreases, thus producing opposite effects. When *venous* pressure rises, especially in the lungs, other pressure-sensitive receptors initiate cardioacceleration, and the result is a more rapid transfer of blood to the arterial side of the circulation. High carbon dioxide is detected by receptors in the arterial locations, and the reflex response is heart acceleration, vasoconstriction, and thus faster circulation. Dissolved gases can also apparently affect neurons of the medullary centers directly. The entire set of reflexes keeps the blood pressure within safe limits when hemorrhage, for example, causes losses; insures the provision of adequate supplies of oxygen during heavy periods of metabolic demand; redirects and reroutes blood flow for controlling temperature or supplying localized oxygen demands. These operations dramatically illustrate the futility of talking about metabolic matters apart from integration—for even the most everyday kind of metabolic function in the multicellular organism is under community control. We now turn to the specific nature of these controlling systems.

7

Integration

No matter how precisely the machinery of development achieves a balanced population of differentiated cells, no matter how exactly these are arranged with respect to one another, *proper functioning of the whole organization is not possible without continued exchange of information between cells.* This, in essence, is what is meant by integration. The definition makes it clear that we are not encountering the problem for the first time in our account of organisms. For example, integration has already been shown to occur during development: the process is seen in all of the regulative aspects of embryonic growth, including cellular cohesion and the inductive interactions between neighboring tissues. Such exchanges of information may conceivably involve the transfer of specific molecules, or instead might depend on the molecular order present in intercellular materials.

In the adult organism cell-to-cell interactions can occur through a variety of means. In plants, where the absence of circulated extracellular fluids and the presence of cellulose walls put special difficulties in the way of distant communication, cell-to-cell interactions are usually mediated by direct communication. As has been noted in Chapter 5, a large proportion of immediately neighboring cells in most higher plant tissues are connected through plasmadesmata—protoplasmic bridges which pass through minute openings in the cellulose walls. These communication channels serve for the exchange of a variety of materials, some of them certainly of informational character in the sense that they serve as stimuli that alter the behavior of the cell. Similar transmission is possible wherever cellular continuity exists, as in all *syncytial* tissues. It is important to realize that such connections may not be structurally obvious. For example, several instances of electrical interaction have been shown between nerve and epithelial cells having no evident connections or junctions; nevertheless it is possible to demonstrate that the cells are coupled through some pathway of low electrical resistance which can serve to coordinate their activity. The most ubiquitous and effective means of communication between cells is the exchange of chemicals. In the simplest cases the molecules involved may have no special informational content: it is a reasonable guess that chemical communication arose simply through the competition of cells for certain nutrients or the production of metabolites. Whenever such substances are in particular demand or have specific effects, they can make the growth or other activity of a given cell dependent on its fellows. Thus the eggs of certain marine fish are prevented from hatching if trimethylamine, an excretory product, is present in too great an amount as a result of the presence of many other eggs in a confined space. Carbon dioxide, another familiar product of cellular metabolism, has an important role in many acts of intercellular modulation of activity, including its control over respiratory rates in many animals and of transpiration systems in plants.

Most of the means of communication just described are effective in near-contact situations; but the demands of large and complex multicellular organisms require coordination involving action at a distance. The regulatory message must often travel quickly and far. Thus all complex organisms have, to some degree at least, evolved specialized communication systems to accomplish integration—specialized in the sense that certain members of the cell population are uniquely differentiated for this function. It is still a general rule that these systems all use specific chemicals as messengers; the hormones released to the circulating fluids by endocrine glands are examples. Communication by nerves is a special case in which electrical signals are used to secure the release of specific chemicals in a faster and more spatially restricted way. These integrative systems, and their influence on the behavior of the whole organism, form the subject matter for this chapter.

HORMONAL CONTROLS

Most biologists have always been satisfied to differentiate between the major integrative systems as above, by calling one *hormonal* (or humoral) and the other *neural*. The first operates by means of specific chemical substances, usually circulated between cells in solution in various *extracellular* fluids (in plants, *within* cells); the second involves the electrical transmission of impulses along nerve fibers.

Although a common and often useful distinction, it is somewhat artificial. Nerves almost always communicate with other nerves, or with muscles, by releasing a chemical transmitter at their endings. Across the motor end plate of a mammalian skeletal muscle fiber, a molecule of acetylcholine must travel a distance of some 300 Å to cause its specific effect on the muscle fiber. A molecule of adrenalin, released into the blood, may travel more than a meter before it reaches the pacemaker region of the heart to participate in speeding its beat. The route for adrenalin is longer, some thirty million times longer. Yet, in principle, where does the difference lie? The important difference between hormonal and neural regulations is that the latter, by interposing a specific communication line, makes the delivery of the chemical message swifter and restricts the audience. Thus hormones, wherever they have a diffuse distribution, provide an integration of preeminently *temporal* character, varying the activity of their targets as a function of time. Like embryonic inductors, the nervous system, because it mediates highly "addressed" messages, can also function to integrate the activities of specific regions with one another—that is, it can accomplish *spatial* integration.

Even within the realm of purely chemical regulations, however, the term *hormone*, partly because of its history, carries with it problems of definition. The first hormone to be characterized clearly was the one that stimulates pancreatic secretion in the vertebrate digestive tract. Rather than continuously discharging digestive enzymes into the ducts that lead to the small intestine, the pancreas is normally quiescent and initiates secretion only when the animal has had a meal. Pavlov, who was largely responsible for showing that acidity of the small intestine was responsible for this pancreatic secretion, believed that it was mediated by nerves. But Bayliss and Starling demonstrated in 1902 that the stimulus can be transmitted to the pancreas from a loop of intestine with all nervous connections between the two structures eliminated. They were able to extract from the gastric mucosa a substance which, when injected into the blood, stimulates pancreatic secretion.

With subsequent discoveries animal hormones were generally defined as blood-borne chemicals, produced by specialized tissues, which influence the activity of other tissues at a distance. But this definition is restrictive. In plants, substances that clearly function in the same sense are not blood-borne, since plants don't have blood. And exactly what does "at a distance" mean? We may be willing to exclude from the definition synaptic transmitter substances in nerve, but there are some borderline cases in which the diffusion distance is considerably longer than 300 Å but never involves transport within the circulation. For present purposes, we will require that the action involve several cells at least, but not that the hormone be circulated in some vascular system. Finally, we shall stipulate that a substance must be primarily produced by certain cells only, and clearly have some specific function in communication; this is to rule out substances like carbon dioxide, which might be said to have a hormone-like action on the respiratory regulatory mechanism but which is a non-specific metabolic product of all cells.

For purposes of illustration rather than memorization, a diagram illustrating the variety of molecules employed as hormones in animals alone is given in Fig. 7-1. In terms of molecular configuration the hormones have considerable diversity. But a single hormone may have many different effects; in short, there are more communication functions to be performed in organisms than there are hormones. Thus arises an important principle of hormonal function: namely, that the specificity of action of any hormone basically resides in the target cell, not in the chemical message. Very different molecules may serve analogous hormonal functions in different organisms; and on the other hand, the same hormone acting on two different cells in the same organism may have entirely opposite results. In other words, a communicative relationship arises during evolution through the development of sensitivities to preexisting molecules, and not through the development of molecules to meet each new requirement for communication.

The broad functions of hormones can be broken down as dealing with (1) growth and differentiation, (2) the regulation of the internal environment, and (3) the regulation of behavior. These are not entirely exclusive; (2) and (3) merge at a number of points, an example being that adrenalin controls much behavior in a mammal as well as a number of its internal regulations. But the division is a useful one, and a starting point.

It seems to us that any attempt at presenting a complete catalog of hormones and their actions is both futile and confusing. Rather, it is wiser to develop the concept of hormones as *communication systems* presiding over a related group of functions by discussion of a few examples. The two major ones that will make the case are, first, the systems controlling a variety of growth functions in plants, and

Fig. 7-1. Sources, chemical nature, and action of some major classes of vertebrate hormones.

Source	Hormones	Chemical Identity	Actions
Adenohypophysis	ACTH	Protein, 39 amino acids	Regulation of adrenal cortex
	Intermedin (MSH)	Polypeptide, 9 amino acids (part of the ACTH sequence)	Regulation of chromatophores
	Growth hormone	Protein, MW 48,000	Stimulation of bone, muscle growth
	Thyrotropic hormone (TSH)	Protein, MW 10,000	Regulation of thyroid secretion
	Lactogenic, follicle stimulating, luteinizing hormones	Proteins, MW all over 25,000	Reproductive controls
Neurohypophysis	Oxytocin and vasopressin (ADH)	Polypeptides, 8 amino acids	Control of uterine contractions and milk ejection in mammals; promotion of water retention
Thyroid	Thyroxin	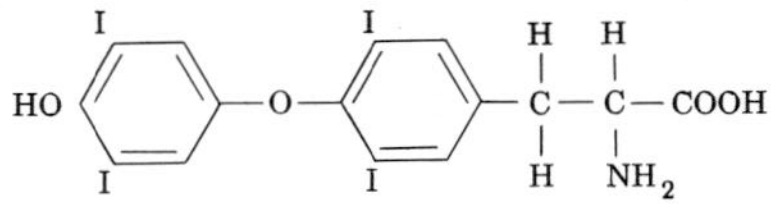 (chemical structure)	Growth promotion and metabolism
Gastrointestinal tract	Several hormones (gastrin, secretin, etc.)	Not known	Regulation of secretion
Gonads and adrenal cortex	Steroids (a large number of types)	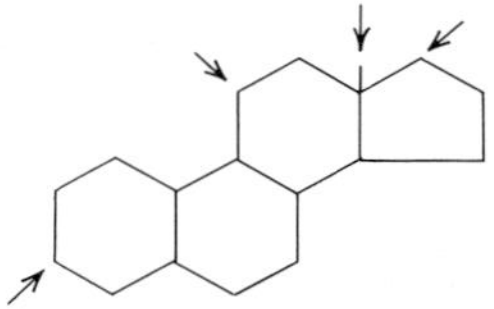 (Basic pattern; arrows indicate substitution positions)	Various sexual regulations, control of salt and water balance, carbohydrate metabolism
Adrenal medulla	Adrenaline (primarily)	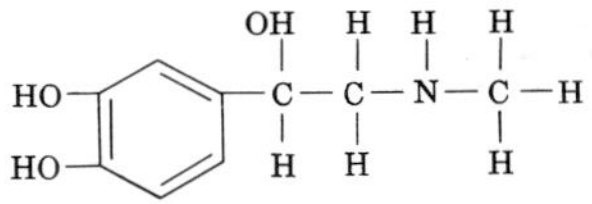 (chemical structure)	Vasodilation, increase of cardiac output, etc.
Various neurons		Other amines	Primarily "local" actions, muscle etc.
Pancreas	Insulin	Protein, MW 6000, sequence known	Carbohydrate metabolism
Parathyroids	Parathormone	Protein, MW 4000 or more	Regulation of calcium metabolism

second, those regulating the constancy of the internal environment in higher vertebrates.

Growth-Controlling Hormones in Plants

We have already emphasized in Chapter 5 that the growth of plants, in contrast to that of most animals, is a uniquely "open" system. There is in the strict sense no embryonic period, but instead a lifelong process of growth and differentiation initiated by the actively dividing regions or meristems at the tips of roots and stems, and in the cambium and other nonapical meristems as well. An important result of this fact is that it gives plants a unique way of responding to the environment; since they are constantly growing, and since their sessile existence makes the speed requirement less pressing, they can adjust by altering growth rates. In fact, hormones form the dominant integrative mechanism governing the relationship of the plant to its immediate environment—in the regulation of which, plants employ a remarkable control over differential rates of growth.

The most prominent class of plant growth hormones is the *auxins*. This term was originally applied to a presumed variety of natural substances; but more recently a single compound, indole-3-acetic acid (IAA) (see Fig. 7-2) has been shown to play the most significant role, all other substances having a similar action being closely related to it structurally. IAA is apparently produced by apical cells, usually but not always by those engaged in active division. The hormone moves down the stem (though under certain circumstances it can move up); its progress is usually from cell to cell. It can be collected by cutting off the apical few millimeters of a stem and

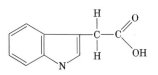

Fig. 7-2. Structural formula for indole-3-acetic acid.

placing its lower end against a block of agar. As the auxin is transmitted down the stem, it enters the block. Its effects can then be studied by placing the block against the cut surface of another plant so that the auxin enters the adjacent cells which then continue to transport it down the stem. When the block is placed over only one half of the decapitated test stem, the covered side grows more rapidly than the other, resulting in a pronounced tip curvature (see Fig. 7-3). Such methods were, in fact, used in the experiments by which diffusible growth hormones were first discovered in plants. The subsequent discovery that indole-3-acetic acid produced a parallel series of effects on the

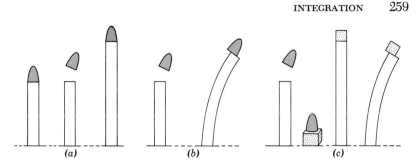

Fig. 7-3.   Tests for auxin. *(a)* Growth is retarded by coleoptile tip removal, accelerated by replacement. *(b)* Tips replaced on one side cause unilateral elongation. *(c)*
Auxin is allowed to diffuse into an agar block, which then is used to promote
elongation or curvature. (From A. Gorbman and H. A. Bern, *A Textbook of Comparative Endocrinology*, Wiley, 1962.)

test plant led to its identification as the most likely chemical structure
of the natural hormones.

The effects of auxin on plant tissues are varied. Usually, auxin
stimulates growth; the response is primarily through cell *elongation*,
but in some cases cell division is accelerated too. Dwarf strains of
plants often show lower auxin production than nondwarf strains,
and application of excess auxin in agar blocks to decapitated plants
can produce increases in internode length. Auxin has also been shown
to be important in fruit formation, in the initiation of root growth,
and in the triggering of growth in the cambium of woody plants.

But the action of auxin, like that of many animal hormones, is not
always positive; the response depends on the target cells. Two very
different systems demonstrate this fact. First, consider the young root
and shoot of the germinating seed, each developing in a horizontal
direction. Auxin accumulates on the lower side. This promotes
accelerated cell elongation on the lower side in the stem; hence the
stem curves upward in a negative geotropism. But the same concentration differential in the root produces the opposite effect; growth
on the lower side is inhibited instead of accelerated, and the response
to gravity is therefore positive instead of negative.

A similar difference in the responsiveness of target tissues to auxin
serves as the basis for a series of *correlative* actions that integrate
growth patterns of the whole plant. The most celebrated of these
effects is the phenomenon of *apical dominance* shown in many plants.
If the growing shoot apex is removed, accelerated growth of lateral
buds results. Replacement of the decapitated apex with auxin-
containing paste prevents the lateral growth once again, though
control experiments show that the paste alone is not effective in

preventing it. Thus apical dominance is exerted by auxin produced in the apical meristem, which in turn affects the growing regions of the developing lateral bud.

In addition, a particular growing region may be quite specifically sensitive to differing concentrations of auxin; a certain amount may result in acceleration, but too much reverses the response and produces inhibition. The borderlines vary for different plant tissues. Thus auxins play a tremendously significant role in the regulation of growth rates and also in the correlation of growth dynamics between different regions.

Light, of course, is an important factor in the regulation of development in higher plants. Their complete dependence on light as an energy source has resulted in a number of adaptations of growth pattern which put the photosynthetic apparatus of the plant into a favorable orientation to the source of light. Leaves are usually arranged in a pattern of minimum overlap; and most plant shoots show extremely sensitive phototropism, growing toward even very dim directional light. The basis for such responses forms one of the oldest problems in plant physiology. Briefly, the current status is as follows: the growing tips of young shoots (of which the oat coleoptile has been the favorite experimental object) bend toward the light, showing good curvature in less than an hour after exposure to even a brief, dim flash (10-meter candles for 60 seconds would be adequate). The light-sensitive tissue is located within a millimeter of the tip. Measurements of the action spectrum (the sensitivity of the response to different wavelengths of light) indicate that the photoreceptive pigment is a carotenoid, as are the visual pigments of animals—though some workers believe that a flavin may be responsible. The curvature resembles that caused by placing an agar block with auxin on one side of a decapitated tin kept in the dark (page 258). It can be tentatively hypothesized that light from one side causes a differential auxin concentration just below the very tip, with the higher concentration feeding down the dark side.

Various means of attaining this differential might work. Light might destroy or inactivate auxin (or some precursor) on the light side, or interfere with its synthesis; on the other hand, it might cause the lateral movement of auxin toward the dark side. The first possibility was considered likelier until recently. However, careful measurements of the amount of auxin which can be trapped by an agar block placed on the cut stem below a unilaterally illuminated tip shows that the *total* quantity emerging is the same as that characteristic of dark controls. But its distribution is quite different: more emerges from the dark side and correspondingly less from the illuminated side. Thus lateral movement (either of auxin or some precursor, or some participant in its synthesis) must be involved. It will be interesting to learn of the biochemical linkages between illumination and this lateral transport.

Auxin is by no means the only hormone with impressive effects on plant growth. Another significant group of substances are the *gibberellins*, first isolated from a rice-infecting fungus. These compounds produce many of the same effects as auxin, especially on cell elongation, though they differ in many specific respects. Sometimes they are effective when auxin is not, and vice-versa; and they appear to play an important role in the promotion of flowering in certain plants. One of the interesting things about the gibberellins is their spectacular and somewhat selective influence in increasing the size of many dwarf plants. There seems at present ample reason to believe that they are naturally occurring regulators of growth in many plants.

In summary, auxins and some other naturally occurring substances exert a hormonal regulation of plant growth, keeping the rate and pattern of that growth in tune with environmental requirements. These effects largely operate through cell *elongation* under hormonal influence. What of cell *number?* It is clear that regulation of division rate is also an important aspect of growth control, but unfortunately we know little of it in plants. A purine derivative, *kinetin*, has recently been shown to have spectacular division-promoting effects on some plant tissues, but it is not certain now whether the substance actually occurs in plants or mimics something else that does.

Control of Plant Reproduction

In plants, to an even greater extent than in most animals, the crucial event in insuring successful reproduction is the provision for synchronous maturation of male and female gametes. This can be done practically by specific interactive relationships between sexes, so that the differentiation of reproductive structures and eventually of gametes is kept in pace. Usually the reproductive maturation of both sexes is under some common environmental control.

Perhaps the most completely known case of the first sort in plants occurs in water molds of the genus *Achlya*. Reproduction depends on the successive action of four hormones, which travel between male and female mycelia (Fig. 7-4). The first, liberated by the female, causes the male mycelium to differentiate sexual branches (antheridia). These branches in turn produce a second hormone, which induces the formation of female reproductive organs (oogonia). The oogonia

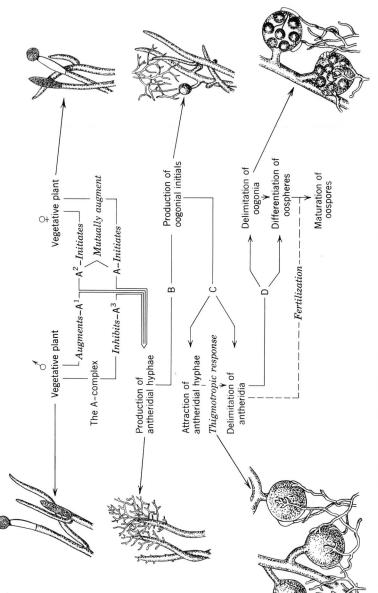

Fig. 7-4. Hormonal control of reproductive differentiation in the water mold *Achyla.* The sequence of events is illustrated by the drawings. (From J. R. Raper, *Amer. Sci.,* **39,** 110 (1951).)

then produce a third, which causes chemotropic growth of the male antheridia toward the female; the antheridia, as they do so, produce a fourth hormone that causes further differentiation in the oogonia. A byword here: it may not be altogether proper to refer to chemical communication between individuals as involving hormones. But more and more "social hormones" (which are sometimes called *pheromones*) are being uncovered. For example termites of the reproductive caste ("kings" and "queens") secrete a substance which, when licked from their bodies by the not-yet-differentiated secondary reproductive individuals in the colony, *prevents* their sexual differentiation. When the king and queen are removed, secondary reproductives do complete their differentiation; this will not happen if the removed king and queen are separated from the colony by a mesh screen which permits the licking to take place but eliminates other kinds of contact.

In higher plants the mechanisms involved in producing flowers do not include such individual-to-individual interactions, but are instead timed by the environment. It was discovered around 1920 that the environmental variable responsible for triggering flowering was light—the *length of day*, which varies systematically with the seasons. Such *photoperiodic* responses are now also known in a large number of animals. It was shortly recognized that most plants fall into two categories: autumn-flowering species, such as the cocklebur, that are stimulated by short days; and spring-flowering, "long-day" plants.

It now appears that it is not actually the length of day that is important in the flowering of short-day plants. In many such plants a few (or only one) long nights are required to do the job; but if that long night is interrupted by a single flash of light in the middle, the plant fails to flower. Thus the duration of *uninterrupted darkness* is somehow crucial. This fact first became interpretable through experiments to identify the light-sensitive pigments involved in photoperiodic responses. As usual in such problems, the first step was to test the relative effectiveness of different wavelengths in determining the response, and to match this "action spectrum" against the absorption spectra of pigments that might be likely candidates. It turned out that the wavelengths most effective in preventing flowering in short-day plants by the interruption of long nights centered around 660 mμ— the red region of the spectrum. These same wavelengths of light are also the most effective in promoting flowering in long-day plants, in stimulating germination of certain seeds, and in producing a wide variety of growth responses. Thus the same pigment seemed to be involved in mediating a number of photoperiodic and other effects;

specifically, the difference between short- and long-day plants seemed not to involve the whole system, but rather different effects from the same pigment. A remarkable corollary of this finding was that illumination in the far red region of the spectrum (actually at 735 mμ, beyond the limits of human vision) reverses the effects of red light in each of these cases. This situation is summarized in Fig. 7-5.

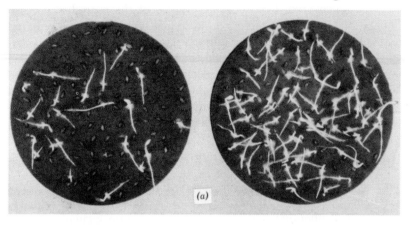

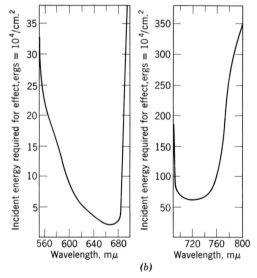

Fig. 7-5. (a) Germination of lettuce seeds is promoted by red radiation. The seeds on the left were last illuminated with far-red light, those on the right with red light. (b) Action spectra for a short period of irradiation to promote germination of lettuce seeds *(left)* and to inhibit it *(right).* (From H. A. Borthwick and S. B. Hendricks, *Science,* **132,** 1224 (1960).)

Subsequent studies have revealed that these effects are mediated by two different pigments which may be jointly responsible for photoperiodic control; they have been termed *phytochromes*. The one absorbing at 660 mμ is converted by red light to another absorbing at 735 mμ; far red light converts this one back to the 660 mμ form. Apparently, some concentration differential between the two forms acts on a variety of growth systems in the living plant to produce this variety of effects. It seems probable that phytochrome 735 is the active form, and that it has differing effects in different plants. Illumination at 660 mμ in short-day plants prevents flowering; but this wavelength is the most effective in promoting flowering in long-day plants, in promoting germination in lettuce seeds, and in making apples turn red! Clearly, the effect of such illumination (or of daylight) is to convert phytochrome 660 to phytochrome 735. What happens then depends on the kind of plant or tissue.

A special hormone, quite different from auxin, participates in flower initiation, and it is of very wide occurrence in plants. The existence of such a chemical substance can be shown, for example, by bringing one soybean plant to flowering state by exposing it to short days. If a shoot of this plant is now grafted to a second plant which has been prevented from flowering by keeping it on a long-day schedule, the flowerless host quickly blooms. The rather universal nature of such *florigen* hormones is shown neatly by the behavior of parasitic plants such as dodder, which always flower with their hosts—on short days if the host is a short-day species, on long days if it is a long-day plant. Florigens are readily transmitted through a graft, but it has not yet been possible to extract them from the plant in an active form. Perhaps they are larger, more complex and delicate molecules than auxin; at any rate they differ sharply from the latter in this and other respects. The role of phytochrome has not been linked to that played by the florigen hormones, although it is obvious that there must be a physiological connection between the two.

A reasonable interpretation, by way of summary, would be as follows. The basic control exerted by light over flowering is operated through its effects on the reversible phytochrome pigment system. The active phytochrome 735 may have different actions. In short-day plants its tendency during long nights is probably to prevent some step important in flowering, and its concentration decreases enough to allow the step to "go." In long-day plants we are forced to assume that phytochrome 735 has the opposite effect, but that the timing mechanism is essentially the same. In both cases the event of flower formation itself is triggered by an unidentified hormone, florigen, whose synthesis is either stimulated or inhibited by phytochrome.

Homeostasis and Hormonal Controls in Animals

As Fig. 7-1 shows, a large number of hormones in animals have been identified and characterized chemically. For example, the adrenal cortex and sex organs of vertebrates produce, in an intricately regulated fashion, some dozen hormones (all belonging to the chemical category of steroids), that regulate the process of gonadal maturation, the presence of secondary sexual characteristics, the timing of ovulation or spermatogenesis, and (in females) the oestrous and menstrual cycles and pregnancy. Other groups of hormones are concerned with a variety of other processes. In terms of general function, a crucial role of the endocrine system is the maintaining of some kind of balance in the characteristics of the blood and extracellular fluid of the body. This principle has had a central place in the thinking of animal physiologists for a long time. The operational freedom of any reasonably complex animal—and especially a terrestrial one—depends on the jealous maintenance of happy circumstances for its constituent cells; the importance of this has already been discussed in Chapter 6 in connection with the circulation. Animals achieve this stability or *homeostasis* by a group of processes which collectively act to maintain the constant condition by compensation for applied change. The implications are worth considering. There must be a capacity to sense change, compensate in the other direction for it, and then evaluate the appropriateness of the compensation. Setting a thermostat, for example, puts the same sort of control system into operation: if the temperature drops at night, the thermostat reports it and the furnace turns on; when the temperature is raised to the preset point, the thermostat senses that too and turns the furnace off. Such systems are routine for the modern engineer; he calls them feedback systems. *Negative* feedback systems normally tend toward stability, since the feedback signal is opposite in sign to the change. *Positive* feedback, however, reinforces the applied change; systems of this kind are highly unstable. In thermostatically controlled operations the action of the furnace in heating the room activates negative feedback from the thermometer, which cuts off the heat.

Feedback systems are routine, too, for the multicellular organism. Nowhere are they more evident than in homeostatic regulation of body fluids; and hormones carry the brunt of the operation. Since it is manifestly impossible to cover all hormones, we will mention several of those important in this regulation with special reference to mammals. The survey will take in most of the principles of hormone action, and will touch on a variety of chemical types of hormones and on a number of different glands that produce them.

Blood Sugar. Glucose, the most important circulating energy source in a vertebrate, is polymerized and stored as glycogen in the liver, whence it is released to the blood as glucose or "blood sugar." The concentration of blood sugar at any given time is critical; it is regulated, of course, by the rate of uptake by cells everywhere which utilize glucose, and also by the rate of glucose release from liver glycogen. The most important hormone involved in this balance is *insulin*, which is produced by special groups of cells in the pancreas called the islets of Langerhans. Insulin is interesting for many reasons, not the least of which is its status as the first protein molecule for which a complete chemical structure has become available. Anyone suffering from diabetes, however, would find it difficult to be academic about this hormone, because an inability to produce it is the cause of his difficulty. The chief clinical symptom of *diabetes mellitus* is an extremely high blood sugar, accompanied by depletion of stored liver glycogen. At such high sugar levels tubular reabsorption in the kidney is no longer able to recover all the glucose, and it appears in the urine and is lost. The action of insulin apparently is involved with the facilitation of glucose uptake by cells. Since glucose cannot be absorbed under insulin deficiency it "piles up" in the blood. The cellular starvation for glucose, not the high blood sugar itself, is actually the serious consequence of diabetes. It has a series of metabolic results including interference with the metabolism of fats and amino acids, which is linked to that of glucose. Under normal conditions insulin output from the pancreas is regulated in turn by the blood sugar levels. The action of insulin is antagonized by several other hormones, most of which are under control of the anterior pituitary, an endocrine gland situated near the base of the midbrain. Experimental diabetes produced in animals by islet cell destruction may therefore be somewhat relieved by removal of this organ. Finally, another pancreatic hormone (glucagon) appears to be functionally related in that it promotes the release of glucose from liver glycogen.

Total Concentration of Blood. Blood and extracellular fluids are poised in a delicate osmotic balance with the cells they bathe; and this balance is also regulated by endocrine factors. Again, the pituitary plays a prominent role. This gland (Fig. 7-6) has two parts—a strictly glandular anterior portion, and a posterior lobe which contains the terminations of nerve fibers whose cell bodies are located in the hypothalamus of the brain above. Two hormones are synthesized in

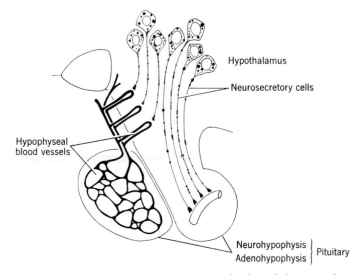

Hypothalamus

Neurosecretory cells

Hypophyseal blood vessels

Neurohypophysis ⎫
Adenohypophysis ⎭ Pituitary

Fig. 7-6. Diagram of the relationships between the hypothalamus and pituitary in mammals. (From A. Gorbman and H. A. Bern, *A Textbook of Comparative Endocrinology,* Wiley, 1962, p. 47.)

these neurons, pass down their axons, and are stored in and released from the posterior lobe of the pituitary. They thus belong to a class of hormones that are elaborated and released by nerve cells, and hence are called *neurosecretory* products. The hormones are *oxytocin* and *vasopressin;* each is a polypeptide containing eight amino acids, and six are identical between the two. Yet these hormones have entirely different primary actions, oxytocin functioning in the promotion of uterine contractions during labor, and vasopressin in increasing blood pressure and promoting reabsorption of water in the kidney.

This latter action now appears to be accomplished in the following way. Increased osmotic pressure in the blood, caused by water loss, affects neurons in the hypothalamus which function as osmoreceptors. The impulse activity of these neurons (which has been recently recorded electrically) triggers the release of stored vasopressin (antidiuretic hormone) from the endings of the neurosecretory cells in the posterior lobe of the pituitary. This reflex may be imitated successfully by localized injections of concentrated salt solutions into the appropriate region of the hypothalamus, or by electrical stimulation. The hormone released in this way affects the reabsorption of water by kidney tubules in mammals, though similar ones in lower vertebrates may act also by reducing the rate of glomerular filtration. As soon as the osmotic pressure of the blood reaches normal values, the osmotic stimulus to the hypothalamic receptors stops, and the secretion of antidiuretic hormone is slowed once again.

Ionic Regulation, the Adrenal Cortex, and the Pituitary. A relationship of particular importance to homeostatic control is that between the anterior lobe of the pituitary and the cortex of the adrenal gland. The pituitary has been called the administrator of the endocrine system, and in fact its anterior lobe does specialize in the production of *tropic* hormones—substances whose primary function is to instruct other endocrine glands to secrete. For example, the *thyrotropic hormone* from this area acts on the thyroid gland to trigger the release of thyroxin, and another pair of hormones likewise has a potent action in causing the release of sex hormones by testes and ovaries. In addition to these, the anterior pituitary also produces ACTH (adrenocorticotropic hormone); its function is to stimulate production of a variety of hormones from the cortical region of the adrenals.

When stimulated by ionic imbalance in the blood or by ACTH released by the pituitary, the adrenals liberate steroids. The primary result is a stimulation of sodium reabsorption in the kidney (in lower vertebrates at other exchanging surfaces as well). This action restores a proper sodium-potassium ratio in blood and extracellular fluids, which is an essential balance for the proper function of nerve, muscle, and other cells. Animals deprived of their adrenal glands quickly show an inability to retain sodium and a rapid leakage of potassium out of the cells; in addition, blood pH may drop due to loss of bicarbonate ions. Thus not only is the total concentration of dissolved substances in blood held (largely by posterior pituitary vasopressin) at controlled levels; the specific balance between these substances is controlled too.

Animals subjected to artificial (or natural) stress frequently show enlarged adrenal cortices, associated with an increased level of production of cortical steroids; this has been hailed as an "adaptation syndrome" of a generalized sort. How the increased cortical secretions actually achieve a more resistant state is not certain, but it is an enticing fact that very crowded populations of small mammals often show enlarged adrenals. It may indeed be that this response does represent a kind of extreme attempt at homeostatic control under severe circumstances.

This sort of "stress" notion actually had an earlier birth, not originally in terms of the adrenal cortex but of the medulla. This region of the adrenal gland consists of cells (chromaffin cells) innervated by nerve fibers belonging to the sympathetic division of the autonomic nervous system. Two closely related hormones, adrenalin and nor-adrenalin (the former predominating in man but not all mammals), are produced when these nerves are activated. The hormones differ little in their action; both stimulate heart rate and increase blood pressure. In general, the effect of stimulation of adrenal medullary secretion may be said to amplify and extend the more specific and local effects of sympathetic nerve stimulation (p. 324). The response of the organism to generalized sympathetic activity was originally described by Cannon as equipping the organism for "flight, fright, or fight"—that is, for a maximum behavioral effort.

General Statements about Animal Hormones. It is illuminating to consider some of the formal differences between different hormones as control systems. The principle of negative feedback has already been mentioned (p. 266); it will be obvious to the reader that most of the endocrine controls described here employ this principle. The essence of negative feedback is that some constant fraction of an output signal is returned to the input, where it causes compensatory decrease in the signal. The feedback thus stabilizes the output. But such systems may operate in different ways (Fig. 7-7) depending on the location of the feedback "loop." For example, the system for

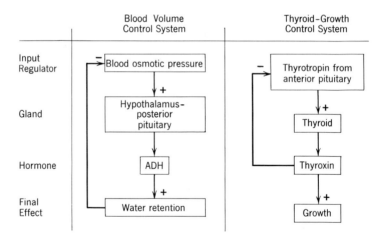

Fig. 7-7. Control diagrams for the hormonal systems controlling blood volume and growth. The thick lines indicate the "loops" for negative feedback; note that because of the position of these loops in the control sequence, the first system stabilizes the value of the output, and the second sets a constant rate of change of the output.

controlling body fluid volume senses the final result of hormone release—namely, the osmotic pressure of the blood—and thus the system operates to stabilize that variable. On the other hand, some processes need to change at a rather constant pace over periods of time, and for these the final output signal is not an appropriate source for the stabilizing feedback. An example would be the thyroid gland, which produces the growth-promoting hormone thyroxin; the liberation of thyroxin is in turn regulated by a *thyrotropic* hormone from the anterior pituitary. The activity of the anterior pituitary in liberating its tropic hormone is increased by low thyroxin in the blood and decreased by high thyroxin. In the latter case the feedback loop is shorter; it stabilizes the *level of hormone* and not the *final effect* of that hormone.

A certain hierarchy of animal endocrine organs is already apparent from the few examples considered in this volume. It is clear that the pituitary gland has, if not a monopoly, at least a sizable corner on control. It may well be that its special significance is concerned with its close relation to the nervous system.

For a number of years endocrinologists and neurophysiologists went about with the attitude that they were working on one or the other of the two great integrating systems in animals, and gave very little thought to their interdependence. But we now know that many hormones are produced under nervous control. The hypothalamus-pituitary relationship, the adrenal medulla, and the powerful effects of local brain stimulation on cortical steroid secretion are examples of the cooperative status between nerves and endocrine organs. Nowhere is this clearer than in the invertebrates, where recent research has turned up an astonishing number of cases of *neurosecretory* hormones, released into the circulation by the endings of neurons specialized for their synthesis. The hormones controlling pigmentation and molting in crustaceans and those controlling various developmental and behavioral events in insects are but two examples. Wherever a generalized effect is required—where many parts of the animal must be stimulated to act simultaneously in different ways—it is more practical to move the messenger in the circulating fluid than to make the substantial investment in neurons required to deliver it at a large number of specific points. But nerves, as we will soon see, are uniquely situated to receive converging sensory information from a variety of external and internal sources. Thus it is not surprising to see that these two mechanisms of integration in the animals have become interdependent in the regulation of growth, homeostasis and other activities.

THE NERVOUS SYSTEM

The control of cellular activities by nerves is faster and more specific than that provided by the endocrine glands and their blood-circulated hormones. A traditional analogy often used to contrast these two integrating systems is the likening of hormonal control to a radio transmitting system and of neural control to a telephone exchange. We have already pointed out the important interrelations of endocrine and neural control, however, and though the radio-and-telephone analogy aptly expresses the relative specificity of "wiring" between stimulus and response, it fails to express an important and basic *similarity* between nervous and endocrine systems. Both modulate the activity of effector cells through the release of chemicals. The ending of a neuron on a muscle fiber or other effector is like a miniature endocrine gland, releasing a local hormone when triggered by an impulse. The specificity of neural control is achieved by the localization of the nerve ending, and its speed comes partly from the fact that diffusion occurs over a very small distance.

The incredibly complex behavior of a whole multicellular animal may involve many thousands of such chemical actions of nerves on the effector cells they innervate, timed in a specific and complex sequence. To understand how this kind of integration is achieved is the aim of this section. The development of complex neural control is one of the most extraordinary achievements of multicellular organization. Studies of its operation in higher organisms are only beginning to explain some of the simpler behavioral patterns in terms of neural control. While neurophysiologists are hopeful of eventually understanding the basis of complex behavior, they realize that in addition to facing mountainous technical obstacles they are also laboring under the unique scientific handicap of asking a device to understand itself. Before ascending to the complexities of neural integration and brains, however, we must ask some questions about the nature of neural signals and their transmission.

Nerve Cells and Membrane Conduction

There is no such thing as a "typical" nerve cell; since neurons serve a wide variety of integrative functions depending on their location, a whole spectrum of morphological types has arisen (Fig. 7-8). In general, the structural differences are correlated with the amount of incoming information the neuron must handle. In relatively simple

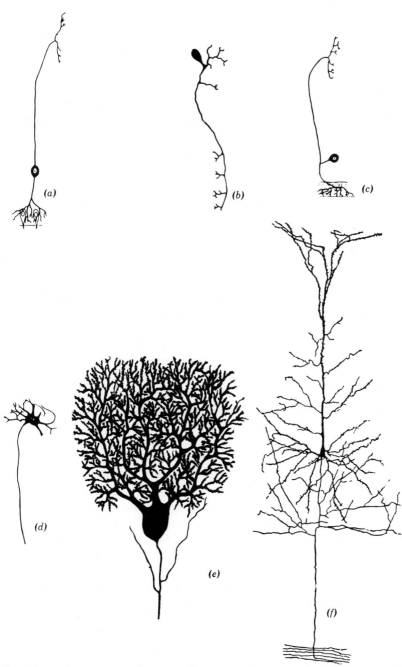

Fig. 7-8. Different types of **nerve cells.** (a) Bipolar sensory cell, vertebrate. (b) Monopolar ganglion cell, invertebrate. (c) Monopolar sensory neuron, vertebrate spinal ganglion. (d) Motor **neuron, mammal.** (e) Purkinje cell, mammalian cerebellum. (f) Pyramidal cell, **mammalian cerebral** cortex.

"relay" situations where one or only a few channels of incoming messages are found, the neuron is often of the *bipolar* type, as in (a). Or the cell body may be off on a side branch of its own (b, c), in which case the neuron is called *monopolar* or *unipolar*. Where many fibers converge on the neuron, it may have several processes, as in (d), or extremely elaborate arborizations as in the neurons of the vertebrate cerebellum and cerebrum shown in (e) and (f).

These cells, different though they are, share at least one important property: the presence of a long process, the *axon*, and the existence of an "input" region through which activity is channeled into the neuron. The shorter processes in the region of the cell body or *soma* are termed *dendrites;* usually these or the soma itself receive the endings of the connecting nerve cells. As we shall see, the electrical activity characteristic of these input regions is often complex, but the axon is highly specialized for the transmission of information over long distances. This function is correlated with some unique structural features. The axon is covered with a closely applied layer of flattened Schwann cells; in most vertebrate nerves these surround the axon during development, laying down a thick lamellar coating of lipoprotein membrane materials. This *myelin sheath* is interrupted by gaps or *nodes of Ranvier* (Fig. 7-9).

The major attribute of the axon is that when it is excited at one end an effect occurs at the other. The time lag is only a few hundredths of a second, even though the two ends may be separated by a distance measuring several meters and connected by a tenuous cytoplasmic process of only a few microns' diameter. The actual velocity of this conduction process was measured by Helmholtz in 1859 by timing the delay between a shock delivered to a nerve and the beginning of contraction in the muscle with which the nerve connected. This measurement was made before much was known about the conduction process. Ultimately, through the direct use of current-measuring instruments connected by metal electrodes to the nerve, it was appreciated that the "excitation" conducted down the nerve was in fact identical with the electrical signal. The term *nerve impulse* refers to the whole complex of propagated electrochemical changes. Our first concern is to find out what this remarkable event involves. (This is a problem in cell biology; but because of its special interest for the topic of nerve and muscle physiology and its incidental occurrence in other types of cells, it is treated here as a part of the problem of neural integration.)

Modern electronic devices permit much more detailed analysis of the nerve impulse than those available to nineteenth century physiolo-

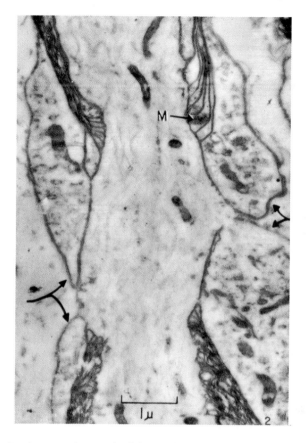

Fig. 7-9. An electron micrograph of the myelin sheath at a node of Ranvier in the mouse. M, layers of myelin. Arrows indicate the boundaries of the Schwann cells at the node. Longitudinal section. (Photograph by B. G. Uzman and G. Nogrueira-Graf, *J. Biophys. Biochem. Cytol.,* **3,** 589, (1957).)

gists. It is now a simple matter to place fine wire electrodes on the outside of a bundle of axons, or even of a single nerve fiber. The signal must be amplified; and since it is very fast, an essentially inertialess instrument should be used to record it. Conventionally a cathode-ray oscilloscope (Fig. 7-10) is the choice. [This instrument utilizes as the voltage indicator a focused beam of electrons which is directed onto a phosphor-coated tube, where the collision of electrons with the coating produces a glow. The beam is swept in a horizontal plane at any speed desired by altering the voltage on a pair of vertical plates, which "sandwich" it. The electrical signal is amplified and put on a second

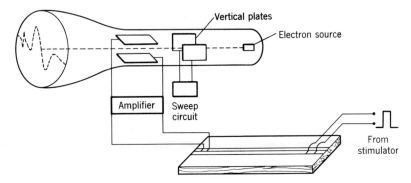

Fig. 7-10. Recording a nerve impulse. The schematic illustration shows the sweep-generating and amplifying systems of the cathode-ray oscilloscope, with the latter connected to a pair of recording electrodes in the nerve chamber. The "square pulse" of current used to stimulate the nerve through the electrodes at the other end is derived from an electronic stimulator.

pair of plates positioned horizontally, so that it deflects the beam up or down from its horizontal path.]

In an actual recording situation involving an isolated nerve, the nerve fiber(s) are contacted by two pairs of metal wire electrodes: one pair, the stimulating electrodes, is used to pass a brief, "square pulse" of current to initiate impulse activity. The second pair is used for recording, to detect the potential changes associated with evoked impulses. These electrodes are connected to a preamplifier and thence to the oscilloscope plates. If the nerve is now excited by passing a brief pulse of current through the pair of stimulating electrodes (Fig. 7-10), the impulse will, after an interval, reach the pair of recording electrodes. The resulting record on the oscilloscope will have two phases; one records the change at the first electrode, the other at the second electrode. The second phase can be eliminated if the second electrode is placed at an inactive location; this can be achieved simply by crushing the nerve between them. If a conduction velocity measurement is to be made, a second pair of recording electrodes is set some distance from the first.

Such experiments reveal the following general properties of the impulse, or *action potential*. First, there are no partial responses; once the stimulating current is of sufficient strength to elicit an impulse, further increases do not affect the magnitude (amplitude) of the action potential. Second, the impulse is conducted without any alteration in size; and the size and duration (about 1 millisecond in most "fast" nerves) of successive impulses are constant. Finally, the conduction velocity is finite and always the same for any given nerve fiber.

If paired shocks are delivered to the nerve within a brief interval, a new property is revealed: although for single stimuli the *threshold* (amount of current barely necessary to evoke an impulse) is constant from trial to trial, each impulse is followed by a brief period in which it cannot be excited by a second stimulus. This *absolute refractory period* is followed by a period of relative refractoriness in which the threshold is elevated over usual values. The usual durations of these periods are 1 and 5–10 milliseconds respectively.

It should be noted that all of these properties—all-or-nothing signals, propagation at finite velocity, and refractoriness—are profoundly different from those of current conducted in a metal wire. The latter propagates instantaneously, can be graded in intensity, and displays nothing like refractoriness. We must ask how and why such a device, almost without analogy in the marvelous world of electronic engineering, arose. For a partial and somewhat hypothetical answer, we may look at some primitive cases such as the muscle fibers that close the oscula of sponges. These muscles regulate the size of the major opening which admits water into the interior of the sponge; they are sensitive to local chemical conditions and respond to changes in their immediate environment by undergoing *graded* responses. Their graded contractions are made possible by graded electrical changes that take place along their membranes. Thus the same cell is responsible for detecting changes in the environment (input) and responding to a degree that is in some way proportional to the extent of the change (output). They are thus *independent effectors.*

A simple organism can manage nicely in this way, but more complex ones must be able to arrange for the simultaneous and coordinated operation of a number of effectors in response to stimuli that may be received at some distant point. Since these distances between effectors and receptors may be large, some way must be found to communicate between them. For this purpose, graded electrical signals analogous to those produced in a wire are not satisfactory: they attenuate too much with distance, particularly if the "wire" is as thin as a nerve axon. The all-or-none action potential in a nerve fiber, on the other hand, arrives at the effector with undistorted amplitude. Two disadvantages, however, result from the adoption of this method of signaling. First, the instantaneous character of conventional electrical propagation is lost; the fastest-conducting nerves only manage speeds of about 150 meters per second. Second, a single all-or-none impulse can convey no information about the intensity of the stimulus which produced it beyond the fact that it was adequate. As we shall see, intensity differences are coded instead by the *frequency* of a series of such impulses.

How nerves (and other kinds of cells) produce such signals has been a matter of speculation for hundreds of years. The nature of biological "electricity" figured importantly in the debates between Galvani and Volta in the eighteenth century, and in fact played a significant role in the development of the Voltaic pile (wet storage battery). It was proposed at the turn of the twentieth century by Bernstein that the nerve membrane acts as a permeability barrier to ions that are maintained at different concentrations inside and out, and that these concentration differences produce a potential difference across the membrane so that the outside of the membrane is positively charged relative to the inside. According to his view, the impulse consisted of a brief increase in permeability which allowed the charged ions to flow together and abolish the potential difference. This concept—a remarkable set of inferences—still dominates our view of the impulse-conduction process. Some ingenious experiments have altered it, however, in many important respects.

The way in which experimental progress was made toward a direct evaluation of membrane events in nerve cells is an interesting and revealing case history in experimental science. The problem obviously had to be attacked by a direct measurement of the current flowing during the impulse—not between two points on the external surface of the nerve, as in our previous example, but *across* the membrane itself. Some algal cells are big enough to have already permitted direct measurements of transmembrane potentials, but it was clear that to accomplish the same thing with a nerve fiber would require one of two advances: either someone would have to invent a rather remarkable electrode, or a very large nerve cell would have to be found. Both were accomplished. In hundreds of laboratories intracellular recording is now accomplished routinely by drawing capillary tubing into tapering tips less than half a micron in diameter, filling them with conducting solutions, and manipulating them into a variety of neurons. It is not surprising, however, that this advance came ten years *after* experiments that depended on the discovery of unusually large neurons. These were found in 1936 in the mantle nerves of the squid; their axon diameter is about half a millimeter, large enough so that a fine wire could be thrust axially up the center *inside* the axon. One can imagine the excitement which attended the accomplishment of this feat and the opportunity to test for the first time a prediction nearly forty years old. When the investigators (Hodgkin and Huxley at Plymouth, England) looked at the resting potential value, it measured 50 millivolts (mV), outside positive; larger values have since been found for this and other nerve cells. The surprise came when an action potential was initiated by a pair of distant stimulating electrodes and allowed to sweep past the recording region. Instead of merely canceling the resting potential, which would be expected if the ions were allowed to mix according to Bernstein's hypothesis, the action potential continued on past the zero potential level, temporarily *reversing* the potential difference so that the potential at the peak of the impulse was about 40 mV, *inside* positive. (See Fig. 7-11.)

To explain this behavior, something must be said of the ion distributions which give rise to the resting potential difference. Imagine a membrane fully permeable to water and ions, but not to large molecules; outside is water, and inside is a solution containing the potassium salt of some protein. The salt will dissociate into negatively charged proteins and positively charged potassium ions. The latter will tend to be driven across the membrane by diffusion down its concentration gradient; but for every K^+ ion that crosses the membrane, a positive charge is accumulated on the outside, which tends to repel succeeding potassium ions. Eventually an equilibrium is set up in which the tendency for potassium to diffuse out along its concentration gradient is just balanced by the electrical charge, which is in the opposite direction.

Table 7-1   Concentrations of Ions in Squid Axoplasm and Squid Blood

Ion	Concentration: Axoplasm	Blood
K^+	400	20
Cl^-	40	560
Na^+	50	440
Isethionate	270	trace
Aspartate	75	trace
Other carboxylic acids: glutamate, fumarate, succinate	29	trace
$[K^+] \times [Cl^-]$	16,000	11,200

From Hodgkin, *Proc. Roy. Soc. B.* 148:1, 1958.

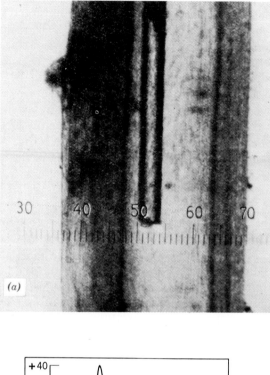

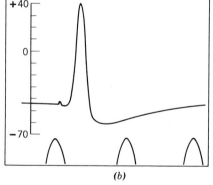

Fig. 7-11. (a) A squid giant axon with metal wire electrode inserted. The scale is 33 μ per division. (b) The impulse recorded across the membrane of the squid giant axon. The potential scale is in millivolts, inside relative to outside; the time marks below are 2 msec apart. (From A. L. Hodgkin and A. F. Huxley, *Nature*, **144** (1939).)

Such *Donnan equilibria* are common in biological systems where semipermeable membranes and ions of widely varying sizes are routinely encountered. Whenever they occur, it is possible to establish a good deal about the ionic distributions involved if we can measure some ionic concentrations on either side of the membrane and/or the potential difference across it. In nerve and muscle cells the resting potential is dependent on an internal excess of negative ions (free aspartic, isethionic, and glutamic acids in various invertebrate nerves, and probably different ones elsewhere) which cannot escape the cell. Experimental studies, some of which are described in the following section, indicate that chloride and potassium distribute themselves passively, just as described above for the model. Sodium, on the other hand, passes the resting nerve membrane with great difficulty; moreover, the cell actively pumps sodium out, using metabolic energy to do so. So sodium has a concentration outside the cell about ten times that within; potassium shows approximately the reverse ratio.

The details of the ionic basis of resting potential differences in cells are usually slighted in books of this kind. We discuss them here as an aside for the especially interested student because questions about the matter often arise.

Figures for the concentrations of sodium, potassium, and chloride in squid giant axons and squid blood are given in Table 7-1. It will be noted that the products (given at the end of the table) of internal and external potassium and chloride concentrations are fairly near one another; equality of the products of diffusible ion concentrations on either side of the membrane is characteristic of all Donnan equilibria, and this shows that sodium may be neglected as a diffusible ion. Of course, if the sodium pump should fail, sodium would leak into the cell slowly, and the potential would run down. This happens in metabolically poisoned axons and in fact is one evidence that a "sodium pump" is present. But a glance at the sodium concentrations will show that sodium cannot possibly be used to predict the value for the resting potential. If it could, the sodium equilibrium potential (the membrane potential value at which its *net* movement would be zero even if permeability were made infinitely great) would have to be the same as that for the measured resting potential. In fact the concentration gradient for sodium is about 10:1 *inward*; the electrical potential necessary to counteract this would obviously have to be positive inside, whereas it is really positive outside. It is a matter of great interest that sodium has such a large driving force tending to push it into the cell, and we shall return to this question in our discussions of the nerve impulse.

It is possible to establish a more formal relationship between the distribution of ions on the two sides of a membrane and the electrical potential developed across it. Strictly speaking, all ions contribute to any stable potential, since all are charged. But they contribute in proportion to their permeability. Potassium and chloride, especially the former, move easily through the membrane and assort themselves passively in response to the electrochemical asymmetries set up by the presence of large anions inside the cell. Since the membrane is relatively impermeable to sodium, and since that ion is pumped metabolically as well, it can be disregarded in predicting the value of the potential difference. The basic equation for calculating membrane potential from ion distribution values contains fractions for the concentration ratios of all ions; but these are multiplied by their individual permeability constants. In effect, then, the entire expression reduces to the concentration ratio(s) of the most mobile ion(s), the others having been eliminated because they contribute relatively insignificantly. Thus the Nernst equation gives the value of the resting potential in terms of the concentration ratio for the ion, the absolute temperature T, Faraday's constant (96,000 coulombs), and the gas constant R:

$$\underset{\text{Potential difference}}{E_o - E_i} = \frac{RT}{F} \ln \frac{(C)_{\text{in}}}{(C)_{\text{out}}}$$

Changing to ten-base logs, assuming a temperature of 20°C, and inserting constants, this becomes (using the potassium ion)

$$E_o - E_i = 58 \text{ mV} \log \frac{[K^+_{\text{in}}]}{[K^+_{\text{out}}]}$$

Substituting the potassium concentration values from Table 7–1 into the Nernst equation, we get a predicted potassium equilibrium potential of 75 mV, outside positive, quite close to the value of 70 mV found for fresh giant axons in squid blood. (Cl⁻ also is near equilibrium at the resting potential value.) Moreover, experimental manipulations of the concentration of potassium outside such axons yield altered membrane potentials that are in reasonable agreement with the predicted 58 mV decrease for a tenfold increase in outside potassium concentration. Sodium alterations, on the other hand, have little effect on the resting potential. Such procedures have now been applied to a variety of nerve cells, and potassium seems to be the determinant ion for the resting potential in most cases. (In the myelinated nerves of vertebrates, chloride may have a special importance.)

What of the alterations in ion distribution which must take place during the millisecond in which a given patch of membrane is involved with the truly impressive voltage changes associated with the nerve impulse? The finding that the resting membrane potential was not merely abolished but actually reversed destroyed the notion that a simple increase in permeability was involved. In its place, biologists have widely accepted a substitute hypothesis generally known as the "sodium theory," which consists of the following elements. (1) Depolarization of the nerve membrane (by an experimentally applied current or some physiological stimulus) increases its permeability to sodium. (2) Sodium enters the cell along its electrochemical gradient, further depolarizing the membrane and increasing its permeability, which in turn accelerates sodium entry still further; in other words, the events form a self-renewing or regenerative system because of positive feedback. (3) Sodium entry is cut short when the equilibrium potential for sodium is reached, that is, when the inside of the membrane is sufficiently *positive* to oppose the concentration gradient for sodium. (4) At about this time the sodium permeability is "turned off" (*inactivated*), and the permeability to potassium undergoes a swift rise; potassium ions flow *out* along their electrochemical gradient, restoring the resting potential to its previous value.

The evidence for this concept, so crucial to our understanding of the operation of neurons and of membrane biophysics in general, is worth some detailed examination—especially since it has come about through some spectacular recent advances. We will restrict our consideration to three crucial points. First, what is the evidence that the "overshoot value" for the impulse really is a sodium potential? Second, can it be demonstrated that approximately equal amounts of sodium and potassium cross the membrane in the appropriate direction during the impulse? Third, are the movements of sodium and potassium sufficient to carry the necessary charge to bring about the observed potential change?

The first question can be approached by using the Nernst equation to calculate the sodium equilibrium potential. Substituting in the equation

$$E_o - E_i = 58 \text{ mV} \log \frac{[\text{Na}^+_{in}]}{[\text{Na}^+_{out}]}$$

the calculated potential is 54 mV, *inside* positive, very near the value for the spike "overshoot." As with the case of the resting potential, variations in the external sodium concentration (achieved by replacing it with choline, a cation which cannot enter the cell) produce predictable changes in the voltage at the peak of the spike.

The second question, involving actual demonstration of ionic flows, is more difficult to answer experimentally. It has been attacked through the use of radioactive sodium and potassium ions. Giant axons may be placed in sea water with Na^{24}; alternatively, the axons are soaked in K^{42} until they have become loaded with the radioactive isotope internally and then are placed in a chamber in sea water without isotopes. Such axons, of course, exchange ions with their surroundings at rest; each experiment thus involves comparison of a stimulated and an unstimulated control axon. In these experiments stimulated axons took up Na^{24} and lost K^{42} much faster than the unstimulated controls, and the results of paired comparisons have proven quite consistent. Typically, stimulation is carried out at 100 impulses per second for a period of several minutes. Both axons are taken out, washed, and counted for radioactivity, then reimmersed and measured again. The surface area of the axon is then calculated, and the net sodium gain of the stimulated axon *over* that of the unstimulated control is given in pmol per cm^2 of membrane per impulse (a pmol, short for picamol, is 10^{-12} mol). An equivalent procedure is carried out with the potassium-loaded axons. Consistently, such experiments have shown that these nerve fibers gain about 3.5 pmol of sodium per cm^2 of membrane per impulse, and lose a nearly equivalent amount of potassium. There can thus be no question that a gain of sodium and a loss of potassium accompanies each impulse, as the sodium theory demands.

Is this enough ionic movement to do the job? This point, the third one on our list, can be evaluated by calculation. The membrane of a cell may be represented physically as a *resistance* (which is the inverse term of its permeability to charged particles) in parallel with a capacitance. A capacitor is a device for storing charge; the physical device itself consists of a pair of metal plates with a nonconducting medium (often oil) between them. The analogy with a neuron is obvious when we consider that the nerve membrane is largely lipid and separates two quite conductive solutions. When we connect the two plates of the capacitor with a battery, current flows until the capacitor is charged up and then stops. The capacitance (the unit for which is the Farad) expresses the amount of charge the capacitor can hold. This value depends on the area of the plates, the distance between them, and the nature of the material in the gap. Now, if a resistor is connected in parallel with the capacitor, some of the current applied across it will flow through the resistor, and this changes the "charging time" of the capacitor. If we measure the charging time (the duration of current flow into the capacitor) and know either the value of the resistance or that of the capacitance, we can calculate the other. Electrophysiologists have been able to derive these constants for a variety of nerve membranes by passing current across them and effectively measuring this "charging time" (or, properly, *time constant*) and the resistance.

A simple relationship exists between capacitance of the membrane and the amount of charge that must be transferred across it to change the resting potential by a given amount. The charge transfer (in millimicrocoulombs) is equal to CV, the capacitance (in microfarads) times the voltage (in millivolts). During the impulse the membrane potential in the squid giant axon changes by about 100mV; the capacitance is about 1.5 microfarads. Thus the current required per cm^2 is about 150 millimicrocoulombs; this would be carried by 1.7 pmol of Na^+ per cm^2. There is, therefore, somewhat more ionic movement, calculated from the isotope studies, than would be necessary to do the job. Part of the explanation for the excess is that near the peak of the impulse potassium is beginning to flow out while sodium is still coming in; the timing of the two permeability changes has some overlap. Thus the two currents are "bucking" one another, and some of the sodium current is wasted as far as transferring charge is concerned.

These are, of course, not the only experiments offered in support of the sodium hypothesis. They are the ones which seem, to the authors, to constitute the most telling fabric of evidence. Of the others, two are worth special mention. First, it has been possible to measure the sodium and potassium currents directly by an ingenious technique known as the *voltage clamp.* In this procedure current is suddenly passed through an internal electrode so as to change the resting potential abruptly. A second electrode measures the potential difference. It is connected to an amplifier which feeds back current so as to keep the membrane potential constant—"clamped." If the new potential level of the cell is depolarized, we would, of course, expect (from the hypothesis) that sodium would flow inward. The amplifier, however, provides feedback current such that the sodium ions which enter are unable to change the membrane potential from its preset value. Thus the current passed by this amplifier provides a record of the sodium current, since the feedback current was exactly what was necessary to keep things constant *in spite of* the sodium current. In this same way the oppositely directed current produced by the outward movement of potassium can be detected.

Voltage clamp experiments produce a current sequence like that in Fig. 7-12. The first current is of a direction appropriate for a positive ion moving in; the second, more prolonged one is opposite. Their time courses agree with those for the rising and falling phases of the action potential. The inward current may be abolished either by reducing the external sodium or by making the initial depolarizing step so large that it carries the membrane to the inside positive value predicted by the Nernst equation to be the equilibrium potential for sodium. The more prolonged current may be varied by altering potassium concentrations.

This sort of experiment elegantly confirms those mentioned earlier, and also has made it possible to ascertain precise values for the permeability of the membrane to sodium and potassium in various phases of the impulse. These values in turn have been used to predict the shape of impulses under various conditions. An even more startling recent achievement has been the removal of cytoplasm from single giant axons and its replacement by perfusion with various artificial solutions. The control over the internal contents of the neuron as well as over its external bathing fluid has made possible a more extended set of observations on the values of resting and action potentials with altered ionic composition. It seems fair to summarize these results so far with the statement that they conform satisfactorily with the demands made by the sodium theory.

These findings demonstrate a remarkable property of the cell membrane. According to the Bernstein hypothesis, the impulse was caused by an increase in membrane permeability allowing the mixing of charges. But the sodium theory states that a much more astonishing thing happens: for a few ten-thousandths of a second, the permeability

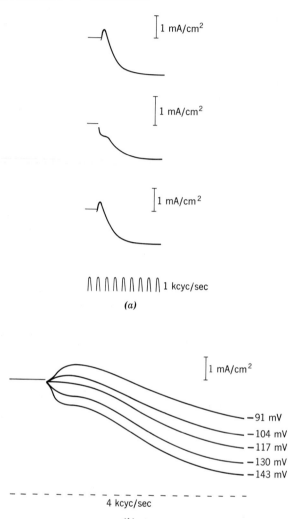

Fig. 7-12. Current records from "voltage clamp" experiments. In *(a)* the membrane potential was reduced by 65 mV; the initial (upward) current is reversed when the sodium is removed from the external solution, and restored (in the lowest record) when the sodium is replaced. The more sustained, opposite current is unaffected, and is therefore presumably carried by potassium moving out. *(b)* The initial potential change has the value shown to the right of each curve. A change of —117 mV completely abolishes the initial sodium current; it does so because it carries the membrane to the equilibrium potential for sodium. Greater changes cause the sodium to move outward instead of inward. (From A. L. Hodgkin and A. F. Huxley, *Cold Sprg. Harb. Symp. Quant. Biol.,* **17,** 43 (1952).)

to sodium is *selectively* reduced without altering that to potassium; and then just as abruptly the permeability to sodium is shut off and that to potassium dominates. The nerve membrane is thus capable of discriminating in some unknown way between these ions.

We must finally ask: How does this delicately balanced series of permeability changes propagate itself down the axon? The simple experiment in which electric current is used to stimulate a nerve fiber provides the clue; this is illustrated in Fig. 7-13. The "active region" of the nerve fiber—that occupied by the impulse—acts essentially like a traveling stimulating electrode. In this zone the outside of the fiber is negative with respect to the region ahead. Current carried by ions will thus flow between the active zone and the adjacent inactive one; and the direction of flow is so as to *depolarize* the resting membrane ahead of the impulse. When this passive current flow produces a certain amount of depolarization—usually about 10-25% below the resting membrane potential—the threshold for the region has been reached. Sodium permeability rises abruptly, and an all-or-none response now takes place in that region. By an infinite series of such steps, the active region is propagated along the fiber. Since the current flow *ahead* of an active region of the nerve fiber propagates decrementally (that is, with an amplitude that falls off in space instead of remaining constant as does that of the impulse), the effectiveness of its spread will determine the velocity of impulse propagation. In turn, the effectiveness of this current spread will depend on the internal and external resistances imposed along its path. If these are low, current spread ahead of the active zone will trigger the active response far ahead of the zone; if they are high, spread is spatially restricted and the conduction velocity low. The two critical resistances are the longitudinal internal resistance of the fiber and the external resistance of the extracellular fluid. The organism cannot change the latter; but the experimenter can. If a nerve fiber is placed in oil, the higher resistance externally results in a considerable drop in conduction velocity. Animals do, however, adjust the internal resistance; since it will depend inversely on the cross-sectional area of the fiber, large fibers would be expected to show higher conduction velocities than small ones (Table 7-2). They do; the rule-of-thumb for the relationship in fibers of the frog sciatic nerve, for example, is $V = 2.5D$. A most impressive experimental demonstration of the importance of this internal resistance pathway has been made by short-circuiting it in the squid axon by inserting a tiny axial wire down the center. Depending on the resistance of the wire —which even for the thinnest one is much less than that of the cyto-

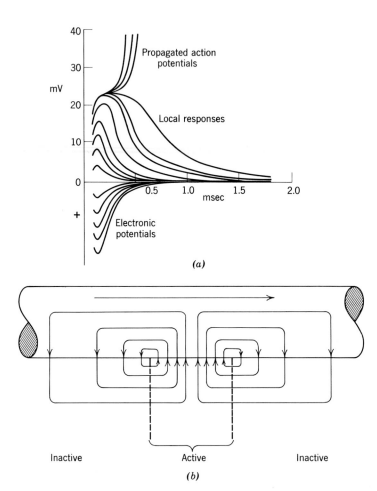

(a)

(b)

Fig. 7-13. (a) The potential changes recorded across a squid giant axon with an internal electrode in response to current of different strengths. Anodal shocks give only local, passive potentials which hyperpolarize the membrane. At low intensity, cathodal shocks give the mirror images of these, but at higher intensities a "local response" and then a full impulse result, the latter when the depolarization reaches a value of 22 mV below the resting potential. (b) The distribution of current around the active region in a squid giant axon. This region (between dashed lines) is defined as the area in which membrane current is inward. The outward current in advance of the active region acts to depolarize the membrane. When it reaches the threshold shown in (a), it in turn becomes active; in this way the impulse spreads along the fiber.

Table 7-2. Conduction Velocity of Various Nerves

Nerve	CV (m/sec)	Av. Diam, μ	T°C.
Large net of jellyfish	0.5	6-12	
Giant fibers of Annelid (Myxicola)	10.0	500	
Squid giant	20.0	200	20
Decapod crustacean motor axons	8 / 10 / 2.0	36 / 40 / 58	
Cat A (myelinated)	78-102	13-17	
Cat B (myelinated)	24-48	4-8	37
C	0.6-2	0.5-1	

From C. L. Prosser, and F. A. Brown, Jr., *Comparative Animal Physiology*. 2nd ed. Saunders, 1961, p. 595.

plasm—the velocity of propagation may be increased up to 200 fold.

In most vertebrate nerves a different adaptation is found. The fiber itself, as shown in Fig. 7-9, is covered by a thick fatty sheath of myelin, interrupted by naked regions called nodes. In such nerve fibers, current flow across the membrane—and therefore the all-or-none active response—takes place only at the nodes, and so in such cases the jumps are finite in length. This arrangement radically increases conduction velocity (as can be seen by Table 7-2, which compares velocities in myelinated and unmyelinated fibers of various diameters.)

The Synapse

The action potential of a nerve cell is a unit of information; but it is useful as a communication signal only if it can *make something happen* when it gets where it is going. Its ultimate destination may be a muscle fiber, or a gland cell, or another neuron; the particular type of response it causes may thus be contraction, secretion, or the initiation of another impulse. But in each case some effect of that impulse must be transmitted across the junction that separates the nerve ending from the subsequent cell.

Such junctions, when they take place between two nerve cells, are called *synapses;* similar joinings between nerve cells and skeletal muscle fibers are *motor end plates*. The problem for both is similar: How is the gap bridged?

We might begin first by asking some questions about the gap itself. It has long been known that the junctions between nerve cells (or nerves and muscles) involve very intimate contact between the cells involved—so close, in fact, that many neuroanatomists of the nineteenth century believed that there was cellular continuity between neurons. It was not until near the end of the nineteenth century, long after the cell theory was well established for other tissues, that the Spanish neurologist Ramon y Cajal demonstrated that the nervous system was not really a "reticulum" after all. The gap between neurons is real; and recent electron microscope studies of synapses show that the membranes of presynaptic and postsynaptic cells are distinct and separate, but that the space between them at the zone of contact may be extremely small—usually between 200 and 500 Å. At the motor end plate on vertebrate skeletal muscle, there is also a complex folding of the muscle fiber membrane under the nerve endings, which run in short channels along the muscle fiber.

A sprightly controversy raged for many years about whether the synaptic gap was bridged by electrical or chemical means. Supporters of the electrical transmission hypothesis felt that electric currents generated by the action potential in the presynaptic nerve were adequate to depolarize the postsynaptic neuron and initiate an impulse directly. The chemical theory, on the other hand, asserted that the presynaptic impulse acted as the trigger for the release of some chemical, which then diffused across the gap and acted to depolarize the postsynaptic membrane.

The proponents of the chemical theory always had on their side the fact that synapses show a sensitivity to drugs and a transmission delay that are quite uncharacteristic of the conduction of impulses down the nerve fiber itself. It is now fully established that transmission across the junction between motor nerves and vertebrate skeletal muscle is chemical in nature, and specifically that it involves the release of the substance *acetylcholine* by the motor nerve endings. The evidence is worth looking at in greater detail. First, acetylcholine can be identified in a solution in which motor nerves (but *not* other sorts of nerves) have been stimulated. Second, acetylcholine applied to the muscle fiber through micropipettes can cause muscle action potentials and contraction, but only if it is delivered right in the region of the motor end plate. In fact, the concentration of acetylcholine applied in this way which is just sufficient to cause a response in the muscle fiber is in reasonable agreement with the amount calculated to be released by a single motor nerve impulse. Moreover, the application of acetylcholine to the end-plate region causes precisely the sequence of electrical events generated by motor nerve stimulation; but these effects cannot be duplicated by passing external currents, as the electrical stimulation hypothesis would demand. Finally, there are a number of drugs that interfere with transmission from nerve to muscle (Fig. 7-14). Claude Bernard, the great nineteenth century French physiologist, was the first to show that the locus of interference was in the junctional region. He injected the Indian arrow poison curare into a frog; though it paralyzed the animal, Bernard showed that direct electrical stimulation of a muscle would still make it contract. He then showed that if the application of curare were restricted to the central portion of the motor nerve, a complete reflex stimulation of the muscle was possible—eliminating the possibility that curare was acting on the main trunk of the nerve itself. Curare and other drugs block the action of applied acetylcholine at the neuromuscular junction in the same way that they block transmission by nerve stimulation: moreover, substances known to block the enzyme that destroys acetylcholine were found to intensify and lengthen the responses of muscles to nerve stimulation.

The conclusion that chemical transmission is the way of bridging the synaptic gap has since been widely applied to neural synapses—and indeed, in a great many of these it has been adequately shown that transmission is chemical. The danger of making such biological generalities, however, has recently been demonstrated by the finding that at certain junctions (one, for example, involving giant nerve fibers in the crayfish) transmission is of the electrical type.

The detailed sequence of events in transmission (see Fig. 7-15) appears to be similar for most synapses of the chemical type. The presynaptic ending contains a store of its particular transmitter agent; in fact, the present suspicion is that it is stored in minute vesicles often seen in electron micrographs of presynaptic endings. At certain junctions, like the motor end plate, there is evidence that transmitter may be released spontaneously from time to time. When an impulse arrives at the nerve ending, it alters the permeability of the membrane and causes the release of a large amount of transmitter, which diffuses across the extremely short synaptic space and then combines (probably with a protein) on the postsynaptic membrane. In some way the transmitter's attachment to its receptor site on the postsynaptic membrane alters the permeability of that membrane so that ions are permitted to flow across it. A microelectrode placed in the postsynaptic cell records at this moment a brief depolarization—a decrease in the

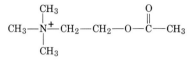

Acetylcholine

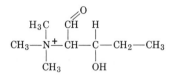

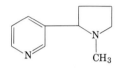

Muscarine

Nicotine

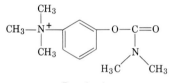

Prostigmine

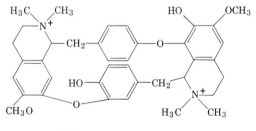

d–Tubocurarine

Fig. 7-14. Acetylcholine and some molecules that interact with it. Muscarine, an alkaloid from certain mushrooms, mimics acetylcholine action on smooth muscle and heart, but is without effect on skeletal muscle or autonomic ganglia. Nicotine, on the other hand, mimics acetylcholine in the latter tissues but not in the former. Prostigmine is one of several competitive inhibitors for the active site of the enzyme acetylcholinesterase, and thus (in low doses) potentiates acetylcholine action by preventing its hydrolysis. Curare (d-tubocurarine) blocks (presumably competitively) the combination of acetylcholine with end-plate receptors in skeletal muscle.

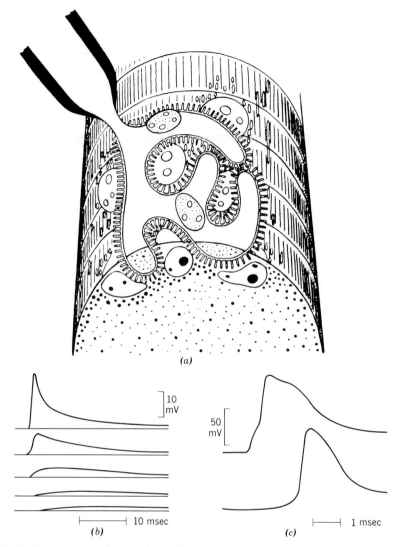

(a)

(b)   10 mV   10 msec

(c)   50 mV   1 msec

Fig. 7-15. Diagram of the relationship between a motor nerve fiber and the muscle fiber it innervates. The branches of the nerve fiber run in grooves in the surface of the muscle; in these grooves the membranes of the two cells are close together and that of the muscle fiber is highly folded. (From G. Hoyle, *The Comparative Physiology of the Nervous Control of Muscular Contraction*, Cambridge, 1957.) *(b)* End-plate potentials produced by stimulating the motor nerve, recorded with a microelectrode inside the muscle fiber; the top one was recorded right beneath the end-plate, and the series below it each 1 mm farther away. Curare had been applied to the end-plate so that the end-plate potentials were reduced below the level necessary to trigger an action potential in the muscle fiber. *(c)* Responses from uncurarized muscle, showing muscle action potential superimposed on end-plate potential. The upper record was made near the end-plate, the lower at a distance. (From P. Fatt and B. Katz, *J. Physiol.*, **111,** 46P (1950).)

resting membrane potential. If this is of sufficient magnitude, it will trigger an all-or-none action potential in the adjacent region of the cell, and a propagated event is thus initiated once again. The action of the transmitter is brief, as it must be if the synapse is to be ready to transmit the next impulse. This is taken care of by the presence in the synaptic region of high concentrations of an enzyme which destroys the transmitter. In the case of the motor end plate, the enzyme is *cholinesterase*, which hydrolyzes acetylcholine into acetate and choline at an extremely high rate. As mentioned, among the drugs which affect transmission at the motor end plate are some which inactivate this enzyme. These anticholinesterases, like *eserine*, have the predictable effect of lengthening the action of the transmitter when applied to the end plate, and (at high concentrations) of *blocking* the junction.

So far, it appears that a number of different substances may serve as chemical transmitter agents. Acetylcholine functions in several places in addition to the motor end plate, most notably between pre- and postganglionic neurons of the vertebrate sympathetic system (see p. 324). Acetylcholine is known *not* to be the transmitter at several synapses; but the identity of the real one is uncertain. Adrenalin and, more especially, noradrenalin are released at the endings of post-ganglionic sympathetic fibers, but generally have their effects on non-nervous cells (smooth muscle, heart muscle, glands, and so on). Of the many transmitter substances that undoubtedly exist in the central nervous system of vertebrates, not a single one has been identified except for a lone case involving acetylcholine.

The motor end plate (in common with many of the neural synapses which have been well studied) is a poor example of a junction in one respect: there is only *one* ending on the postsynaptic cell. The importance of synapses in complex nervous systems is that they are seldom simple relays in which one cell in a chain excites the next. Instead, many synapses usually occur on a single nerve cell; and the firing of that cell is determined in an intricate way by the timing of impulses which arrive over a number of pathways. Hence significant events may be differentiated from trivial ones, and appropriate responses may be given to specific *patterns* of arriving messages.

An example of such a synaptic system is shown in Fig. 7-16. It represents a vertebrate motor neuron, whose cell body would be located in the ventral horn region of the spinal cord. Hundreds to thousands of presynaptic fibers may end on the cell body and dendrites of such a neuron. Each one, when an impulse arrives at the ending, discharges some transmitter and thereby causes a local membrane de-

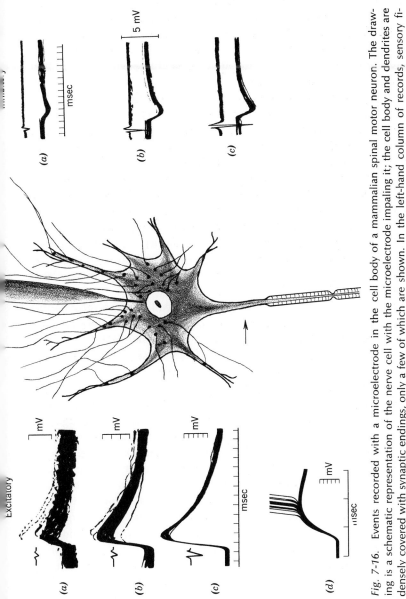

Fig. 7-16. Events recorded with a microelectrode in the cell body of a mammalian spinal motor neuron. The drawing is a schematic representation of the nerve cell with the microelectrode impaling it; the cell body and dendrites are densely covered with synaptic endings, only a few of which are shown. In the left-hand column of records, sensory fibers from the same muscle innervated by the motor nerve are stimulated at various strengths, increasing from (a) to (c); the synaptic potential depolarizes the cell more and more, eventually (d) sufficiently strongly that on a number of the trials the synaptic potential flares up into a propagated impulse. The right-hand column of records resulted from stimulation of the sensory fibers from an *antagonist* muscle; the result is a hyperpolarization of the cell, which would act to inhibit the excitatory process shown on the left. (After J. C. Eccles, *The Physiology of Nerve Cells,* Johns-Hopkins, 1958.)

polarization measurable by a microelectrode inserted into the post-synaptic cell. Depolarizations of this kind occurring simultaneously can add up and, if their sum is sufficient, will trigger an all-or-none impulse. Usually there is a very specific location for the initiation of the action potential; in this and some other cases, it is the hillock of the axon, indicated by the arrow in the diagram. One or even ten synapses may not contribute enough depolarization to achieve the triggering value; it may take fifty.

Another property of certain junctions is revealed in such cells: not all synapses are excitatory. Anyone who has ever tried to operate a car with an accelerator but no brakes realizes that complex devices are better off with negative as well as positive controls; neurons are no exception. Some synapses on cells like the one in Fig. 7-16 are *inhibitory* in function; they come from specific sources and operate to prevent firing of the cell. This is accomplished by the release of a different transmitter, which instead of depolarizing the membrane affects its permeability in such a way that excitatory depolarizations are blocked. If enough of these inhibitory synapses are activated together, the effect of simultaneous excitation can be prevented from reaching threshold.

It is helpful in thinking about synapses to recall that the subsynaptic membranes of nerve cells—those regions of membrane which are specialized for receiving and responding to some chemical transmitter substance—are probably quite different from those regions of membrane, like that surrounding the axon, which support all-or-none impulses. Evidence suggests that subsynaptic membrane never actually undergoes the high specific sodium permeability that accompanies real impulse propagation in an axon. Certainly impulse-propagating membrane is relatively insensitive to transmitter substances. It may even be that the presynaptic ending exerts a kind of inductive control, in addition to its transmitter function, which serves to maintain or localize some specifically differentiated state of those two kinds of membrane. Such a conclusion is suggested by what happens when a muscle fiber is denervated. Acetylcholine sensitivity spreads quickly along the muscle fiber until, after twenty days or so, the entire muscle fiber membrane is as sensitive to the transmitter as the end plate region formerly was. Such information emphasizes that we cannot separate the integrative influences that pass from cell to cell during differentiation and those that do so in the adult organism. There is, quite clearly, a critical set of intercellular controls operating across synapses in addition to the transmission process; and these do not cease with the establishment of the differentiated state.

Receptors

Most central nerve impulse traffic begins with the activation of a variety of receptor cells which signal changes in the state of internal and external environments. Each receptor type responds to one (occasionally more) kind of stimulus energy—light, mechanical deformation, temperature, chemicals, or even electric currents. These sensory endings occur in muscles and joints, in visceral structures where they respond to changes in the internal environment, and on the outside surface where they sense changes in external conditions.

We know from subjective experience that such receptors can provide information about the intensity of any stimulus as well as about its duration and location. Since the single nerve impulse discharged along the axon of a sensory nerve is all-or-none in character, the sensation of intensity clearly cannot depend on alteration in amplitude of the impulse. Instead, receptor cells communicate intensity differences by variations in the *frequency* of a series of impulses— the more intense the stimulus, the faster the discharge rate. Long before it was possible to record these impulses electronically, psychologists had shown that the level of sensation was related to stimulus intensity in such a way that over at least most of the intensity range the sensation level was approximately proportional to the logarithm of the intensity. In practical terms this means that a given sense organ can respond to a wider range of intensities than it could if the relationship were a linear one. Studies on the discharge of single sensory nerves have since shown that, as expected, the frequency of firing is related to the logarithm of the stimulus intensity; in most cases the frequency doubles for a tenfold increase in intensity (Fig. 7-17).

How are these frequency-coded trains of impulses initiated by receptor cells? Recent studies on some of the simpler mechanoreceptor cells have provided a partial answer to this question. If we record electrically from a receptor ending, we see that the discharge of impulses is accompanied by a depolarization of the receptor membrane, which has a resting potential like that of the nerve axon. This depolarization resembles in almost every respect that produced at the synapse by transmitter substances: it is graded in amplitude, and leads to the production of all-or-none impulses. In sensory cells this depolarization has been referred to as the *generator potential*, because it appears to be the cause of impulse generation. The generator potential arises, by means which are at the moment obscure, at the site of absorption of stimulus energy. It spreads in a decremental

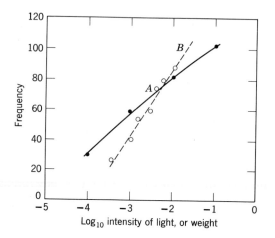

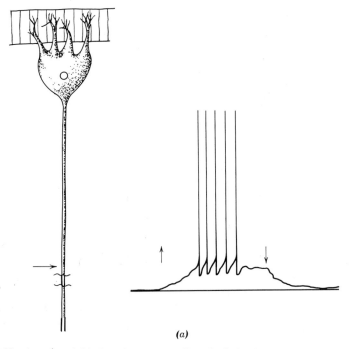

Fig. 7-17. The proportionality between the frequency of impulse discharge and the logarithm of stimulus intensity for single sensory nerve fibers. Data from two very different receptors are illustrated: the muscle spindle of a mammal (open circles; data from B. H. C. Matthews, *J. Physiol.*, **71**, 64 (1931)) and a single ommatidium from the eye of Limulus, the horseshoe crab (closed circles; data from H. K. Hartline and C. H. Graham, *J. Cell. Comp. Physiol.*, **1**, 277 (1932).)

(a)

Fig. 7-18. Impulse initiation in two well-studied kinds of mechanoreceptor neuron. *(a)* Muscle receptor organ of the crayfish. The dendrites are embedded in a special group of muscle fibers, and are thus deformed when the muscle is stretched. The record on the right shows a depolarization (generator potential)

fashion, just as all other graded potentials do, and triggers impulses usually at a point some distance away. Figure 7-18 illustrates the process for two rather different kinds of mechanoreceptors: the muscle receptor organ found in crayfish and some other crustaceans, and the Pacinian corpuscle of mammals. The former discharges in response to stretch of the muscle fiber in which its dendrites are embedded; the generator potential is set up in the dendrites, but impulses are initiated at a point well down the axon. The Pacinian corpuscle, on the other hand, consists of an unmyelinated nerve ending surrounded with a layered connective tissue capsule. The capsule transfers mechanical stress to the ending, where the generator potential is set up. Impulses are initiated at the first node of Ranvier, which occurs along the sensory nerve just inside the capsule.

Mechanoreceptors. In addition to the types of deformation-sensitive cells just described, a variety of others exist. Muscle spindles, for example, occur in almost all vertebrate muscles. (See p. 328.) When the muscle is stretched, the spindle is compressed, and the main

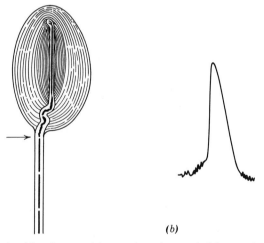

(b)

initiated in the dendrites by a quick stretch and recorded by a microelectrode in the cell body. It evokes five impulses, which actually arise at the point on the axon indicated by the arrow and propagate in both directions. (*Left,* from C. Edwards and D. J. Ottoson, *J. Physiol.,* **143,** 138 (1958); *right,* from C. Eyzaguirre and S. W. Kuffler, *J. Gen. Physiol.,* **39,** 87 (1955).) *(b)* A Pacinian corpuscle from cat connective tissue. The generator potential, which underlies the spike in the record on the right, is produced by the unmyelinated region of the ending within the capsule; the impulse is generated at the first node of Ranvier (arrow). The response was produced by a quick mechanical deformation applied to the capsule. (*Left,* from T. A. Quilliam and M. Sato, *J. Physiol.,* **129,** 167 (1955); *right,* from W. Lowenstein and R. Rathkamp, *J. Gen. Physiol.,* **41,** 1245 (1958).)

spiral nerve ending fires. If the muscle contracts back against the stretch, however, the pressure is released; thus contraction *inhibits* spindle discharge.

Other mechanoreceptors depend on the movement of hairs to which the sensory nerve cell is attached. Such hair receptors are common in invertebrate animals; they are found all over the bodies of many insects and crustaceans and also line the cavity of the *statocysts* in many invertebrates. These organs (which appear in coelenterates and may be the first true organs to have evolved in metazoa) provide their owners with a way of determining primary orientation—in other words, which end is up. An approximately spherical cavity is lined with sensory hairs; it contains a limey concretion called the statolith. This object presses different hairs depending on the orientation of the whole statocyst, and thus the organ as a whole can interpret for the central nervous system the direction "down."

Hair receptors in vertebrates comprise a very large group having a common evolutionary origin in the *lateral line* of primitive fish. This organ is composed of receptors resembling that shown in Fig. 7-19b, distributed along the body in tiny canals open to the exterior. The system to which it belongs also gives rise to the semicircular canals,

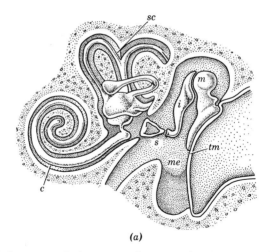

(*a*)

Fig. 7-19. (*a*) Structure of the mammalian ear, showing tympanic membrane (*tm*), middle ear bones (*m, i, s*), semicircular canals (*sc*), and cochlea (*c*). (From A. S. Romer, *The Vertebrate Body*, Saunders, 1955.) (*b*) Hair cell from the cochlea. Such a cell from anywhere in the vertebrate acoustico-lateralis system (e.g., the lateral line of a fish or the semicircular canal of a mammal) would look much like this. Reconstructed from electron micrographs. [From H. Engström and J. Wersäll, *Exp. Cell. Res. Supp.*, **5**, 463–492 (1958).]

the otolith organs, and the cochlea of higher vertebrates—in short, to every inner ear sensory system. (See Fig. 7-19a.) Studied in cross section with the electron microscope, the hairs reveal the basic structure of cilia, and are undoubtedly derived from them. The receptor cells themselves are not neurons, as the previous examples were; they are columnar epithelial cells, and the sensory neuron (which is thus not really primary at all) synapses with the base of the receptor.

In the semicircular canals, (Fig. 7-19a) such receptors occur in swellings or *ampullae* that are located at one end of the canal; their hairs project into a gelatinous cupula which extends like a swinging door

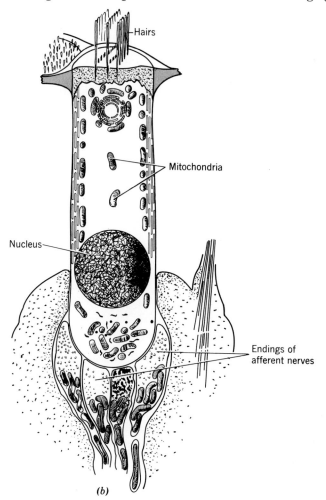

(b)

across the ampulla. Any acceleration in the plane of the canal tends to increase impulse discharge, but acceleration in the other direction slows it. Thus the spontaneous discharge allows the receptor to respond in a bidirectional fashion, and a man or any other vertebrate can distinguish between opposite horizontal accelerations with the labyrinth of only one side.

Some otolith organs located just below the array of semicircular canals respond in much the same way as the invertebrate statocysts. Some of the sensory hair cells in the otolith organs, however, are not associated with the otoliths themselves; these are free to respond to higher-frequency vibrations, and do so even in many fishes. From such hair cells located near the base of the labyrinth the sense organ responsible for hearing in mammals evolved. The *cochlea* in mammals is a coiled, fluid-filled structure (Fig. 7-19a). It is divided internally for almost its entire length by a thin partition, the basilar membrane (Fig. 7-20), on which the hair cells are carried. Their hairs are em-

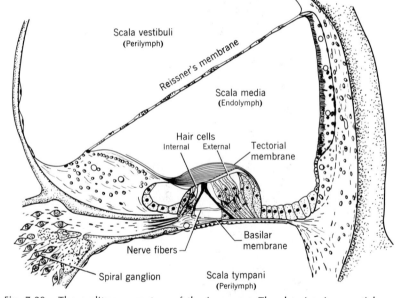

Fig. 7-20. The auditory receptors of the inner ear. The drawing is a partial cross section of the guinea-pig cochlea at the level of its second spiral turn. If we imagine that the spiral is unrolled to create a cylinder, the basilar membrane would partition the cylinder lengthways; this membrane, as shown in this section, bears the hair cells, whose hairs contact the tectorial membrane. Vibration of the basilar membrane produces shear on the hairs, and this somehow fires the nerves that innervate the hair cells. (From H. Davis, in: *Handbook of Physiology,* Vol. I, American Physiological Society, Washington, 1959, p. 567.)

bedded in an overlying flap, the tectorial membrane. As the basilar membrane vibrates up and down in response to pressure waves transmitted to the cochlea from the tympanic membrane via the three bones of the middle ear, a shearing force is placed on the hairs, and this results in impulse discharge.

How does this system give the capacity to discriminate pitch (frequency)? Sounds of different frequencies cause the basilar membrane to vibrate with maximum amplitude in different places—near the base for high frequencies, and at the apex or final turn of the cochlea for low frequencies. Although a large number of receptors are excited even by a pure tone (since a large area of basilar membrane vibrates), those in a certain region, different for each frequency, will respond most actively. The purity of the sensation, however, must depend on the action of the central nervous system in sharpening this peak, which it appears to accomplish by inhibiting or rejecting responses from the receptor cells that are firing less strongly than those at the center.

Photoreceptors. The visual organs of animals present a remarkable array of complex structures serving the same functional end. For this reason they have long been favorites of the anatomist, embryologist, and evolutionist. The simplest photoreceptors are a variety of neurons and muscle cells which are able to respond to light. Isolated clusters of sensory cells appear in the skin of many lower invertebrates; in annelids and flatworms these may be congregated beneath a refractile structure that serves as a lens and is backed by an absorbing pigment layer, which assures that the structure will respond to light only from a particular direction. Such "simple" eyes also occur in arthropods (ocelli) and even in vertebrates (the parietal or pineal eyes of some reptiles). But complex and active groups of animals, in general, have developed visual organs of either the *compound eye* or *camera eye* type. The first solution is characteristic of the arthropods generally; the second has been reached (in a stunning example of evolutionary convergence) by both vertebrates and cephalopod mollusks. The general plan of these structures is shown in Fig. 7-21.

The vertebrate eye is frequently and aptly likened to a camera; but any camera enthusiast will instantly recognize that it has some very remarkable and expensive features. The diameter of the pupil can be controlled directly or by reflex action, so that the optical system admits an amount of light appropriate for the brightness at any time. The lens, suspended in position by ligaments, can be changed in shape or moved back and forth (in some fish) to adjust

Fig. 7-21.   The Structure of Eyes at Different Levels.

(1) Eye of the scallop, *Pecten*. (1a) A section through the eye showing the dual structure of the retina. (From W. Dakin, *Quart. J. Microscop. Sci.* **4**, 49 (1910). (1b) Electron micrograph (X 20,000) of the sensory organelle from a distal retinal cell. (From W. H. Miller, *J. Biophys. Biochem. Cytol.* **4**, 227 (1958).) (2) The eye of the horseshoe crab, *Limulus*. (2a) Surface, and (2b) longitudinal section showing the array of ommatidia that compose this compound eye. (2b) is a silver-stained preparation showing the nerve fibers connecting with one another as they exit from the ommatidia (by W. H. Miller; from Ratliff, F., in *Sensory Communication*, W. A. Rosenblith, Ed., M.I.T. Press, 1960, p. 183.) (2c) Cross-section of a single ommatidium showing the rosette of retinula cells with the spoke-like arrays of *rhabdomeres* dividing their inner borders. (2d) Electron micrograph of the rhabdom region showing the tubelike microvilli cut in cross section. (From W. H. Miller, *Ann. N. Y. Acad. Sci.* **74**, 204 (1958).) (3) Mammalian eye. (3a) Diagrammatic section, showing the thinness of the sensory retina; (3b) The receptor cells and neural elements of the retina; many receptors converge onto one bipolar cell, and many bipolar cells onto one ganglion cell. (Redrawn from S. Polyak, *The Retina*, Univ. Chicago Press, 1941.) (3c) Reconstruction from electron micrographs of the fine structure of a single rod. The outer segment is a stack of discs formed by out-pocketings from a cilium that forms the stalk connecting the outer segment to the nucleated inner segment. (From E. de Robertis, *J. Biophys. Biochem. Cytol.*, **2**, 319, 1956.) The important thing to note is that in these very different photoreceptors the visual pigment is organized into a receptor structure consisting of tightly-packed membranes that are whorled in the scallop, arranged in tubules in *Limulus*, and stacked as discs in the vertebrate rod.

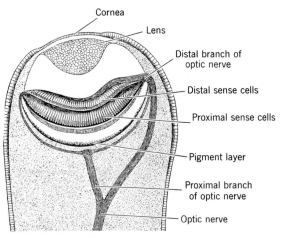

1(*a*)

Fig. 7-21.   (continued)

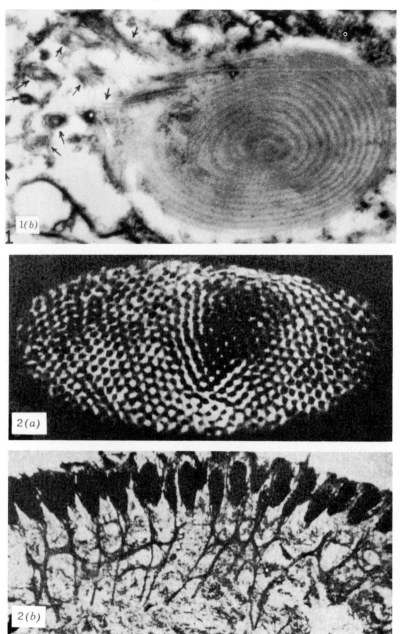

Fig. 7-21.   (continued)

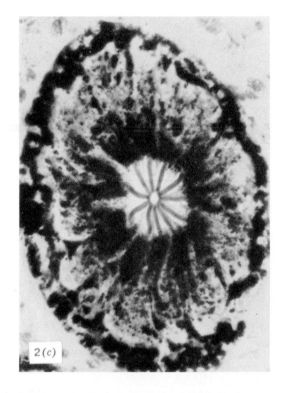

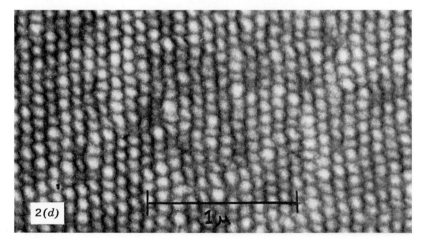

Fig. 7-21.   (continued)

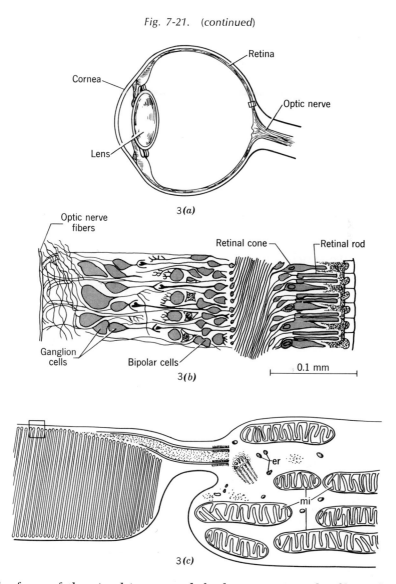

3(a)

3(b)

3(c)

the focus of the visual image; and the lens contains color filters that
further alter the quality of light reaching the retina. The retina itself
consists of two types of visual cells, rods and cones; the former function in dim light and yield a rather fuzzy visual image, but they are
extremely sensitive. The latter operate in bright light. They are concentrated in a central area, the *fovea*, which is directed at any object

of close scrutiny. The retinal grain is extremely fine here, and vision of high acuity is therefore possible.

In order to respond to light, a receptor cell must first absorb it. Electron microscope observations on a variety of photoreceptor cells from different animals reveal the presence of layered fine structures like those illustrated in Fig. 7-21. It may be no accident that in this respect these visual cells resemble the chloroplasts of plants, which are also in the business of absorbing and converting light energy. In both the rods and cones of vertebrates, these membranes are derived from cilia. Photoreceptor cells all have (probably incorporated into these layers) some photosensitive pigment—a colored substance that absorbs light of certain wavelengths and, as a result, undergoes a chemical change. In the vast majority of photosensory cells, this substance is a carotenoid protein of one kind or another; the best-known example is the *rhodopsin* found in the rods (dim-light receptors) of the vertebrate retina. It consists of a protein component and a carotenoid, *retinal*, which is closely related chemically to vitamin A (hence the connection between vitamin A deficiency and night blindness). Of five isomeric forms of the carotenoid, only one, the 11-*cis* isomer (Fig. 7-22), will combine with the protein to make rhodopsin. When quanta of light are absorbed by rhodopsin, the

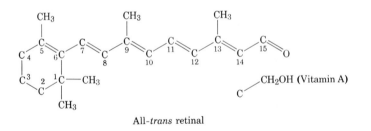

All-*trans* retinal

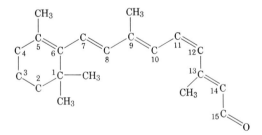

11-*cis*-retinal

Fig. 7-22. Structure of two retinal isomers.

protein and retinal split apart; as they do so, the red color of the rhodopsin is lost, that is, the pigment bleaches. The retinal molecules released are not in the same isomeric form as when they first combined with the protein; they have been converted to the all-*trans* form. In a biochemical cycle involving the interconversion of vitamin A and retinal (and which may in certain instances even short-circuit vitamin A), new retinal of the proper form is supplied, and it combines with the protein to regenerate rhodopsin. Thus in the visual process the same light that stimulates also depletes visual pigment, thereby reducing sensitivity. The recovery of sensitivity after exposure, which we experience ourselves going into a dark room from full sunlight, is called *dark adaptation;* its rate is dependent ultimately on the biochemical restitution of rhodopsin. These cycles are summarized in Fig. 7-23.

How is it possible to show that a particular pigment is responsible for vision in any given photosensory cell? The method of proof resembles that given (Stern & Nanney, Chap. 9) concerning photosynthesis and other light-dependent processes. The pigment has a particular *absorption spectrum;* that is, it absorbs some wavelengths of light more efficiently than others. These same wavelengths should also be most effective in the visual process, if the pigment is indeed responsible for the primary absorption of light.

Such correlations have been established for a variety of visual systems. As an example, Fig. 7-24 shows the comparison for the rods of the human retina. Similar curves could be shown for rhodopsins from a remarkable variety of animals. Certain receptors, however,

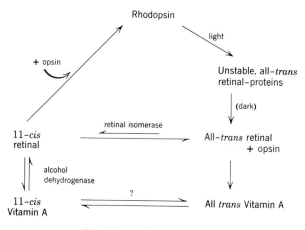

Fig. 7-23. Rhodopsin cycle.

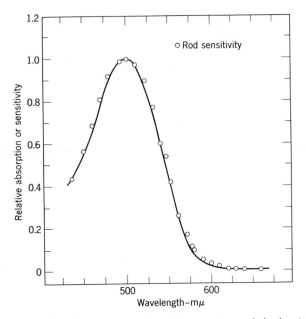

Fig. 7-24. Comparison between the absorption spectrum of rhodopsin in human rod particles (solid line) and the spectral sensitivity for human dim-light (rod) vision (points). (From G. Wald and P. K. Brown, *Science,* **127,** 222, (1958).)

contain visual pigments with rather different absorption properties, though these pigments too depend on retinal. Most notable are the pigments contained in the *cones* of the vertebrate retina. These receptors are less sensitive than the rods, but to them we owe acute vision and color perception. The only cone pigment so far isolated chemically has an absorption spectrum with its peak much toward the red end of the spectrum from that of rhodopsin: when we move from dim to bright illumination and begin using our cones, red becomes a *relatively* brighter color for us. (This alteration in brightness was long ago named the "Purkinje shift" after its discoverer.) In the particular case of the human retina there happens to be more than one cone pigment—as our ability to distinguish hue requires, and as had been predicted more than a hundred years ago. The subject of retinal photochemistry should not be left without a tribute to the marvelous sensitivity of the rod system. A trained, dark-adapted visual observer can see a flash of green light consisting of only 100 to 200 *quanta;* calculations of the loss of light in the optical apparatus of the eye make it clear that less than a dozen or so quanta must be absorbed by the rods in order to produce a visual sensation. Since the field occupied by the stimulus contains many thousands of rods, the probability that any *one* rod absorbs two quanta is negligible. It is thus statistically inescapable that a single rod can give a response when it absorbs *one quantum* of light; this is equivalent, of course, to saying that the single rod has reached its theoretical sensitivity limit.

The absorption of light by receptors in the retina, however, only begins the visual process. Streams of impulses from each of these elements in the visual mosaic must be integrated into the image that is finally perceived and then acted on by the organism. In a mammal this involves five different sets of synapses between the cells comprising the visual pathway: as Fig. 7-21 shows, rods and cones are connected to bipolar cells and these to ganglion cells; the ganglion cell axons proceed in the optic nerve to a relay station in the thalamus of the midbrain, from which fibers in turn project to the visual cortex. The retina is thus not merely a sensing "film"; beyond the receptor cells lies a neural network which acts in every way like a part of the brain, which in the embryological sense it really is (p. 169). Experiments in which the activity of single optic nerve fibers is recorded show that each one may be activated by light falling in a circle about 1 mm in diameter on the retina; thus the *receptive field* of such a nerve fiber includes many thousand receptor cells. To this point, then, the visual pathway is a *convergent* one: about a hundred thousand optic nerve fibers (in a mammal) carry the traffic produced by seven million receptors.

Already in the optic nerve fiber, as Fig. 7-25 shows, the message has become complex. A tiny spot of light directed onto the center of the receptive field may produce discharges in the nerve only when it is turned on, whereas one near the edge produces impulses only when it is extinguished; in other receptive fields the reverse may be true. In the visual cortex of the cerebrum (see p. 342), single nerve cells show even more complex responses. Their receptive fields when mapped on the retina frequently turn out to be arranged in linear rather than circular fashion, and "off" and "on" areas are often side by side or in a sandwich. In some of these cortical cells, for example, only a straight edge moved through the visual field at a particular angle and direction will evoke responses. Through the convergence and interaction of nerve elements a message which begins as a series of spatially distinct impulse trains is converted to the exquisitely organized conscious event of perception.

Some of the basic mechanisms involved in this complex task are shown by simpler visual systems, which apart from their own considerable interest can serve as models in our attempt to understand

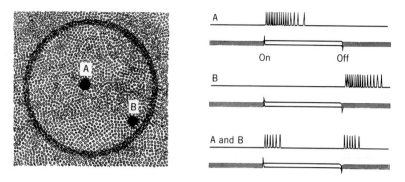

Fig. 7-25. The organization of receptive fields in the retina of a vertebrate. The circle represents the area of receptors (encompassing several thousand of them) that converge upon and activate a single optic nerve fiber, from which the electrical records at right are taken. When a spot of light is shone upon the center of the field, it evokes responses at "on"; when it is shone in the periphery, it evokes responses at "off" instead. When the two spots are put on together, an "on-off" response is produced; but each discharge is weaker than it was alone, indicating that there is mutual inhibition between the receptors. (From D. Kennedy, *Sci. Amer.*, **209**: 122, (1963); experiment done originally by S. W. Kuffler.)

the process. The best-studied example is that of the compound eye of the horseshoe crab, *Limulus* (see Fig. 7-21). Each unit or ommatidium of this eye contains eight receptor cells; but only a single functional nerve fiber passes from it into the optic nerve, and a train of impulses can be recorded from it on illumination. Each fiber, however, interacts with each of its neighbors in the following way: when a particular ommatidium (*A*) is illuminated so as to produce a certain frequency of impulses in its nerve fiber and then the adjacent one is also illuminated, the discharge frequency of *A drops.* All ommatidia thus *inhibit* their neighbors; this is accomplished by cross connections among the nerve fibers, which act as inhibitory synapses. The important consequences of this for the horseshoe crab appear to lie in improvement of contrasts: at any boundary between light and dark which falls across the eye, units at the light edge are exerting a relatively strong inhibition on those on the darker side, and the border is thus enhanced. The *Limulus* eye also shows us something of what may be happening in cells of the vertebrate visual system that discharge at "light off." The sudden extinction of light falling on one ommatidium will, to be sure, cause it to stop firing impulses; but this cessation will release a neighboring one from inhibition, and permit it to discharge again. From this relationship, illustrated in Fig. 7-26, it is possible to predict much of the complexity

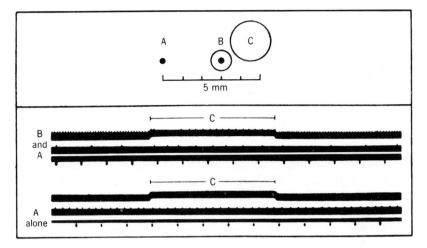

Fig. 7-26. Complex responses from the *Limulus* eye. A, B, and C are three light stimuli directed onto the mosaic of ommatidia (see Fig. 7-21). Nerve impulses are recorded from ommatidium A and ommatidium B; they appear in the upper and lower traces respectively. In the first experiment, B and A are illuminated together, B with a more intense stimulus; then, in the middle of the record, C is illuminated. The result is a suppression of impulse discharge in B, through lateral inhibition; but this in turn releases A from inhibition, and its discharge speeds up. The lower records show that if B is not illuminated, the same stimulus to C has no effect upon the discharge frequency of A. It is through such regional inhibitory inter-actions as this that the responses of optic nerve fibers in vertebrates (see Fig. 7-25) are thought to be produced. (From F. Ratliff, in *Sensory Communication,* W. A. Rosenblith, Ed., M.I.T. Press, 1960, p. 183.)

of responses found in vertebrate optic nerve fibers. Helpful though this may be, we are still very far indeed from being able to bridge the gap between the behavior of sensory nerves and the process of perception.

Chemoreceptors. For many organisms chemical sensitivity is as important a window on the environment as hearing and vision are for man. Male moths fly through a dark night to a female, guided by receptors on the antennae sensitive to a few molecules of volatile chemical produced by the mate-to-be; salmon guide themselves past innumerable choice points in a river system to find the same spawning bed they fled as fingerlings five or six years before. Unfortunately, our understanding of the workings of such chemoreceptor systems, in-cluding the mammalian olfactory epithelium, has not progressed very far. We know that many neurons respond to chemical stimuli; this is, after all, the usual method of transmission across synapses. But in no case is it known how a stimulating molecule is absorbed on a chemoreceptor cell, or how it initiates impulses once it is there. In particular, the ability to *discriminate* odors, as the mammalian olfactory epithelium does so well, is a mystery: molecules that smell alike may be radically different chemically, and there are so many classes of molecules that we can tell apart that it seems hard to believe that one kind of receptor cell responds specifically to each.

Other Types of Receptors. Receptors sensitive to other modes of stimulation are known, and still more may remain undiscovered. Temperature-sensitive cells in a variety of animals, for example, respond with increased discharge on warming; perhaps the most sensitive are those in the pit organ of rattlesnakes, which detect their prey largely by heat. Other temperature receptors fire faster when cooled. Certain fish use weak electrical pulses in their orientation, and possess electroreceptors in the lateral line which alter their discharge rate in response to minute changes in the electrical field surrounding them.

All of these energy channels represent the information on which the organism must base his response and on which his survival depends. What, now, of the apparatus of response itself?

Effectors

Strictly speaking, any cell that *does* something in the organism is an effector; the definition is not very exclusive. Biologists have come to think of effectors in a more restrictive way: as those cells which initiate movement of parts of the organism, or which produce other kinds of energy acting on the environment. Muscles, electric organs, and luminescent organs are all effectors; so are many cells that produce hormones and thus affect the activity of other cells. In simpler organisms such effectors are often of the *independent* kind— like the oscular muscles of sponges discussed earlier, or the nematocysts ("stinging cells") of coelenterates, or the guard cells surrounding the stomata of plants. These are called independent because their action is triggered by the cell itself; the effector, in other words, has its own receptor mechanism. In many kinds of cells organelles act as effectors: familiar examples discussed in Chapter 2 are the cilia and flagella, important organelles of locomotion in microorganisms and in some metazoan cells. In the remainder of this section, we shall be concerned with effector systems that are under the corporate control of the organism, and are therefore usually brought into action by nervous or endocrine stimuli.

This restriction still leaves a lot of ground to cover, but we shall devote virtually all of our attention to a single effector system—muscle. Of all of the properties possessed by organisms, movement is surely one of the most impressive and crucially important. Multicellular plants, most of which are committed to a sessile existence by virtue of being autotrophic, can rely on the slower kinds of movement provided by differential growth. Only occasional jobs in a higher plant require faster methods, and for these (for example, the closing of stomata, the fast "drooping" of *Mimosa* leaves, or the forceful expulsion of a seed or spore from its case) plants usually employ turgor pressure brought about through active transport mechanisms. Animals in general must be capable of relatively fast movements of the whole body or parts thereof, and for this kind of directed action muscle is almost universally employed.

The Structure of Muscle. Muscle cells all perform work exclusively by shortening, and the kind of movement they produce will depend on how they are connected. In all of the invertebrates that lack skeletons, and in the visceral muscles of vertebrates (p. 323), the muscles cells form circular and/or longitudinal sheets; they can thus act to change the diameter or the length of a tube, but the softness of the structure limits sharply the precision of the movement. When, however, muscles are present along with a rigid skeleton, a new opportunity arises: by spanning two movable parts of the skeletal structure, the muscle can use the mechanical advantage present in the joint arrangement and thus operate with greater versatility as well as greater efficiency.

The arrangements of skeletal muscle differ in interesting ways. We often hear of the remarkable efficiency of insect muscle; for their size, grasshoppers achieve truly astonishing feats of strength. One reason is that an external skeleton affords unique opportunities for attachment of muscles: fibers may end all along the skeleton of a particular limb, and inside it the muscle fibers may be packed in a pinnate (featherlike) arrangement in a very small space. Vertebrate muscles, on the other hand, generally consist of parallel fibers connecting with a tendon, which attaches them at either end to the skeleton, and permits force to be applied only at one point.

In the most primitive muscular systems, such as that found in the coelenterates, the contractile portion of the muscle cell is merely a tail attached to an otherwise normal epithelial cell. More advanced muscle fibers are long and cylindrical or cigar shaped in appearance. They usually consist of bundles of much smaller *fibrils;* and in the skeletal muscles of most invertebrates and all vertebrates, the fibrils have a banded appearance—this is why they are called *striated*. In the arthropods and the vertebrates, which together share the honor of having evolved efficient, jointed skeletal systems, these striated muscles are multinucleate—the "single muscle fiber" is thus formed from long rows of cells between which, during development, the separating membranes are eliminated. Visceral muscle (of the gut, for example, or the bladder, or blood vessels) in vertebrates consists of uninucleate cells which lack cross-banding, and it is therefore called "smooth" muscle. But it is a mistake to suppose that all animals maintain this difference between visceral muscle and skeletal muscle: fibers of the gut in crustaceans and insects, for example, are cross-striated. Vertebrate heart muscle is also cross-striated; but the fibers within it branch, rebranch, and connect with one another so that the entire structure behaves in many ways like a single unit. Some of these features are shown in Fig. 7-27.

Fine structure and contractile behavior. The internal structure of the vertebrate striated muscle fiber has been subjected to considerable scrutiny with all of the tools available and at all levels. The results are a unique testimony to the inseparability of structure and function. At every point, the studies of the internal architecture of muscle have had implications for studies of the mechanism of contraction, and vice versa; and it is only fitting that they be talked about together. The inside of most mammalian striated muscle fibers is filled with tiny *myofibrils*, about 1μ in diameter in mammalian skeletal muscle. These are shown in Fig. 7-28; the figure also shows (as revealed by the electron microscope) that the fibrils are in turn composed of very small filaments, which are either thick or thin and arranged in a very orderly pattern. The fibrils are (in many muscles) cross-striated; the striations, looked at with the conventional microscope, are also orderly. The dark regions, labeled *A* bands, are bisected by a zone called the *H* region; the lighter areas, called *I* bands, are bisected by very dense Z lines. The letters *A* and *I* stand respectively for *anisotropic* and *isotropic*. This means, in simple terms, that the *A* (anisotropic) region consists of highly oriented longitudinal elements, and the *I* (isotropic) region of less ordered or unordered ones. These terms, strictly speaking, refer to the passage of polarized light through the substance: anisotropic solutions preferentially transmit light of one particular plane of polarization, whereas isotropic ones transmit all planes equally well.

Of the two kinds of observations just cited, the one concerning

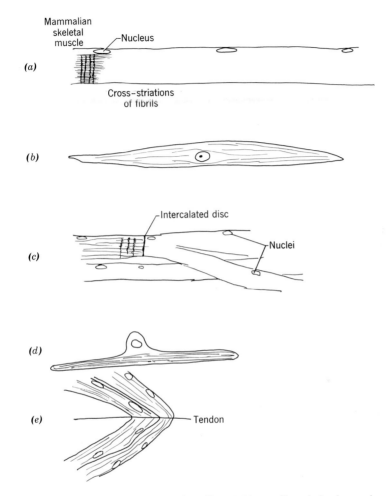

Fig. 7-27. Sketches of types of muscle cells. (a) Mammalian skeletal muscle. (b) Mammalian smooth muscle. (c) Mammalian cardiac muscle. (d) Coelenterate epithelio-muscular cell. (e) "Pinnately" arranged arthropod skeletal muscle fibers.

the A and I bands is very much older, and caused speculation about the source of order in the A region of the muscle fiber. It turned out that over half the dry weight of the muscle fiber is accounted for by one protein, *myosin;* since this protein has an extremely elongated shape (about 30 times as long as it is wide), it was a likely candidate for the orientation found in the A bands. This protein is often associated with another, *actin;* and a remarkable achievement was made when a complex between them, *actomyosin,* was

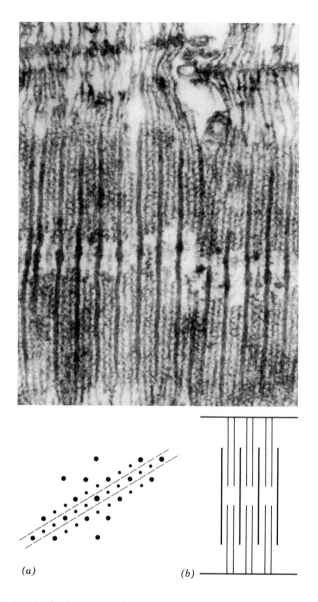

(a)   *(b)*

Fig. 7-28. Longitudinal section of striated muscle; one *sarcomere* is shown. The bottom of the figure shows diagrammatic views of the thick and thin filaments in cross section (a) and longitudinal section (b). (From H. E. Huxley, *J. Biophys. & Biochem. Cytol.*, **3,** 631 (1957).)

extracted from muscle. The precipitated actomyosin could be formed into a thread, and under certain conditions such threads could actually contract just like a muscle fiber. The conditions are of some interest. Biochemists have come to realize that cells employ the energy-rich phosphate compound adenosine triphosphate (ATP) to power a huge variety of energy-requiring tasks; and one of its most spectacular roles is the supplying of energy for muscular contraction. Actomyosin, in addition to its other roles in the muscle fiber, was found to act as an enzyme to split ATP and thus release its energy. And, indeed, it turned out that application of an ATP-containing solution to the actomyosin threads caused them to shorten.

We can be reasonably sure, then, that the proteins myosin and actin, together with ATP as a source of chemical energy, produce shortening of the muscle fiber. How? The first biochemical suppositions were based on analogy: the protein fibers of wool, for example, can fold on heating into a supercontracted state (as anyone can discover for himself by boiling wool socks). Some such folding process, it was believed, might be responsible for the shortening of muscle. At this point, however, we must return to the more recent results of electron microscopy. The thick and thin filaments seen within the fibril shown in Fig. 7-28 turn out to have a very specific relationship to the pattern of cross-striation. The A region is composed of overlapping thick and thin filaments. The thin filaments (probably mainly actin) are attached to the Z band, and the I region consists of thin filaments only; the lighter H zone in the middle of the A band is an area occupied only by thick filaments, which are composed of myosin. There is plenty of "room" for telescoping between the two kinds of filaments, and this appears to happen during contraction. The thick and thin filaments slide along one another, the thin ones crumpling in the H zone where they meet; in electron micrographs of contracted muscle they are seen to overlap completely.

The cross-striation patterns change accordingly, the Z lines appearing to move closer together and the A regions to expand in contracted muscle. In this way the folding concept of contraction has been replaced with one featuring telescoping. Apparently, the energetics of the sliding process involve a kind of ratchet mechanism. Electron microscope sections show cross-bridges between the thick and thin filaments, and it is hypothesized that during shortening these cross-bridges are successively attached to active sites on the actin of the thin filaments, thus pulling the thin filaments along. Although this theory has gained wide support for mammalian striated muscle, it is unlikely to help us explain the contraction of those muscles in invertebrates and lower vertebrates which lack alternating thick and thin filaments.

Finally, it should be mentioned that recently substances (associated with microsomes) that can induce relaxation after ATP-produced contractions have been extracted from muscle fibers. Since some constituents of muscle are known to inhibit this "relaxing factor" system, it seems possible that contraction results from the inhibition of relaxation. Hypothetical though this scheme may be, it at least focuses our attention on another level of the muscle story—the identity of the *trigger* that arranges for the muscle to be activated at the convenience of the organism.

The Innervation of Muscle. "Muscle is the servant of nerve." As old as this axiom is, it expresses the very basic fact that under normal conditions all skeletal muscles are activated only on the demand of the nerve fibers that connect with or *innervate* them. The chain of events in the neural activation of mammalian skeletal muscle has been well worked out up to a point (p. 290–294). The arrival of a nerve impulse at the junction between nerve and muscle fibers causes the release of a chemical transmitter which depolarizes the end-plate region of the muscle fiber and generates an all-or-none action potential. This impulse sweeps down the muscle fiber in both directions and causes it to contract. In response to a single nerve impulse, the contraction of the single muscle fiber is always all-or-none; but this feature is due simply to the fact that the muscle action potential is all-or-none. If partial depolarization of the muscle fiber membrane is evoked by passing a small electric current through it locally, partial contractions can occur. Thus there is nothing fundamentally all-or-none about the contractile apparatus itself.

The contraction caused by a single nerve impulse is a brief affair, called a *twitch;* it requires about 50 msec to reach contracted length, and about twice this time to relax fully again. It is thus very different from the usual actions that muscles perform. A far more common mode of activation under natural conditions is by sequences of motor nerve impulses. Since the action potential of the muscle fiber is followed by a refractory period which is short compared to the durations of the mechanical events we have talked about, it is possible to stimulate the muscle a second time before it has relaxed from the first stimulus—in fact, even before it has become fully contracted. The train of nerve impulses may be so timed that partial (but not complete) relaxation occurs between each; if the intervals are shorter still, so that no chance is given the muscle to relax, the individual contractions are fused into a smooth, steady tension called *tetanus*. Such responses have the advantage not only of steadiness but of greater strength, since the closely timed responses summate with one another to yield *greater tension than that produced by a single twitch*. The single muscle fiber is really "all-or-none" only when one is talking about twitches (Fig. 7-29).

Even with the considerable aid of such temporal variations in impulse sequence, however, there remains the problem of getting finely graded contractions out of a muscle mass composed of units that are individually all-or-none. This is not actually the contradiction it seems; the muscle is able to grade its action because it is composed of a great many such units. The quantum of muscle action is, in fact, not the single muscle fiber but the single motor nerve fiber. As the axon enters the tissue of the muscle, it branches many times and innervates a number of muscle fibers (in different muscles, anywhere from 3 or 4 to several hundred). The motor nerve and the muscle fibers it serves are referred to collectively as the *motor unit* (Fig. 7-30). Almost all muscles are composed of hundreds of such motor units. It is up to the central nervous system's switchboard to activate only the percentage of motor neurons, and hence of motor units, that are necessary to produce a contraction of the appropriate strength. Temporal regulation, too, is important; not all motor units in the muscle respond simultaneously. Smooth contractions are produced by temporal asynchrony between responding motor units, which are centrally activated at different frequencies.

Is this the only way of doing things? It clearly is a most expensive one; for in order to produce finely graded movement, the muscle must be composed of a great many motor units, and this in turn requires a larger number of central neurons with complex regulatory systems for proper operation. Consider, for example, whether it is likely that a gnat's leg (which includes five joints, each capable of graded movement in two or more directions) could successfully employ such a system. In fact, a quite different one is in use, not only in insects and

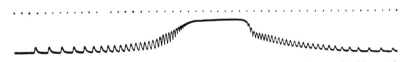

Fig. 7-29. Tension development in a single, isolated skeletal muscle fiber. The nerve supplying the muscle fiber is stimulated at steadily increasing frequency from 2 to 50 per second; the individual twitches fuse gradually into a tetanic contraction, which develops a tension several times that in a single twitch. Time marks above the record are 0.2 sec. (From F. Buchthal, *Dan. Biol. Medd.*, **17**(2): 1 (1942).

other arthropods but also in almost all other invertebrates and many vertebrates as well. The key to the operation of this other kind of muscle is that graded contractions do not result from the progressive recruitment of all-or-none units, but rather from graded tension development in each individual muscle fiber. The major difference is that the nerve fibers, instead of having a single ending at a motor end plate, branch and rebranch to make contact with the muscle fiber at a number of sites along its length (Fig. 7–30). Moreover, in most instances, activation of the nerve does not produce a conducted, all-or-none muscle action potential. When the nerve is stimulated, arrival of the

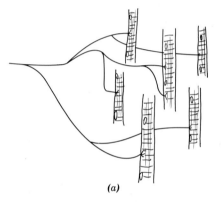

(a)

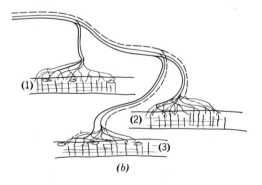

(b)

Fig. 7-30.   Diagram of the innervation of (a) mammalian and (b) arthropod skeletal muscles. In mammals a single motor nerve supplies several muscle fibers, usually with a single ending each; the whole group is a *motor unit*. In arthropods several types of motor nerves exist; each supplies a number of muscle fibers (1, 2, 3) and has *multiterminal* endings on each. The motor nerves branch and rebranch together, as shown in (b).

impulse at the endings depolarizes the muscle at a number of closely spaced points. If the impulses arrive in sequence, the second often produces a larger depolarization than the first; this process, called *facilitation*, results in a smooth build-up of tension. Some muscle fibers may develop tension rather slowly. In others a single impulse may produce such a large depolarization that the response resembles the twitch of a mammalian muscle. These "fast" and "slow" types may be mixed in the same organism or even in the same muscle. The latter are frequently used for posture-maintaining types of activity, the former for swift movements. In the arthropods, especially crustacea, the *same muscle fiber* may even show both kinds of response; and it has been shown in such cases that the muscle fiber receives endings from two different nerves which, when active, produce different types of responses in the muscle fiber. A final trick, known only among arthropods, is the use of a third kind of nerve in which impulses arriving at the muscle fiber prevent or *inhibit* contractions in response to activity of the other nerves. Thus the skeletal muscle fiber of these animals is a much more versatile instrument, and in most ways a more complex one, than that of mammals.

The important result of this versatility is that with a small number of muscle fibers and a very few nerves, these organisms can still accomplish smooth movements. Some larval insects, for example, have whole functional muscles that consist of but a single fiber; and a crab can operate an entire claw-bearing appendage (often with disastrous effectiveness) with only about 12 motor nerve cells.

In the evolution of vertebrates, however, some new possibilities opened up. The expanding mass of the nervous system offered new opportunities for control; the internal skeleton permitted bulkier, meatier muscles. Terrestrial life, too, put a greater stress on speed of action, and for speed the all-or-none impulse conducting muscle fiber has undeniable advantages. Even so, the replacement of graded muscle fibers with all-or-none "twitch" fibers has proceeded with caution. Frogs, birds, and reptiles all have many graded muscle fibers mixed in with the newer kind. And the mammals, complete though the transition has been in almost all skeletal muscle, still require multiply innervated muscles in at least one place: the extraocular muscles, which are responsible for some of the most exquisitely controlled movements we know.

Smooth muscle and autonomic nerves. Smooth muscle in vertebrates is found in a number of places—in the walls of the gut and bladder, in the pupil of the eye, in the walls of blood vessels, and so forth. Like the muscles of most soft-bodied primitive animals, vertebrate smooth muscle fibers do not have attachments with solid skeletal elements. Rather they form circular or longitudinal sheets. And like these primitive muscular systems, the smooth muscles are usually shot through with a network or plexus of nerves.

Although some smooth muscles are activated by nerve in the same "motor-unit" pattern shown by skeletal muscle, most do not depend in a rigid way on nervous control. Almost all vertebrate intestinal muscle, for example, exhibits spontaneous contractions when isolated from the animal; but this spontaneous activity is subject to regulation by hormones and by nerves. The nerve supply to vertebrate smooth muscle constitutes a readily separable division of the nervous system, the *autonomic nervous system*. Some autonomic motor nerves leave the brain as parts of the cranial nerves, or come from the extreme posterior (sacral) end of the spinal cord; these are the *parasympathetic* nerves. Others, constituting the *sympathetic* subdivision, leave the spinal cord at intermediate levels as parts of the spinal nerves. They then diverge and enter a chain of ganglia that runs parallel to the spinal cord. There the so-called preganglionic nerve fibers of the sympathetic system synapse with postganglionic fibers, which run to the heart, digestive tract, blood vessels, and other structures. The parasympathetic division, too, has pre- and post-ganglionic fibers; the ganglia where the synapses between them occur are located in or near the various tissues or organs innervated by the postganglionic fibers. Many, though not all, of the visceral organs receive double innervation from both sympathetic and parasympathetic nerve fibers.

The action of autonomic nerves, like that of other motor nerves, is to release a chemical substance at their endings when an impulse arrives there. In general, however, endings of autonomic nerves in smooth muscle are more diffuse and less rigorously associated with single muscle fibers than those we have previously described for skeletal muscle. Moreover, the substances released have a longer duration of action because they are destroyed less quickly. The chemicals liberated by autonomic nerves may thus be thought of as intermediate between typical hormones on the one hand and transmitter substances on the other. An example of the closeness of this relationship is provided by the adrenal medulla, which is innervated by preganglionic sympathetic fibers and releases a blood-borne hormone (adrenalin) on stimulation. In fact, the cells of the adrenal medulla may be considered modified postganglionic sympathetic neurons, the latter release a virtually identical substance on stimulation. This may be related to their common embryonic origin from neural crest material.

The identity of the parasympathetic transmitter—and indeed the whole chemical basis of autonomic neuroeffector transmission—was provided by Otto Loewi in a justly famous experiment performed in 1921. He stimulated the vagus nerve supplying the heart of a frog. Activity of these parasympathetic fibers resulted in inhibition of the beat. The fluid perfusing this heart was conveyed to a second heart, which subsequently also was inhibited, showing that a chemical substance was responsible for the effect. Later the responsible chemical was identified as acetylcholine; and this substance has since been shown to be released by the endings of all postganglionic parasympathetic fibers. Its distribution, of course, is even wider than this; it functions as the transmitter between motor nerve and skeletal muscle, and also between pre- and post-ganglionic fibers in both sympathetic and parasympathetic ganglia.

The heart, incidentally, also receives sympathetic innervation; and the adrenalin produced by activity in the sympathetic nerve supply results in acceleration of the heartbeat. This combination of positive and negative effects is the usual rule for dual autonomic innervation. But sometimes (as with intestinal smooth muscle) the parasympathetic effect may be excitation and the sympathetic effect inhibition, so that the sign of the response depends on the target organ and not on the nature of the released chemical.

In summary, the autonomic nervous system provides a set of controls over the operation of smooth and cardiac muscle which is reasonably quick and direct, even though it usually lacks the precision of connection and the speed of action found in the junctions between nerve fibers and skeletal muscle. In thinking about the whole evolution of mechanisms coordinating and controlling the actions of effectors, it may be useful to consider the autonomic system (and possibly also some primitive nerve nets) as a kind of intermediate between a hormonal and a neural control. Smooth muscle, since it is usually capable of spontaneous activity in the absence of nerve signals, has not been brought under the domination of the nervous system to the extent that skeletal muscle has. Nevertheless, free though these muscles are to function by themselves, the development of diffuse nervous connections enables their rate of activity to be controlled closely—especially when dual innervation allows both positive and negative effects. The fact that these chemical modulators are delivered by nerve endings allows greater speed and a greater selectivity than would be possible with blood-carried hormones alone.

Reflexes

Equipped now with receptors and effectors, we can put them together and get out some integrated activity. The complexity of arrangements of neurons and synapses involved in even the most simple reflex is far more than one would suspect in view of the rather straightforward nature of neuronal conduction and transmission across "relay" synapses like the motor end plate. As an example, we shall describe what is in many ways the simplest behavior shown by a mammal. It will illustrate both the elegance of neural reflexes and the difficulty of achieving physiological analyses of behavior.

The observation is a simple one. If we suddenly stretch the extensor muscle of a mammalian limb (the great muscle of the thigh responsible for extending the lower limb is especially suitable), a very fast shortening of the muscle against the stretch occurs. Physicians and small boys frequently test this reflex by tapping the tendon of this muscle below the kneecap, which provides the effective stretching stimulus; the result is the well-known knee jerk. It was ascertained long ago that this response, along with a variety of other "spinal" reflexes, does not depend on any central nervous elements outside that segment of the spinal cord involved in the innervation of the limb; animals with transected spinal cords show the behavior perfectly well.

To understand how this behavior is produced, we must look at its anatomical basis (Fig. 7-31). A cross section of a mammalian spinal cord at the exit point of a lumbar spinal nerve shows that the nerve divides as it approaches the cord; sensory fibers enter as part of the dorsal root, pass through the external white matter of the cord (which consists of nerve *fibers*), and enter the dorsal horn of gray matter

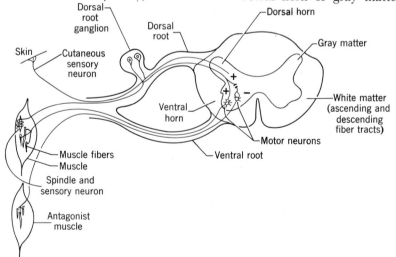

Fig. 7-31. Diagram of a mammalian spinal segment and a pair of antagonist limb muscles innervated by it. The synapses are shown symbolically; excitatory synaptic actions indicated by +, and inhibitory actions by —.

(where cell bodies and synapses occur). These incoming sensory fibers, which have their own cell bodies located just outside the cord in the dorsal root ganglion, may do a number of things: they may turn and pass up (or down) the cord in fiber tracts bound for the brain or other spinal segments, they may cross to the other side, or they may turn downwards and connect synaptically with other nerve cells in the same segment. In the ventral horn lie the cell bodies of motor nerve cells, whose axons pass out through the ventral root. Each spinal nerve, peripheral to the junction of ventral and dorsal roots, is thus a mixed nerve containing both sensory and motor fibers.

Much was learned about the organization of spinal reflexes by physiologists who stimulated peripheral nerves and measured the tension produced in various muscles. Notable among these men was Sir Charles Sherrington, whose book *The Integrative Action of the Nervous System* remains a classic of biological investigation. When techniques of electrical recording became available, others were quick to see that the division into pure sensory and motor roots constituted a remarkable convenience to the investigator. If we were to record from the entire ventral root and stimulate the entire dorsal root with a high intensity shock, the ventral root response would appear as a composite of Fig. 7-32 *a* & *b*, consisting of a rapid, highly synchronized discharge of impulses in motor nerve fibers followed by later, more prolonged, and

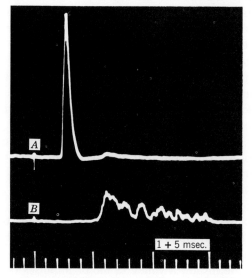

Fig. 7-32. Responses recorded from the ventral root following stimulation of a muscle nerve (a) and a cutaneous nerve (b). (From D. P. C. Lloyd, *J. Neurophysiol.*, **6**, 111, (1943).)

much more spread-out firing. It was established through careful studies of the timing of the early discharge that it must result from the direct synaptic transfer of impulses from sensory fibers to motor neurons, and hence it is called the *monosynaptic* reflex discharge. The later outburst, on the other hand, clearly involves longer, *polysynaptic* pathways. Finally, stimulation of various peripheral nerves showed that the mono-synaptic reflex response is elicited only by receptors in muscle, and never by skin receptors, as shown by the experiment of Fig. 7-32. It is still widely stated that the "hot stove" kind of reflex, involving withdrawal of a painfully stimulated limb, is the fastest of spinal reflexes. In fact it is a relatively slow one.

By applying stretch to an extensor muscle and recording motor nerve responses in the same segment, allowing for the time required for impulse conduction along both sensory and motor nerves, it can be shown that stretch reflexes of the knee-jerk type are indeed mediated by monosynaptic central connections—that there is time for only one synapse in the pathway. The responsible sense organs are the muscle spindles; stretching of the muscle compresses their spiral primary nerve endings, and causes impulses in a number of these large sensory fibers to sweep at high velocity into the central nervous system. In the ventral horn of the same spinal cord segment, the arriving impulses exert a powerful excitatory effect on the motor neurons innervating that muscle, and the result is a synchronous motor bombardment causing contraction. One important thing to note is that the reflex "returns" primarily to the muscle of origin; it goes more weakly to cooperative muscles having the same action, but *never* does it excite antagonist muscles.

Impulses in many motor neurons, produced by activity in sensory fibers from muscle spindles, constitute the monosynaptic reflex responsible for the knee jerk. The willingness of any individual motor nerve to respond, however, will depend on the activity of endings from other sources. If these are providing a good deal of background depolarization, the threshold will be lower than if they are not. Thus the potentiality for firing is distributed among the *pool* of motor neurons serving a particular muscle in such a way that some are very likely to respond to activation and others are not.

This brings us to another important part of the story. Since the junction between the motor neuron and the muscle fiber is a simple relay which never normally fails, the course of action of the muscle is determined the instant a volley of motor impulses departs from the spinal cord. For this reason, the *prevention* of muscle contraction must be accomplished centrally. Consider the inefficiency (and danger) that would result if, during reflex contraction of a muscle, its antagonist were also to contract as the result of a different stimulus. This problem is circumvented by accessory central reflex pathways which simultaneously *inhibit* the responses of motor neurons supplying antagonist muscles. Thus the sensory fibers from muscle spindles, in addition to contacting motor neurons going to the muscle from which they come, also connect with motor neurons supplying antagonist muscles—in this case flexor muscles of the thigh. This connection is *not* monosynaptic. Rather, a short central neuron (interneuron) is interposed between the sensory fiber and the antagonist motor neuron. Activity of the sensory fibers, set up by stretch, passes to these interneurons; their effect on the antagonist motor neuron, viewed with a microelectrode inside the cell, is the very opposite of the excitatory one described earlier. Instead of a depolarization, a graded, brief hyperpolarization or *increase* in membrane potential occurs (p. 296); and this acts to block the effect of excitation from any other source since it subtracts from the depolarization and increases the threshold requirement. In this way the very same sensory barrage that produces the stretch reflex in its *own* muscle prevents simultaneous action by its antagonists.

In describing the behavior of the muscle spindle (p. 300) we referred to the fact that contraction of the muscle actually relieves the spindle ending of compression, and causes it to become silent again. This, of course, ends the stimulus for the monosynaptic reflex, and brings the action to a close. However, the muscle at this point is in a rather bad way, because the spindles, having just been decompressed and quieted, are relatively insensitive to slight additional length changes. Here a remarkable second-level adjustment takes place. Inside the spindle capsule are a set of small *intrafusal muscle fibers,* and these are innervated by a special class of small motor nerves. When these intrafusal muscle fibers are stimulated and contract, their action —in contrast to that of the surrounding muscle—is to compress the sensory nerve ending associated with them, and they thus make the spindle more sensitive. Apparently, the same reflex connections that fire the large motor neurons to the muscle also activate the small; their activity arrives somewhat later than the volley which causes contraction of the muscle, because the nerves carrying it are smaller and conduct more slowly. The effect is to "take up the slack" in the muscle spindle so that even during contraction of the surrounding fibers it remains poised near its discharge threshold. Thus the spindle is an effective sentinel even during the reflex activity of its own muscle.

Other, related reflexes occupy these motor neurons as well. One example is the so-called lengthening reaction or "clasp-knife" reflex.

If we started at the point where we evoked the stretch reflex in the above example but then kept pulling against the muscle harder and harder, it would soon suddenly cease its reflex contraction and lengthen abruptly—much as a jackknife blade, when closed halfway, suddenly snaps into its handle. The reflex is the result of activation of another sort of stretch receptor, this one located in the tendon and hence activated both by stretch and contraction. These tendon organs have relatively high thresholds. In the spinal cord they connect (always via central interneurons) in a way exactly opposite to that established for the spindles: in other words, they inhibit motor neurons going to the muscle of origin but excite antagonists. The most obvious function for this reflex is safety; too much tension will cause the muscle to go limp, and will prevent tearing of the muscle or its tendons.

These examples, complex though they may be, have been deliberately restricted to the simplest spinal reflexes we know of—the only ones for which a clear and reasonably complete anatomical and physiological basis has been established. The motor neurons in the spinal cord respon-sible for them have a huge variety of incoming connections which we have not discussed at all, but which profoundly affect their participation in these tasks. For example, sensory connections from the opposite limb exist, and these are important in locomotor "stepping" reflexes. Im-portant descending fibers involved in volitional movement come from the cerebral cortex; another significant descending system comes from the cerebellum, which plays an important role in fine motor adjustment because it integrates information from equilibrium receptors in the labyrinth and from stretch receptors.

The analysis of such reflexes can now be taken to the cellular level; and at that level *spatial* organization has a special significance. The cell body and dendrites of each motor neuron receive hundreds of endings (illustrated in Fig. 7-16). It is the sum of activity of all of these (whether excitatory or inhibitory) that determines whether or not the cell will fire an impulse. The individual synaptic potentials must, in order to produce an impulse, depolarize the axon hillock of the motor neuron by about 15–20 mV in order to initiate an impulse. Since these synaptic potentials lose amplitude with increasing distance, the location of any particular ending assigns to it a *weight* in terms of its ability to excite or inhibit: endings far from the critical impulse-initia-tion zone (i.e., endings on the dendrites) have a lesser weight than those on the cell body near it.

There are also, of course, temporal factors that enter the picture. In order to sum, activity must arrive over the various pathways at nearly the same time, and thus synchrony of action is important. We have already mentioned other temporal factors: for example, the case in which a second response across a synapse is larger than the first (facilitation).

The variation of synaptic effectiveness with time is a matter of considerable importance. Nerve physiologists, in common with everyone else, are interested in learning; and it has been widely held that the important neural correlate of learning would be some long-lasting alteration in synaptic effectiveness. Most facilitation, unfortunately, lasts for only a few seconds at most; but in the spinal cord repetitive stimulation can produce enhanced transmission lasting for an hour or more. In many other nervous systems, however, the balance is quite the other way, and repeated use of the pathway depresses it. Cockroaches, for example, possess at the end of the abdomen receptors which respond to mechanical stimuli; these synapse with ascending "giant" nerve fibers which in turn set off motor impulses in leg nerves. If you blow at the end of a cockroach, he scuttles away; but repeated stimuli become less and less effective, so that the animal finally begins to act quite unconcerned about the proceedings. Psychologists call such a decline in responsiveness to a repeated stimulus *habituation*. For the cockroach, the neural locus of decreased synaptic effectiveness appears to be at the junctions between the giant interneurons and the motor nerve fibers, while in other arthropods the change takes place between sensory fibers and interneurons.

Levels of Organization in Nervous Systems

In order to understand the basis of complex organization, it is often helpful to trace the levels of complexity shown by a given system, using where possible the simpler versions as models for the more complicated ones. Consider, for example, a shore crab and a mouse, both of the same weight. We tend to think of the mouse as a more admirable creature, partly because he is more like us and partly because of his obviously more plastic behavioral talents. Mammals have clearly evolved a highly adaptable central nervous system; it is the realm of learned, modifiable behavior in which the mouse owns significant advantages over the crab. But a comparison of crab and mouse in terms of the more routine behavior of which each is capable reveals a surprising similarity in complexity.

The crab moves quickly, operates ten five-jointed limbs (and a number of other appendages as well) with great precision, catches fast-moving food, recognizes and escapes from enemies, indulges in some fairly fancy courtship rituals, and may show territoriality and other social behavior. The crab does all these things with 10^5 to 10^6 neurons, whereas the mouse needs perhaps 10^{11}—at least a hundred thousand times as many. The mouse is not guilty of profligate waste; the vastly greater number of neurons is necessary because the evolution of the vertebrate nervous system has proceeded along entirely different lines from that of the arthropods. It has a basically different kind of organization; and the nature of such differences is what concerns students of the evolution of the nervous system. Let us not mislead you, however; we cannot proceed through the animal kingdom from simple to complex forms and label the kinds of organization we find as "stage I," "stage II," etc. in an evolutionary continuum. All we can do is describe some well-known examples and use each to represent a particular line of development. Often it is a highly specialized one—a kind of end point of some direction taken in a particular group. The results of such comparative studies, however, are useful because they point to trends in the phylogeny of nervous control, and because they tell us that very efficient, adaptive ends can be reached by very different kinds of basic organization.

This is a good point at which to review the important generalizations on which the comparative analyst of nervous systems can rely. In the first place, he can safely assume that impulses in almost all nerve cells have the same basic properties (p. 272): an all-or-none character, depending on transient permeability changes to sodium and then potassium; a refractory period following the single impulse that limits the firing frequency; a finite velocity of propagation. Moreover, the events at synapses between neurons (p. 289) show broad similarities in all nervous systems. With only a few exceptions, transmission occurs by the release of a chemical transmitter at the presynaptic ending, which is followed by quick diffusion across a small synaptic space and the subsequent production of graded depolarization which (if it is large enough) leads to the generation of an impulse in the postsynaptic nerve cell. Such synapses may be of another type, in which the effect of the transmitter substance is *inhibitory* and acts to prevent discharge. Although the specific identity of the molecules used as transmitters differs, these two kinds of synaptic junctions—excitatory and inhibitory —exist in the nervous systems of almost all animals studied, and wherever found appear to operate in fundamentally similar ways.

We can press this point further by asking another question, still at the level of very small groups of neurons but not of whole nervous systems. What ways are known by which a neuron can *integrate* information coming from some number of presynaptic sources? By integrate, we mean to *change* or to *express in a different way*; for this is the

essence of what the central nervous system does. Under normal conditions a vertebrate muscle fiber does not integrate; a single impulse
reaches the end plate over the motor nerve fiber, and the impulse is there
relayed to the muscle fiber. The output is the same as the input. But
in reflex systems, as we have seen (p. 330), this almost never happens;
many sensory fibers connect with a single motor neuron, and simultaneous activity in several of the former is required to fire the latter.
One way of integrating, therefore, is by *spatial summation*, which involves the setting of a threshold requirement to a value equal to the
excitation of a certain percentage of the endings. In many cells the
endings vary in their closeness to the point at which impulses are
actually initiated. Since the individual electrical event produced at each
synapse is a *graded* one and decreases in size as it propagates, the
nearest junctions will have greater effect than the farther ones. In a
system of junctions involving inhibitory as well as excitatory endings,
the effect produced will be the arithmetic sum of positive and negative
effects. In addition to these spatial factors, integration depends in a
critical way on temporal events—on the spacing in time of incoming
activity, resulting in summation, or facilitation or its opposite (p. 323).

These different ways of achieving neural integration are known from
virtually the entire range of nervous systems that have been studied.
We may therefore have some confidence that nervous systems are all
built out of similar units, that these units are connected according to
certain rules, and that there are a limited number of ways at the unit
level in which they can act to alter and recode the stream of impulse
traffic that passes over them. This does not mean that we *know* all the
ways, only that there are a limited number of them. Having said this,
but realizing at the same time that neurons in large numbers present
grossly different patterns of organization, we are ready to attempt
comparison of different nervous *systems*.

How may we proceed to do this? Basically, there are only a few
techniques. First, we can study the arrangements of neurons and groups
of neurons by anatomical means—either through gross structure or by
tracing individual pathways. Since nerve fibers degenerate when
separated from their cell bodies, the job of pathway tracing is made
much easier when a given bundle of nerves is sectioned in one place
and degenerating fibers are searched for in another. Such methods have
been useful in determining, for example, the existence of connections
between structures in the mammalian brain, to the extent that rather
complete wiring diagrams are now available for some major areas.
Second, it is possible to do electrical recording with gross electrodes,
which "see" the activity of large numbers of nerve cells. Placement of

such recording electrodes, combined with the stimulation of distant structures, may enable us to establish connections and also to specify some of the properties of intervening junctions. A particularly important result of this kind of work during the past thirty years has been the demonstration that various brain areas in vertebrates concerned with the reception of particular sensory information are organized topographically—that is, the central neurons are grouped in such a way that they form a replica map of the arrangement of the receptive area. Thus on the somatic sensory region of the human cerebral cortex, lying just behind the central gyrus (Fig. 7-33), there are "active points" that correspond to specific skin areas, so that a map of the body surfaces can be drawn on it. This map, though somewhat distorted, represents the

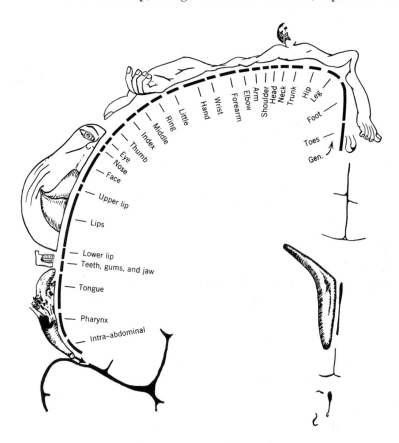

Fig. 7-33.   Schematic representation of the homunculus formed by the regions of sensory cortex that respond to local stimulation of the skin. (From W. Penfield and A. Rasmussen, The Cerebral Cortex of Man, Macmillan, 1950.)

body areas in an orderly relation to one another, not "scrambled up," and the map itself thus forms a figurine that looks rather like a man. Similarly, in the area of cortex (near the back of the brain) which forms the primary receiving area for visual stimuli, the visual field is plotted out in the same map-like way.

A similar kind of experiment can be performed by *stimulating* regions of the central nervous system, and then simply watching what happens. In the motor region of the human cerebrum, which lies just on the opposite side of the central gyrus from the somatic sensory area, local stimulation produces local contraction of muscles. Again, the points are arranged like the corresponding body regions, and the figurine so mapped is a near-duplicate of the one formed on the sensory cortex. Recently the same kind of thing has been tried with insect brains, and the results are quite different. Instead of producing regionally defined muscle contraction, local stimulation gives rise to whole patterns of behavior, often occurring in an orderly sequence and involving many different muscle groups in different parts of the body. So far there does not appear to be any suggestion in any invertebrate brain that the organization is topographic. Rather, individual regions seem concerned with the release of whole patterns of neural output. A similar result comes from stimulating certain subcortical regions in mammals.

The final technique available to the investigator is at once the most promising and the most capricious and difficult. It involves recording in the intact nervous system the activity of *single* neurons, using fine electrodes. This method achieves the finest resolution of any, since it specifies what the basic units are doing. In order to learn from such information about whole populations of nerve cells, however, we must have data from a great many neurons of any given category, and must at the same time be certain that we are sampling the group adequately. Finally, it will require ingenious experiments and imaginative analysis to see how the individual patterns fit together to make the whole system work. This is one more salient example of the difficulty in analyzing organisms in terms of cells.

Even the very analysis of discharge can be a complex thing, for interpreting the activity of central neurons is much more than a matter of saying whether or not an impulse is present. A large percentage of the cells in any complex nervous system is active most of the time, even when the experimenter tries to keep the animal "unstimulated." The problem is thus to separate, from this ceaselessly shifting pattern of activity, the events which have special functional significance; there may be many of these, each important in specific contexts. To be really exact about this, we would have to know something of the nature of the neurons that are receiving this activity, and of the connections that are initiating it in the recorded cell. The task is not hopeless, but it is difficult.

Having made some cautionary comments and discussed methods, we should now be ready to look at what is known of the structural and functional relationships within some nervous systems of increasing complexity, and see whether we can really draw some comparative conclusions that might lead to the identification of trends in complexity.

Nerve Nets in Coelenterates. Hydra, sea anemones, and other coelenterates present a diffuse and apparently simply organized nervous system which is usually described as a nerve "net" simply because the nerve fibers cross one another in a reticular fashion, all mixed in with the muscle fibers and other cells of the body layer in which the net is located (Fig. 7–34). Thus the nervous system is not *segregated* from other tissues in a rigorous way. Yet a good deal of complexity is possible. It is an easy matter to take a sea anemone or a jellyfish, for example, stimulate it electrically at one point, and then follow the progress of

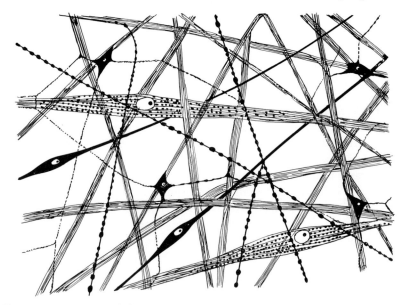

Fig. 7-34. A portion of the nerve-net of a coelenterate. Multipolar and bipolar neurons are scattered among other cells in the muscle layer, and occasionally synapse with one another where they cross. (After E. Bozler; from B. Hanström, *Vergleichende Anatomie des Nervensystems der Wirbellosen Tiere*, Springer-Verlag, 1928.)

conduction in the nerve net by watching the progressive wave of muscle contraction that proceeds from the point of stimulation. What can we see? First, a need for *facilitation* is a common finding. Often one shock will not suffice to produce contractions, but two or three or more are required; and still more may cause a more extended spread of the response. Second, the direction of propagation sometimes shows a polarity, indicating the presence of synapses of the conventional sort. Recent studies have revealed that within the coelenterates we can already identify trends of increasing complexity. In some of the more advanced members of the group, there are two nets that join at a few points, and in some cases stimulation of one net will inhibit spontaneous activity in the other. Junctions may thus be inhibitory or excitatory even in such simple systems. Moreover, some jellyfish show special aggregations of larger nerve fibers that serve to connect different regions of the net and conduct more rapidly than does the net itself.

In the main, however, the coelenterate nervous system appears to be concerned with local action, though the modes of controlling that action may be fairly complex. It represents in its degree of localization, a series of intermediates between the simplest possible situation, in which one cell serves as receptor and effector (for example, the pore cells of sponges described earlier) and more complex ones in which chains of true neurons are interposed between a specialized receptor cell and a specialized effector. Often a short neuron-like process may connect a receptor directly to a muscle cell; and even in some of the more complex nerve nets, the nerve fibers are seldom long. Nevertheless, the presence of occasionally distinct, faster-conducting bundles shows us that the nervous system even at this primitive level of organization is already moving toward the concentration of cells and the more rapid conduction that is so characteristic of advanced systems.

Worms and Arthropods. In the evolution of body form, a remarkable property becomes really clear for the first time in the annelid worms and in the arthropods. This property—which we vertebrates share, albeit somewhat masked by additional complexities—is the division of the body into a series of segments. Along with other structures, the nervous system shares in this segmental arrangement. In the simplest case, this involves the aggregation of neurons into *ganglia,* one of which occurs in each segment; often, however, ganglia from several segments may fuse into one during development. Thus the most evident change from the "nerve net" condition is *centralization;* and this trend carries with it profound implications for neural organization. For one thing, it establishes a distinct separation between the periphery, where the effector and receptor cells for the most part lie, and the center, which is now clearly differentiated as a system for conduction of excitation over distances and, more important, for the integration of information. The classic parts of the reflex arc (receptor or sensory neuron, central neuron and effector or motor neuron) are now clear as they never are in the coelenterates.

This centralization involves much more than the mere aggregation of certain neurons into a series of ganglia. These systems show in addition an orderly arrangement in which *parts* of neurons are anatomically separated in accordance with their function. Within a ganglion (Fig. 7-35) central and motor neurons are almost always unipolar —that is, equipped with a single process which branches. These cell bodies form a layer, often ventral in the simplest ganglia; and their branches form an elaborate dorsal meshwork called the *neuropile*, in which all synaptic junctions are located. There, contacts are made not only among central and motor neurons, but also between these and the sensory fibers which enter through nerve roots connecting the ganglion with the periphery. The cell bodies of these sensory fibers are always located out in the periphery of the animal, near the receptor structure with which they connect; and they are nearly always bipolar

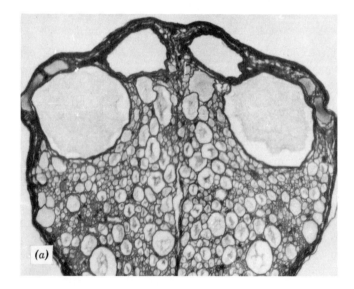

Fig. 7-35. Cross-section of a connective (a) and part of a ganglion (b) from the nervous system of the crayfish. Four giant fibers are visible in (a), a pair of very large lateral fibers and a pair of smaller median ones. There is an extremely wide

in form. The ganglia, where cell bodies and neuropile are primarily located, are linked with one another by thick bundles of nerve fibers called *connectives*. Fibers within these may be sensory, passing up or down from the ganglion in which they enter; but most are central neurons (interneurons) which are involved in the relay and integration of neural messages between ganglia. Often they pass for great distances along the nerve cord, making a variety of connections with other fibers in the neuropiles of several ganglia.

In addition to this impressive centralization and regional division of function, these nervous systems also show another trend, that of *cephalization*, the aggregation of especially complex and large masses of nervous system in the head region. This has happened for very obvious reasons. Active animals have concentrated sensory structures at the anterior end, since it is obviously important for their survival to perceive what's going on up ahead rather than in the other direction. The additional receptor "load" requires more central neural mass for pro-

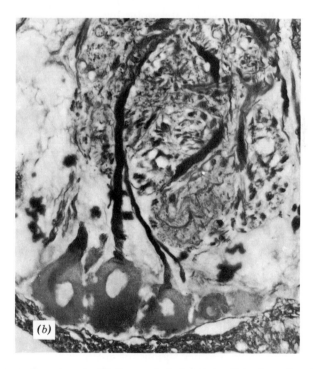

range of axon diameters. In (b) the ventrally-located cell bodies of motoneurons and interneurons each send a single process dorsally into the tangled neuropile, where all synaptic junctions occur. Photographs by D. Kennedy.

cessing the information. Thus the brain or supraesophageal ganglion and the optic ganglia of annelids and arthropods are by far the most impressive structures found in these nervous systems. They are impressive not only because of their mass, but because they show intimate features of organization that are more complex and more ordered than those characteristic of other ganglia. Fig. 7-36, for example, is a reconstruction from sections of the optic ganglion of an insect. Instead of the diffusely tangled fiber mass of neuropile found in most ganglia, this structure is orderly and layered, or stratified. Moreover, the cells themselves are more complex, and the cell bodies of the neurons more involved in the synaptic region. Many cells are multipolar, and have localized synapses in special regions. It is a good guess that such complexity results from the necessity of handling the information coming in over the many separate sensory channels of the eye in an orderly but highly integrative way. A few invertebrates have in addition large masses of brain which are not devoted in any specific way to some sensory system. Octopuses, for example, have an area—the so-called "verticalis complex" of the optic lobe—that appears to be an association area of great importance. They can be trained to discriminate various patterns visually, and "remember" them for days. With this structure removed, the animal can be trained but quickly forgets.

A word of caution is needed against assuming that complex nervous structures in the head end of an animal always represent the kind of cephalic dominance that vertebrates show—that is, the situation in which a volitional, "higher" area dominates and regulates other parts of the nervous system. All the evidence indicates that in most invertebrates segmental ganglia have a great deal of reflex autonomy. They do get information from other regions of the body; and their output is clearly regulated in terms of what is happening everywhere in the organism. But there appears to be no one center which has exclusive prerogatives to command and to override. Instead, the pattern of action is determined by information from a variety of local and outside sources. Some of it may be peremptory in the sense that it inevitably results in specific motor activity; other information may simply modify actions by contributing a little more excitation or inhibition. The whole system is thus best described as distributed rather than hierarchical; and no single center appears to have a marked monopoly on control.

In addition to their greater centralization, the arthropod and annelid nervous systems show another significant advance over lower invertebrates: they have evolved neurons of much greater conduction velocity, capable of mediating a number of fast, specifically connected reflexes. Especially prominent among these are the so-called *giant* fibers

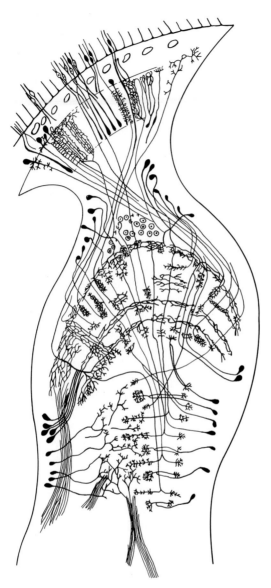

Fig. 7-36. Optic ganglion of a fly. (After S. Ramon y Cajal and D. Sanchéz; in B. Hanström, *Vergleichende Anatomie des Nervensystems der Wirbellosen Tiere,* Springer-Verlag, 1928.)

(Fig. 7-35). Conducting at speeds up to 20 or 25 m/sec, these fibers usually run the length of the nervous system and produce responses in motor neurons at all ganglionic levels. In crayfish and lobsters, for example, the two pairs of giant fibers in the ventral nerve cord synapse with flexor motor neurons in each of the abdominal segments, and when stimulated cause the massive flexor contraction that we recognize as the "tail-flip" swimming reflex. Similar fibers in earthworms produce the quick retraction in the burrow familiar to fishermen who attempt to catch their own bait. Though these giant fiber systems constitute a kind of "emergency control" they are not operated from any particular center; often, impulses may arise in them at a number of different points, propagating from there to other regions.

Vertebrates. In gross anatomical terms, the central nervous system of a vertebrate differs from that of an annelid or an arthropod in consisting of a dorsal instead of ventral nerve trunk. At the spinal cord level, the cell bodies of central neurons and the synapses are located in the central gray matter; in the brain, these cellular layers are on the outside instead. The vertebrate nervous system, though segmented, thus does not restrict cell bodies of neurons to one nonsynaptic region, as is the case in arthropod ganglia; they are in general much more closely involved with the synaptic field.

Actually, the greatest difference in vertebrate nervous systems from those discussed so far is their much greater mass—caused not by an increase in cell size, but in number of cells. The largest expansion, of course, has occurred in those cephalic segments composing the brain. Primitively the vertebrate brain develops a series of three expansions. The anterior forebrain, early in vertebrate history, was involved primarily with the processing of olfactory sensations, the midbrain with vision, and the hindbrain with other sensory (and motor) functions—notably those connected with equilibrium and later with hearing. Subdivisions of these three regions are given in Table 7-3.

Within the vertebrate line there have been marked trends toward the addition of new brain structures overlaying the old, with accompanying shifts in function (Fig. 7-37). Thus the cerebral cortex of mammals represents a "new" mass of forebrain, derived from structures only modestly developed in lower vertebrates (and primitively associated with smelling). In amphibians, for example, which lack a well developed cerebrum, the midbrain (especially its roof or tectum) represents the "highest" integrating area for special sensory systems. With the growing prominence of the cerebrum, however, the midbrain structures are shifted from functioning as final projections to being

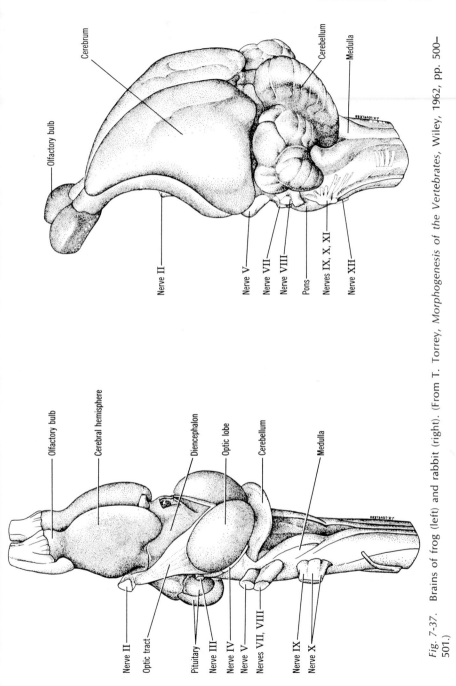

Fig. 7-37. Brains of frog (left) and rabbit (right). (From T. Torrey, *Morphogenesis of the Vertebrates*, Wiley, 1962, pp. 500–501.)

Cerebrum

Olfactory bulb

Cerebellum

Medulla

Nerve II

Nerve V

Nerve VII

Nerve VIII

Pons

Nerves IX, X, XI

Nerve XII

Olfactory bulb

Cerebral hemisphere

Diencephalon

Optic lobe

Cerebellum

Medulla

Nerve II

Optic tract

Pituitary

Nerve III

Nerve IV

Nerve V

Nerves VII, VIII

Nerve IX

Nerve X

Table 7-3   Subdivision of Vertebrate Brain

Prosencephalon (forebrain)	Telencephalon	Cerebral cortex Rhinencephalon (olfactory lobes)
	Diencephalon	Thalamus Hypothalamus Neurohypophysis
Mesencephalon (midbrain)		Optic lobes, optic tectum
Rhombencephalon (hindbrain)	Metencephalon	Cerebellum, pons
	Myelencephalon	Medulla

synaptic relay (and integration) stations beneath the new "higher" cortical centers. Even within mammals, further evolutionary expansion of the dorsal and posterior area of cerebral cortex occurs, the added material being usually called neocortex. Thus the mammalian brain is not merely a large mass; it is a series of them, which have had a serial phylogenetic origin and which appear to have *some serial aspects in function*. We are saying, in effect, that these brain regions form a hierarchy.

This hierarchy can be illustrated both by motor systems—those regulating the spinal motor neurons that control muscle actions—and by sensory pathways. In the former, cells from the motor cortex of the cerebrum form an impressively large tract of fibers (the cortico-spinal or pyramidal tract) that passes down the dorsal spinal cord to synapse with the motor neurons of each spinal segment. Other brain areas may also influence spinal motor outflow: the cerebellum, for example, and the reticular core of the hindbrain. In sensory systems, ascending primary fibers from receptors in the skin as well as in the "special" senses of the head region (visual, auditory, etc.) will show a series of relays, almost always including one in the thalamus, before the final pathway to their destination in the cerebral cortex. Each relay is actually a set of synapses, and each set processes the information in a more and more complex way, so that in a real sense the so-called higher centers *are* higher in that they are dealing with the most integrated messages.

It is thus reasonable to view the vertebrate brain as a set of centers which, though primitively developed as processing areas for different sensory systems, have become correlative regions of the greatest importance, regulating much complex behavior including all of that relating to the "special" senses. These centers form a hierarchy not only in terms of the complexity of their functions but in terms of their connections, which enable them to impose controls over lower centers. The apex of this tower of control is occupied by the cerebral cortex, which receives in its sensory areas a highly complex report of the outside world and sends this to its motor areas for translation into commands for the spinal cord.

In this respect the vertebrate brain contrasts remarkably with the central nervous systems of all invertebrates, for none of the latter have so segregated the function of command. In particular, as we said earlier, no invertebrate appears to have organized its central nervous system in terms of a regional topography of control. Why these differences? The answer is a very simple one: the vertebrates alone could afford to because they were able to give house room to a hundred thousand times more neurons than even the most behaviorally sophisticated arthropod. This is the significant evolutionary achievement of the vertebrate nervous system. Along with it have proceeded a number of coordinated changes. The vertebrates have gradually dropped out muscle fibers capable of graded contraction, and built their muscles instead of many all-or-none fibers. This has been possible only because there can be a motor nerve population dense enough to innervate groups of these independently.

It is probable, too, that vertebrates would never have been able to achieve this state of affairs had they not found means to get along with smaller nerve fibers. For their fastest reflexes, invertebrates employ "giant" nerve fibers; a nervous system of the vertebrate design, employing giant fibers to attain fast conduction, would have to be inordinately huge. The myelin sheaths on the faster-conducting vertebrate nerve fibers permit a nerve of 8μ in diameter to conduct with the speed of a giant axon of 150μ in the crayfish, making a kind of miniaturization practicable which in turn allows tremendous increases in the number of fibers in a given space.

This story would be an unfair chronicle indeed if it did not pay tribute to what perhaps is the most celebrated achievement of higher vertebrate nervous systems—namely, the tremendously expanded capacity for the adaptive behavioral control that we call learning, and for the complex associative functions that we (being higher vertebrates ourselves) know collectively as consciousness. To be sure, invertebrates learn; but their numerically limited neural equipment allows very little of the plasticity we vertebrates possess in this regard, and it is a fair conclusion that they rely primarily on a more stereotyped, push-button kind of response pattern. The ability of vertebrates to perform a wider repertory of adaptive learned behavior is clearly a product of the presence of a mass of brain that assumes "higher" functions: the tectum of the midbrain in lower vertebrates, and the cerebral cortex in mammals. Even in an evolutionary series of mammals alone, one sees that there is a progressive reduction in the percentage of area in such a higher center concerned with *specific* sensory or motor systems. In the cerebral cortex of primates, to take an end point, large regions, especially of the frontal and temporal lobes, seem to be free of special concern with vision or audition or tactile sense, or in fact, of anything we can put a label on. Local stimulation of the temporal regions of cortex in human patients undergoing brain surgery produces astonishing sensations of recall of past events; and occasionally the necessary surgical procedure of frontal lobe removal produces a well characterized set of symptoms involving, to put it simply, a kind of loss of "responsibility" and a defective organization of the business of living. We can only guess at the physiological events that go on in these misty regions, but they surely have something to do with the property of "mind" which, much more than the opposable thumb and upright posture, separates the higher primates from almost every other animal of the earth.

We can recapitulate the vertebrate part of this story by saying that a significant advance was made in the development of small, fast conducting nerve fibers, a great many of which can be packed in a limited space; and that with this development a hierarchy of "control from above" began to evolve. This does not mean that local, segmental autonomy has been abandoned; it is still available for simple survival responses. But for all complex acts, it is modulated and controlled from the brain. The simultaneous abandonment of graded muscle fibers and adoption of all-or-none, twitch motor units lent to the apparatus of motor control a central specificity previously lacking, and generated the opportunity for topographic laying-out of brain regions. Finally, the selection of brain areas as centers of nervous control had an important by-product: parts of the brain were able to evolve away from primary concern with special sensory or motor functions, and develop instead as centers for association, memory, and those operations to which we subjectively refer as "thought."

The Nervous System and Behavior

A major goal for the organism biologist in studying the nervous system is to achieve an understanding of how behavior is controlled. Basically, behavior is anything an organism does in response to some input from the environment (which may be internal as well as external), which changes its relation to that environment. As such, behavior is obviously an important component of all functions of the multicellular organism, playing critical roles in the process of feeding, sexual reproduction, finding a compatible environment, and in a variety of internal metabolic regulations.

It is quite clear that many responses that fit this definition do not fit with our ordinary use of the term behavior. In plants, for example, the entire task of controlling orientation to the environment is handled by the hormonal integration of development. Equivalent mechanisms also exist in animals, and the importance of endocrine systems for behavior has been indicated previously. But the fastest and most obvious responses in animals are those produced through the nervous control of muscular contraction.

One general property of all behavior is that it defies classification in terms of *ends*. It is, instead, a complex set of (often) species-specific strategies that have little in common beyond the nature of the neuromuscular mechanisms that operate them. We thus come once again to the central problem in organism biology: coping in a general way with a diverse set of attributes. The diversity of behavior patterns comes out of the fact that organisms are specialists in their activities, and that specific behaviors are as "adapted" as specific structures. Since the control system is common to all, however, we may hope to attack the general problem by trying to account for behavior on the basis of the neural organization that underlies it.

Kinds of Behavior. A good deal can be done, even in very complex animals, when the complexity of the behavior is at the spinal reflex level, or at the level of giant fiber "escape" reflexes in arthropods like the cockroach. Before evaluating how much more one can hope for, it may be convenient to make a division of behavior into two kinds, which we shall call *innate* and *learned*. The division is artificially strict; most behavior is modifiable by experience, and even the most classically learned behavior may have innate components. But the two kinds are still separable, perhaps especially by their widely different scientific traditions: investigation of learned behavior has a history associated with experimental psychology, which until recently resisted almost all temptations to correlate the process with neural events. Innate behavior, on the other hand, has been looked at primarily by zoologists, especially in recent years by a European school led by K. Lorenz and N. Tinbergen. The ethologists, as the practitioners of this discipline have been called, have been on their part almost too willing to engage in speculations about the neural organization of innate behavior.

Fundamentally, the distinction between the two kinds of behavior is that the innate sort is shown by animals reared in isolation from others, and thus must depend upon neuronal linkages the architecture of which is genetically specific for the species. The very stereotyped courtship movements of ducks and other birds, the hunting behavior of wasps, and the specific songs of some birds are examples of innate behavior. Learned behavior, on the other hand, is by definition more highly modifiable by contact with the environment. Classic examples of such behavior are the improvements in maze running abilities of animals with experience, or the development of *conditioned responses*—the most famous of which is the one described by the Russian neurologist Pavlov involving a dog that salivated in response to the ringing of a bell. In such experiments, the bell is termed the conditioned stimulus; it is first paired with the presentation of food (unconditioned stimulus) a number of times, and subsequently when presented alone evokes the conditioned response. It should be remembered, however, that all behavior is a product both of heredity and environmental influences. The distinction between learned and innate behavior is thus arbitrary in many respects, owing more to tradition and pedagogical convenience than to good sense.

Learning. We cannot discuss learned behavior extensively in this book. It is such an overwhelmingly significant problem that it deserves and receives the attention of an entire discipline, psychology; yet its roots are fundamentally biological. In particular, biologists are now showing a widespread interest in how the nervous connections responsible for some behavioral process might change to produce the effect of "learning" or "memory."

Unfortunately, neurophysiologists have not brought their technique to the point where they can be of much help to the student of behavior in explaining how the learning process comes about. The present status of this rapidly expanding field may be summarized by the following statements. (1) Isolated nervous structures of a fairly simple sort are capable of internally changing so that particular motor patterns become associated with specific stimulus situations; this has been shown, for example, with isolated ganglia in an insect thorax. Thus learning is not specifically characteristic of large and highly organized masses of central nervous system, nor is it a monopoly of the vertebrates. (2) We can record in the brains of mammals electrical activity (electroencephalograms or EEG's) from the surface which presumably comes from a very large number of nerve cells; whether it represents summed spike activity from these cells or slow changes in membrane potential is not altogether certain. Changes in the form of such activity in different regions can, however, be correlated with the formation of a conditioned response, and these changes frequently form defined regional sequences. Thus there *are* correlations between the electrical activity of nerve cells and the process of learning. (3) It is clear that the performance of much behavior is influenced by some internal state, which has always been referred to as *motivation*; and in the development of learned responses, the relationship of a response to a stimulus is established through the occurrence of rewarding or *reinforcing* events. Classically, of course, the experimenter uses as reinforcement the presentation of food of some sort. Recently, the whole matter of reinforcement (and, less directly, of motivation) has been brought more into the realm of physiology by the discovery of a new kind of "reward" for which experimental animals will often work even harder than for food. If stimulating electrodes are implanted permanently in the anterior hypothalamus or in certain regions of the forebrain septal area, rats will persistently press a bar that allows electric current to pass. Such self-stimulation may also be used instead of food as a reward in teaching rats to run a maze or to perform other tasks. (4) Numerous attempts have been made to discover processes at the level of the synapse which could account for the altered neural pathways that must accompany the laying down of a conditioned response. There is no shortage of mechanisms that can alter the probability of firing of synapses over periods of seconds or minutes; but days and weeks are another matter. It may well be that long-term facilitation or *post-tetanic potentiation* (p. 331), or circuits of nerve cells endlessly reexciting one another in a daisy chain, could be involved in short-term processes; but is very unlikely that they function in the more resistant, long-term kind of memory. (5) Molecular coding systems for memory have been proposed; though some evidence for the exchange of ribose nucleic acid (RNA) between cells in the central nervous system has been provided, nobody has suggested how such a chemical code could be repeatedly translated back and forth into an electrical signal—and nobody is likely to do so reasonably until we understand more about ordinary neural communication. (6) Although we tend to think of the vertebrate central nervous system as one that—in contrast to those of most invertebrates—relies largely on *learned* behavior to carry out an adaptive relationship with the environment, there is much evidence that only certain kinds of behavior are subject to this kind of modification. In short, the nervous system is not as plastic as we once thought.

Amphibians whose eyes are rotated 180° in their sockets never learn to strike at food in the proper way. Rats whose tendons are connected to leg bones in an inappropriate way by experimental surgery never regain normal use of the limb—instead, they keep on making the same mistakes in locomotion.

Learning is an adaptive property of nervous systems that may be found at different levels of complexity but is not shown by all nervous systems nor even by all portions of the most advanced ones. While there is intense effort to find neural mechanisms for the process, no complete one has been suggested—let alone proven—at this writing.

It is important to realize that even the most rigorously innate piece of behavior has a developmental history and may reflect some of that history. We can experimentally bring many kinds of innate behavior under the control of a new stimulus by conditioning procedures. On the other hand, many examples of learned behavior function at specific times in the life cycle of the organism and in such specific ways that they might be confused with innate behavior. For example, in many young birds there is a period during which following responses may be evoked to a variety of objects which fall within certain size limits and move at approximately the right rate. Normally, of course, this results in appropriate responses to the mother; but the substitution of other stimuli can produce bizarre and inappropriate reactions—like persistent following of the experimenter. This kind of process has been called *imprinting*. There is probably no need to separate it from other kinds of learning by a special term, but its existence does emphasize a special quality of the relationship between learned and innate behavior: that there may be specific times or situations when the learning system is peculiarly receptive to the establishment of a stimulus-response relation. Such receptiveness is itself "innate"; we might suppose that the next step in the evolution of a species-specific stimulus-response relation would be the limitation of the system of perception to the point where only objects with a few specific qualities would be acceptable; at that point, the behavior itself would become innate.

Reflexes and Taxes. Reflexes are actually instances of innate behavior, though they are considered insufficiently interesting as behavior to have excited much attention from ethologists. Animals show various patterns of greater complexity than reflexes involving directional locomotion towards or away from some stimulation: these movements are called *taxes* (*phototaxis* if light is the stimulus, *geotaxis* if it is gravity and so on). Many animals (including insects, frogs, and higher vertebrates) alter the direction of their movements so as to "follow" apparent motion in the visual field. Such *optomotor* responses are both ubiquitous and interesting; they depend upon the coordinating influence of not only the eyes, but of proprioceptive sense organs as well—in the case of vertebrates, especially the semicircular canals. A simple demonstration of this can be made by whirling a person on a special chair (a swivel bar stool is an acceptable substitute); during and just after the rotation, the eyes show a repeated pointing movement (nystagmus), following the visual field as it rotates and then snapping back to follow it again. Some ingenious experiments have recently been devised to analyze analogous behavior in beetles. The insects in question usually walk upside down on a blade of grass; to mimic the natural situation the experimenter gives the beetle a balsa toy to hold. The toy weighs exactly what the insect does and consists of a series of strips intersecting at angles of 120° which form a globe. The beetle holds the toy and, fixed in position, "walks it around," encountering the choice points just as he would if he were walking upside down on his grass blade. The direction taken at each choice point is recorded as either a right or left taxis. The fixed insect may now be surrounded by a drum in which vertical slits occur, each slit corresponding in position to the view of a single vertical row of ommatidia in the compound eye. When the slits are illuminated in sequence from right to left, it is as though stimuli were successively applied to each adjacent row of ommatidia, as they might be if the beetle were actually turning itself. The arrangement is shown in Fig. 7-38.

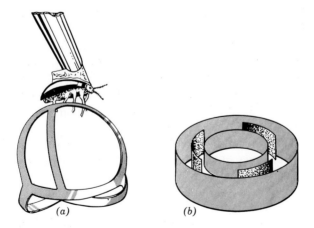

Fig. 7-38. Apparatus for investigating phototaxis in the beetle. The insect is fixed in position and holds a Y-maze globe (a); he is then placed in the center of slotted cylinders, which illuminate his eye with a sequence of stripes (b). See text. (From W. Reichart, in *Sensory Communication*, W. A. Rosenblith, Ed., M.I.T. Press, 1961.)

If the slits are illuminated in order, the beetle turns (or actually, turns his toy) so as to follow the wave of illumination just as many other organisms tend to follow movements in the visual field. The same thing happens when every *other* slit is successively illuminated, but fails to happen if every third slit (and thus, every third row of light receptors) is illuminated. This result immediately reveals something about the neural organization of the visual system: namely, that adjacent and next-to-adjacent ommatidia constitute an ordered sequence in the correlation process which yields the perception of a direction, but that ommatidia separated further than that are connected in some other way. Many other conclusions have been drawn from more sophisticated stimuli, but this one example is enough to demonstrate the power of a cleverly conceived behavioral experiment in giving clues to the kinds of nervous connection that underlie "innate" behavior.

Centers. The orderly pattern and sequence of limb movements in locomotion is also a piece of innate behavior that appears to be more complex than that found in simple reflexes involving one appendage. Like many important kinds of behavior, it consists of sequences of movements, each related in a specific way to the preceding one. A very old question about the neural basis of such behavior has to do with the order and timing of the sequence. We might suppose that sense organs (muscle spindles and other proprioceptors in the involved parts of the body) report the completion of each individual movement of the series, and that this signal then initiates the next movement. According to this view, the sequence would be programmed in a *chain reflex* pattern. On the other hand, there might be centers in the nervous system which, all by themselves, produce orderly patterns of neural output and complete the sequence without feedback from the periphery. Recent experiments on the flight of locusts have investigated this question directly; similar results have come from work on other invertebrate systems and from work on swimming in fish.

Locusts, like other insects, fly by elevating and depressing the wings by means of changes in the shape of the thorax. These shape changes work on a complex joint that affixes the wing to the side of the thorax. The muscles that power flight form a large mass in the thorax; the elevators simply compress the thorax in a dorsal-ventral direction, but the depressors are more complex and may twist the wing in either direction during the downstroke to change its angle of attack. More advanced, fast-flying insects such as bees and flies have a unique system in which a single nerve impulse can trigger a whole series of beats of the flight muscle; but locusts evoke contraction in each muscle group by sending one or two impulses to it along a few motor nerve fibers (another example of the economical innervation usually practiced by arthropods). The entire sequence, involving forewings and then hindwings, takes about 60 msec and is thus repeated about 17 times per second.

The sequence of bursts in motor nerves which results in this coordinated flight pattern may be initiated and maintained in a variety of ways. Blowing air on the head can produce flying by stimulating wind-sensitive hairs there; removal of a platform upon which the insect's feet are resting will initiate flight but not maintain it. Neither of these sensory stimuli is specifically required for the performance of the act. Even when the ganglion of the central nervous system that supplies motor nerves to the flight muscles is isolated from the rest of the central nervous system but left connected to the wings, it continues to produce a pattern of nerve impulses appropriate for flying (Fig. 7-39). It still might be thought, however, that sensory information fed back from the wing itself might be acting to direct the pro-

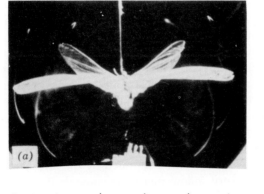

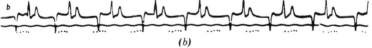

Fig. 7-39. (a) Experimental arrangement for studies of locust flight. The animal is mounted in a wind tunnel with recording electrodes implanted in various flight muscles; stroboscopic pictures, of which this is an example, may be correlated with records of nervous activity during flight. (From D. Wilson and T. Weis-Fogh, *J. Exp. Biol.*, **39,** 643 (1962).) (b) Discharge of motor neurons in flight muscles in a preparation which has been isolated from all sensory input by severing nerves. During the time of recording one sensory nerve was stimulated to provide excitation, but the stimulation frequency bore no relation to the flight rhythm. (From D. Wilson and E. Gettrup, *J. Exp. Biol.*, **40,** 171 (1963).)

duction of the sequence—especially since recording from sensory nerves during flight shows a considerable amount of such information coming in. But this cannot be the case: when the ganglion is totally isolated *even from the wings* and the output of its motor nerves is recorded, the sequence remains intact (though it occurs at a lower frequency) as long as *some* sensory activity is coming in. It does not matter which of a number of sensory nerves are stimulated, nor at what frequency one stimulates them. Their only contribution is to raise the "central excitatory state" within the ganglion to a level at which the output may emerge. The pattern depends upon the center for its specific timing, not on incoming signals, which probably function in additional fine regulation of the already-present pattern, and may *block* it if they are inappropriate to the phase being executed.

The little information so far available indicates that there are, in some central nervous systems, centers that are organized to produce a complex, formed behavioral act whose properties depend upon those of the center. The need for such centers is perhaps emphasized by the abundance of extremely complex behaviors that have extraordinarily simple triggers. Sensory hairs on the legs of flies are innervated by several nerve cells, one of which is responsive to various sugars and another to salts. If a single sensory nerve is stimulated by putting a tiny drop of sugar solution at the end of its hair, the insect will extend its proboscis and drink. So will an isolated head; and experiments with these show that the behavior lasts only as long as does the train of impulses in the sensory nerve. Clearly, the single sensory fiber "controls" the behavior; but just as clearly, a single train of impulses in one nerve fiber does not contain the information required to program the complex sequence of contractions in the several muscles involved. Thus the *organization* must be supplied by the arrangement of central neurons; the sensory inflow merely commands its release.

We may justifiably ask whether there is any more direct evidence for such centers. If a particular behavior can be released by a specific stimulus, and if the output pattern depends only on the properties of the center, then electrical stimulation of particular regions of the central nervous system ought to produce it as well. In an increasing number of cases, behavior can be evoked in this way. Electrical stimulation of certain regions of the brain in birds, for example, can produce stereotyped display movements or induce the experimental subject to sing the song characteristic of its species. Similar results have been obtained from the insect brain, where local stimulation can evoke respiratory movements or perfectly normal sound production. All these results indicate an inherent organization in particular parts of the nervous system which enables these regions to produce an ordered output even when triggered by such a crude procedure as a shock delivered through two metal wires.

Innate Behavior. This concept of nervous centers is very close to one developed by ethologists in interpreting innate behavior: they, too, often refer to behavior as originating in a center, and the specific command that initiates it is called the *releaser*. A wealth of evidence has been accumulated which shows that various complex responses can be evoked by one certain aspect of the stimulus. For example, the fighting response by which male sunfish defend the territory around their nests is specifically elicited by the red belly that is characteristic of males in breeding condition. Models have been extensively used to investigate this type of phenomenon: in this particular example, a block of wood approximately the size of a sunfish will elicit fighting responses from breeding males as long as it is painted red; it need not be a very good model in other respects.

Early in the history of ethology, such data were taken to indicate a very rigid organization of the systems controlling behavior, with particular stimuli having lock-and-key relationships with the center (an "innate releasing mechanism"); moreover, the center was thought by some to contain its own "energy," which was built up over time, sometimes resulting in spontaneous performances of the innate act when the appropriate releaser was not forthcoming. Currently ethologists are being less specific about central nervous models and are concentrating more on the nature of the behavior itself and in particular on how it is evolved.

It is evident that "innate" behavior must depend on specific arrangements of neurons, and that it can thus be inherited and altered through evolution in just the way any structure is. One of the great contributions of ethology has been to strengthen this concept by pointing out the evolutionary sequences themselves and attempting to decide how they may have come about.

One of the kinds of behavior most studied by ethologists is communicative in nature—that is, it involves two participants of either the same or different species. The behavior of one serves as the signal for the second, which responds to it in a particular way; then the roles may be changed, the second becoming the actor and the first the audience. Such relationships may hold for courtship rituals, aggressive behavior and territory defense, parental care rites, communication in social organisms, and for a variety of displays between species, as, for example, prey-to-predator. These behaviors often involve stereotyped displays or movements that serve as stimuli for other organisms, and more often than not these signals resemble acts from an entirely different behavioral context. For example, when certain moths are confronted with a predator they make movements with the front wings which reveal a pair of large spots located on the hind wings; this in turn evokes fright reactions in the predator. The movements made by the moths look very much like flight movements, but are elicited in entirely different circumstances. The process by which the behavioral act is converted from its previous context to a new one is called *ritualization*.

We are beginning to understand how such a process might work. For example, the ingenious experiments of von Frisch have shown that a remarkable communication system exists among worker bees in a hive; it is based on dances performed by scout bees when they return from a promising food source. In brief, the dance indicates by its form and its angle with respect to gravity on the vertical side of the comb, the direction (relative to the sun's position) of the food; and the frequency with which a wagging motion of the abdomen (Fig. 7-40) is performed signals the distance to the food. It may be hard to imagine how such a complex communication system might have arisen; but recently it has been noticed that many insects make turning movements upon arrival at a food source, and that others may produce, when alighting from a flight, wagging movements of the abdomen which are proportional in frequency to the distance flown. These insects are not social; these movements can have no communicative significance. But they apparently have evolved such significance in bees. As in

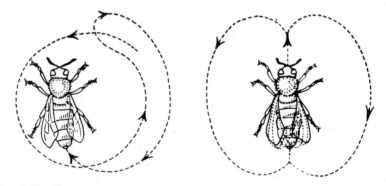

Fig. 7-40. The communication dances of worker honeybees. On the left, the round dance is performed when food is close to the hive; on the right, the wagging dance indicates the distance and direction of more distant food. The angle of the straight portion away from "straight up and down" indicates the bearing away from the sun, and the number of wags gives distance. (From Karl von Frisch, *Bees*, Cornell Univ. Press, 1950.)

other cases, the communication system evolves through the development of responsiveness to a pre-existing signal—a signal that already had a certain appropriateness in terms of stability and information content.

It may be that transfer of motor patterns from one set of muscles to another also plays a role in the origin of new signals. When impulse patterns in motor nerves of locusts are observed while the animals are behaving naturally, it has been noted that the patterns of discharge to one set of muscles are mirrored at lower frequency by those in other (and irrelevant) motor channels. For example, the stream of impulses sent to the legs in walking is accompanied by discharge of an identical pattern to the wings—though the frequency of impulses to the wings is a bit too low to produce any actual movement of the wings. It is easy to see that the control sequence for a novel piece of behavior is already present; if brought accidentally to the threshold for expression, it might be selected for in an entirely different context from that of the leg movements to which it is related.

Having said something of the mechanisms which may underlie the control and perhaps the evolution of behavior, we should reemphasize that individual behavior is selected for very specific, strategic purposes. Nowhere is this better illustrated than in the kinds of stereotyped "innate" behavior that are directed at other species—especially at predators. The intricate measures and countermeasures of such behavioral strategies are suggestive of a war game between predator and prey—fought over millions of years instead of days. A case in point is the relationship between bats and many of the small moths on which they feed. Bats orient their flight by producing brief, ultrasonic clicks (above the frequency range for human hearing) and receiving echoes from them; this "sonar" system is used in insect-catching as well as general navigation, and is astonishingly efficient at detecting even very small objects. Several genera of moths fed upon by bats possess acoustic receptors that are sensitive to the frequencies emitted by bats in their echolocation; they are capable of detecting the cries of an approaching bat at distances of over 100 feet. In response to nerve impulses in a single sensory fiber, the moths then either drop by folding their wings or engage in elaborate evasive action. (Fig. 7-41). It has even been reported recently that one group of moths can itself produce pulses of sound in such a way that they interfere with the bat's own system for echolocation.

These illustrations are intended to show that behavior serves an immense number of special purposes, each adapted for the circumstances under which the organism lives. This huge assortment of

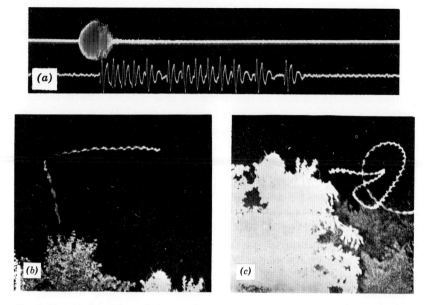

Fig. 7-41. (a) Response of the moth "ear" (tympanic organ) to the orientation signal of a nearby bat. The upper trace of the oscilloscope is the bat cry, recorded with an ultrasonic microphone. The lower trace shows the train of impulses generated in the sensory nerve from the tympanic organ of the moth, which was several feet from the bat. (b) and (c) Evasive action taken by moths when exposed to a series of artificial bat cries generated by a loudspeaker. The moths were photographed on a brightly floodlit outdoor arena; the sound was turned on shortly after the camera started. Thus the first tracks are of level flight, and responses to the sound appear later. These involve an abrupt power dive (b) or an erratic series of turns (c). (From K. D. Roeder and A. E. Treat, *Amer. Sci.,* **49,** 135 (1961).)

species-specific response patterns does point the way to some common mechanisms of control by the central nervous system. But the unique sets of responses with which individual organisms cope with their environment have been individually perfected through generations of selection by that environment from among the various meaningful outputs of which a central nervous system is capable. Much of behavior is directed toward other organisms, and takes us away from the single organism and into the province of population biology, the subject of MacArthur and Connell's third volume in this series.

ADDITIONAL REFERENCES

The references cited in the figure captions are convenient sources of additional information. We particularly recommend the following texts as general references for the material covered in each chapter.

CHAPTER 1 THE PROBLEM OF DIVERSITY

MacArthur, R. H., and J. Connell, 1965. *The Biology of Populations.* Wiley, New York.
Simpson, G. G., C. S. Pittendrigh, and L. H. Tiffany, 1957. *Life: An Introduction to Biology.* Harcourt, Brace, New York.
Stern, H., and D. Nanney, 1965. *The Biology of Cells.* Wiley, New York.

CHAPTER 2 THE BIOLOGY OF MICROORGANISMS

Burnet, F. M., and W. M. Stanley (Eds.) 1959. *The Viruses; Biochemical, Biological, and Biophysical Properties,* v. 1–5. Academic Press, New York.
Gunsalus, I. C., and R. Y. Stanier (Eds.) 1960–64. *The Bacteria; a Treatise on Structure and Function,* v. 1–4. Academic Press, New York.
Jahn, T. L., and F. F. Jahn, 1949. *How to Know the Protozoa.* Wm. P. Brown, Dubuque.
Luria, S. E., 1953. *General Virology.* Wiley, New York.
Mackinnon, D. L., and R. S. J. Hawes, 1961. *An Introduction to the Study of Protozoa.* Oxford, London.
Smith, G. M., 1955. *Cryptogamic Botany,* v. 1, 2nd ed. McGraw-Hill, New York.
Stanier, R. Y., M. Doudoroff, and E. A. Adelberg, 1963. *The Microbial World.* 2nd ed. Prentice-Hall, Englewood Cliffs, N. J.
Tartar, V., 1961. *The Biology of Stentor.* Pergamon, London.
Thimann, K. V., 1963. *The Life of Bacteria.* 2nd ed. Macmillan, New York.

CHAPTER 3 MULTICELLULAR ORGANISMS

Barnes, R. D., 1963. *Invertebrate Zoology.* Saunders, Philadelphia.
Bloom, W., and D. W. Fawcett, 1962. *A Textbook of Histology.* 8th ed. Saunders, Philadelphia.
Bonner, J. T., 1959. *The Cellular Slime Molds.* Princeton University Press, Princeton, N.J.
Buchsbaum, R., 1948. *Animals without Backbones.* University of Chicago Press, Chicago.
Esau, K., 1965. *Plant Anatomy.* 2nd ed. Wiley, New York.

360 THE BIOLOGY OF ORGANISMS

Foster, A. S., and E. M. Gifford, 1959. *Comparative Morphology of Vascular Plants.* Freeman, San Francisco.
Romer, A. S., 1962. *The Vertebrate Body.* 3rd ed. Saunders, Philadelphia.
Smith, G. M., 1955. *Cryptogamic Botany,* v. 1, 2nd ed. McGraw-Hill, New York.
Young, J. Z., 1962. *The Life of Vertebrates.* 2nd ed. Oxford, Clarendon.

CHAPTER 4 REPRODUCTION IN MULTICELLULAR ORGANISMS

Gorbman, A., and H. A. Bern, 1962. *A Textbook of Comparative Endocrinology.* Wiley, New York. (Chapters on the endocrine control of reproduction).
Maheshwari, P., 1950. *An Introduction to the Embryology of Angiosperms.* McGraw-Hill, New York.
Rothschild, L., 1956. *Fertilization.* Methuen, London.
Simpson, G. G., C. S. Pittendrigh, and L. H. Tiffany, 1957. *Life: An Introduction to Biology.* Harcourt, Brace, New York.

CHAPTER 5 DEVELOPMENT

Balinsky, B. I., 1960. *An Introduction to Embryology.* Saunders, Philadelphia.
Barth, L. J., 1964. *Development: Selected Topics.* Addison-Wesley, Reading, Massachusetts. (Deals especially with genetic problems in development).
Esau, K., 1965. *Plant Anatomy.* 2nd ed. Wiley, New York.
Saxen, L., and S. Toivonen, 1962. *Primary Embryonic Induction.* Legos, London, (Prentice-Hall, Englewood Cliffs, N. J.)
Smith, G. M., 1955. *Cryptogamic Botany,* v. 1, 2nd ed. McGraw-Hill, New York.
Waddington, C. H., 1956. *Principles of Embryology.* George Allen and Unwin, London.

CHAPTER 6 METABOLISM OF MULTICELLULAR ORGANISMS

Davson, H., 1959. *A Textbook of General Physiology.* 2nd ed. Churchill, London.
Greulach, V., and J. E. Adams, 1962. *Plants: An Introduction to Modern Botany.* Wiley, New York.
Krogh, A. M., 1941 (New ed. 1959). *The Comparative Physiology of Respiratory Mechanisms.* University of Pennsylvania Press, Philadelphia.
Prosser, C. L., and F. A. Brown, Jr., 1961. *Comparative Animal Physiology.* 2nd ed. Saunders, Philadelphia.
Ray, P. M., 1963. *The Living Plant.* Holt, Rinehart and Winston, New York.
Smith, H. W., 1953 Jan. The Kidney. *Scientific American.*
Steward, F. C. (Ed), 1959. *Plant Physiology,* v. 2. Academic Press, New York.
Wiggers, C. J., 1957 May. The Heart. *Scientific American.*
Zimmermann, M., 1963 March. How Sap Moves in Trees. *Scientific American.*
Zweifach, B., 1959 Jan. Microcirculation of the Blood. *Scientific American.*

CHAPTER 7 INTEGRATION

Bliss, E. L. (Ed.), 1962. *The Roots of Behavior.* Harper, New York.
Butler, W. L., and R. J. Downes, 1960 Dec. Light and Plant Development. *Scientific American.*
Davson, H. 1959. *A Textbook of General Physiology.* 2nd ed. Churchill, London. (Chapters on nerve, muscle, and sense organs are a thorough account).

Eccles, J. C., 1963. *The Physiology of Synapses*. Academic, New York.

von Frisch, K., 1950 (New ed. 1956). *Bees: Their Chemical Sense, Vision and Language*. Cornell University Press, Ithaca, N. Y.

Galston, A., 1964. *The Life of the Green Plant*, 2nd ed. Prentice-Hall, Englewood Cliffs, N. J.

Gorbman, A., and H. A. Bern, 1962. *A Textbook of Comparative Endocrinology*. Wiley, New York.

Griffin, D. R., 1958. *Listening in the Dark*. Yale University Press, New Haven.

Hillman, W. S., 1962. *The Physiology of Flowering*. Holt, Rinehart and Winston, New York.

Hodgkin, A. L., 1964. *The Conduction of the Nervous Impulse*. Sherrington Lectures, #7. C. C Thomas, Springfield, Ill.

Hubel, D. H., 1963 Nov. The Visual Cortex of the Brain. *Scientific American*.

Huxley, H. E., 1958 Nov. The Contraction of Muscle. *Scientific American*.

Katz, B., 1952 Nov. The Nerve Impulse. *Scientific American*.

Leopold, A. C., 1955. *Auxins and Plant Growth*. University of California Press, Berkeley.

Miller, W., F. Ratliff, and H. K. Hartline, 1961 Sept. How Cells Receive Stimuli. *Scientific American*.

Penfield, W., and L. Roberts, 1959. *Speech and Brain Mechanisms*. Princeton University Press, Princeton, N.J.

Prosser, C. L., and F. A. Brown, Jr., 1961. *Comparative Animal Physiology*, 2nd ed. Saunders, Philadelphia. (A useful reference source for comparative treatment of various special topics).

Salisbury, F. B., 1957 April. Plant Growth Substances. *Scientific American*.

Society for Experimental Biology Symposia, 1962. *Biological Receptor Mechanisms*. Cambridge, London.

Sperry, R. W., 1959 Nov. The Growth of Nerve Circuits. *Scientific American*.

Wilson, E. O., 1963 May. Pheromones. *Scientific American*.

INDEX

363

370 INDEX